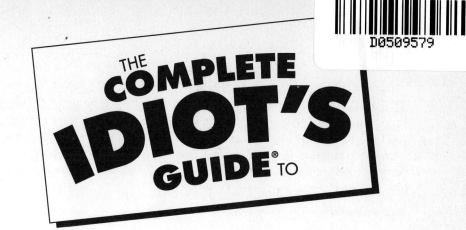

THE
COMPLETE
IDIOT'S
GUIDE® TO

The Civil War

Second Edition

by Alan Axelrod, Ph.D.

ALPHA

A member of Penguin Group (USA) Inc.

For Anita—again

ALPHA BOOKS

Published by the Penguin Group

Penguin Group (USA) Inc., 375 Hudson Street, New York, New York 10014, U.S.A.

Penguin Group (Canada), 10 Alcorn Avenue, Toronto, Ontario, Canada M4V 3B2 (a division of Pearson Penguin Canada Inc.)

Penguin Books Ltd, 80 Strand, London WC2R 0RL, England

Penguin Ireland, 25 St Stephen's Green, Dublin 2, Ireland (a division of Penguin Books Ltd)

Penguin Group (Australia), 250 Camberwell Road, Camberwell, Victoria 3124, Australia (a division of Pearson Australia Group Pty Ltd)

Penguin Books India Pvt Ltd, 11 Community Centre, Panchsheel Park, New Delhi—110 017, India

Penguin Group (NZ), cnr Airborne and Rosedale Roads, Albany, Auckland 1310, New Zealand (a division of Pearson New Zealand Ltd)

Penguin Books (South Africa) (Pty) Ltd, 24 Sturdee Avenue, Rosebank, Johannesburg 2196, South Africa

Penguin Books Ltd, Registered Offices: 80 Strand, London WC2R 0RL, England

Copyright © 2003 by Alan Axelrod

THE COMPLETE IDIOT'S GUIDE TO and Design are registered trademarks of Penguin Group (USA) Inc.

International Standard Book Number: 1-59257-132-8
Library of Congress Catalog Card Number: 2003106941

08   07   10   9   8   7

Interpretation of the printing code: The rightmost number of the first series of numbers is the year of the book's printing; the rightmost number of the second series of numbers is the number of the book's printing. For example, a printing code of 03-1 shows that the first printing occurred in 2003.

Printed in the United States of America

Note: This publication contains the opinions and ideas of its author. It is intended to provide helpful and informative material on the subject matter covered. It is sold with the understanding that the author and publisher are not engaged in rendering professional services in the book. If the reader requires personal assistance or advice, a competent professional should be consulted.

The author and publisher specifically disclaim any responsibility for any liability, loss, or risk, personal or otherwise, which is incurred as a consequence, directly or indirectly, of the use and application of any of the contents of this book.

Most Alpha books are available at special quantity discounts for bulk purchases for sales promotions, premiums, fund-raising, or educational use. Special books, or book excerpts, can also be created to fit specific needs.

For details, write: Special Markets, Alpha Books, 375 Hudson Street, New York, NY 10014.

Publisher: *Marie Butler-Knight*
Product Manager: *Phil Kitchel*
Senior Managing Editor: *Jennifer Chisholm*
Acquisitions Editor: *Gary Goldstein*
Development Editor: *Tom Stevens*
Production Editor: *Billy Fields*
Copy Editor: *Rhonda Tinch-Mize*
Illustrator: *Jody Schaeffer*
Cover/Book Designer: *Trina Wurst*
Indexer: *Brad Herriman*
Layout/Proofreading: *Angela Calvert, John Etchison*

Contents at a Glance

Contents

Foreword

It was an incredible stroke of luck.

At about ten o'clock on the morning of Sept. 13, 1862, while bivouacked in a field that had just the day before been occupied by Confederates, a Union private found in the grass three cigars, wrapped in a two-page letter. While the private, Barton W. Mitchell of the 27th Indiana, divided the cigars among his comrades, Sgt. John M. Bloss examined the important-looking document. It was headed "Special Order 191" and was signed by Robert E. Lee, commander of the Army of Northern Virginia. Realizing the importance of the find, Bloss stopped the soldiers from lighting up.

Located about a mile southeast of Frederick, Maryland, the meadow had been the headquarters of Confederate General D.H. Hill. A week earlier, Hill had been part of the ragtag 60,000-man force that Lee had led across the Potomac to invade the North. It was a bold move, and one that Lee hoped would shake Yankee morale and bring a swift victory because he knew the South could not fight a long war against an enemy so rich in men and supplies.

The piece of paper that Private Mitchell found wrapped around the cigars was nothing less than Lee's battle plan for the invasion, and it contained a vital piece of information: Lee was going to risk splitting his force in two.

Lee had given copies of the plan to his best generals, including Stonewall Jackson. Jackson copied the orders for his brother-in-law, D.H. Hill. It was either Hill or one of Jackson's staff that lost the copy of the orders eventually found by Private Mitchell.

With the advantage of knowing Lee's strategy, McClellan should have crushed the Army of Northern Virginia. Yet, he hesitated. The secret orders did not give troop numbers, and because of bad Union intelligence, McClellan believed Lee had far more men than he actually did.

McClellan hesitated.

Four days later, George McClellan and Robert E. Lee fought to a bloody draw near a creek in Maryland called Antietam. And while McClellan succeeded in driving Lee out of Maryland, he did not finish him off. The war would drag on for another three years, causing untold suffering on both sides.

The story of "Lee's Lost Dispatch" is just one of the fascinating and true tales from the Civil War that await you in this book. The author, Alan Axelrod, is not only an expert on American history, but is a natural storyteller as well.

Here, Dr. Axelrod presents the panorama of the war that probably did more to shape the American character than any other conflict, and yet he still manages to paint telling (and often chilling) details: the abolitionist John Brown hacking to death pro-slavery settlers along Pottawatomie Creek with swords, a wounded Union private calling piteously for water on the Chickamauga battlefield and being left a full canteen by a rebel soldier, a Confederate saboteur riding a horsecar through New York with a stinking carpetbag full of "Greek fire" between his legs, intent on burning down a few of the city's best hotels.

Also, in this new edition, you'll find details on Civil War–era weapons, from the ubiquitous Springfield muzzle-loading rifle to "secret" weapons like the CSS *Hunley*, the first submarine to successfully sink another vessel. On Feb. 17, 1864, the *Hunley* rammed the USS *Housatonic* with a torpedo, then sank while making its getaway—with eight Rebel sailors inside.

You'll also discover tips on tracing your Civil War ancestors, visiting the best battlefields and parks across the country, and—if you've truly been bitten by the Civil War bug—how to become a living history reenactor.

As a novelist who often places his stories in Civil War settings, I know how interesting researching the era can be. You have an exciting adventure in store. And whether you're just brushing up on the Civil War or are planning to plunge in-depth into this defining moment in American history, you could have no better guide than Alan Axelrod.

Huzzah!

—Max McCoy, journalist and award-winning author of *Sons of Fire, Home to Texas,* and *Jesse: A Novel of the Outlaw Jesse James.*

Introduction

Of the 1,556,000 soldiers who served in the Union army during the Civil War, 359,528 were killed and 275,175 were wounded. Of the approximately 850,000 men of the Confederate forces, at least 258,000 died, and some 225,000 were wounded. This means that 41 percent of the Union soldiers and 56 percent of the Confederate soldiers who fought were either killed or wounded.

The population of the Northern states in 1860, the year before war began, was 22 million, including 4 million men of combat age. That of the Confederate states was 9 million (of whom almost 4 million were slaves), including 1,140,000 men of combat age. The 1,117,703 casualties on both sides represented 3.6 percent of the total U.S. population; however, 21 percent—more than one fifth—of the nation's young men were killed or wounded between 1861 and 1865.

The United States spent $15 billion on the war in an era when an unskilled laborer earned about a dollar a day. The South, of course, emerged from the war having lost its chief agricultural labor system—slavery—and with most of its factories and railroads destroyed, along with some of its richest croplands.

The Civil War, then, was death and pain and ruin, all of it self-inflicted, and all on a scale that, even after two world wars, is still difficult to imagine. That we now drive on broad interstate highways, crossing North to South at 70 miles per hour without a thought, makes the devastation even harder to picture. Beyond place names, a few historical markers and monuments, a handful of battlefield parks, exhibits in museums, and some cemeteries, all traces of the Civil War are gone.

Except in memory.

None of us lived through the war, yet the war seems, somehow, a part of us. It is a kind of hunger, judging from the rate at which we consume books on the subject. No fewer than 65,000 volumes have been devoted to the Civil War since it ended in 1865, and in any recent year, 1,500 to 2,000 Civil War titles are actively in print. *Gone with the Wind* was a box-office phenomenon when it was released in 1939 and remains at the top of many filmgoers' list of favorites. And, in 1990, millions of television viewers turned from the commercial networks to watch Ken Burns's somber multi-episode Civil War documentary on PBS.

We continue to argue about the war, too. Was it *really* about slavery? Should Lincoln have just let the Southern states go their own way? Was the cause of the South evil, just misunderstood, or, at least in some ways, right? Were Lee and Stonewall Jackson overrated? Was Grant a "butcher" and Sherman a "war criminal"? Was Lincoln a great man or a single-minded tyrant?

No events in nineteenth-century American history—and only a handful of *current* events—seem more important to us, more relevant to us, or more familiar to us than those of 1861–1865. Yet no matter how important, relevant, or familiar, those events are not only distant in time, but often complex and confusing to interpret. The Civil War is one of those subjects we both care about and feel we *should* care about. We know *something* about it, but feel we should know *more*. The names of battles and generals are familiar to us, but only vaguely. We are attracted to the subject of the Civil War, but we're not quite sure why. And schoolbook history, with all its dates, midterm exams, and pop quizzes—well, none of that was much help.

The Complete Idiot's Guide to the Civil War, Second Edition will not tell you *everything* you need to know about the Civil War. But it *will* tell you all you need to know to get started in an exploration of a true-life drama by which we can measure the remarkable heights and unspeakable depths humanity touches, and through which we can learn something about who we were, are, and might yet be.

Part 1, "Fire-Bell in the Night," takes us to the very hour at which the Civil War began, then looks back before this time, to the roots of slavery in the New World. For it was in slavery that the war began, despite all the effort to avoid it through argument, excuse, and compromise.

Part 2, "Rally Round," shows how the Americans, a most unmilitary people, suddenly transformed themselves into soldiers, and how the North, many times greater in wealth and population than the South, saw its army beaten in opening battles more terrible than either side had imagined possible.

Part 3, "Die to Make Men Free," takes us to the moral turning point of the war. The Battle of Antietam was the first in which the Union could claim a victory, however narrow and however bloody, and this gave President Lincoln the platform from which to issue an emancipation proclamation. From now on, whatever else the war meant, it was officially a war to end slavery, a struggle "to set men free."

Part 4, "That the Nation Might Live," begins with the military turning point of the war: Gettysburg, not only the most momentous battle of the Civil War, but also the largest battle ever fought on this continent, and one of the great military contests in all history. Despite Union victory here, the North, we will see, was plagued by riot, racism, subversion, and other forms of dissension.

Part 5, "The Last Full Measure," begins with the installation of Ulysses S. Grant as the Union's general-in-chief. Now, increasingly, the war became a contest in deadly earnest between Grant and Lee, while Grant's principal subordinate, William Tecumseh Sherman, fought Joseph E. Johnston, John Bell Hood, and, ultimately, the people of the South. This section of the book concludes where, for all practical purposes, the Civil War ended, at Appomattox Court House, with Lee's surrender of the Army of Northern Virginia.

Part 6, "Taps and Reveille," begins with the assassination of Abraham Lincoln, whose death doomed the nation, and the South in particular, to more than a decade of punitive and destructive Reconstruction policy, which created, in turn, a climate of regional resentment, social intolerance, and racial hate. The section concludes with an acknowledgment of the war's unfinished business and a look at how the Civil War continues to live in our collective memory.

Extras

In addition to the main narrative and photographs, portraits, and maps in *The Complete Idiot's Guide to the Civil War, Second Edition*, you'll also find other types of useful information, including definitions of key terms, an array of historical sites open to the public, a collection of eyewitness accounts and other period documents, battle statistics and other war-related numbers, and a collection of Civil War facts, anecdotes, and trivia. Look for these features:

Words of War

The Civil War was fought with words as well as bullets. Here are definitions of the era's key words.

Voices

This feature presents Civil War eloquence, eyewitness accounts, and a few official documents.

Count Off!

Here you will find battle statistics and other informative numbers related to the war.

War News

This feature offers Civil War anecdotes, trivia, and informative facts.

Sites and Sights

Many Civil War battlefields and other sites are maintained today as public parks, historical monuments, and museums. This feature presents some of the most interesting and important.

Special Thanks to the Technical Reviewer

The Complete Idiot's Guide to the Civil War, Second Edition, was reviewed by an expert who double-checked the accuracy of what you'll learn here, to help us ensure that this book gives you everything you need to know about the Civil War. Special thanks are extended to Max McCoy.

Trademarks

All terms mentioned in this book that are known to be or are suspected of being trademarks or service marks have been appropriately capitalized. Alpha Books and Penguin Group (USA) Inc. cannot attest to the accuracy of this information. Use of a term in this book should not be regarded as affecting the validity of any trademark or service mark.

Part 1

Fire-Bell in the Night

When did the Civil War begin? Answer at Fort Sumter, on April 12, 1861, and you'd be right—partly. But the deepest roots of the war can be found in August 1619, when Virginia tobacco farmers purchased their first consignment of 20 slaves from Dutch traders. From that moment, the slavery issue festered through the colonial and early national periods, inexorably tearing the nation apart.

In this section, you'll read about the tortured attempts to compromise on slavery, about men who could tolerate no compromise, and about one man who tried to arm the slaves to win their freedom for themselves. This section ends with the inauguration of Abraham Lincoln, come to Washington to preside over a "house divided against itself" and a people rushing headlong toward war.

Beginnings

In This Chapter

◆ The fall of Fort Sumter

◆ Slavery comes to America

◆ Opposition to slavery

◆ Attempts to compromise on the slavery issue

◆ The Missouri Compromise

What caused the Civil War? Most schoolbooks say it was the issue of slavery—the South wanted it; the North wanted to abolish it—but get into any serious discussion of the subject, and you're likely to hear that slavery was secondary to "economics" or "states' rights" or some other issue.

True, slavery was by no means the only matter at issue in the Civil War, and, later in this book, we'll look at how various people fought the war for various reasons. Nevertheless, these reasons notwithstanding, the fact of slavery always looms behind or towers above all other motives for the war. The fact is this: If there had been no slavery, there would have been no other reasons to fight.

And so this chapter begins with the first day of the war—April 12, 1861—then reaches back to the seeds of war, planted some 242 years earlier.

Fort Sumter, South Carolina, April 12, 1861

Life moved at a leisurely pace in the peacetime army of what had been the *United States of America*. The construction of Fort Sumter, on an artificial island of New England granite transported to Charleston Harbor, had begun in 1829 and was still unfinished on the day after Christmas 1860, when Major Robert Anderson assumed command. Anderson commanded a garrison of two U.S. Army artillery companies—68 soldiers, 9 officers, and 8 bandsmen, along with a handful of civilian workers. Less than a week earlier, on December 20, 1860, South Carolina had *seceded*—proclaiming itself no longer a state of the Union. Backed by militiamen and volunteers loyal to their state, South Carolinians quickly seized federal property, including military installations and arms.

Words of War

To **secede** is to withdraw from membership in an organization, association, alliance, or, in the case of what became the 11 Confederate states, to withdraw from the union of the United States.

In the predawn hours of April 12, 1861, the Confederates (that's what the citizens of seven Southern states now called themselves) aimed against Sumter the bristling guns of batteries at Morris, James, and Sullivan islands and Forts Moultrie and Johnson, as well as the town of Mount Pleasant.

Pierre Gustave Toutant Beauregard, a dashing Louisianian, was an excellent engineer and a fine artillerist, having been educated in that art by his West Point instructor, Major Anderson. Now in command of the Confederate forces that had laid siege against Sumter since January, Beauregard sent, under a flag of truce, two men rowing out to the fort in Charleston Harbor. They presented Anderson with a chivalrous note demanding surrender:

> All proper facilities will be afforded for the removal of yourself and command, together with company arms and property, and all private property, to any post in the United States which you may select. The flag which you have upheld so long and with so much fortitude, under the most trying circumstances, may be saluted by you on taking it down.

For his part, Anderson, a Kentuckian married to a Georgian, was torn between loyalty to the Union and sympathy with the South. To Beauregard's messengers he handed a reply resigned rather than defiant: The general's demand was one "with which I regret that my sense of honor, and of my obligations to my government, prevent my compliance." As he gave the rowboatmen this message, he remarked: "Gentlemen, if you do not batter us to pieces, we shall be starved out in a few days."

Dashing, chivalrous, not brilliant but competent, Confederate general Pierre Gustave Toutant Beauregard (1818–93) commanded the bombardment of Fort Sumter, firing on his former West Point artillery instructor, Maj. Robert Anderson.

(Library of Congress)

Four more rowboatmen, including South Carolina politician Col. James Chesnut, called on Anderson after midnight on April 12, 1861, with a warning that bombardment was about to commence. Anderson replied that, barring further orders or supply from "my government," he would evacuate the fort by April 15. But that would not do, Beauregard's emissaries declared; the bombardment would begin in one hour.

The honor of letting fly the first shot was offered to the Virginian Roger Pryor. He had resigned his seat in the U.S. Congress to join the Confederate Army on March 3, 1861, and was what the divided nation called a "fire-eater," a rabid advocate of secession, who had exhorted the people of South Carolina to "Strike a blow!" But now he shook his head, protesting weakly that he "could not fire the first gun of the war." According to some accounts, 67-year-old Edmund Ruffin, a rural Virginia newspaper editor and a crusty, wild-eyed defender of slavery, pulled the lanyard for the first shot at 4:30 A.M.

Words of War

On the eve of civil war, a **fire-eater** was a Southerner who enthusiastically and unconditionally advocated secession.

(although a Capt. George S. James had actually fired a small signal gun before this). In any event, some 4,000 rounds followed the first shot through Friday the 12th and into Saturday the 13th.

Edmund Ruffin, 67-year-old rural Virginia newspaper editor and rabid defender of slavery, is generally credited with firing the first shot of the Civil War, although a Capt. George S. James actually fired a signal gun before Ruffin fired.

(National Archives and Records Administration)

Four thousand rounds! Some artillery ammunition of this period was explosive, but most of what was used against Fort Sumter was solid shot—12- or 20-pound iron projectiles propelled at great velocity. It penetrated or battered down most of whatever it hit. Yet, astoundingly, when Major Anderson finally "struck his colors" (lowered the flag in surrender), content after two days and nights of continuous bombardment that honor had been satisfied, no one had been killed or even seriously wounded. Although the battle was over, the casualties were yet to come.

The first was Roger Pryor. Reluctant to fire the first shot of the war, he now rushed into the shattered fort as one of Beauregard's emissaries presiding over the installation's surrender. Taking a seat at a table in Sumter's empty hospital while the terms he had dictated were put into writing, he was overcome with thirst, seized a bottle that was close to hand, quaffed it, found that it tasted strange, and *then* thought to read the label: "Iodine of Potassium."

Pryor the "fire-eater" had poisoned himself. The fort's surgeon hauled him outside, pumped his stomach, and saved his life.

Sites and Sights

The Fort Sumter National Monument, administered by the National Park Service and encompassing Forts Sumter and Moultrie, can be reached by ferries operated by Fort Sumter Tours, Inc. Call 1-803-722-1691 for hours of operation and fees. Boats depart from the City Marina in downtown Charleston and from Patriots Point in nearby Mount Pleasant. Admission requires a fee. For information, contact Park Superintendent, Drawer R, Sullivan's Island, SC 29482.

The Confederate flag flies over the ruins of Fort Sumter.

(Massachusetts Commander, Military Order of the Loyal Legion, and the U.S. Army Military History Institute)

The next day, Beauregard lived up to the chivalrous terms he had originally offered Anderson. The Union commander was permitted to order a 50-gun salute to his fallen colors. When the Federal artillery thundered, a stray ember touched off some powder in a keg. The blast injured five people and killed one, Union Private Daniel Hough, the first soldier to die in the American Civil War. In the next four years, at least 618,000 others would join him.

Jamestown, Virginia, August 1619

What could have so violently torn apart a nation founded on the unalienable rights to life, liberty, and the pursuit of happiness? What could drive the country to sacrifice more than 600,000 (some say nearly 700,000) of its young men?

In fact, the war began *long* before the spring of 1861.

In May 1607, a group of English settlers led by Captain Christopher Newport sailed into Chesapeake Bay, proceeded 30 miles up what they called the James River, and planted Jamestown, the first permanent English colony in America. Just 12 years later, in August 1619, Virginia tobacco farmers purchased their first consignment of 20 slaves from Dutch traders.

These 20 souls, bought and sold, were hardly the first slaves transported to the New World. By 1619, Spanish and Portuguese slavers had brought more than a million Africans, in bondage, to their Caribbean and South American colonies. Unlike the wealthy planters in the colonies of Spain and Portugal, however, few of the hard-scrabble English farmers could afford African slaves.

At first, *indentured servitude*, whereby Englishmen and women bound themselves to a *limited* period of service in return for passage to the New World, was a far more common source of cheap labor. But, by the close of the seventeenth century, the price of slaves fell and American colonists' wealth increased. Planters were now able to make the investment in a slave who, though he or she cost twice as much as an indentured servant, would yield a lifetime of labor. More than a lifetime, in fact. For the children of slaves were born slaves, and their children likewise—and so on, generation after generation, in perpetuity. Slavery was an eternal bargain.

Words of War

Indentured servitude was a form of voluntary servitude, in which a person bound himself to work for another for a fixed period (usually seven years) in return for passage to the New World.

A "Peculiar Institution"

At least it was a bargain in places where much land was controlled by a few wealthy planters. It was a bargain where vast amounts of cheap labor were required. It was a bargain where the work was so back-breakingly miserable that free white laborers shunned it. As the seventeenth century gave way to the eighteenth, slavery had taken little hold in the Northern colonies, where farms were small and typically worked by the families who owned them. Slaves were simply unnecessary. In the North, too, certain religious groups actively opposed slavery on moral grounds, with the Quakers taking the lead in this opposition as early as 1724.

But in the South, where the plantations were vast, slavery became essential to the region's economy. Nowhere was this more true than in South Carolina, whose planters were always the most ardent defenders of what came to be called (in polite circles) the "peculiar institution." Many Southerners were small farmers and owned few or no slaves, but slavery was very much a part of Southern life and society whether one owned slaves or not.

By the 1720s, rice plantations covered the tidal and inland swamps of the Low Country, and indigo thrived in the higher, drier elevations. At this time, African slaves accounted for 64 percent of South Carolina's population. They lived, many of them, in malarial swamps, worked by their masters until disease or exhaustion brought them the death that finally set them free.

Words of War

Peculiar institution was the euphemism Southerners (and some others) adopted when referring to slavery.

Three-Fifths of a Man

Tyranny: a word that rang in America through the later eighteenth century. The word swelled in volume and repetition, hurled by increasingly disaffected North American colonists against the government of the mother country, until a "shot heard 'round the world" was fired in 1775, a Declaration of Independence was proclaimed in 1776, a long and bitter war was fought to secure that independence, and, ultimately, a Constitution was wrought to "secure the blessings of liberty to ourselves and our posterity."

One meaning of *tyranny* is absolute power, cruelly wielded—an apt description, too, of slavery. Yet the irony seems to have been all but lost on the Founding Fathers. To be sure, Thomas Jefferson (himself an owner of slaves) proposed addressing slavery in the Declaration of Independence and, later, in the Constitution with an aim to abolishing it, but more conservative voices prevailed concerning both documents. By the final quarter of the eighteenth century, slavery was just too much a part of Southern life to be so readily disposed of.

Not that the Constitution entirely ignored the subject. The document stipulated that the importation of slaves—the slave trade—would cease by 1808 (Article I, Section 9). At the same time, however, the Constitution recognized and protected the institution of slavery, specifying that slaves who escaped into a free state were not thereby freed and had to be "delivered up on claim of the party to whom such labor may be due" (Article IV, Section 2.3).

There was another matter as well. Patrick Henry had helped stir the Revolution by declaring that "Taxation without representation is tyranny." Now the framers of the new U.S. Constitution sought to hammer out an equitable *representative* government. But they were bedeviled by the stubborn fact that the more *representatives* a state could claim, the more influence it would have in the federal government. For most purposes, Southerners were pleased to count their slaves as property. But when it came to apportioning representation in Congress, they suddenly preferred to count them as human beings. Seeking to minimize Southern influence, Northerners argued that slaves should be altogether excluded from the calculation.

At length, a compromise was reached. For purposes of levying taxes and apportioning representation, slaves were to be counted in the official census, but only as three-fifths of a person. The so-called "*Three-Fifths Compromise,*" embodied in Article I, Section 2.3 of the Constitution, was the first of many tortured and tortuous compromises American slavery would spawn. Like those later acts, the Three-Fifths Compromise was expedient in that it put off immediate conflict, but it *settled* nothing. The issue of slavery continued to smolder, and, with each subsequent compromise, it burned hotter and hotter—until it exploded.

Words of War

The **Three-Fifths Compromise** is represented in Article I, Section 2.3 of the U.S. Constitution. It stipulates that slaves (though that word is not used) may be counted as three-fifths of a person for purposes of levying taxes and apportioning representation in Congress.

Words of War

Those who advocated abolishing slavery altogether were called **abolitionists**. To some Northerners, the label was a badge of honor; to most Southerners, it was a mark of scorn.

Against the American Grain

If the Constitution condoned or at least countenanced slavery, growing numbers of Americans were finding the South's "peculiar institution" intolerable. Almost all of these people—the most radical of whom were called "*abolitionists*" because they wanted to abolish slavery entirely—lived in the North, where slavery had never taken root and where there had never been a demand for cheap agrarian labor on a vast scale. (However, at least in 1861, most Northerners were not abolitionists, and certainly racism was pervasive in the North.)

Freedom-Loving Quakers and Enlightened Colonists

As already mentioned, the Quakers mounted organized opposition to slavery by 1724. The colony of Rhode Island, a haven of toleration since its founding by dissident minister Roger Williams in 1636, legally abolished slavery in 1774. Elsewhere in the North, individual protests grew in number and volume.

The Feds Take a Stand

And even the federal government took action. A year before the Constitution was ratified, Congress enacted the *Northwest Ordinance* of 1787. The ordinance spelled out the basis for the government of what was then called the Northwest Territory (the vast region west of Pennsylvania, north of the Ohio River, east of the Mississippi River, and south of the Great Lakes) and for the eventual admission into the Union of its constituent parts. Under the ordinance, the territory was eventually to comprise a minimum of three and a maximum of five states.

Most important, the ordinance outlawed slavery in the lands of the Northwest Territory. The implications of this were profound. Not only was it the first federal pronouncement against slavery, but inasmuch as the ordinance regulated the expansion of the country—the nation's future—it more than hinted that this future should be one *without* slavery. On a more pragmatic and immediate level, the ordinance ensured that, at some time, three to five more "free" states would counterbalance the slave states, thereby checking and diminishing slaveholding interests and influence in Congress.

A Simple Machine

The thought behind the antislavery aspects of the Northwest Ordinance was to end slavery gradually, reducing through the machinery of representative government the influence of slaveholding states. Thus the "peculiar institution" would eventually just go away.

It might have happened just that way. As immigration from Europe increased after the Revolution, cheap labor became more plentiful, and there were growing indications that the economic utility of slavery was diminishing. Moreover, the markets for the chief slave-produced crops of the South—tobacco, rice, and indigo—though large, were finite, what today would be called "mature markets," with little potential for growth. Maybe, just maybe, as the years went by, slavery would disappear of its own accord as part of a natural economic process.

But there *was* another Southern crop of some importance. Along the Southern coast, black-seed, long-staple cotton was cultivated. Before it could be exported for weaving into cloth, it had to be cleaned of its seeds. This was easy to do with black-seed cotton; the seeds could be expelled simply by passing the cotton bolls through a pair of rollers.

The trouble was that black-seed cotton could be grown only in a limited coastal area. The vast interior lower South grew only green-seed, short-staple cotton—the seeds of which stubbornly resisted cleaning. There was only one way to separate seeds from fiber: slowly and tediously by hand, one cotton boll at a time. Even with slave labor, the work was time-consuming and expensive, and the potential of cotton as a source of profit for the lower South was proportionately limited.

Eli Whitney, Inventor

Eli Whitney was about as Yankee as a boy could be. Massachusetts born and Yale educated, he took the offer of a teaching job down in Georgia in 1792, only to find, on his arrival, that the promised post had somehow evaporated. Jobless, cashless, marooned far from Massachusetts and Connecticut, Whitney was rescued by Catherine Lidfield Greene, owner of Mulberry Grove, a large Georgia plantation. She befriended Whitney and introduced him to another Yankee and Yalee, Phineas Miller, who was the manager of Greene's property.

The pair hit it off and, among other things, fell to discussing how much export money could be made if only the green-seed, short-staple cotton produced at Mulberry Grove and other plantations of the Southern interior could be processed economically. Great Britain, in the throes of an Industrial Revolution, was building mill after mill to turn out cotton cloth on new automated looms. Its hunger for raw cotton looked to be insatiable.

Words of War

The **cotton gin** was a device for separating the seeds from cotton fiber so that the fiber could be woven into cloth. "Gin," short for engine, was what the eighteenth century called any labor-saving mechanical device.

Whitney transformed the discussions into action. With funding from Greene (some even claim that the initial idea was hers), the young man put together a crude model of a simple four-part machine. It had a hopper from which the cotton was fed onto a revolving cylinder studded with hundreds of short wire hooks. These hooks were closely set in rows that matched fine grooves cut into a stationary piece that strained out the seeds as the fiber flowed through it to the "clearer," a cylinder sporting bristles that brushed the cotton from the hooks, letting it fly off by centrifugal force.

In 1794, Whitney perfected his crude prototype, secured a patent, and partnered with Miller to make and service the new "*cotton gins.*" The machines were so successful—and so elegantly simple—that the partners found themselves pirated out of business by 1797. Planters made their own gins or bought cheaper knockoffs from any number of unscrupulous manufacturers. "An invention can be so valuable as to be worthless to the inventor," Whitney later moaned.

A New Economy

Valuable? During the first half of the nineteenth century, cotton exports came to exceed the value of all other American exports *combined*. The cotton gin made cotton king in the South and the leading product of the United States.

Constitutional compromise ended the importation of slaves in 1808. Eighteen years earlier, in 1790, the first U.S. census had counted 697,897 slaves. The census of 1810, two years *after* the slave-trade ban, counted 1,191,354 slaves, an increase of 70 percent. On the eve of Civil War, in 1860, the census enumerated 3,953,760 slaves. The cotton gin created a new economy for the South and had, in the process, renewed, reaffirmed, and increased the demand for slave labor to pick the cotton, feed the gins, bind the bales, and load them for shipment.

Count Off!

In 1790, the United States produced about 3,000 bales (500 lbs. each) of cotton. In 1801, after the widespread introduction of the cotton gin, production was 100,000 bales; in 1820, 400,000 bales; on the eve of the Civil War, cotton production reached 4,000,000 bales.

A Major Purchase

The vast Louisiana Territory, some 90,000 square miles of land west of the Mississippi River, was French until the defeat of France in what Europe called the Seven Years' War and America called the French and Indian War. In 1763, France ceded the territory to its ally Spain as compensation for the Caribbean territories Spain lost in the war. In 1800, however, Napoleon Bonaparte reacquired the territory by secret treaty in exchange for parts of Tuscany, which the "Little Corporal" pledged to conquer on behalf of Spain. Napoleon also promised to maintain Louisiana as a buffer

Voices

On March 4, 1858, as war loomed, Southern Senator James H. Hammond warned his Northern colleagues: "You dare not make war upon cotton! No power on earth dares make war upon it. Cotton is king." And "King Cotton," one of the great catch phrases of the nineteenth century, was born.

between Spain's North American settlements and the United States. But no sooner was the secret treaty concluded than Napoleon abandoned his Tuscan campaign, and France and Spain fell to disputing. Beginning in 1802, Spain responded to its ally's broken promise by closing the Mississippi River to *American* trade—the first step in Spain's plan to retake the Louisiana Territory.

President Thomas Jefferson could not tolerate so complete a disruption of western trade. However, neither did he relish the prospect of Napoleon entering North America. True, the French armies were currently bogged down in the Caribbean, vainly fighting tropical diseases and the brilliant Haitian revolutionary Toussaint-Louverture. Just now, they posed little threat to the continent, but Jefferson also feared that the ongoing warfare between France and England would likely result in the *English* seizure of the Louisiana Territory. Any way he looked at it, it was a bad situation, and, short of going to war with France, President Jefferson decided to resolve the crisis by sending James Monroe to Napoleon with an offer for the purchase of Florida and the port city of New Orleans.

The president's plan was not only to reclaim the right to Mississippi River navigation, but also to capitalize on a discovery that had been made years earlier, in 1790, when U.S. Navy Captain Robert Gray found and named (after his ship, the USS *Columbia*) the Columbia River on the Northwest coast. With a presence established at the mouth of the Mississippi, and with the Columbia already claimed for the United States, Jefferson could find justification for laying claim to the vast territory lying *between* the rivers as well.

Buying New Orleans was a very good idea. But Monroe, as it turned out, was offered something even better. Resolving to cut his Caribbean losses, Napoleon decided to withdraw from the Americas altogether. For him, all of Louisiana was now a liability. Even as Monroe was crossing the Atlantic, Napoleon's minister Talleyrand asked Robert R. Livingston, U.S. foreign minister to France, how much Jefferson would offer not just for New Orleans and Florida, but for the entire Louisiana Territory. A bargain was struck for 60 million francs.

Words of War

By the **Louisiana Purchase** of 1803, the United States acquired from France territory extending from the Mississippi River to the Rocky Mountains between the Gulf of Mexico and the Canadian border for the bargain price of $15 million.

Yet even Jefferson did not at first grasp the full scope of the *Louisiana Purchase*. He saw it as a means of avoiding war, of protecting western trade, of staking a claim on the continent all the way to the Pacific, and, most immediately, of providing a convenient space for the peaceful "relocation" of the Indians from east of the Mississippi to west of the river.

In the South, however, many saw the vast territory as a virtually unlimited cotton field.

"Title Page to a Great Tragic Volume"

But more cotton also meant more slaves. Abolitionists eagerly pointed to the Northwest Ordinance, which had (they said) established a nonslavery precedent for *all* new territories. Pro-slavery factions responded with legalistic brilliance: True, the Constitution specified an end to the slave trade, but it did not restrict slavery itself, and, furthermore, by the fugitive-slave provision and the Three-Fifths Compromise, it frankly acknowledged the legitimacy of slavery. Moreover, the Fifth Amendment, in the sacred Bill of Rights, guaranteed the security of property, which, after all, is what slaves were. Finally—and this was, for the South, the most compelling argument in support of their "peculiar institution"—the Constitution gave to the individual states all powers and authority not specifically reserved to the federal government.

The regulation of slavery was nowhere reserved to federal authority; therefore, it must be a right of the individual states. Those states that opposed slavery, Southerners argued, could abolish it within their own borders, but states that wished to protect, preserve, and perpetuate slavery had, within *their* borders, the right to do so as well.

The years following the Louisiana Purchase widened the gulf that slavery gouged between North and South. A major crisis came during 1818–19, when the United States Senate consisted of 22 Senators from Northern states and 22 from Southern states. Precariously, ever since the end of the Revolution, the balance between the nonslaveholding North and the slaveholding South had been preserved with the addition of each new state. Now the territory of Missouri petitioned Congress for admission to the Union as a slaveholding state. The balance suddenly threatened to shift.

Representative James Tallmadge of New York responded to Missouri's statehood petition by introducing an amendment to the statehood bill, calling for a ban on the further introduction of slavery into the state (but persons who were slaves in the present territory would remain slaves after the transition to statehood) and for the emancipation of all slaves born in the state when they reached 25 years of age. Thus, by attrition, slavery would be eliminated from Missouri. The House passed the Tallmadge amendment, but the Senate rejected it, adjourning afterward without reaching a decision on Missouri statehood.

When the Senate reconvened, a long, rancorous debate began. Northern Senators held that Congress had the right to ban slavery in new states. Southerners asserted that new states had the same right as the original 13: to determine whether or not they would allow slavery.

At last, in March 1820, a compromise was cobbled together. It was agreed that Missouri would enter the Union as a slave state, but, simultaneously, that Maine (hitherto a part of Massachusetts) would be admitted as a free state. So, for the moment, the slave state/free state balance was maintained. Looking toward the future, the so-called Missouri Compromise called for a line to be drawn across the Louisiana Territory at a latitude of 36°30', north of which slavery would be permanently banned, except in the case of Missouri.

As some saw it, the *Missouri Compromise* staved off civil war. Others, among them Thomas Jefferson and John Quincy Adams, looked at it differently. To the aging Jefferson, the rickety compromise, "like a fire bell in the night, awakened and filled me with terror." With equal foresight, Adams read it as what he called the "title page to a great tragic volume."

The Least You Need to Know

- ◆ The bloodless fall of Fort Sumter was the first battle of the Civil War, in which 620,000 Americans would eventually die.

- ◆ The large-scale cultivation of such Southern crops as rice, indigo, tobacco, and, most of all, cotton created and perpetuated the demand for slave labor.

- ◆ By the end of the eighteenth century, slavery showed signs of diminishing, but the introduction of the cotton gin in 1794 made large-scale cotton cultivation economically feasible and renewed the demand for slave labor.

- ◆ Men would fight the Civil War for many reasons, but the root cause of the war was slavery. The North wanted ultimately to end it, and the South refused to part with it.

- ◆ The Missouri Compromise of 1820 staved off civil war, but also showed that violent conflict over the slavery issue was almost certainly inevitable.

Chapter 2

Liberty and Union, Now and Forever?

In This Chapter

- The Nullification Crisis
- The abolitionist movement and its leaders
- The Underground Railroad
- Texas independence and the Mexican War
- California gold rush

As mentioned in the first chapter, those who scoff at the "schoolbook" notion that slavery was the root cause of the Civil War will typically tell you that the *real* cause of the war was economic. Well, they do have a point: Aside from the moral obscenity of involuntary servitude, slavery was very much an economic issue, and, in this sense, the Civil War was indeed fought for reasons of economics. To be sure, bigotry and racism permitted slavery to flourish, but it was the large-scale plantation economics of the South that drove, fed, and sustained the "peculiar institution."

This chapter explores the brutal, brute forces of an economy bound to slavery—a way of life that tore apart a people who had, less than a century earlier, declared themselves one.

The South Says No

Slavery was part and parcel of the South's agrarian economic system, dedicated to producing raw materials for manufacture by others. Some of these raw materials, chiefly cotton, were shipped to textile mills in the North, but most of what the South produced was exported. Raw cotton was spun into cloth in the great mills of England, which in turn exported the manufactured product back to the United States.

Through the first quarter of the nineteenth century, the South enjoyed relatively free trade with its European customers, little hampered by tariffs and duties. But although this was a boon to the agricultural economy of the South, it was a burden to the fledgling industrial economy of the North. When Americans imported their manufactured goods from abroad, homegrown industry suffered, struggled, and was stunted.

Words of War

A **protective tariff** is a tax imposed on imported goods with the purpose of discouraging importation and, therefore, promoting the manufacture and sale of domestic goods.

To help foster American industry, Congress passed a stiff *protective tariff* law in 1828, levying a hefty duty on manufactured goods imported from abroad. Predictably, the Northeast embraced the legislation, whereas the South voiced its outrage. If tariffs made it too costly for Americans to buy European goods, Europe would buy less of the South's raw materials and the region's export business would dry up. Southerners decried the 1828 measure as a "Tariff of Abominations."

Calhoun's Theory

John C. Calhoun, son of the South Carolina Piedmont region at the foot of the Appalachians, was a congressman whose fiery nationalism moved him to introduce the declaration of war against Britain in June 1812. So ardent was he during the War of 1812 that a colleague dubbed him the "young Hercules who carried the war on his shoulders." After the war, his advocacy of nationalism continued to know no bounds. He promoted federal funding of a permanent road system and the creation of a standing army and modern navy. He even voted in favor of a protective tariff in 1816. The following year, President James Monroe appointed him secretary of war, and John Quincy Adams, Monroe's secretary of state, declared Calhoun to be "above all sectional and factious prejudices more than any other statesman of this Union with whom I have ever acted."

But the admiration of his president and his colleagues was not enough to satisfy the ambitions of John C. Calhoun. He wanted desperately to be president himself, but although he served as vice president to both John Quincy Adams and Andrew Jackson, the higher office repeatedly eluded him. Calhoun became increasingly cantankerous and began to execute a 180-degree turn away from passionate nationalism and toward fanatical regionalism. In 1828, while serving as Adams's vice president, he responded to the "Tariff of Abominations" with an anonymous pamphlet, the *South Carolina Exposition and Protest*, arguing that the tariff could be declared "null and void" by any state that deemed it unconstitutional.

Words of War

Nullification is the concept that a state may nullify and refuse to obey or enforce any federal law it considers unconstitutional. The concept rested on the related principle of **states' rights,** which is the doctrine that the individual states do command all powers and authority not *explicitly* assigned to the federal government by the Constitution.

The idea of nullification was not original with Calhoun. Indeed, James Madison and Thomas Jefferson introduced the concept when they wrote the Virginia and Kentucky resolutions of 1798 and 1799. The resolutions declared that the Alien and Sedition Acts (repressive, reactionary legislation enacted by the Federalist administration of J. Q. Adams's father, John Adams, and a skittish Congress) violated the Bill of Rights. Because they were therefore unconstitutional, Jefferson and Madison argued, they could and should be nullified by any state that chose to do so.

Despite this impressive precedent, Calhoun had difficulty garnering support for nullification in 1828. Even most Southern states repudiated the concept, and Jefferson Davis himself, the Mississippian destined to become the president of the Confederate States of America, argued forthrightly against nullification, asserting that the states had no such right. In any case, a major battle over the Tariff of Abominations was averted by the 1828 election of Andrew Jackson, a Southerner, who pledged tariff reform.

Yet the promised reform proved disappointing in scope, and the Tariff Act of 1832, passed during Jackson's administration, again offended the South. Calhoun abruptly resigned as vice president, gained election to the Senate, and the state of South Carolina called a convention that, on November 24, 1832, passed an Ordinance of Nullification forbidding collection of tariff duties in the state. Another South Carolina senator, Robert Y. Hayne, first presented Calhoun's nullification theory in the Senate, arguing not only that a state could nullify an unconstitutional law, but also that it could, as a last resort, even secede from the Union.

In reply to Hayne, Daniel Webster, senator from Massachusetts, made an eloquent defense of the powers of the federal government versus the alleged rights of the states, concluding with the stirring appeal, "Liberty and Union, now and forever, one and inseparable!"

Nullification had brought the nation to a crisis, a showdown between the will of a state and the law of the nation. And the scope of the crisis went well beyond the issue of the tariff. Calhoun and the other advocates of nullification were really fighting for protection of slavery, which, they saw, would in all likelihood someday be abolished by a Northern majority in Congress—unless the doctrine of states' rights could be made to override the national will, which the South feared would soon be dictated by the North. One need look no further than the nullification crisis for proof that, for the South, slavery was an intensely economic issue.

Jackson Acts

Calhoun hoped and believed that Jackson (a Southerner, after all) would back down on the tariff. To the senator's chagrin, however, the president responded on December 10 with a declaration upholding the constitutionality of the tariff, denying the power of any state to block enforcement of a federal law and threatening armed intervention to collect duties. He secured from Congress passage of a Force Act, empowering him to use the military to enforce the tariff.

With passage of the Force Act, outright civil war suddenly loomed; but, that same year, a compromise tariff was enacted, and although South Carolina did "nullify" the Force Act, it also accepted the new tariff, which made the nullification moot because the Force Act would not be used. Bloodshed was averted for now, but the nullification and states' rights concepts refused to die and would provide a rationale for the break-up of the Union less than three decades later. The times were dangerous indeed.

The Liberators

The times were dangerous for the nation in general, and for the South in particular. With each passing year of the nineteenth century, Northern opposition to slavery grew stronger, better organized, more loftily eloquent, and increasingly militant. For Southerners, the issue of slavery might have been based on economics, but, in the North, moral passion was now speaking louder than the collective purse.

Genius of Universal Emancipation

At first, William Lloyd Garrison (1805–1879) was typical of the liberal white Northerners who opposed slavery. A native of Newburyport, Massachusetts, he became co-editor of a genteel abolitionist periodical called *The Genius of Universal Emancipation*. But the more Garrison thought and wrote about slavery, the less genteel he became until, on January 1, 1831, he published the first issue of *The Liberator*—a radical and eloquent abolitionist periodical that declared slavery no less than an abomination in the sight of God—and called for the immediate emancipation of all slaves.

The radical *Liberator* rapidly galvanized the abolitionist movement. Three years after the debut of *The Liberator*, Garrison founded the American Anti-Slavery Society and embarked on a national campaign of what he called "moral suasion." Slavery would end, he declared, when a majority of white Americans experienced a "revolution in conscience." Garrison sought just such a revolution. In 1842, he exhorted *Northerners* to break with the Union because the Constitution protected slavery. A pacifist who abhorred violence, Garrison nevertheless hailed John Brown's bloody 1859 raid on Harpers Ferry for the purpose of stealing guns to arm slaves for a general uprising (see Chapter 13).

Voices

William Lloyd Garrison, from the first issue of *The Liberator*, January 1, 1831:

> … I determined, at every hazard, to lift up the standard of emancipation in the eyes of the nation, within sight of Bunker Hill and in the birthplace of liberty. That standard is now unfurled; and long may it float, unhurt by the spoliations of time or the missiles of a desperate foe—yea, till every chain be broken, and every bondman set free! Let Southern oppressors tremble—let their secret abettors tremble—let their Northern apologists tremble—let all the enemies of the persecuted blacks tremble ….

> … I do not wish to think, or speak, or write, with moderation. No! No! Tell a man whose house is on fire to give a moderate alarm; tell him to moderately rescue his wife from the hands of the ravisher; tell the mother to gradually extricate her babe from the fire into which it has fallen—but urge me not to use moderation in a cause like the present.

A Life in Search of Liberation

A tonic too strong for many, even in the North, *The Liberator* was the most forceful white voice in support of abolition. In 1845, a gripping account of slavery and liberation by an escaped Maryland slave named Frederick Douglass was heard as the most compelling African American voice of liberation. Garrison thrilled his readers with violent eloquence, but the autobiographical *Narrative of the Life of Frederick Douglass* brought home the collective inhumanity of slavery and the individual humanity of the slaves. Although both Garrison and Douglass sought to end slavery, Douglass disagreed with Garrison over breaking with the Union. Douglass wanted to work within the Constitution.

Frederick Douglass, an escaped Maryland slave whose autobiography and stirring oratory brought home the collective inhumanity of slavery and the individual humanity of the slaves.

(UPI/Corbis-Bettmann)

Murder in Virginia

As the South saw it, violent words were dangerous enough, but seething under the chivalrous surface of Southern society was fear of a violence beyond mere words.

In much of the South, black slaves outnumbered white owners, and fear of *servile insurrection* was never far from the thoughts of slaveholders. Nat Turner was a slave on the plantation of Joseph Travis in Southampton County, Virginia. A fiery lay-preacher, Turner gathered a band of rebellious fellow slaves. Just before dawn of August 22, 1831, he and his followers killed every white member of the Travis household. They then swept through the countryside, killing every white they encountered during the next 24 hours—perhaps 60 people in all.

Words of War

Southerners feared a massive **servile insurrection**—their term for a slave rebellion.

The white response was, in turn, swift and bloody. Turner and 50 of his band were captured and summarily tried. Twenty were hanged. Dissatisfied with this display of "justice," bands of white avengers ranged the countryside, torturing and killing whatever blacks they happened to run across.

It was all well and good to speak of tariffs, economics, and states' rights, but in Southern society, slavery was clearly an issue of life—and of death.

> **Count Off!**
>
> By 1861, one third of the Southern population of 12,000,000 were slaves; 384,000 whites were slave owners, but only about 1,800 whites owned more than 100 slaves.

Notes from Underground

Legislative pressure, public eloquence, and physical violence were not the only weapons wielded against slavery. Beginning in the 1830s, a loose network of white abolitionists and free blacks created an *Underground Railroad* to smuggle slaves out of the South and into the free states of the North. The "conductors," as the secret operatives of the system were called, transferred the fugitives ("passengers" or "freight") gradually northward from one secret safe house ("station") to another. During the 1830s, '40s, and '50s, 50,000–100,000 slaves "followed the North Star" to freedom by way of the Underground Railroad (even though the railroad's "terminals" never reached into the *deep* South—southern Georgia, Alabama, and Mississippi).

> **Words of War**
>
> The **Underground Railroad** was a secret network that helped fugitive slaves escape from the South to the free states of the North and, sometimes, into Canada.

Although the rewards of freedom were greatly prized, the risks were grave. "Conductors" were menaced, beaten, and even killed, and fugitive slaves, once retaken, were often severely punished as an example to others. When the Supreme Court ruled in 1842 (in *Prigg* v. *Pennsylvania*) that states were not required to enforce the Fugitive Slave Law of 1793 (which provided for the return of slaves who escaped to free states), Southern opposition to the Underground Railroad became especially intense and bitter.

War and Gold

As the nation inexorably tore along the seam dividing North from South, increasing numbers of Americans turned their eyes westward. In the years before the Civil War, traffic on the Oregon Trail and the other overland trails multiplied. In the nation's time of trouble, the West held hope and, it seemed, the future.

Mexican Sunset

While the prairies of the Midwest and the plains of the West began to fill, the Southwest, still the territory of the Republic of Mexico, was also being settled by a growing number of American colonists. The most important of these was Moses Austin, who secured a Texas land grant from what was then the Spanish government of Mexico. In 1821, before he could begin the settlement, Austin fell ill and died. From his deathbed, he asked his son, Stephen F. Austin, to carry out his plans.

By this time, Mexico had won independence from Spain and, under terms established by a special act of the new Mexican government, Stephen Austin brought more than 1,200 American families to Texas. By 1836, the American population of Texas had swelled to 50,000, while Mexicans numbered a mere 3,500.

The large American colony chafed under Mexican rule. The colonists, predominantly Protestant, had religious differences with the overwhelmingly Catholic Mexicans, and they also felt themselves culturally and "racially" superior to the Mexicans. Most of all, however, the Texas colonists objected to Mexican laws forbidding slavery. Austin tried to negotiate with the country's president, Antonio Lopez de Santa Anna, for a degree of autonomous Mexican statehood for Texas, but failed and was even imprisoned in Mexico City for two years. Released in 1835, embittered and broken in health, Austin urged Texans to support a Mexican revolt against Santa Anna, thereby triggering the Texas Revolution.

Santa Anna led troops into Texas during January 1836 and reached San Antonio in February. There, against the advice of independence leader Sam Houston, a force of perhaps 189 Texans made a stand behind the walls of San Antonio de Valero, a decayed Spanish mission better known as the Alamo because of its proximity to a grove of cottonwood (in Spanish, *alamos*) trees. The little Texas band held off 1,800 troops for 10 days, until March 6, when 1,400 men of the Mexican siege force breached the mission's wall and all the Alamo's defenders were killed. (The most famous defender, Davy Crockett, probably survived to be taken prisoner and was then executed.)

This Mexican "victory" made martyrs of the Alamo band and spurred Texans, now united under Houston's brilliant leadership, to victory at the Battle of San Jacinto (April 21, 1836), where Santa Anna was defeated and Texas won its independence.

The new republic immediately agitated for annexation to the United States. Congress and the president met this with reluctance, however. Not only would it mean adding another slave state to the Union, upsetting the delicate balance of compromise, but it would also surely touch off a war with Mexico. But when France and England made overtures of alliance to Texas, outgoing President John Tyler finally urged Congress to adopt an annexation resolution, and Tyler's successor, James K. Polk, admitted Texas to the Union on December 29, 1845.

Sites and Sights

The Alamo, a Franciscan mission officially known as the Mission San Antonio de Valero, became an American icon as the site of the battle between a small band of Texans led by Jim Bowie, William B. Travis, and including Davy Crockett and a large contingent of Mexican soldiers commanded by Antonio Lopez de Santa Anna during February 23–March 6, 1836. Recent scholarship suggests that the number of Alamo defenders, traditionally believed to be 189, might have been closer to 257.

Located on the Alamo Plaza in San Antonio, the Alamo is one of the nation's most-visited tourist attractions. Contact: 1-210-225-1391.

In the meantime, England and France also demonstrated undue interest in California, held so weakly by Mexico that it was ready to fall into any waiting hands. Polk offered Mexico $40 million for California. When the offer was spurned, Polk threw his support behind the so-called Bear Flag Rebellion staged by the small American colony in California, and the territory's independence from Mexico was proclaimed.

During this time, too, Mexico disputed the boundary of the new state of Texas. Polk dispatched troops to Texas and, on May 13, 1846, responding to a Mexican attack, declared war on Mexico. Although some, especially in New England, protested that war with Mexico was nothing less than an exercise in U.S. imperialism, the conflict garnered overwhelming popular support, and in some states, volunteers were so numerous that many had to be turned away from recruiting offices.

U.S. forces enjoyed victory after victory, often against superior Mexican numbers, and, on September 13, 1847, Chapultepec Palace, the seemingly impregnable fortress guarding Mexico City, fell to General Winfield Scott. On September 17, Santa Anna surrendered.

By the Treaty of Guadalupe Hidalgo (ratified by the U.S. Senate on March 10, 1848), Mexico ceded to the United States New Mexico (which included parts of the present states of Utah, Nevada, Arizona, and Colorado) and California. Mexico also renounced claims to Texas above the Rio Grande.

Optimists believed the vast new Western territories would relieve some of the North-South tension; pessimists pointed to the necessity of making any number of urgent and potentially explosive decisions as to whether an acquired territory would join the Union as a free state or a slave state.

The Mexican War meant something else as well. It was the baptism in blood of commanders such as Ulysses S. Grant, Robert E. Lee, and many other Northern and Southern officers destined in less than two decades to meet, as foes, on fields much closer to home.

Gold Rush

Johann Augustus Sutter was a hard-luck case. Born in Kandern, Germany, in 1803, he went bankrupt there and, one jump ahead of his creditors, fled to the American Southwest, where he plunged into the Santa Fe trade, going bust two more times before he settled in Mexican California in 1838 and built a large ranch in the country of the central valley. On January 24, 1848, one of his employees, James Wilson Marshall, went out to inspect the race of a new mill Sutter had built. Something shiny in the sediment at the bottom of the mill race caught his eye. It was gold.

Sutter's luck had changed.

Or so it seemed. Within a month and a half, all of Sutter's employees had deserted him in search of gold. Unstaffed, the Sutter ranch began to fall apart. Worse, his claims to the land adjacent to the mill were judged invalid. As those around him (it seemed) grew gold rich, Sutter went broke—again. He died bitter and bankrupt in 1880.

Tough luck for him. For the rest of the country, the California Gold Rush of 1849 was on! All over the nation, men dropped their tools, left their jobs, kissed their families good-bye, and headed for the south fork of the American River to find their fortunes. Although most who prospected never stuck it rich, the Gold Rush lasted through the eve of the Civil War and exploded the region's population.

This rapid influx hastened the entry of California into the Union. It became the 31st state in 1850, and once more the delicate balance shifted. Once more Congress was compelled to rush to bitter, divisive compromise, and the nation, bathed in the warm glow of California gold, drifted even closer to civil war.

The Least You Need to Know

- The Nullification Crisis of 1832–1833 was an early contest between the sovereignty of individual states and the authority of the federal government. It almost triggered civil war in the 1830s.

◆ John C. Calhoun turned the Nullification Crisis into a battle over "states' rights," which ultimately meant a struggle to preserve and protect slavery.

◆ In the years leading up to the war, slavery was under multiple attacks. While abolitionist leaders brought moral pressure to bear against slavery, the Underground Railroad smuggled a small but significant number of slaves to freedom, and slave revolt loomed in the Southern consciousness as a constant fear.

◆ The opening of the Southwest dramatically upset the balance between slave states and free states, propelling the nation to its final great crisis before the war.

Descent into War

In This Chapter

- ◆ The Compromise of 1850 and the Kansas-Nebraska Act
- ◆ John Brown and the raid on Harpers Ferry
- ◆ The birth of the Republican Party
- ◆ Enter President Lincoln
- ◆ The first states secede

The awkward Missouri Compromise of 1820 (see Chapter 1) bent, wheezed, and broke under the weight of California gold. At the height of the Gold Rush, in 1849, more than 80,000 fortune seekers poured into the region. Statehood for the newly acquired territory was now an urgent issue; so urgent, South Carolina Congressman John C. Calhoun warned, that it could lead directly to civil war.

This chapter tells how the very steps that averted civil war for one more decade also made that war inevitable.

The Tortured Course of Compromise

During the first year of the Mexican War, 1846, Congress wanted to bring the conflict to a quick end and debated a bill to appropriate $2 million to compensate Mexico for what the lawmakers euphemistically termed "territorial adjustments." Seizing opportunity, Pennsylvania Congressman David Wilmot introduced an amendment called the Wilmot Proviso, which would have barred the introduction of slavery into any land acquired by the United States as a result of the Mexican War.

South Carolina's Calhoun angrily countered with four proposed resolutions:

- ◆ First, that all territories, including those acquired as a result of the war, were to be regarded as the common and joint property of the states

- ◆ Second, that Congress acts as agent for the states and can, therefore, make no law discriminating between the states and depriving any state of its rights with regard to any territory

- ◆ Third, that the enactment of any national law regarding slavery violates the Constitution and the doctrine of states' rights

- ◆ Fourth, that the people have the right to form their state governments as they wish, provided that such government is republican in principle

Nor did Calhoun leave his resolutions suspended in midair for leisurely contemplation. Action was required, he urged, for failure to maintain a balance between the demands of the North and the South would surely mean "civil war."

The Compromise of 1850

Action was not immediate, however. The year 1846 saw the commencement of a three-year debate on ways to brace and bolster the Missouri Compromise. That task was complicated by the accumulated eloquence of three decades of abolitionist voices (see Chapter 2), which made most Northerners unwilling to stand by while slavery was extended into any new territory above or below the line drawn by the 1820 Compromise.

Words of War

Popular sovereignty was the doctrine and policy introduced in the Compromise of 1850. It provided for the people of a territory to vote on whether the territory would apply for admission to the Union as a free state or a slave state. The federal government would be bound by the people's decision.

Stalemate, Senator Lewis Cass of Michigan saw, was fatal. He therefore advanced the doctrine of *popular sovereignty*, which provided for the organization of new territories without mention of slavery one way or the other. Only when the territory wrote its own constitution and applied for admission as a state would the people of the territory itself vote whether it would be slave or free.

To solve the immediate issue of California statehood, it was decided that California would be admitted to the Union directly instead of going through an interim territorial status. At this Southerners recoiled, assuming that California would vote itself free. (It did, as would, later, New Mexico.) So Senators Henry Clay of Kentucky and Daniel Webster of Massachusetts worked out a new compromise. California would be admitted as a free state, but the other territories acquired as a result of the Mexican War would be subject to popular sovereignty. Moreover, the slave trade in the District of Columbia (an embarrassment to foreign diplomats and other visitors from nations where slavery had long ceased to be tolerated) would be discontinued.

However, to appease the South, a strong fugitive slave law was passed, explicitly forbidding Northerners from giving refuge to escaped slaves. Finally, the federal government agreed to assume debts Texas (admitted as a slave state in 1845) incurred before it was annexed to the United States.

As with previous compromises, that of 1850 offended as many interests as it placated. Abolitionists were appalled by the Fugitive Slave Law, whereas states' rights supporters saw the slave/free balance in Congress tilting ever northward.

Kansas Bleeds

The Compromise of 1850 augmented the Missouri Compromise, but, four years later, when the territories of Nebraska and Kansas applied for statehood, Congress responded by repealing the Missouri Compromise altogether and passing the Kansas-Nebraska Act. This extended the doctrine of popular sovereignty beyond territory acquired as a result of the Mexican War, eliminating the 1820 slave/free line.

If the situation four years earlier had been explosive, the Kansas-Nebraska Act applied a match to the fuse. For although there was never any doubt that Nebraskans would vote themselves a free state, Kansas, to the south, was another matter. Pro-slavery Missourians and antislavery Iowans streamed across the territory's border—each side striving to achieve a majority. Many of the Missourians retreated to their home state after successfully electing a pro-slavery territorial legislature for Kansas, but the Iowans remained, and soon a chronic state of civil warfare developed between pro- and antislavery factions in what came to be called "Bleeding Kansas."

Typical of the violence was the 1856 raid against the antislavery stronghold of Lawrence. *Border ruffians* (pro-slavery Missourians) raided the town

Words of War

Border ruffians were pro-slavery Missourians who periodically raided eastern Kansas, intimidating and sometimes murdering antislavery settlers. For many border ruffians, the slavery issue was little more than an excuse for robbery.

in 1856, setting fire to a number of buildings, destroying a printing press, and killing several townspeople.

On the night of May 24, John Brown, a radical abolitionist who had taken command of the territory's so-called Free Soil Militia, led four of his sons and two other followers in an assault on pro-slavery settlers along the Pottawatomie Creek. Brown and his militia put five unarmed settlers to the sword, and then proudly claimed responsibility for the act, pronouncing it retribution for the sack of Lawrence. Although Kansas was ultimately admitted as a free state in 1861, guerrilla violence was repeated there throughout the Civil War.

John Brown, avenger of the abolitionist cause in Lawrence, Kansas, and leader of a later raid on Harpers Ferry in an effort to arm the slaves.

(Author's collection)

Beyond Compromise

By the 1850s, the people of the United States were traveling inexorably beyond all compromise. The journey was made on roads emotional as well as legal.

The Little Woman Who Made This Great War

Harriet Beecher was born in 1811 in Litchfield, Connecticut, one of eleven children of a prominent Congregationalist preacher, Lyman Beecher. Harriet's brother, Henry Ward Beecher, would earn fame as a Brooklyn-based abolitionist. Harriet embarked on a career as a teacher at a school her sister, Catherine, founded in Cincinnati, Ohio. In 1836, she married a theology professor, Calvin Ellis Stowe, and began writing books.

During the eighteen years she lived in Cincinnati, Stowe came to know slave owners from neighboring Kentucky, and she also met fugitive slaves. Slowly, the experience made its impression on her. In 1850, her husband was appointed to a professorship at Bowdoin College, in Brunswick, Maine. There Harriet Beecher Stowe began to write a book about slavery.

Uncle Tom's Cabin, or Life Among the Lowly tells the story of old Tom, a slave devoted to his kindly but debt-burdened Kentucky master, who is sold to the cruel Simon Legree. The story was published serially during 1851–1852 in a magazine called *National Era* and then appeared in book form later in 1852. A publishing sensation, it was aggressively promoted by abolitionists even as it was denounced by Southerners, who passed local legislation to suppress distribution of the book throughout the region. Doubtless, this only stimulated sales, which topped 300,000 in its first year of publication. Soon, the book was dramatized by a host of playwrights and thus reached an even wider audience, who were moved by the humanity of the slaves and horrified by the details of slave life Stowe depicted.

 Voices

In response to the enormous popularity of *Uncle Tom's Cabin*, some Southern writers decided to fight fire with fire, and a number of pro-slavery novels were published—the best known of which was Mary Henderson Eastman's paean to the culture of master and slave, *Aunt Phillis' Cabin, or Southern Life as It Is* (1852). In her next novel, Stowe herself took a different approach to portraying the evils of slavery. Her 1856 *Dred: A Tale of the Great Dismal Swamp* did not detail the misery of slave life, but attempted to portray how slavery corrupted and destroyed slaveholding society.

Uncle Tom's Cabin did much to humanize the slavery issue, winning the hearts and minds of many Northerners hitherto lukewarm on the issue of abolition. Reportedly, when President Lincoln received Stowe at the White House in 1862, he greeted her by saying, "So you're the little woman who wrote the book that made this great war."

Dred Verdict

The mayhem of Bleeding Kansas and the explosive popularity of *Uncle Tom's Cabin* were opening chords in the overture to the greater conflict to come. Another note was struck, to even more resounding effect, within the orderly confines of the Supreme Court. In 1857, the high court heard the appeal of one Dred Scott, fugitive slave.

Scott had belonged to John Emerson of St. Louis. An army surgeon, Emerson had been transferred first to Illinois and then to Wisconsin Territory, taking his slave with him. After Emerson's death in 1846, Scott returned to St. Louis, where he sued Emerson's widow for his freedom. He made his claim on the basis that he was now a citizen of Missouri, having been freed by virtue of his terms of residence in Illinois, where slavery was banned by the Northwest Ordinance, and in Wisconsin Territory, where the provisions of the Missouri Compromise made slavery illegal.

When the Missouri state court decided against Scott, his lawyers appealed to the Supreme Court. Predictably, the high court's antislavery Northern justices sided with Scott, while the pro-slavery Southerners upheld the Missouri court's decision. Chief Justice Roger B. Taney, native of the slave state of Maryland, had the final word. He held, in the first place, that neither free blacks nor enslaved blacks were citizens of the United States and, therefore, could not sue in federal court.

That alone would have settled the case, but Taney had more to say: He ruled that the Illinois law banning slavery had no force on Scott once he returned to Missouri, a slave state. The law in Wisconsin was likewise without force, because, he said, the Missouri Compromise was unconstitutional, a violation of the Fifth Amendment, which bars the government from depriving an individual of "life, liberty, or *property*" without due process of law. If slaves were indeed nothing more than "property," no state could liberate them by simply taking them from their owners.

Voices

Chief Justice Roger B. Taney, from the 1857 Supreme Court decision in *Dred Scott v. Sandford*:

> [The framers of the Declaration of Independence] regarded [blacks] as beings of an inferior order; and altogether unfit to associate with the white race ....

> [I]t is too clear for dispute, that the enslaved African race were not intended to be included, and formed no part of the people who framed and adopted this Declaration .... [They] knew that ... the negro race ... , by common consent, had been excluded from civilized governments and the family of nations, and doomed to slavery.

The Dred Scott Decision galvanized the abolitionist movement. Had the nation come to *this*—that the highest court in the land could use the Bill of Rights to *deny* freedom to a human being? Where presidents and legislators had waffled and compromised, the Supreme Court, third branch of the federal government, boldly ordered that government to honor the ownership of human beings *everywhere* in the nation.

By making slavery a Fifth Amendment issue, the Dred Scott Decision put the matter beyond compromise. If the constitutional rights of slave holders had to be universally upheld as long as slavery existed, slavery had to be universally accepted or universally abolished. There was no middle course, and, without a middle course, the people of the North and the South knew that war was all but a certainty.

Some More Blood: The Raid on Harpers Ferry

At Pottawatomie Creek, Kansas, John Brown had demonstrated that he was a man of sharp, swift, bloody deeds. In 1857, he moved from Kansas to Boston, the national hotbed of abolitionism. There, with the support of six of the most prominent abolitionists—Samuel Gridley Rowe, Thomas Wentworth Higginson, Theodore Parker, Franklin Sanborn, George L. Stearns, and Gerrit Smith—he raised cash to finance a raid he was planning on the federal arsenal at Harpers Ferry, Virginia (present-day West Virginia).

"One man and God can overturn the universe," he declared as he explained his plan to use the guns and ammunition appropriated from the arsenal to arm the slaves of the South for a massive rebellion.

The Raid Begins

John Brown led 16 white men and 5 black men to the federal arsenal and armory at the confluence of the Shenandoah and Potomac rivers. He and his band quickly took the armory and Hall's Rifle Works nearby, and then hunkered down to defend the prize, holding hostage some 60 residents of Harpers Ferry and the surrounding area, including the great-grandnephew of George Washington. Brown dispatched two of his black "soldiers" to alert local slaves. He counted on this pair to rouse thousands to "swarm."

None came. And when the fighting started, the first civilian Brown's men killed was a free black man.

The fighting began as the citizens of Harpers Ferry, surrounding Brown's position, opened fire and killed two of the abolitionist's sons. Sporadic fighting continued through the morning and afternoon, when the survivors barricaded themselves and their hostages in a firehouse adjacent to the armory.

Enter Lieutenant Colonel R. E. Lee

At this point, Lt. Col. Robert E. Lee, U.S. Army, and his former West Point student, Lt. James Ewell Brown Stuart—known familiarly as Jeb—arrived with a company of

U.S. Marines. Having been hurriedly called away from leave at his estate in Arlington, Virginia, where he was wrestling with the financial affairs of his late father-in-law, he was still wearing civilian clothing. Nevertheless, even out of uniform, Lee was a commanding presence: handsome, dignified, soft-spoken, and of aristocratic bearing. His intellect had put him at the top of his West Point class in 1829.

Arriving at Harpers Ferry amid wild rumors of a slave rebellion, Lee, trained at the Academy as a military engineer, moved deliberately. He let the night of the 17th pass; then, come morning, he sent Jeb Stuart under a flag of truce to demand Brown's surrender.

War News

The United States was so resolutely nonmartial in attitude and spirit before the Civil War that no army troops were available, even in the vicinity of a federal arsenal. A small marine detachment was handiest, so Lee became the only U.S. Army officer ever to command U.S. Marines.

His fiery eyes flashing, Brown refused. Stuart emerged from the parley and waved his broad-brimmed cavalryman's hat in a prearranged signal for the marines to charge. They made short work of the firehouse door and rushed in; doing their best to protect the hostages, they put two of Brown's men to the bayonet.

The battle lasted all of three minutes. Marine Lt. Israel Green stabbed and pummeled Brown with his sword, and all but four of the raiders were killed. Four citizens of Harpers Ferry, including the town's mayor, died, along with one marine.

John Brown's Body

The state of Virginia charged the wounded Brown and his surviving followers with treason, conspiracy to foment servile insurrection, and murder. Trial came swiftly, 10 days after the raid, and all were sentenced to hang.

War News

Like other executions of the day, the hanging of John Brown was a public event. Professor Thomas Jackson took his Virginia Military Institute class to bear witness. (Two years later, after his performance at the First Battle of Bull Run, he would be better known as General "Stonewall" Jackson.) Edmund Ruffin, destined to fire the first shot in earnest against Fort Sumter, was there, too. And so was a popular matinee idol by the name of John Wilkes Booth.

But, to the embarrassment of the Virginia government, John Brown did not die like the crazed fanatic southerners thought him to be. At his sentencing, he spoke calmly, reasonably, and eloquently, arguing that he had behaved in harmony with the New Testament injunction to "remember them that are in bonds, as bound with them." Brown concluded:

> Now, if it is deemed necessary that I should forfeit my life for the furtherance of the ends of justice, and mingle my blood further with the blood of my children and with the blood of millions in this slave country whose rights are disregarded by wicked, cruel, and unjust enactments— I submit; so let it be done.

Voices

John Brown left a haunting note to be read after his execution:

I, John Brown, am now quite certain that the crimes of this guilty land will never be purged away but with Blood. I had as I now think vainly flattered myself that without very much bloodshed, it might be done.

On the day of Brown's execution, December 2, 1859, the nation's most respected philosopher and man of letters, Ralph Waldo Emerson, joined William Lloyd Garrison to memorialize Brown before a mass gathering of abolitionists in Boston. By hanging John Brown, the Southern state of Virginia had given the North a martyr to its most radical cause. The song that, in 1862, would become immortal as "The Battle Hymn of the Republic" was originally called "John Brown's Body," with the opening lines, "John Brown's body lies a-mouldering in his grave,/But his soul goes marching on." For its part, after the Harpers Ferry raid, the South grew far less inclined to negotiate and talk peace. The die, it seemed, had been cast.

The Shattered Party

Following passage of the Kansas-Nebraska Act in 1854, the Whig Party, traditional opponent of the pro-Southern Democratic Party, lost credibility as the voice of abolition. Antislavery voters resented the repeal of the Missouri Compromise and its replacement by popular sovereignty. In 1854, a host of small abolitionist parties, most importantly the Free-Soil Party, the Conscience Whig Party, the Liberty Party, and the Anti-Nebraska Democratic Party, joined forces as the Republican Party.

The new party failed to capture the White House with their first presidential candidate, the famous Western explorer John C. Frémont, but it did win more than 100 congressional seats. Four years later, the party's candidate for senator from Illinois, Abraham Lincoln, made a national name for himself by his eloquence in a series of debates against incumbent Senator Stephen A. Douglas. Douglas won reelection, but Lincoln emerged as the party's standard bearer—even though his position on slavery was not dramatically different from Douglas's. Both Lincoln and Douglas favored banning slavery in the territories, but neither thought it constitutionally possible to abolish slavery outright by political action.

As the Republicans swept the Whigs aside, their influence and relatively strong stand against slavery drove radical Democrats in the South to claim that if a Republican were elected president in 1860, the Southern states would secede from the Union.

Had they presented a united front and a single candidate, the Democrats might have defeated Lincoln in 1860. However, going into the elections, the Democratic Party was fatally splintered. Stephen A. Douglas sought the Democratic nomination, but, by denouncing the pro-slavery constitution initially adopted by Kansas, he had alienated the South. (Although not an abolitionist, Douglas didn't want to see the spread of slavery.) Douglas did capture the nomination, but as the candidate of a shattered party. John C. Breckinridge was nominated by a breakaway group called the Southern Democratic Party, and another splinter group, the Constitutional Union party, fielded its own candidate, further splitting the party.

In the end, 123 electoral votes were divided among the various Democratic candidates, and 180 votes went to the Republican candidate, Abraham Lincoln.

Count Off!

Although clearly victorious in electoral votes, Lincoln won only a plurality (more than any other *single* candidate) of the popular vote. He received only 1,866,452 popular ballots against 2,815,617 cast for *all* his opponents.

Abraham Lincoln, 16th president of the United States.

(Harper's Pictorial History of the Civil War, *1866)*

The Union Dissolves

James Buchanan (1791–1868), 15th president of the United States, is remembered chiefly for two things: first, for his bachelorhood (he still stands as the only unmarried president the nation has ever elected); second, for his complete absence of moral strength and leadership in the final crises leading to the Civil War.

Personally opposed to slavery on moral grounds, he had done nothing to oppose it officially and, indeed, usually caved in to pro-slavery interests. His only strategy for preserving the Union consisted of placating the South by suppressing Northern anti-slavery agitation and by enforcing the Fugitive Slave Act of 1850. To the suffering citizens of Bleeding Kansas, he appealed for their acceptance of the unpopular pro-slavery "Lecompton Constitution" proposed for that state.

Once Lincoln was elected, the lame-duck Buchanan did not act when seven Southern states seceded. To be sure, he denounced their going, but he claimed he could find no Constitutional means to stop them.

But what of the president-elect? With the country he would soon lead falling to pieces about him—in part, falling to pieces *because of* him—Abraham Lincoln said nothing. He was determined to be silent until inauguration day.

Buchanan waited, too, eager now for the arrival of March 4, 1861, when the gangly figure from Illinois (unfriendly newspapers compared him to an ape or a baboon, and it was a cruel slur that his enemies, both in the North and the South, eagerly repeated) would lift a terrible burden from his unwilling shoulders.

The Least You Need to Know

- The Compromise of 1850 and the Kansas-Nebraska Act staved off civil war, even as they further polarized the nation.

- Guerrilla warfare between pro-slavery and antislavery forces in Kansas was a violent prelude to the Civil War.

- Harriet Beecher Stowe's *Uncle Tom's Cabin* (1852) put a human face on slavery and thereby greatly aided support for the abolitionist cause.

- The Supreme Court's decision in the Dred Scott Case outraged even moderate Northerners and made it clear that the slavery issue had gone beyond compromise.

- John Brown's Harpers Ferry raid failed to incite a universal slave insurrection, but it galvanized the abolitionist cause, further polarized the nation, and brought civil war closer.

Chapter 4

Bleak Inaugural

In This Chapter

◆ Secession follows Lincoln's election

◆ The South's economic and industrial handicaps

◆ A plot to assassinate President-elect Lincoln

◆ Lincoln's inaugural message

After Lincoln's election, seven Southern states immediately made good on their threat to secede:

1. First to leave the Union was South Carolina, on December 20, 1860

2. Mississippi followed on January 9, 1861

3. Florida on January 10

4. Alabama on January 11

5. Georgia on January 19

6. Louisiana on January 26

7. Texas on February 1

Four days later, delegates from these states met in Montgomery, Alabama, where they wrote a constitution for the Confederate States of America and named Mississippi's Jefferson Davis provisional president.

This chapter details the critical months and weeks before the fall of Fort Sumter.

"Black" Lincoln

No "transition teams" existed in Abraham Lincoln's day; no highly paid staff of advisors, "spin doctors," and consultants to make the change of office less turbulent. The president-elect did not even think to huddle with James Buchanan during the troubled interval before his inauguration. And even when Lincoln learned that Jefferson Davis had offered to negotiate peaceful relations with the United States, he kept silent.

Lincoln also knew that Senator John J. Crittenden of Kentucky was proposing, as a last-ditch alternative to war, the Crittenden Compromise—a set of six constitutional amendments to protect slavery while absolutely limiting its spread. Still, Lincoln stubbornly refused to commit himself to any position before taking office.

This might have done little harm had the president-elect not permitted others to *attribute* positions to him. When radical Republicans voiced their victorious candidate's unalterable opposition to compromises that might result in protecting, let alone extending, slavery, Lincoln was silent. Yet, in truth, Lincoln's primary objective was not to end or even limit slavery, but to save the Union. To save the Union, Lincoln was quite willing to consider protecting slavery where it existed, even by constitutional amendment, if necessary. The president-elect also believed that the Fugitive Slave Act, a duly enacted law, *should* be—and legally *had* to be—enforced.

These positions might have placated Southern extremists and staved off war a bit longer, but, by remaining silent between his election and his inauguration, Lincoln conveyed the impression that he fully shared the radical Republican opposition to compromise. So, calling him "Black Lincoln," state after state below the Mason-Dixon Line renounced the Union.

The Wayward Sisters

Because there were, at first, seven secession states, the press sometimes called them the Seven Sisters—a reference from Greek mythology to the daughters of Atlas and Pleione, who were changed into the stars of the constellation Pleiades, even as the breakaway states transformed themselves into the stars of a new flag. In response to the first wave of secession, Winfield Scott, the aged general-in-chief of the U.S. Army, advised President Lincoln simply to say to the seceded States, "wayward sisters depart in peace!" This advice came not from Buchanan-like timidity and indecision—Scott had been an aggressive hero in the War of 1812 and in the Mexican War—but from Scott's conviction that the Southern states could not long survive without the North and that, if allowed to go, they would, by and by, return. It was a view shared by William H. Seward, Lincoln's secretary of state, who likewise counseled, "let the erring sisters go."

Scott and Seward were not alone in their belief that the South—its industries poorly developed, its population one-third slave, and many of its free people dirt poor—was economically inferior and incapable of long sustaining itself. Certainly, few outside of the South believed that, if the conflict came to a fight, the "Sisters" could put up much of a show. One evening during the secession crisis, as the divided nation continued its march toward war, William Tecumseh Sherman tried to explain the odds to a Southern dinner companion. An Ohioan, Sherman had graduated near the top of the West Point Class of 1840, received his commission as second lieutenant, was dispatched to fight Seminole Indians in Florida, and then was forced to sit out the Mexican War as an administrative officer in California. Disappointed by the dearth of long-term prospects in a military career, he resigned his commission and joined a banking firm. Failing at this pursuit during the national financial panic of 1857, he took equally frustrating stabs at a few more ventures and, through old army buddies Braxton Bragg and Pierre Gustave Toutant Beauregard (both destined to become generals in the Confederate army), found a job as superintendent of the newly established Louisiana State Military Academy.

On Christmas Eve 1860, when news reached him that South Carolina had seceded from the Union, Sherman declared to the academy's classics professor, with whom he was dining, that "this country will be drenched in blood, and God only knows how it will end. It is all folly, madness, a crime against civilization! You [Southern] people speak so lightly of war; you don't know what you're talking about. War is a terrible thing!" Sherman continued:

> Besides, where are your men and appliances of war …? The North can make a steam engine, locomotive, or railway car; hardly a yard of cloth or a pair of shoes can you make. You are rushing into war with one of the most powerful, ingeniously mechanical, and determined people on earth—right at your doors. You are bound to fail. Only in your spirit and determination are you prepared for war. In all else you are totally unprepared, with a bad cause to start with. At first you will make headway, but as your limited resources begin to fail, shut out from the markets of Europe as you will be, your cause will begin to wane. If your people will but stop and think, they must see that in the end you will surely fail.

Sherman's assessment of the South's incapacity for a sustained struggle, though exaggerated, had a solid core of truth. The 11 states that eventually made up the Confederacy had a population of 12 million, of which 4 million were slaves. By contrast, the 23 states of the Union (to which even more would be added in the course of the war) had a combined population of some 22 million, all free.

Count Off!

Union banks held 81 percent of the nation's deposits, as well as $56 million in gold bullion. The Union's international credit was virtually unlimited, whereas the South was cash poor, gold poor, and, in order to establish credit in the world, would have to gain international recognition as a sovereign nation.

Sherman was wrong to assert that the South had no industry—on the eve of war, some 20,000 Southern factories employed about 100,000 workers—but Northern factories numbered well over 100,000 and employed in excess of a million workers. As to railroads, essential for transporting goods, war materiel, and troops, the South boasted a mere 9,000 miles of track—much of it limited by nonuniform and mutually incompatible gauges (track widths)—whereas the North was thoroughly networked with 20,000 miles of uniform-gauge track. How *could* the South hope to prevail?

Olive Branches

Representatives from the first secessionist states convened in Montgomery, Alabama, on February 8, 1861, and declared themselves a new nation, the Confederate States of America. Jefferson Davis of Mississippi was elected president and Alexander Stephens of Georgia vice president. Nevertheless, there were those in the North who thought that war could still be averted and the Union glued back together. One of these hopeful men was John J. Crittenden, senator from the *border state* of Kentucky.

Words of War

The **border states** were slave states that did not secede. They included Delaware, Maryland, Kentucky, and Missouri.

West Virginia declared itself loyal to the Union and seceded from the rest of Virginia when that state left the Union. On June 20, 1863, West Virginia was admitted to the Union as a new state; ushered in as a slave state, it is usually counted among the border states.

As for Kentucky, it declared itself neutral, but Kentuckians fought on both sides.

Crittenden Tries

Crittenden not only wanted to preserve Kentucky for the Union, he wanted to preserve the Union. In December 1860, he presented a series of six constitutional amendments that would effectively revive the old Missouri Compromise of 1820 and extend the line dividing slave states from free all the way to the Pacific. In addition, the federal government would see to the strict enforcement of the Fugitive Slave Law and would even indemnify owners of fugitive slaves whose return was prevented by antislavery elements in the North. Popular sovereignty would be extended to all the territories, and slavery in the District of Columbia was to be protected from congressional action.

Lame-duck president James Buchanan said nothing about the Crittenden Compromise, and President-elect Lincoln declined to address the proposal directly, but he instructed a Republican colleague to "entertain no proposition for a compromise in regard to the extension of slavery." And that was quite sufficient to deliver a mortal wound to the proposal. In January 1861, Crittenden tried to get a public hearing on the compromise, introducing a resolution calling for a national referendum on his proposals. The Senate never acted on the resolution.

Buchanan Acts—More or Less

On the night after Christmas, six days after South Carolina seceded, Major Robert Anderson moved his small garrison from the highly vulnerable Fort Moultrie, on Sullivan's Island, South Carolina, to the stronger Fort Sumter. As if it were a sovereign nation, South Carolina protested this action to President Buchanan. At last, the bachelor president was roused to action. Instead of surrendering the fort, he sent supplies and reinforcements, albeit via an unarmed civilian merchant steamer, the *Star of the West.*

As she passed Charleston, South Carolina gunners drew a bead and opened up on her. The *Star* turned back. Fort Sumter would neither be reinforced nor resupplied, and James Buchanan once again settled back uneasily to await the transfer of authority to the new president, who would have to deal with Sumter and everything else.

Farewell

The morning of February 11, 1861, came to the town of Springfield, Illinois, chill and dreary, with a cold, pelting drizzle. The victor in the presidential election of 1860, Abraham Lincoln, stood in the waiting room of the Great Western Railway depot and shook the hands of friends and local associates. There were no lighthearted congratulations, no bursts of laughter, nothing but kind, hopeful words and well-meaning, if wan, smiles.

At 8:00, the engineer in the idling locomotive blew the all-aboard, and the president-elect, together with his family and a handful of others, ascended the steps of the single passenger car. Lincoln stood on the observation platform and spoke to those who would remain behind:

> My friends, no one not in my situation can appreciate my feeling of sadness at this parting. To this place and the kindness of these people I owe everything. Here I have lived for a quarter of a century, and have passed from a young to an old man. Here my children have been born, and one is buried. I now leave, not knowing when, or whether ever, I may return, with a task before me greater than that which rested upon Washington. Without the assistance of that Divine Being who ever attended him, I cannot succeed. With that assistance I cannot fail. Trusting in Him who can go with me and remain with you and be everywhere for good, let us confidently hope that all will yet be well. To His care commending you, as I hope in your prayers you will commend me, I bid you an affectionate farewell.

The next day would be Abraham Lincoln's fifty-second birthday. Although he called himself an old man, he was the youngest president the nation had yet elected.

Dangerous Inaugural Journey

The president-elect's train was scheduled to make stops at Indianapolis, Cincinnati, Columbus, Pittsburgh, Cleveland, Erie, Buffalo, Albany, New York City, Trenton, Newark, Philadelphia, and Harrisburg. At Baltimore, Lincoln was not only to stop, but also to change trains, going by carriage from the Calvert Street depot to Camden Station. But the day before Lincoln left Springfield, Allan J. Pinkerton, the eminent private detective hired by the president of the Philadelphia, Wilmington, and Baltimore Railroad, received a disturbing tip from the railroad's master mechanic. It seemed that "a son of a distinguished citizen of Maryland said that he had taken an oath with others to assassinate Mr. Lincoln before he gets to Washington, and they may attempt to do it while he is passing over our road."

Pinkerton sent his best operatives undercover in Baltimore and was soon satisfied not only that an assassination plot was afoot, but also that it was being planned as the opening shot in a lightning campaign that would culminate in a rebel invasion of Washington, whereupon (the plotters hoped) the demoralized North would abandon its design to enforce its will upon the South. Pinkerton learned that the assassination was to take place at the Calvert Street Station, where, by pre-arrangement, a crowd of secessionists would effectively choke off all passages leading to the street and Lincoln's carriage. The president-elect would have to thread his way through the throng, a diversionary disturbance would be staged, and Lincoln would be shot.

Pinkerton dispatched Kate Warne, one of his female operatives, from Baltimore to New York, where she met the president-elect's train and conveyed the details of the assassination conspiracy to Norman Judd, a member of the inaugural party traveling with Lincoln. They decided to lay all the facts before the president-elect when he arrived in Philadelphia on February 21.

According to recollections published in Pinkerton's memoirs, Abraham Lincoln received the news not with fear, but sadness. Pinkerton favored cutting short Lincoln's itinerary and rushing him immediately to Washington. The president-elect was hesitant, protesting that he had "promised to raise the flag over Independence Hall tomorrow morning, and to visit the legislature at Harrisburg in the afternoon." After these promises were fulfilled, however, he was willing to put himself entirely in Pinkerton's hands.

Pinkerton decided that, after the ceremonies at Harrisburg, a special train consisting of a baggage car and one passenger coach would carry Lincoln back to Philadelphia. There Pinkerton would personally escort Lincoln from one depot to another, where he would board a Baltimore-bound train—not the one directly from Harrisburg, which the conspirators were expecting, but the regular 11:00 train from Philadelphia. To ensure that no telegraph message could reach the conspirators to advise them of the change, George H. Burns, the American Telegraph Company's confidential agent, was assigned to see to it that telegraph traffic between Harrisburg and Baltimore was intercepted and delivered to Pinkerton.

At 5:45 P.M. John G. Nicolay, Lincoln's private secretary, handed the president-elect a note while he and his traveling party were in the dining room of a Harrisburg hotel. The men abruptly rose, and the president-elect changed out of his dinner clothes and into a traveling suit. According to Joseph Howard Jr., a reporter for *The New York Times*, Lincoln, acting on Pinkerton's instructions, carried a shawl upon one arm, as if he were an invalid, and had a soft felt hat tucked into his coat pocket. Lincoln was spirited into a coach, which took him to the depot. The train arrived in Philadelphia shortly after 10:00 P.M. He was then transferred by coach, with Pinkerton, to another depot.

Kate Warne had engaged the rear half of a Baltimore-bound sleeping car to accommodate (she said) "her invalid brother." At the depot, Warne approached the president-elect (who, it is said, still carried the shawl over one arm) and greeted him loudly as her brother. Together with Pinkerton and Lincoln's longtime friend Ward H. Lamon, she and Lincoln entered the sleeping car by its rear door.

Baltimore Transfer

It was 3:30 A.M. when the train pulled into Baltimore. Lincoln did not leave the sleeping car, which was drawn by horses over the horsecar tracks from the Philadelphia, Wilmington, and Baltimore depot to the Camden Street Station. The train that would take Lincoln's car to Washington was delayed almost two hours. Although those in the president-elect's party were nervous, Lincoln remained in his berth, joking easily with them. Even at so early an hour, the depot was active, and Lincoln and the others caught snatches of rebel tunes, including "Dixie," a song introduced by the popular minstrel entertainer Dan Emmett in 1859 and that had been taken up by the South as an unofficial anthem. "No doubt there will be a great time in Dixie by and by," Lincoln dryly observed to his companions.

Voices

"Dixie" was composed in 1859 by Daniel Decatur Emmett (1815–1904), originator of the minstrel show (a very popular form of variety show originally performed exclusively by whites in black-face make-up). Emmett was an Ohio-born New Yorker, whose fake black-dialect homage to an idealized plantation South became the Confederacy's unofficial anthem:

> I wish I was in de land ob cotton,
> Old times dar am not forgotten,
> Look away! Look away!
> Look away! Dixie Land.

> In Dixie Land whar I was born in,
> Early on one frosty mornin',
> Look away! Look away!
> Look away! Dixie Land.

> Den I wish I was in Dixie,
> Hooray! Hooray!
> In Dixie Land I'll take my stand,
> To lib and die in Dixie,

> Away, away, away down south in Dixie,
> Away, away, away down south in Dixie.

Ironically, "Dixie" was one of Abraham Lincoln's favorite tunes.

The belated train arrived at last, set off, and reached Washington some time after 6:00 in the morning. As journalist Howard reported it, Lincoln wrapped his invalid's shawl around his shoulders and left the sleeping car with Lamon and Pinkerton. The crowd outside did not recognize him.

Two Failures and a Tariff

The president-elect's party disembarked from the train, and Lincoln was bundled into a carriage, which set off for Willard's Hotel, on 14th and Pennsylvania Avenue, where the soon-to-be First Family would lodge prior to the inaugural ceremony.

The Peace Convention Fails

Elsewhere in Willard's, a "Peace Convention," called to order under sponsorship of the state of Virginia on February 4, was grinding on in vain and to little notice. It was a gathering of old men, presided over by former president John Tyler, aged 71, with 131 delegates from 21 states (including Southern states, but none of the seceded states). On March 1, the Peace Convention presented a handful of proposals to Congress, which simply refused to consider them.

Crittenden Fails

In Lincoln's time, Inauguration Day was in March, and, on March 2, 1861, two days before the ceremony, Senator Crittenden's proposal was narrowly defeated in the Senate. Unlike in 1820, 1850, and 1854, there would be no peace-patching compromise.

Sites and Sights

Today, Willard's Hotel is the pricey Willard Inter-Continental, a magnificent Washington landmark at 1401 Pennsylvania Avenue NW, Washington, D.C. 20004 (phone 1-202-628-9100).

War News

Senator John J. Crittenden's frustrated reconciliation efforts symbolized not only Kentucky's predicament, torn between the Union and the Confederacy, but the entire nation, plunging headlong into a war between brother and brother. The senator's son, George Bibb Crittenden, became a Confederate general; his other son, Thomas Leonidas Crittenden, served as a Union general.

The Morrill Tariff

Also on March 2, Congress passed the Morrill Tariff Act, sponsored by Vermont Representative Justin S. Morrill, a founder of the Republican Party. As a protective tariff intended to block importation of manufactured goods, the Morrill measure out-did even the "Tariff of Abominations," which brought on the Nullification Crisis and talk of secession some three decades earlier. The timing of the tariff could not have been more inflammatory to the South. It was the final—and entirely gratuitous—nail in the coffin that had been the *United* States.

The "Essence of Anarchy"

By the time James Buchanan called upon the president-elect at Willard's to escort him, as tradition dictated, to the inauguration platform, the weather had changed from fair at dawn to overcast and cold and then to sunny again. The ceremony took place on the east portico of the Capitol—its dome under construction, unfinished. It appeared, eerily, decapitated, a highly disturbing image. Disturbing, too, was the bronze statue representing Freedom, a classically robed woman with a sword in one hand and a wreath in the other, lying prostrate on the grass now, awaiting the completion of the dome, whose top she would grace.

The U.S. Capitol under construction, its dome yet to be completed.

(Harper's Pictorial History of the Civil War, 1866)

After witnessing the swearing-in of his vice president, Hannibal Hamlin of Maine, it was Abraham Lincoln's turn to speak. He addressed a crowd of some 10,000. "I have no purpose," Lincoln told the crowd, "directly or indirectly, to interfere with the institution of slavery in the states where it exists. I believe I have no lawful right to do so."

Thus "Black Lincoln" finally broke his silence, with words intended to ring loudly through the South. But, he continued, "no government proper ever had a provision in its organic law for its own termination …. No state upon its own mere motion can lawfully get out of the Union." And he went on to pledge that the "power confided in me will be used to hold, occupy, and possess the property and places belonging to the government, and to collect the duties and imposts." With calm, clear, eloquently humane logic, Lincoln explained his view of the present crisis:

> Shall fugitives from labor be surrendered by national or State authority? The Constitution does not expressly say. Must Congress protect slavery in the Territories? The Constitution does not expressly say.

> From questions of this class spring all our constitutional controversies, and we divide upon them into majorities and minorities. If the minority will not acquiesce, the majority must, or the government must cease. There is no other alternative; for continuing the government is acquiescence of one side or the other.

> If a minority in such case will secede rather than acquiesce, they make a precedent which in turn will divide and ruin them; for a minority of their own will secede from them whenever a majority refuses to be controlled by such a minority ….

> Plainly, the central idea of secession is the essence of anarchy. A majority held in restraint by constitutional checks and limitations, and always changing easily with deliberate changes of popular opinions and sentiments, is the only true sovereign of a free people. Whoever rejects it does, of necessity, fly to anarchy or to despotism. Unanimity is impossible; the rule of a minority, as a permanent arrangement, is wholly inadmissible; so that, rejecting the majority principle, anarchy or despotism in some form is all that is left ….

> In your hands, my dissatisfied fellow countrymen, and not in mine, is the momentous issue of civil war. The government will not assail you. You can have no conflict without being yourselves the aggressors. You have no oath registered in Heaven to destroy the government, while I shall have the most solemn one to "preserve, protect and defend it."

> I am loath to close. We are not enemies, but friends. We must not be enemies. Though passion may have strained, it must not break our bonds of affection. The mystic chords of memory, stretching from every battlefield and patriot grave to every living heart and hearthstone all over this broad land, will yet swell the chorus of the Union when again touched, as surely they will be, by the better angels of our nature.

The inaugural address concluded, Abraham Lincoln placed his broad palm on the Bible, shakily proffered by the aged hand of Chief Justice Roger Taney, and took the oath of office.

The Least You Need to Know

◆ Even after the first seven Southern states seceded, efforts to compromise further and thus maintain peace continued. The most important of these was the Crittenden Compromise.

◆ Economically and in numbers of population, the South's prospects for victory in a civil war were poor.

◆ Allan J. Pinkerton and others successfully foiled an apparent plot to assassinate President-elect Lincoln.

◆ Lincoln's inaugural address made it clear that his purpose was to preserve the Union, not to abolish slavery in the states where it currently existed.

Part 2

Rally Round

This part begins with a view of the governments and armies of the North and South at the start of the war. You'll see how both sides sought European allies, how President Lincoln walked a tightrope across the "border states" (those slave states that had chosen—so far—not to leave the Union), and how the people of the North tasted the bitterness of defeat in the first major contest of the war—the battle at Bull Run.

You'll understand why the North looked to George B. McClellan, "the Young Napoleon," to save the nation, while an obscure commander named Ulysses Simpson Grant almost lost his army at a place called Shiloh. You'll witness a new kind of war on the sea, fought with ships of steel and iron. You'll understand how "Stonewall" Jackson was able to roll up one Confederate triumph after another, while the "Young Napoleon" was out-generaled by Robert E. Lee, and the Union lost a *second* battle at Bull Run.

Chapter **5**

"We'll Manage to Keep House"

In This Chapter

- ◆ The vulnerable U.S. capital
- ◆ Espionage and counterespionage
- ◆ Lincoln and his cabinet
- ◆ Davis and his cabinet
- ◆ The armies

Not the least dramatic aspect of the Civil War, especially during its opening weeks and months, was the fact that Washington, D.C., the muggy, sleepy little seat of the Union government, was essentially a *Southern* city, and Virginia's secession on April 17, 1861, suddenly put a hostile nation just across the Potomac. The newly declared enemies could see, hear, and even smell one another.

A mere three or four hundred marines at the U.S. Marine Barracks on 8th and I Streets and another 100 army troops at the Washington arsenal were the only regular U.S. military forces stationed in Washington at the outbreak of the war. The citizens of the United States weren't militaristic, and they didn't like to maintain standing armies. But now it was reveille in Washington. The city would change. The people would change.

A Meeting with the President

William Tecumseh Sherman, having resigned from the Louisiana State Military Academy in February, came to Washington to pay a visit to the new president, report on the situation in the South, and offer his military services.

Sites and Sights

The Marine Barracks at 8th and I St. SE, Washington, was the first USMC headquarters and today houses the "Eighth and Eye Marines," the Commandant of the Marine Corps, and The President's Own, the Marine Corps orchestra that traditionally plays at White House state functions. Although there are no official tours of the facility, a ceremonial Evening Parade is held each Friday evening after nightfall from May through October. The public is welcome to see and hear the Marine Band, Marine Corps Drum and Bugle Corps, a special exhibition drill platoon, and a Battalion of Marines from the barracks. Marines regard "Eighth and Eye" as the spiritual center of the Corps.

"Ah," Lincoln greeted him, "how are they getting along down there?"

"They think they are getting along swimmingly. They are preparing for war."

"Oh, well," the president replied, "I guess we'll manage to keep house."

To Sherman, it was as if Lincoln were in a trance. Sherman immediately dropped the idea of reenlisting, bade the president farewell, and left Washington for St. Louis to head up a streetcar company.

Lincoln's response to the crisis was typical of most Northerners. If Southerners were exhilarated by the prospect of war, Northerners, but for a handful of the most ardent abolitionists, seemed enervated, as if the realities of the crisis had not yet penetrated.

City of Spies

Sherman returned to Washington and to military command soon enough, shortly after the fall of Fort Sumter. By then, the capital's torpor had turned to panic. The public parlors of Willard's Hotel buzzed with rumors of a rebel army massing in Virginia for an assault on Washington.

On Saturday, April 20, the city awoke to find itself entirely cut off from the North, pro-Confederate rioters in Baltimore having blockaded railroad traffic and seized the telegraph office. Many Washingtonians deserted the capital. Boards went up on the windows of many shops and homes. Workmen were busy at the Treasury offices, installing iron bars on doors and windows, and some people said the building was also being mined with explosive charges. Another rumor had it that old Ben McCulloch, most famous of the Texas Ranger captains, was putting together 500 men in Richmond to make a lightning raid on Washington, kidnap the president and his cabinet, and carry them to the South.

The four or five hundred regular troops stationed in Washington were augmented by armed volunteer groups, including the Potomac Light Infantry (one company), the National Rifles (one company), the Washington Light Infantry (a skeleton battalion of 160 men), and the National Guard Battalion. None of these was worth much. The Potomac Light Infantry moved quickly into action—taking an emergency vote to *disband* until peace was restored. One shamefaced corpsman proposed a toast: "The P.L.I., invincible in peace, invisible in war!"

Other local militia companies hurriedly formed, including the Silver Grays' Home Guard, made up of veterans of the War of 1812. The only man older than those in the ranks of the Silver Grays was the U.S. Army's general-in-chief, hero of the War of 1812 and the Mexican War, and now a corpulent 75-year-old, Winfield Scott, known as "Old Fuss and Feathers." To Colonel Charles P. Stone, whom he had just appointed inspector-general for the District of Columbia, Scott wheezed in horror: "They are closing their coils around us, sir!"

> ### War News
>
> The panicky Prussian attaché in Washington sought to secure his official residence from attack by placing a large sign over the doorway to his building. He also wanted a Prussian flag, but couldn't get one delivered because of the disruption in rail service.

But Just Who Were "They"?

"They" weren't just the army supposedly massing in Virginia. As master detective Allan J. Pinkerton saw it, "they" were a

> secret enemy, who [were] conveying beyond the lines the coveted information of every movement made or contemplated …. Men who formerly occupied places of dignity, power and trust …. Aristocratic ladies, who had previously opened the doors of their luxurious residences to those high in office and who had hospitably entertained the dignitaries of the land.

These and others "were now believed to be in sympathy with the attempt to overthrow the country, and engaged in clandestine correspondence with Southern leaders."

"They," in fact, were almost anyone in Washington. Although the city could breathe a sigh of relief when the Seventh New York Regiment marched in to garrison the capital, spies were everywhere. Army officers and federal officials defected to the South daily.

Samuel Cooper, U.S. Army adjutant-general, joined the Confederate cause in March. Quartermaster General Joseph E. Johnston did the same soon afterward. Captain John Magruder (not to be confused with the soon-to-be celebrated Confederate commander "Prince John" Bankhead Magruder), charged with command of the First U.S. Artillery and brought to Washington with that unit specifically to see to the defense of the capital, was openly disloyal.

The commander of the Washington Navy Yard, Marylander Franklin Buchanan, was a rebel sympathizer. He resigned in April, protesting that his loyalties lay with Maryland—a deeply divided border state that did not leave the Union—but honorably admonished his men to remain faithful to their government. (Soon after Buchanan's departure, it was discovered that many of the bombshells manufactured at the Navy Yard had been filled with inert sand and sawdust instead of explosive black powder.)

In the civil government, disloyalty was rife, from bureau clerks to Supreme Court Justice John A. Campbell—who carried on a correspondence with Confederate officials at Montgomery even as he continued to sit on the high court.

In Lincoln's own White House, John Watt, employed as a gardener, confessed that he had sold official secrets, though not directly to the Confederates, he said, but to a newspaper. Watt had been trusted without reservation because he was a favorite of the president's wife, Mary Todd. Of course, as many saw it, *her* loyalty was very much in doubt, she being a Kentuckian with a brother and three half-brothers enlisted in the Confederate army.

A Question of Intelligence—and Counterintelligence

Espionage and counterespionage were highly developed professions among the great powers of Europe, but they were virtually unknown to the U.S. civil and military establishment at the outbreak of Civil War. There was nothing like the CIA in existence, and, indeed, no official intelligence organizations. The army did employ "scouts," civilians who sometimes functioned as spies. But, aside from soldiers attached to the Provost Department (military police), no resources were devoted to counterintelligence.

Allan J. Pinkerton, a Scottish immigrant who created the nation's first private detective agency in the 1850s, did private security work for the Illinois Central Railroad before the war. There he became acquainted with the railroad's president, former U.S. Army officer George McClellan, and was assigned to protect President-elect Lincoln during the rail journey to his inauguration (see Chapter 4). In November 1861, McClellan, who had returned to military service at the beginning of war, was appointed general-in-chief of the Union army. He hired Pinkerton to conduct espionage work for him.

As we will see, the intelligence Pinkerton provided his employer was grossly inaccurate and helped to scare McClellan into excessive caution and even inaction. Pinkerton proved far more successful as a director of counterespionage efforts (see "The Rebel Rose" in Chapter 6). When President Lincoln relieved McClellan as general-in-chief following the Battle of Antietam (see Chapter 11), Pinkerton's work in military intelligence came to an end. He had called himself "chief of the Secret Service," but in fact, there was no such government agency, and the Union's chief spymaster was never more than a contract employee.

A Tale of Two Governments

The now-warring governments of the United States and the Confederate States of America were actually very much alike, at least on paper. The constitution adopted on February 8, 1861, at Montgomery, Alabama, "for a provisional Confederate government" was quite similar to the U.S. Constitution, except that it very explicitly guaranteed the protection of slavery. And if the rebels were faced with the task of creating an instant government, they at least did not have their enemies at their doorstep, as did the 85-year-old government in Washington.

Lincoln and His Cabinet

What American does not have the face of Abraham Lincoln etched in memory? Ugly-beautiful, manly-motherly, it is a face that seemed to have the backcountry of Kentucky and Illinois written all over it, despite a gentleness about the mouth and a penetrating wisdom in the eyes.

He had been born on February 12, 1809, in a log cabin in Hardin (now Larue) County, Kentucky. In 1816, the family moved to Indiana and, finally, to Illinois in 1830. Lincoln was mostly self-taught, driven by an insatiable thirst for knowledge. He tried any number of occupations, including militiaman in the war against the Indian leader Black Hawk during 1832. He discovered that military life held little appeal for him, but he did take "much satisfaction" in having been elected captain of his militia company and found in himself a talent for leadership. This moved the young backwoodsman to run for the Illinois state legislature. He lost, but ran again and was elected to four consecutive terms from 1832 to 1841.

Settling in the state capital of Springfield, Lincoln established a prosperous law practice, served a term (1847–1849) in the U.S. House of Representatives, and then returned to the law, having, he admitted, lost "interest in politics."

Then came the Kansas-Nebraska Act of 1854. Lincoln was no abolitionist, but the doctrine of popular sovereignty, which potentially threw open to slavery vast new territories, reawakened the political animal in him. Lincoln believed that, for better or worse, the Constitution protected slavery in states where it already existed, but he also thought that the Founding Fathers had put the "peculiar institution" on the way to extinction with the Northwest Ordinance, which banned its spread to new territories.

Lincoln ran unsuccessfully for the U.S. Senate in 1855; then, the following year, he left the Whig Party to join the newly formed Republicans. In 1858, he ran for the Senate against the Illinois incumbent, Stephen A. Douglas, accepting his party's nomination on June 16, 1858, with a powerful speech against what he saw as the efforts of Douglas, Chief Justice Roger B. Taney, and Democratic presidents Franklin Pierce and James Buchanan to nationalize slavery. Rejecting their efforts, he also declared that compromise on slavery was doomed to fail, that the country could not endure half slave and half free, and that (paraphrasing the Gospel of Mark), "A house divided against itself cannot stand."

As a result of his debates with Douglas, Lincoln gained national recognition for his eloquence, decency, and morally upright moderation, even though he lost the senatorial bid to his opponent. More than any other politician in 1860, Lincoln seemed to speak the Northern mind and, against a splintered Democratic field, was elected president of a disintegrating nation.

Once he was in office, some venerated him, others found him too timid with regard to abolishing slavery, and still others thought him too bold. A great many simply doubted his ability to lead.

Edwin M. Stanton derided the new president as the fabled missing link—the evolutionary step between ape and human—the "original gorilla." However, even though he knew what Stanton thought of him, Lincoln brought him into his cabinet to replace the corrupt Simon Cameron as secretary of war (January 11, 1862). That said a great deal about Lincoln. He understood that Stanton was ruthless, power-hungry, always conniving with the radical Republican wing, and, yes, even contemptuous; yet he also saw that Stanton was a vigorous, tireless, and singularly acute administrator: the man to get the job done.

Edwin M. Stanton, ruthless and power-hungry, was also extremely capable. Lincoln took him into his cabinet to replace the corrupt Simon Cameron as secretary of war.

(Harper's Pictorial History of the Civil War, *1868*)

The same was true of another key cabinet member, Secretary of State William H. Seward. He had lost the nomination to Lincoln in 1860 and entered the cabinet with great misgiving, believing that Lincoln was hardly equal to the job. At first, he high-handedly attempted to outmaneuver the president, thinking it best for the nation if he, Seward, pulled the strings and ran the government. But Lincoln, little by little, transformed Seward into a loyal subordinate and trusted advisor, and he made the best use of his critically important diplomatic talents.

Most troublesome of all was Salmon P. Chase, secretary of the treasury. Lincoln recognized that Chase served brilliantly in a post so vital to the war effort, but Chase had also unsuccessfully contended for the 1860 presidential nomination and, unlike Seward, could never reconcile himself to the belief that the abler man had won. Persistently disloyal and insubordinate, he was finally dismissed by Lincoln in 1864, though the president, never a petty man and wanting to keep Chase's judgment and intellect in service to the nation, nominated him to the post of chief justice of the Supreme Court after Taney's death later in the year.

Davis of Mississippi

Like Lincoln, Jefferson Davis had been born in a log cabin, a son of the Kentucky backwoods. But the similarities ended there. Whereas Lincoln's father remained a poor backwoodsman, Davis's father settled the family on a plantation called Rosemont at Woodville, Mississippi, when the boy was only three, and prospered. In contrast to the self-taught Lincoln, Davis was sent away, at seven, to a Dominican boys' school in Kentucky, and, at 13, was enrolled in Transylvania College, at Lexington. Subsequently, he spent four years at West Point, graduating in 1828 with a second lieutenant's commission.

After serving in the Black Hawk War, he resigned his commission in 1835 and became a planter near Vicksburg, Mississippi. His bride, Sarah Knox Taylor, daughter of his commanding officer, Zachary Taylor, succumbed to malaria three months after the couple moved to the plantation, and a devastated Davis secluded himself on his property, enlarging and developing it, replete with slaves, as he devoted himself to the study of philosophy, law, and constitutional law.

At the conclusion of seven years in virtual isolation, Davis was elected to the U.S. House of Representatives in 1845 and remarried. The following year, he resigned his seat in Congress to serve in the Mexican War as colonel of the First Mississippi volunteers. His brilliant victory at the Battle of Buena Vista in 1847 won him not only national but also international renown. Subsequently wounded, he entered the Senate, served as chairman of the Military Affairs Committee, and then was appointed secretary of war by President Franklin Pierce in 1853.

Jefferson Davis, hero of the Mexican War, U.S. senator, secretary of war to President Franklin Pierce, and president of the Confederate States of America.

(Author's collection)

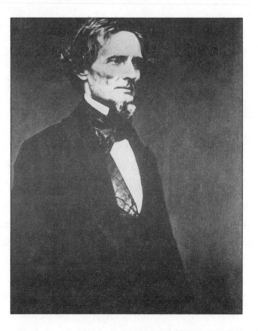

As civil war approached, Davis, strangely enough, came once again to resemble Lincoln. He was no secessionist, but instead made many public speeches urging reconciliation, compromise, and harmony. Even after South Carolina became the first state to secede in December 1860, Davis voiced his opposition to secession. But he did believe that states had a Constitutional right to secede, and he also believed that Abraham Lincoln, if elected, would coerce the South into renouncing slavery, thereby bringing economic disaster.

On January 21, 1861, 12 days after his home state of Mississippi seceded, Davis bade farewell to his Senate colleagues and made a last, impassioned plea for peace. Commissioned major general to lead Mississippi's army, he was soon chosen provisional president of the Confederacy by the Confederate Convention in Montgomery, Alabama.

Even now, he continued to seek an alternative to war, sending, shortly after his inauguration on February 18, 1861, a peace commission to Washington, D.C. Unwilling to recognize the Confederacy as a sovereign nation, President Lincoln refused to see the commission. Early in April, when Lincoln sent armed ships to resupply Fort Sumter, Davis, with great reluctance, ordered the bombardment of the fort.

Once the fight began, Davis showed himself a man of iron determination, which meant that he was strong, but also unbending, inflexible, and, ultimately, brittle. His task was to prosecute a paradox: to carry out a *conservative* revolution, a rebellion to *preserve* the status quo. That put one great stress on Davis's iron spine. Another was the necessity of creating an instant government, but not just *any* government: a government with sufficient central authority to fight a war. The trouble was that states' rights, the doctrine at the very heart of the rebellion, was by definition incompatible with strong central government. Any claim Davis laid to broad wartime powers, however necessary, would be met with a storm of criticism.

Finally, there was the Confederate Cabinet. Davis lacked Lincoln's skill in managing volatile but creative personalities. The result was a mostly undistinguished cabinet, unequal to the task of fighting a war or managing a government.

Of all the cabinet members, only Judah P. Benjamin, former U.S. senator from Louisiana, would show real brilliance, first as attorney general, then as secretary of war, and, most of all, as secretary of state. Benjamin was to serve only briefly as secretary of war, but, then, so did everyone else who tried his hand at that thankless job. No fewer than six men would occupy the post in four years. In modern terminology, Davis insisted on "micromanaging" his cabinet, and in no case was this more true than in the War Department. He would shoulder the entire burden of the war, often to the detriment of the war effort.

Jefferson Davis with his first Confederate Cabinet. Seated (left to right): Attorney General Judah B. Benjamin, Secretary of the Navy Stephen R. Mallory, Vice President Alexander H. Stephens, President Jefferson Davis, Postmaster General John H. Reagan, Secretary of State Robert Toombs; standing (left to right): Secretary of the Treasury Charles G. Memminger, and Secretary of War Leroy P. Walker.

(Harper's Pictorial History of the Civil War, *1868*)

Grim Realities

In contrast to many of the nations of Europe, the United States shunned the maintenance of a large standing army. In most crises, as in the War of 1812 or the Mexican War, local and state militias as well as other "irregular" forces were called on to supplement the tiny "regular" army. Just before the fall of Fort Sumter, the U.S. Army consisted of a mere 16,000 officers and men. Until March 3, 1863 (for the Union), and April 16, 1862 (for the Confederacy), there was no such thing as a military draft. The army was an all-volunteer force.

The Arsenal of 1861

By 1861, the world's weapon makers had significantly advanced the technology of killing, introducing improved high-velocity artillery and replacing smooth-bore muskets with far more accurate rifles.

The most important innovations were the percussion rifle-musket and the *minié ball.* Named after its French inventor, Claude Etienne Minié, who designed it in 1848, the minié ball was not a ball at all, but was shaped like a bullet. Smaller than the barrel of the rifle-musket, it was easy to load. Its hollow base filled with gases when the gun was fired, forcing the minié ball to expand into the rifling (spiral grooves) within the rifle barrel. The rifling imparted a spin to the minié ball, making it far more accurate than a conventional projectile fired from an old-fashioned smooth-bore musket. Yet because the minié ball expanded only as it was fired, it lost minimal velocity as it left the rifled barrel.

The combination of musket-rifle and minié ball greatly improved the speed and accuracy of fire, but the reality was that, in 1861, American arsenals were stocked not with state-of-the-art weapons, but obsolescent firearms of Mexican War vintage.

Words of War

The **minié ball** was named for its inventor, the Frenchman Claude Etienne Minié, who designed it in 1848. The bullet-shaped projectile was a great advance on conventional long-arm ammunition. Fired from a rifle-musket, it was highly accurate and was the ammunition of choice in the Civil War.

The same was true of artillery. Most that was immediately available was outmoded, even though, just before the war, two important innovations had been introduced.

The "Napoleon" was a 12-pounder (meaning that it fired a 12-pound projectile), smooth-bore weapon originally developed by the French and named after Emperor Napoleon III. The American-made Napoleon was developed in 1857 and had a range of 1,619 yards. Production of Napoleons proceeded apace on both sides, and by 1863, this weapon made up some 40 percent of the artillery used by the Union as well as the Confederacy.

The Ordnance Rifle, patented by weapons maker John Griffen in 1855, was used mainly by the Union army and featured a wrought-iron barrel, which was stronger than conventional cast iron and could therefore be loaded with a bigger, more powerful charge without risk of exploding. Unlike the Napoleon, the Ordnance Rifle had a rifled bore, which imparted a spin to the projectiles, giving them greater accuracy.

The Ordnance Rifle was lighter than the third important piece of Civil War artillery, the Parrott Gun (or Parrott Rifle), which was patented in 1861 by Robert P. Parrott. Manufactured in 10- and 20-pound versions, the Parrott Gun featured a breech reinforced with wrought iron, rather than made entirely of it. This made the gun cheaper to manufacture than the Ordnance Rifle, but also made it more vulnerable to explosion.

In the heat of war, both sides rushed to manufacture or import all these new weapons, but, in the early months of the conflict, they had to rely on whatever obsolescent artillery was available.

The Art of War, 1861

A battle typically consists of attackers and defenders. In the course of the Civil War, weapons technology consistently gave the advantage to the defenders. Improved rifles, including repeating rifles, enabled increasingly rapid and accurate fire, making it easier to defend a position and, conversely, harder to attack it. Advances in heavy artillery likewise gave the advantage to those who occupied fortified positions, whether forts, dugouts, or trenches, and, again, made the attacker's task more difficult.

One of the great and tragic paradoxes of the Civil War was that the art of war—strategy and tactics—failed to keep pace with the technology of the war's weapons. Although that technology gave the edge to defenders, the most widely accepted strategy and tactics were those born of the age of Napoleon I and therefore emphasized the attack. Surely this is in part responsible for the terrible toll the Civil War exacted on both sides. Commanders repeatedly ordered foolhardy, futile, even suicidal attacks against defensive weapons of terrible destructiveness.

Although the Civil War saw some great tacticians, most officers, especially at the highest levels, were slow to adopt strategy and tactics to a war that technology made unlike any other that had come before.

The Armies

To fight the great wars of the twentieth century, the federal government enlisted or drafted vast numbers of men directly. During the Civil War, however, the central governments of the North and the South relied on the individual states to raise the necessary forces. This was a cumbersome and unreliable process, which resulted in much duplication of effort and a good deal of conflict among command authorities.

> ### War News
>
> The Army of the Confederate States of America was established by act of the Confederate Provisional Congress on March 6, 1861, but never actually came into existence. The war was fought with volunteers of the Provisional Confederate Army, established by acts of February 28 and March 6. In April 1862, the Confederate government passed a conscription act, which inducted soldiers into the Provisional Army through the individual states.

Taking Command

If mustering rank-and-file soldiers into the army was a difficult process, finding the officers to command them was even harder. The U.S. Army made for a thankless career. Promotion proceeded at a glacial pace, and opportunities were severely limited. Good officers, then, were always in short supply, and as the Southern states seceded, 313 of the very best resigned to join the Confederates. Despite a few truly extraordinary commanders such as Grant, Sherman, and Sheridan, Union forces were usually less ably led than those of the South.

It was not just an issue of inexperience, but of politics. So-called *political generals*—commanders appointed for reasons of political patronage rather than for proven military accomplishment—infested the armies of both sides, but were especially rife in the Union Army. This was partly because the fledgling Republican Party was attempting to build a power base; staunch Republicans and pro-Union Democrats were rewarded with military rank and command.

> **Count Off!**
>
> When Fort Sumter fell, the United States Regular Army (that is, the Federal army) consisted of a mere 16,000 officers and men. Of its most experienced officers, 313 resigned their commissions to fight with the Confederacy. Except for this number, Confederate "regular" forces started the war with no personnel. State and local militia forces fired the first shots.

> **Words of War**
>
> **Political generals** were inexperienced commanders taken from civilian life and given high military rank as a reward for political services.

Worst and Best

We shall meet some of the commanders, good, bad, and indifferent, in the pages that follow. But what of the soldiers in the ranks? Overwhelmingly, they were ordinary citizens, not professional hirelings of a warlike state. In the North, African Americans, whom Justice Taney's Dred Scott Decision had excluded from citizenship, nevertheless agitated from the very beginning of the war for the right to fight. It was not until the autumn of 1862 that African-American troops were admitted into the Union Army, in wholly segregated units commanded by white officers. (In the South, during the final, desperate months of the war, the Confederate Congress authorized the recruitment of 300,000 black soldiers, but the public raised such an outcry that no African-American Confederate soldiers were ever committed to battle.)

The typical soldier on either side was a white Protestant, a farmer, unmarried, aged 18 to 29—though there were also much older men (Southerner Edmund Ruffin was 67, and Northerner Curtis King was 80 when he enlisted) and younger (Charles C. Hay joined an Alabama regiment at age 11, and Edward Black enlisted in the 21st Indiana as a nine-year-old musician). Most men on both sides were native born, although one out of four Northern soldiers was a first- or second-generation immigrant, mostly of German or Irish origin. Three brigades of Cherokees,

Choctaws, Chickasaws, and Seminoles fought for the Confederacy, whereas one brigade of Creeks enlisted in the Union army. Most of the time, most of the soldiers, North and South, were highly motivated, and acts of heroism were more common than instances of cowardice or failure of morale.

Voices

In August 1861, escaped slave and noted abolitionist Frederick Douglass wrote:

> Our Presidents, Governors, Generals and Secretaries are calling, with almost frantic vehemence, for men.—"Men! men! send us men!" they scream, or the cause of the Union is gone; and yet these very officers, representing the people and Government, steadily and persistently refuse to receive the very class of men which have a deeper interest in the defeat and humiliation of the rebels, than all others .... What a spectacle of blind, unreasoning prejudice and pusillanimity is this! The national edifice is on fire. Every man who can carry a bucket of water, or remove a brick, is wanted; but those who have the care of the building, having a profound respect for the feeling of the national burglars who set the building on fire, are determined that the flames shall only be extinguished by Indo-Caucasian hands ....

The boys of war: An unidentified member of an Ohio regiment (left) and Pvt. Edwin Francis Jamieson, 2nd Louisiana Regiment (right). Jamieson would fall in the Seven Days' Battles during June 1862.

(Library of Congress)

In April 1862, the Confederacy enacted a draft law, and the Union followed the next year. On both sides, the laws were unjust and unpopular. In the South, those who owned or oversaw 20 or more slaves were exempt from service, which meant that the well-to-do need not fear becoming cannon fodder. As if that weren't enough, one could pay a cash "commutation fee" in lieu of service or could hire a substitute to serve in one's stead. Both alternatives required wealth beyond that of the common working man. In the North, the commutation fee was $300—at a time when unskilled labor earned about a dollar a day. Substitutes could also be hired. The inequity of the Northern draft law sparked a series of riots across the country and a near-revolution in New York City during July 13–16, 1863: a paroxysm of looting, arson, and murder carried out by poor Irish immigrants outraged by the notion of being drafted to free black slaves who would then come up north to "steal" their jobs. We will return to this bloody episode in Chapter 16.

Commanding officers on neither side valued conscripts highly, describing them with such epithets as "depraved" and "degenerate." But even the best soldiers, the volunteers, stubbornly resisted military discipline. In companies that had been raised locally, the men now charged with command had been, just days before, friends, neighbors, or even employees. Moreover, most newly minted officers were no more experienced in military art than the men they were supposed to lead.

> ### War News
>
> Civil War soldiers, mostly laborers and farm boys, were unaccustomed to handling firearms. Once mustered in, they were poorly trained, doing much marching, but little shooting. As a result, the level of marksmanship was abysmal in both armies. It has been calculated that some 900 pounds of lead and 240 pounds of powder were consumed for each of the enemy killed.

It is understandable that citizen-soldiers would be reluctant to take arms against other citizen-soldiers, but, contrary to the myth that most Civil War recruits were frontiersmen accustomed to firearms, shooting was so alien to most young men of the period that, despite the extraordinarily poor rations issued to the armies of the North and the South, few men seized the obvious alternative of hunting one's supper.

Count Off!

By the end of the war, 2,128,948 men had served in the Union Army (359,528 are known to have died). Of those who served, 75,215 were "professional" soldiers—soldiers by vocation. An even smaller number, 46,347, were draftees, and 73,607 were substitutes. (The conscription laws of both the North and the South permitted a draftee to hire a surrogate soldier to serve in his place.) The average strength of the Union Army was probably a little over 1.5 million.

Just *how* bad were Civil War rations? The Union's staple ration was *hardtack*; salt pork, called *salt horse* or *sowbelly*; and coffee beans the men crushed and boiled. Fabled for its staleness, it was rumored that hardtack—half-inch-thick, three-inch-square crackers the troops called "sheet-iron crackers" or "teeth dullers"—had been warehoused since the Mexican War. Another fragment of folklore asserted that the initials "B.C.," stamped on crates of hardtack, stood not for "Brigade Commissary," but referred to the date of manufacture.

And it got even worse. "Fresh" meat rations, often hard to come by, were typically flyblown and rotten. Food poisoning and dysentery killed many more soldiers than bullets in the Civil War.

Count Off!

Confederate forces kept poor records, and most of those burned in the fires that consumed much of Richmond toward the close of the war. Estimates of the strength of the Confederate Army range from 600,000 to 1,500,000, but the generally accepted figure is a little over a million, of whom at least 200,000 died.

Nonprofessional, undisciplined, poorly trained, poorly fed, often inadequately clothed (especially in the South), sometimes equipped with hopelessly obsolescent firearms, the Civil War soldier would endure disorder, discomfort, disease, and death. Yet he would carry out combat on an unprecedented scale. The commanders who struggled with their men in the early weeks and months of the war doubtless shook their heads in despair over having been saddled with possibly the worst soldiers America had ever fielded. Yet these commanders would soon come to recognize that, although their men might be the worst of *soldiers*, they were also the best of *fighters*—fierce, determined, tireless, and uncomplaining.

The Least You Need to Know

- At the outbreak of the war, Washington, D.C., was virtually a city under siege, vulnerable to a hostile army from without and to untold numbers of spies from within.

- Abraham Lincoln struggled with his cabinet, but succeeded in forging a strong administration and was generally well advised.

- Jefferson Davis, an intelligent but inflexible leader, was faced with creating an instant government, but the states resisted giving up authority to the central government. Davis's cabinet, in contrast to Lincoln's, was weak.

- The armies of both sides were similar in that the overwhelming majority of the soldiers were poorly trained, distinctly un-military citizen-soldiers.

- Although the Union could field a larger, better-equipped army than the South, Southern forces were usually better led.

Chapter 6

The Anaconda and a Picnic Party

In This Chapter

- ◆ Winfield Scott and his Anaconda Plan
- ◆ The role of international diplomacy
- ◆ The *Trent* Affair
- ◆ Contest for the "border states"
- ◆ First Battle of Bull Run

On the face of it, this war was a simple thing. The "Confederate States"—by June 8, 1861, there were 11 of them—were fighting for independence, while the Federal army was fighting to get them all back into the Union. The South, with a much smaller population, a severely limited economy, and comparatively puny industrial capacity, seemed doomed.

But the situation wasn't as simple as it seemed. The North was hardly unified in its will to fight. Lincoln needed to keep the focus on preserving the Union, even though his more radical Republican colleagues wanted it to be a war against slavery. But Lincoln knew that the majority of Northerners were not radical Republicans and, at least at this point, would probably not be willing to fight a war to end slavery. The border states—committed wholly neither to North nor South—would likely embrace the Confederacy if the war become a struggle for abolition.

The South enjoyed more unity, at least at first. Its people saw themselves as defending their homeland, and this gave them a strength and advantage beyond what their numbers or "national" economy would suggest.

Truth to tell, neither side was really ready to fight a war.

Old Fuss and Feathers

No one, North or South, had more military experience than Winfield Scott (introduced in Chapter 5). Born in 1786 in Petersburg, Virginia, he was commissioned a captain of artillery in 1808, fought in the War of 1812, and rose rapidly through the ranks to major general. After the War of 1812, he studied tactics in Europe, and in 1841 was named general-in-chief of the U.S. Army. Already corpulent in middle age, he generously filled out the immaculate, epauletted, braid- and medal-bedecked uniforms he favored, which, along with his punctilious insistence on adherence to all military formalities, earned him the epithet of "Old Fuss and Feathers."

Winfield Scott, "Old Fuss and Feathers," general-in-chief of the U.S. Army, was a hero of the War of 1812 and the Mexican War.

(Harper's Pictorial History of the Civil War, *1866*)

But Scott was neither a hollow martinet nor a fat figurehead. At 60, during the Mexican War, he conceived and commanded the seaborne invasion of Mexico, the first amphibious operation in U.S. military history, capturing Veracruz in March 1847 and, piling victory upon victory, making an advance on Mexico City so daring that no less than the Duke of Wellington, vanquisher of Napoleon, predicted Scott's defeat. Wellington was wrong, and Scott entered Mexico City on September 14, 1847, thereby ending the Mexican War.

Now, at 75, pained by gout and much too fat even to mount a horse, Scott was the leader of the Union army.

The Anaconda Plan

Scott had a plan. He understood the economic, population, and industrial advantages the North enjoyed over the South. But he also understood that the North would have to take the offensive—to attack and invade the South—and his tiny regular army and undisciplined state and local militia units were not prepared to fight an offensive war. For all its disadvantages, the Confederate army would be fighting a defensive war, close to home and close to sources of supply. Scott decided that he needed time— time to prepare the Union Army to attack, and time to start a slow process of constriction around the very vitals of the South.

Scott proposed a two-pronged blockade of the Confederacy. He wanted to cut off Atlantic and Gulf ports, simultaneously sending some 60,000 troops ("rough-vigor fellows," Scott called them) and a flotilla of naval gunboats down the Mississippi to take New Orleans. By these two means, Scott proposed to cut off the South economically (it would be unable to import or export goods) and cut it in two geographically, East severed from West. While the breakaway states thus slowly but surely suffocated, additional assaults and offensives could be planned and then launched at will.

On the map, Scott's strategy was certainly sound. The only catch was that the Southern coastline, with all its gulfs, inlets, twists, and turns, was about 3,500 miles long and offered some 180 ports, while the Union navy had pitifully few ships. Still, it *was* a plan. Abraham Lincoln bought it, and announced it on April 19.

Count Off!

In April 1861, the Union Navy consisted of 42 ships mounting 555 guns and manned by 7,600 sailors. (Only three of these vessels were modern steam-powered craft.) By year's end, after a crash shipbuilding program, purchases of commercial vessels, and an enlistment drive, the Navy had grown to 264 ships mounting 2,557 guns and manned by 22,000 sailors—still hardly adequate to patrol so much Southern coastline and so many Southern ports.

War Without Glory

The president might have bought it, but the press, on both sides of the Mason-Dixon line, was not so easily persuaded. They derided it as "Scott's Anaconda" and published fanciful cartoons featuring a great constrictor snake (often with the head of Scott or Lincoln) coiling around the Southern coast. Journalists not only found the plan impractical, even worse, they judged it inglorious. Many believed the war could and should be fought and won in a matter of months, if not weeks. Some Northern editors even questioned the loyalty of Virginia-born Scott, who, they pointed out, had been among those counseling the evacuation of Fort Sumter.

Blockade of Chesapeake Bay

Initially, Union forces focused on seizing the waterways leading into Virginia. For their part, the Confederates aimed to choke off access to Washington via the Chesapeake Bay and the Potomac River.

Union gunboats bombarded Confederate shore batteries—which returned fire—at Sewell's Point, near Norfolk, Virginia, during May 18–19, 1861 and then, during May 29–June 1, at Aquia Creek. Following this action at sea, Union regiments fought at Big Bethel (or Great Bethel), Virginia, on June 10. It was hardly the glorious commencement of land action Union partisans had hoped for. Poorly led Union forces became confused and soon withdrew. "Friendly fire" was a major problem because uniforms had not been standardized, and many Union troops wore gray uniforms, which drew fire from their own side.

Immediately following Big Bethel, Union gunboats accomplished what they could to patrol Chesapeake Bay, but it was the Confederate artillery that seized the initiative and did a creditable job impeding Washington-bound traffic on the Potomac.

What the World Thought

Despite initial disappointments in and around Chesapeake Bay, time would prove the soundness of Scott's Anaconda. To survive a war, let alone fight and win one, the South now needed even more of everything it used to get from the North. Because its own manufacturing capacity was so limited, the Confederacy would have to import goods, especially arms, ammunition, and warships, from abroad. To do this, it needed money. One source, of course, was the export of such raw materials as cotton, which the Anaconda blockade would sharply curtail. Another source was foreign credit. But that required either international allies or, failing that, at least international recognition as a sovereign nation.

Yet what stake did Europe have in this American struggle?

The most important of the two European powers, France and England, viewed the South as a trading partner. British cloth manufacturers, in particular, needed Southern cotton. The South understood this fact and relied heavily on the cotton export trade—ultimately, *too* heavily. Having chanted the mantra of "King Cotton" for so many years, Southerners forgot that the English and the French also traded with the North, and that the grain produced on the *Northern* plains had become, for the English, just as important an American import as cotton.

But, for Europe, more than trade was at stake. England and France were monarchies existing in a part of the world that had been swept by waves of republican revolution, most recently in 1848. On the face of it, this should have prejudiced them against rebellion in North America; however, the Confederacy, though ostensibly democratic, presented itself as a conservative "empire" actually ruled by a landed aristocracy. Moreover, the very fact that the Union had been dissolved could be pointed to as an object lesson proving that republican government could *not* work. Of course, for the lesson to stand, the Union had to *remain* dissolved. Aristocratic, reactionary Europe had some economically and politically compelling reasons to recognize, perhaps even openly side with, the Confederacy.

Dixie Diplomacy

But there was one huge obstacle to alliance. Even conservative European governments could not countenance slavery. Fortunately for the South's new diplomats, Abraham Lincoln had done them the favor of stipulating that the preservation of the Union, not the abolition of slavery, was the issue of this war, and Congress formally backed him with the Crittenden Resolution asserting just that. Southern emissaries were therefore in a position, albeit a delicate one, to persuade the English and French governments that they could come to the aid of the Confederacy without becoming involved in a fight to preserve and perpetuate slavery.

The English Question

Jefferson Davis was quick to dispatch two able diplomats to Europe to negotiate recognition, possibly even alliance, and certainly trade in war materials. He appointed James M. Mason of Virginia minister to England and Louisiana's John Slidell minister to France. They slipped out of Charleston harbor on a *blockade runner* (a ship that specialized in evading the Union naval blockade) early in October and made for Havana, Cuba, via Nassau in the Bahamas. At Havana, they boarded the British mail packet *Trent*.

As fortune would have it, the USS *San Jacinto*, returning from a tour of duty along the African coast, touched port at Cuba during this time in search of intelligence concerning the activities of Confederate *commerce raiders* (private, civilian vessels that intercepted U.S. merchant ships and seized their cargo). But Captain Charles Wilkes received far more momentous intelligence than he had counted on. Learning that Mason and Slidell had set sail on the *Trent*, he steamed out to the Bahama Channel, intercepted the British craft on November 8, and fired two shots across her bow.

Words of War

A **blockade runner** was a vessel—or captain—specializing in evading the Union naval blockade of the South. The ships were generally small, sleek cargo vessels built for speed and with a sufficiently shallow draft to negotiate the treacherous waters along Southern coastlines without running aground. A **commerce raider** was a private, civilian vessel authorized by the Confederate government to intercept U.S. merchant ships and seize their cargo. Commerce raiding was, in effect, government-sanctioned piracy.

"What do you mean by heaving my vessel to in this way?" the *Trent*'s skipper called through a speaking trumpet.

Wilkes made no answer other than to dispatch a boarding party in two boats under the command of Lt. D. MacNeill Fairfax.

Slidell manfully introduced himself to the lieutenant, and Mason followed. Acting on the orders of Wilkes, who reasoned that if a nation at war had the right to remove enemy dispatches from neutral ships, it also had the right to remove human emissaries from them, Fairfax took Mason and Slidell back with him to the *San Jacinto*. The American ship delivered the pair to Fort Warren in Boston harbor, and Wilkes was hailed as a national hero and even given the official thanks of Congress.

But the British government, already inclined to sympathize with the Confederate cause, was outraged. Eleven thousand British soldiers were dispatched to Canada, and the British fleet was put on alert. An apology was demanded, along with the release of the prisoners.

"One War at a Time"

As secretary of state, it was up to William Seward to advise President Lincoln on how to respond to the British demands. Far from rushing to apologize, Seward counseled that war with Britain might be just what the nation needed to reunite itself.

Certainly, Jefferson Davis didn't see the incident as a cause to reunite with the North. The gaunt and somber Davis was rubbing his hands together with unaccustomed glee at the prospect of the *Trent* affair's propelling England into a Confederate alliance. And Abraham Lincoln didn't see it Seward's way, either.

"One war at a time," he told his secretary of state, and Seward at last agreed. He ordered the release of Mason and Slidell and composed a note of apology that was left-handed enough to include a sting of censure.

A major crisis for the Union was thus averted, but the British continued to lean toward the Confederate cause and, although officially neutral, turned a blind eye toward English munitions works and shipyards that were selling war materiel to the American South. On May 13, 1861, Queen Victoria recognized the Confederacy as a "belligerent," which lent a certain international legitimacy to the cause. The situation, we shall see, would build to a new crisis in the fall of the war's second year, after the North suffered reverses at the Second Battle of Bull Run.

States on the Border

Closer to home, another kind of diplomacy was called for. The border states, Delaware, Kentucky, Missouri, Maryland, and the mountain counties of Virginia that would become West Virginia, were slave states, but had not voted to secede. For the Union, losing them might well mean losing the war before it had hardly begun; for the Confederacy, gaining the border states would mean a great advantage won.

Although slavery was legal in Delaware, secession was never a significant issue there, and the small state's loyalty to the Union was certain. Kentucky, however, sat on the fence. Its governor was inclined to secede, but its legislature was solidly Unionist. The result was the state's declaration of neutrality, and neither Lincoln nor Davis wanted to risk disturbing this delicate situation. Although both the Union and the Confederacy *unofficially* raised troops in Kentucky, *officially* they left the state alone.

Civil War in Missouri

Missouri was another matter altogether. As in Kentucky, the legislature favored the Union, while Governor Claiborne F. Jackson was a secessionist. Shortly after the fall of Fort Sumter, Jackson attempted to seize the federal arsenal at St. Louis. When an aggressive Union army captain named Nathaniel S. Lyon blocked this effort, the governor's troops set up Camp Jackson on the outskirts of the city and bided their time. Authorities in Washington, deciding that the Union general in command of the area, William A. Harney, was far too passive about the continued threat the pro-Confederate troops posed, put Lyon in temporary command of Harney's brigade. He was soon jumped in rank to brigadier general of volunteers.

On May 10, 1861, Lyon moved against Camp Jackson, arrested the state militiamen, and, as he marched his prisoners through St. Louis, suddenly found that he had incited a riot. Civilians shouted catcalls and pelted the Union soldiers with rocks. After one drunken St. Louisan wounded an officer with a random pistol shot, the Union troops returned fire, killing more than 20 civilians.

Carthage and Wilson's Creek

General Harney's policy had been to maintain something between a standoff and a truce with the governor's pro-Confederate forces. As in Kentucky, neither side wanted to take action that might propel Missouri into the opposite camp.

There was a clash at the town of Carthage, on July 5, 1861, when Claiborne Jackson himself—who had defied the state legislature by setting up a breakway Confederate state "government" at the town of Neosho—led a ragtag group of rebels against the forces of Brig. Gen. Franz Sigel. Sigel prudently withdrew. But it wasn't until the impetuous Lyon decided to march into southwestern Missouri to confront Confederate forces under Ben McCulloch that real combat took place.

Fiery U.S. Army Captain Nathaniel Lyon attacked superior Confederate forces at Wilson's Creek, Missouri, on August 10 and lost his life.

(Harper's Pictorial History of the Civil War, *1866)*

Outnumbered more than two to one, Lyon nevertheless attacked at Wilson's Creek on August 10 and fought an incredibly intense battle, which resulted in his death and the retreat of his army.

While the Confederates remained in control of southwestern Missouri, the state never seceded, although it was plagued throughout the war by an especially bitter and brutal brand of murder and mayhem that military commanders chose to call guerrilla warfare.

> ### Count Off!
>
> The Battle of Wilson's Creek (August 10, 1861) accomplished nothing, but cost both sides much. The Union fielded 5,400 men against the Confederacy's 11,600. Among the Federals, 223 were killed, 721 wounded, and 291 went missing. The Confederates lost 257 killed, some 900 wounded, and 27 missing. Although the Union forces lost the engagement, they fought more effectively than the rebels. For every 1,000 Union troops engaged, 241 Confederates were killed or wounded; whereas for every 1,000 Confederates engaged, only 81 Union soldiers became casualties.

Montani Semper Liberi

The Latin motto adopted by the state of West Virginia, *Montani semper liberi* ("Mountaineers are always free"), expresses the attitude of backwoods western Virginia toward coastal Virginia more than it proclaims any love of the Union. The struggling frontier people of the state's mountainous western counties had long been hostile to relatively prosperous Tidewater Virginia, the seat of a government (the westerners felt) that cared and did little for them. Secession presented an opportune time for the western counties to break away and seize their own destiny.

As we shall see in the next chapter, the dashing young Maj. Gen. George B. McClellan won a small but significant victory against the Confederates at Philippi, in western Virginia, on June 3, 1861, thereby essentially securing the region for the Union. On June 20, 1863, West Virginia was admitted to the Union as a new state.

Brawl in Baltimore

On April 19, 1861, the Sixth Massachusetts Regiment, commanded by Colonel Edward F. Jones, was on the rails, heading toward Washington to garrison the besieged capital. When the troops changed trains in Baltimore, they were mobbed by Confederate sympathizers, so-called *plug uglies*, who hurled stones and

Words of War

The pro-Confederate citizens who took part in the attack on the Sixth Massachusetts were known as **plug uglies.** The name came in part from the plug-style hats they wore and perhaps also from the spikes plugged into the front of their boots, the more effectively to kick with. They not only rioted in Baltimore, but also wreaked havoc throughout Maryland.

bricks at them, killing four of their number. The soldiers opened fire, killing 12 Balti-moreans and wounding others. Three days after this, a citizens' committee called on President Lincoln to protest the "pollution" of Maryland soil.

On April 19, 1861, Baltimoreans rioted against the Sixth Massachusetts Regiment, which was passing through Baltimore on the way to garrison Washington, D.C. Four soldiers and twelve civilians were killed.

(Harper's Pictorial History of the Civil War, *1866*)

"Our men are not moles, and cannot dig under the earth," Lincoln replied to the committee members. "They are not birds, and cannot fly through the air. There is no way but to march across, and that they must do." In response, Baltimoreans cut tele-graph lines, sabotaged railroad tracks, and destroyed bridges. For a time, Washington was cut off from communication with the North.

War News

Despite opposition from Chief Justice Roger B. Taney, Lincoln suspended *habeas corpus* twice more, including "throughout the United States" on September 24, 1862. In the course of the war, probably more than 13,000 Americans were held, for varying periods, without formal charges, hearing, or trial.

Habeas Corpus Held Hostage

Lincoln responded by ordering Gen. Benjamin F. Butler to occupy the city, empowering him to arrest and jail all pro-Secessionists, including nine mem-bers of the state legislature, Mayor William Brown, and the city's chief of police. Butler was an ambitious "political general," who, originally a Massachusetts Democrat, had supported the nomination of Jefferson Davis as his party's presidential candidate in 1860, but who became a zealous Unionist once war broke out. Now he carried out his assignment in

Baltimore with relish, giving Baltimoreans a taste of the deportment and attitude that would prompt the citizens of New Orleans to christen him "Beast" Butler when he occupied that city later in the war.

In Baltimore, Abraham Lincoln effectively suspended one of the most cherished democratic rights of Americans: *habeas corpus*, the basic protection from imprisonment except as a result of due course of law. For this, some, in the North as well as the South, condemned the president as a tyrant.

The Battle of Bull Run

In the wake of Fort Sumter's fall, Northern newspapers, spearheaded by Horace Greeley's *New York Daily Tribune*, called for decisive action. Instead, as the weeks ground on, there were more secessions from the Union:

- Virginia, April 17

- Arkansas, May 6

- North Carolina, May 20

- Tennessee (though deeply divided over the issue), June 8

There were also two minor (albeit promising) Federal victories in West Virginia, tempered by the Federal failure at Big Bethel. At last, in July, with an army of some 35,000 men massed in Alexandria, Virginia, General Irvin McDowell was directed to make a major move. He was to attack a Confederate force of about 20,000 men under P.G.T. Beauregard at Manassas Junction, on a creek called Bull Run, squarely athwart the best direct route to Richmond.

McDowell was a West Pointer who had also been educated in France and had a fine command of the classical texts on military tactics. He was also notable for his prodigious appetite, and was known to have polished off an entire watermelon as dessert after a large meal, pronouncing the fruit "monstrous fine." He was not so much chosen to command the first great Union offensive of the war as he was given it by default. He was one of relatively few fully qualified officers who hadn't defected to the Confederacy after the fall of Sumter.

Certainly, McDowell was savvy enough to recognize that, while he enjoyed a numerical advantage over Beauregard, some 9,000 more rebels under the command of Joseph Johnston were facing 16,000 Federals under 69-year-old Gen. Robert Patterson near Harpers Ferry. If Johnston somehow got around Patterson and reinforced Beauregard, the tables could well be turned against the Federal attack at

Manassas Junction. Patterson was assigned, therefore, to keep vigilant pressure on Johnston.

If McDowell was at least a trained military man, his soldiers, almost everyone of them, were not. True, many of his men relished parading to battle in their new uniforms—but the weather was oppressively hot, and when they got winded or just bored, they broke ranks and rested or wandered off to pick blackberries.

War News

Union uniforms were by no means *uniform*. In addition to the standard blue blouses of the U.S. Army, there was a variety of state regimental and militia uniforms, including some that were as gray as anything the rebels wore, as was made all too evident in the confusion at Big Bethel. Other uniforms were patterned in imitation of French Zouaves (with ballooning bright red pants, blue coats, brightly colored sashes, and turbans or fezzes for headgear) and Scottish Highlanders, tartans and all.

McDowell's skylarking troops had their first contact with the enemy on July 18, and one Union division was driven back. Worse, while these preliminaries were going on near Bull Run, Johnston, in the Shenandoah Valley, managed to give Patterson and his superior Federal numbers the slip so that, when the battle finally took place, on July 21, some 35,000 Union troops were pitted against reinforced Confederate forces of almost 30,000.

The Rebel Rose

Unknown to the Union commander, the Confederates had a secret weapon at Bull Run—a weapon that had come into play before a shot had been fired. After the death of her husband, Department of State official Dr. Robert Greenhow, in 1854, Rose O'Neal Greenhow became a kind of merry widow, ingratiating herself with any number of influential men, young and not so young, in Washington and the military. When the war began, Greenhow was recruited by Thomas Jordan, rebel spymaster (and former West Point roommate of William Tecumseh Sherman), to gather information for the Confederacy.

Greenhow considered herself "a Southern woman, born with revolutionary blood in my veins," and she enthusiastically embarked on a career as secret agent, plying highly placed civil and military authorities with her charms. She was able to obtain a wealth of information concerning Union plans for the Bull Run battle, which she transmitted via a female courier, Betty Duvall, a comely Washingtonian, who hid Greenhow's enciphered messages in what Confederate general M.L. Bonham called "the longest and most beautiful roll of hair I have ever seen."

The information Greenhow supplied proved valuable in prompting General Beauregard to deploy his forces advantageously behind Bull Run Creek.

The espionage career of Rose O'Neal Greenhow, whom the tabloids of the time would later dub "The Rebel Rose," was cut short by no less a figure than Allan Pinkerton, who ran her to ground on August 23, 1861. She was held under house arrest and then consigned to the Old Capitol Prison—originally built after the War of 1812 as temporary quarters for Congress until the original Capitol, burned by the British, was rebuilt—but was ultimately paroled to the South. On September 1, 1864, she drowned in the wreck of the ship *Condor*, running the Union blockade off the coast of North Carolina. She was smuggling gold for the Confederate cause, and the weight of one of the bags she carried pulled her under the waves.

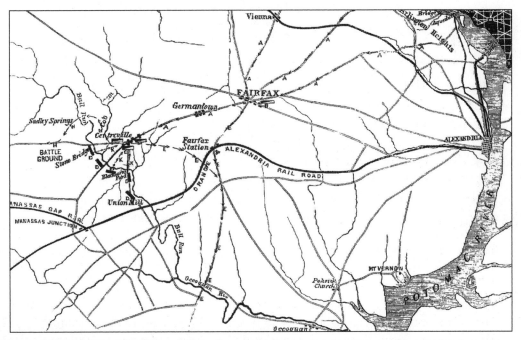

A map of the vicinity of Bull Run. The battleground is just to the west of Centreville, which is west and slightly south of Washington.

(Harper's Pictorial History of the Civil War, *1866*)

Cheers

The morning of the battle, flocks of fashionably dressed Washingtonians rode out to Centreville, Virginia, 18 to 20 miles from the city, in carriages filled with picnic baskets and bottles of champagne to view, through field glasses and telescopes, the action some three miles off.

Despite the rebel reinforcements, McDowell's forces at first drove the Confederates from their defensive positions and even managed to turn the Confederate left flank. The picnic parties cheered.

Like a Stone Wall

Then something extraordinary happened. The Confederate Beauregard was a good soldier, but overly fond of tactics too complex for his indifferently trained and untested men to execute. Union general McDowell was knowledgeable but uninspired. But Confederate Brig. Gen. Thomas J. Jackson was made of stuff, it seemed, from another world altogether. Anyone who looked into his gimlet-blue eyes—"Old Blue Light," his men called him—would attest to the otherworldly power of his presence.

Words of War

Skedaddle was the word Civil War soldiers used to describe the act of fleeing under fire.

While men stumbled over one another in confusion or ran off in panic (*skedaddled*), Jackson materialized with his brigade of unwavering Virginians.

Gen. Barnard Bee, destined to sustain a mortal wound later in the battle and die the next day, saw Jackson and his stalwarts hold their ground against the Federal onslaught.

"There's Jackson standing like a stone wall!" Bee shouted. Then, grandly gesturing with his sword, Bee called out, "Rally behind the Virginians!"

And so they did. As for Jackson, he was known as "Stonewall" from that day on, and his command earned the nickname "Stonewall Brigade."

War News

General Bee might have actually expressed himself more mundanely: "Yonder stands Jackson like a stone wall; let's go to his assistance." It is also *possible*, according to some witnesses, that Bee did not intend the "stone wall" remark as a compliment, but thought that Jackson should be on the move rather than just standing "like a stone wall."

Pursued by Furies

For the rest of the afternoon, the fighting seesawed, first one way, then the other. Finally, late in the day, the Confederates, hitherto fighting mainly a defensive battle, massed for a decisive counterthrust.

"Yell like furies," Jackson ordered his men as they charged, and, for the first time on any battlefield, friend and foe alike heard the "rebel yell"—a high-pitched keening that seemed to come from the same otherworldly place as the eerie blue of Old Blue Light's eyes. The effect was electric. The Federal lines broke, crumbled, dissolved, and panic-stricken soldiers fled the enemy along roads choked with erstwhile picnickers, now as panic-stricken as the soldiers.

Anyone searching for a symbol of "civil war" would have found it that afternoon: dust, death, terror, confusion, and chaos. Yet if McDowell's army had fallen apart in defeat, the army of Beauregard and Johnston was not much better organized. Jefferson Davis, always the micromanager, arrived on the scene to supervise. It crossed his mind to order a pursuit of the routed Union forces, but, over the fruitless urgings of Jackson, he did not. Instead, the rebels settled into camp, feeling now that the war might be over quickly. For its part, the Union started looking around for a new general.

Count Off!

Union losses at Bull Run were 2,896 killed, wounded, and missing. Confederate casualties amounted to 1,982.

The Least You Need to Know

 ◆ Winfield Scott planned to strangle the South with a naval blockade, even though the Union navy was far too small for the task.

 ◆ International diplomacy—especially relations with England—was a crucial aspect of the war, as was control of the border states.

 ◆ Rose O'Neal Greenhow, seductive and effective, was one of many Confederate spies in the very heart of the Union military and civil government.

 ◆ The First Battle of Bull Run, or First Manassas, was a contest of amateur armies, but nevertheless deadly; for most of the battle, the fighting was indecisive, until "Stonewall" Jackson rallied the Confederates and triggered a rout of the Union troops.

Chapter 7

The Young Napoleon and a Man Who Fights: McClellan and Grant

In This Chapter

- ◆ McClellan's victories in western Virginia
- ◆ The Ball's Bluff disaster
- ◆ Lee's and Grant's maiden battles
- ◆ Grant takes Forts Henry and Donelson
- ◆ The bloody battle at Shiloh

The Civil War names we think of as the greatest—Grant and Lee—belonged to more or less obscure figures during the opening months of the war, with Grant even more obscure than Lee. In the North, early on, the names of Winfield Scott and George B. McClellan were on every lip. In the South, it was Pierre Gustave Toutant Beauregard and Albert Sidney Johnston—the latter active in Tennessee and considered by many to be one of the most promising Confederate commanders. The South looked to the recent victory at Bull Run for encouragement, while the North could only cling to the future—and the hope that it would bring a great heroic general to deliver the Union in its darkest hour of need.

This chapter focuses on the maiden battles of McClellan, Lee, and Grant, ending with Grant's bloody trial at Shiloh.

A Saddle and Small Victories

From the Union's confused and shamefaced post-Bull Run perspective, no man appeared more competent than George Brinton McClellan. He'd graduated from West Point in 1846, second in his class, and was thrice *breveted* (promoted for bravery) in the Mexican War. An official observer of foreign armies, McClellan had introduced a number of innovations in uniforms, tents, and drill, and, in 1856, designed a new-style cavalry saddle that was adopted by the Army. Brilliant though he was, like other brilliant young officers, he had advanced only to the rank of captain after 10 years' service and resigned his commission in 1857 to become vice president of the Illinois Central Railroad. In this capacity, he first met Abraham Lincoln, who was a lawyer for the ICRR.

Words of War

A **brevet** is a promotion for conspicuous bravery or meritorious service. The promotion usually comes without an increase in pay and is often of an honorary or temporary nature.

Philippi

When the war started, Pennsylvania-born McClellan became major general of the Ohio volunteers and was quickly promoted to major general in the regular army, with command of the Department of the Ohio. Dispatched to western Virginia, McClellan attacked the sleeping Confederate camp at the mountain settlement of Philippi. He routed about 1,500 on the night of June 3, 1861. Although this was a minor skirmish, especially by comparison to the First Battle of Bull Run, the Confederates retreated with such haste that the Northern newspapers seized on it as a great triumph, dubbing it the "Philippi races."

Rich Mountain

The next victory, at Rich Mountain, on July 11, was more important. McClellan's subordinate, Brig. Gen. William Rosecrans, skillfully advanced through an unguarded mountain trail to cut off a Confederate unit, seize more than 500 prisoners, and open the way for deeper Union penetration. Although the battle involved small numbers, it essentially secured for the Union the region that would break away from Confederate Virginia to become the loyal state of West Virginia.

While Rich Mountain was a significant gain, both it and Philippi were on a small scale. Nevertheless, in the gloom of Bull Run, they glowed, and Lincoln gave McClellan command of the Department (later Army) of the Potomac—the forces around Washington—which he set about transforming from a rabble into a fighting force. He proved himself a brilliant administrator, quickly earning respect and affection from his men and admiration from the press. Short in stature, McClellan was nevertheless a very youthful general at 35 and cut a dashing figure. The papers called him the "Young Napoleon."

Death Leap

In late October, McClellan sent a reconnaissance force under Brig. Gen. Charles P. Stone across the Potomac River to Ball's Bluff, a steep, wooded hill about 30 miles upriver from Washington. Pressing the reconnaissance aggressively, the Federals got trapped on the top of the bluff. Among the first to fall in the fighting on October 21 was Col. Edward D. Baker, a U.S. senator and a close personal friend of Lincoln. Demoralized by the sight of the colonel's body being carried from the front, a knot of inexperienced Union soldiers panicked and commenced an unauthorized retreat.

The only path to safety was down the bluff and into boats that would take the men across the Potomac to the Maryland shore. The retreat became a rout, as, under intense fire from the Confederates, the Federals backed up to the top of the bluff, all wanting desperately to get to the boats. Bunching together, the soldiers made an obscenely opportune blue-coated target.

Count Off!

Federal losses at Ball's Bluff were 49 killed, 158 wounded, and 714 captured or missing. Confederate losses were 33 killed, 115 wounded, and one missing.

War News

Gen. Charles P. Stone was suspected of treason for the Ball's Bluff disaster. Imprisoned for 189 days without charges or trial, he was ultimately released and returned to duty, but never again given an important assignment. He resigned in 1864 to become chief of the general staff of the army of the Khedive of Egypt. Retiring in 1883 as a pasha, Stone returned to the United States and served as chief engineer for the design and erection of the pedestal of the Statue of Liberty.

"A kind of shiver ran through the huddled mass upon the brow of the cliff," one Confederate soldier later recalled. "It gave way; rushed a few steps; then, in one wild, panic-stricken herd, rolled, leaped, tumbled over the precipice."

Men jumped down, one on top of another, some skewering themselves on the bayonets of those who had leaped first.

A grandson of Paul Revere was captured; a son of Oliver Wendell Holmes wounded; a nephew of James Russell Lowell killed—all were casualties at Ball's Bluff. But it was the death of Senator Baker that sent shock waves through the White House and Congress. The latter body formed the Joint Committee on the Conduct of the War and set about looking for someone to blame. They settled on General Stone, who was arrested and imprisoned with neither charge nor trial.

McClellan emerged blameless from Ball's Bluff, and, in November, was named general-in-chief of the Union armies, replacing "Old Fuss and Feathers" Scott, who, pressed by an excess of age and flesh, retired.

"Supreme command of the Army will entail a vast labor upon you," Lincoln told McClellan.

"I can do it all," the Young Napoleon replied.

> ### Sites and Sights
>
> Ball's Bluff Regional Park (Ball's Bluff Road, Leesburg, Virginia) surrounds the Ball's Bluff National Cemetery and preserves the battlefield. The park is open year-round from dawn to dusk and is staffed by volunteer battlefield interpreters (Phone: 1-703-737-7800).

A Granny and a Tannery Clerk

Before the Civil War, few people knew Robert E. Lee and far fewer knew Ulysses S. Grant. Both men served with distinction in the Mexican War; Winfield Scott called Lee "the very best soldier I ever saw in the field," and Grant was breveted captain. But the public had a short memory for heroes of the Mexican War. Lee rose quietly in the peacetime army, and Grant settled into a dreary assignment at Fort Humboldt, California, where he acquired a reputation for little more than heavy drinking and finally resigned his commission in 1854 to take up farming and then real estate. Failing miserably at both, he became a clerk in a Galena, Illinois, leather goods business owned by his father and operated by his brothers.

The Civil War seared the names of Lee and Grant in American memory. But not right away.

Lee Retreats from Cheat Mountain

Robert E. Lee was so highly regarded in professional military circles that, before Lee resigned, Abraham Lincoln repeatedly offered him command of the Union armies. Jefferson Davis, no less an admirer than Lincoln, made Lee his personal military advisor. But Lee's first field command, in western Virginia, proved worse than disappointing. Saddled with unruly subordinates and operating amid a hostile local populace, Lee nevertheless mounted an assault on Cheat Mountain, a position that controlled a major turnpike and several mountain passes. On September 11, 1861, he attacked a Union position, only to be tricked by some Federal POWs, who persuaded Lee that the Cheat summit was held by 4,000 Federals, far outnumbering Lee.

Robert E. Lee, commander of the South's Army of Northern Virginia and, by the end of the war, general-in-chief of the Confederate armies. No commander, North or South, was more respected or beloved than Lee.

(National Archives and Records Administration)

In fact, only 300 Union soldiers held the summit, but Lee was suckered; he hesitated, lost the element of surprise, and soon found himself facing all-too-real Union reinforcements. After a two-day skirmish, Lee withdrew. His casualties were light, but it had been an inauspicious maiden battle for the general, whom the Richmond papers derided as "Granny Lee" and "Evacuating Lee."

Grant Retreats from the Battle of Belmont

Ulysses S. Grant's first Civil War battle was also less than impressive. Leading some 3,000 troops in boats out of Cairo, Illinois, across the Mississippi to Belmont, Missouri, he defeated Confederate forces under Gen. Gideon Pillow. So far so good—not that besting Pillow was any great accomplishment. Although the Union army became notorious for harboring large numbers of incompetent "political generals," few could match in sheer ineptitude Confederate General Pillow, a Jefferson Davis political appointee.

Ulysses S. Grant, a hard-drinking business failure, became the brilliant commander of the Union forces. He understood the essential nature of this Civil War: The populous North could afford to lose men, while the more thinly populated South could not. Some would call Grant a butcher; others would say he saved the Union.

(National Archives and Records Administration)

In any event, Grant allowed his men to revel in their achievement by looting the abandoned Confederate camp. At this point, Gen. Leonidas Polk, a close friend of Davis but a West Pointer and no political hack, trained his artillery against Grant's men, and then massed some 10,000 troops below Belmont in an attempt to cut Grant off from his river transports.

Count Off!

Grant suffered 607 casualties out of 3,114 engaged at Belmont, while the Confederates lost 642 (killed, wounded, and missing) out of some 4,000 engaged.

It was a most embarrassing position for the Union commander, but if Grant made a terrible mistake in his first engagement with the enemy, he also demonstrated a remarkable presence of mind in recovering from it. To a subordinate who bellowed that they were surrounded, Grant calmly replied, "Well, we must cut our way out as we cut our way in." Grant gave up the camp, but managed to preserve his command.

Hope for the Young Napoleon

As 1861 drew to a close, Southerners tried to bask in what was left of Bull Run's glow, while Northerners had little or nothing tangible to base their hopes on. They did have, however, the prospect and promise of the "Young Napoleon."

Little Mac Takes Command

The press might have called George McClellan the Young Napoleon, but his soldiers, with great affection, referred to him as Little Mac. In the demoralized wake of Bull Run, McClellan had reorganized, augmented, and trained the Army of the Potomac, and now he did the same thing for the rest of the Union forces. He made farm boys, clerks, and factory hands feel like soldiers, and that was no small accomplishment.

Yet as the final months of 1861 dissolved into 1862, McClellan did nothing but continue to train and drill his army. As he repeatedly delayed committing it to combat, Lincoln began to doubt his general.

The "Young Napoleon," George Brinton McClellan, posed for this imperial portrait with his wife, Ellen Marcy McClellan. Lincoln and the North pinned their hopes on him as general-in-chief of the army. This old photograph is badly stained and streaked.

(National Archives and Records Administration)

Triumph at Fort Donelson

The attention of most Americans, North and South, was fixed on the East Coast. Being assigned to an army command in and about Virginia was prestigious, whereas leading soldiers into battle in the war's western theater—that is, west of the Appalachians—was regarded as something of a backwater assignment.

In the opening months of the war, the Union entrusted command of operations in the area to John Charles Frémont, a Western explorer who had fought in the Mexican War, yet who was at best a gallant but marginally competent commander. Frémont did have sufficient sense to order the construction of a gunboat fleet—invaluable in a region watered by the Mississippi, Tennessee, and Cumberland rivers—and he also elevated Grant, at that point a brigadier, to command the key position of Cairo (pronounced Kay-ro), Illinois, where the Ohio joins the Mississippi River.

Words of War

In the Civil War era, a **gunboat** was a squat, shallow-draft vessel, often clad in iron plates to deflect cannonballs, designed mainly for use on rivers as a floating artillery platform.

In September 1861, Kentucky ended its neutrality and declared itself for the Union, whereupon Confederate general Polk invaded the state and occupied Columbus, situated on commanding bluffs above the Mississippi. Grant answered by taking Paducah, which controlled the mouths of the Tennessee and Cumberland rivers.

Also in September, Davis appointed Albert Sidney Johnston (no relation to Joseph E. Johnston, the ranking Confederate officer at First Bull Run), at the time considered the most capable of the Confederate army's officers, to command in the West. Johnston well understood the vital importance of the rivers in the area. He secured the Mississippi by reinforcing Columbus, and he fortified the Cumberland and Tennessee rivers, which he figured to be principal highways of potential Northern invasion. He built Fort Henry on the Tennessee and Fort Donelson on the Cumberland.

Albert Sidney Johnston, whom many considered the South's ablest commander, headed the Confederate army's Western Department until his death at the Battle of Shiloh.

(Harper's Pictorial History of the Civil War, *1866)*

In November of 1861, the Union made some changes of its own in command. Maj. Gen. Henry Wager Halleck—known as "Old Brains" because, back in 1846, he had written a textbook called *Elements of Military Art and Science*—was put in charge of the area west of the Cumberland, and Brig. Gen. Don Carlos Buell was given command east of that river. Between them, Halleck and Buell commanded more men than Johnston, but neither Union general was very aggressive, and, even worse, neither liked the other. They worked grudgingly together and consistently failed to coordinate plans and movements.

Nevertheless, the first assault on Johnston's army went well as Union general George H. Thomas defeated Confederates under the command of George B. Crittenden at Mill Springs, Kentucky, on January 19, 1862. After this, Halleck dispatched Grant with 15,000 men and a squadron of ironclad gunboats under navy Flag Officer Andrew Foote against Fort Henry on the Tennessee. That bastion fell quickly, on February 6.

> **Words of War** _____
>
> Nowadays, a **flag officer** in the U.S. Navy or Coast Guard is the generic term for anyone holding a rank above captain, such as a rear admiral, vice admiral, or admiral. During the Civil War, flag officer was a discrete rank, above captain, but below rear admiral.

Wasting no time, Grant turned sharply east and marched to the Cumberland to attack Ft. Donelson, again coordinated with Foote's gunboats. Johnston did not wish a repeat of Ft. Henry, so he had reinforced the Cumberland River position with some 15,000 troops pulled out of Bowling Green, Kentucky. In consequence, Ft. Donelson held out against the Union onslaught for three days, until Grant received reinforcements and was able to pound the position with artillery.

U.S. Navy Flag Officer Andrew Foote was U.S. Grant's collaborator in the capture of the Confederate forts on the Mississippi.

(Harper's Pictorial History of the Civil War, *1866*)

At an inn in the little town of Dover, adjacent to the fort, four Confederate commanders held a counsel of war. The subject was surrender. Neither Gen. John Buchanan Floyd nor Gen. Gideon Pillow wanted the burden of surrender on *their* shoulders, so Floyd, in charge of the fort, declared to Pillow, "I turn command over, sir," and Pillow declared to Gen. Simon Bolivar Buckner, "I pass it," to which Buckner replied, "I assume it." A disgusted witness to this was cavalry general Nathan Bedford Forrest, whom no less a figure than William Tecumseh Sherman would later call the most remarkable commander, of either side, in the war. "I did not come here for the purpose of surrendering my command," Forrest fumed and, with his cavalrymen, rode out of the fort, to fight another day.

As for Floyd and Pillow, they simply fled and thereby evaded capture. (Jefferson Davis cashiered Floyd out of the army and suspended Pillow, who never again received an important command.) Buckner was left to pen a note to Grant proposing the "appointment of commissioners to agree upon the terms of capitulation of the forces and fort under my command." Receiving the note, Grant, wrote a reply that rang—at last—triumphantly in Northern ears: "No terms except an unconditional and immediate surrender can be accepted. I propose to move immediately upon your works."

Grant's given name was Hiram Ulysses, but somehow the papers appointing him to West Point listed him as Ulysses S. Grant. Knowing the folly of trying to punch through government red tape, Grant adopted the new name (even saying the "S" stood for Simpson, his mother's maiden name). In any case, he liked the sound of "U.S. Grant," as did his West Point classmates, who dubbed him "Uncle Sam" and even nicknamed him Sam. After Ft. Donelson, however, the North insisted jubilantly that the initials stood for "Unconditional Surrender."

Words of War

In military parlance, **works** are fortifications.

Place of Peace

Grant and Foote had won a significant victory. With the fall of the river forts, General Johnston was forced to evacuate Nashville, leaving behind supplies the Confederacy could ill afford to lose. The strongly fortified and strategically critical position at Columbus was also abandoned. P.G.T. Beauregard, transferred from Virginia, arrived as Johnston's second in command; his first assignment was to take the Columbus garrison south to join up with Johnston's troops—and whatever reinforcements could be found—at Corinth, Mississippi, a key rail connection. With luck, Johnston and Beauregard would be able to field about 50,000 men.

Of course, it was the Union army's job to meet this combined force with overwhelming numbers. And they *could* do it. If Halleck and Buell managed their movements swiftly and efficiently, they *could* hurl some 70,000 troops against the Confederate's 50,000. Yet, all too typically, the Union failed to capitalize on the gains it had made. Grant, having been promoted to major general, was still subordinate to Halleck. He urged "Old Brains" to press the pursuit of the retreating rebels, but Halleck and Buell moved slowly, giving Beauregard and Johnston ample time to meet and regroup at Corinth.

Grant's Mistake

Grant established his camp with some 42,000 men at Pittsburg Landing, Tennessee, on the west bank of the Tennessee River, just northeast of the Confederate position at Corinth, Mississippi. Nursing a badly sprained ankle, Grant set up his headquarters tent next to a log-built Methodist meeting house called Shiloh Chapel, after the Canaanite town mentioned in the Old Testament as the place where the Tabernacle and the Ark of the Covenant were lodged. The Hebrew name means "place of peace."

And that is precisely what Grant expected. Believing the Confederates would stay in Corinth for the present, Grant did not adequately defend his camp: no entrenchments, no cavalry patrols, and no remote pickets. On Sunday morning, April 6, Albert Sidney Johnston and P.G.T. Beauregard attacked.

Words of War

During the Civil War, **picket** was another name for sentry, and a **picket line** was an outer perimeter, usually around a camp, which was patrolled by sentries.

Voices

Famous as the journalist and explorer who found the long-lost African missionary, physician, and explorer Dr. David Livingstone, Henry Morton Stanley fought as a youth at Shiloh with the Dixie Greys, a Louisiana regiment:

> [I saw] a young Lieutenant, who, judging by the new gloss on his uniform, must have been some father's darling. A clean bullet-hole through the centre of his forehead had instantly ended his career. A little further were some twenty bodies, lying in various postures, each by its own pool of viscous blood, which emitted a peculiar scent, which was new to me, but which I have since learned is inseparable from a battlefield. Beyond these, a still larger group lay, body overlying body, knees crooked, arms erect, or wide-stretched and rigid according as the last spasm overtook them. The company opposed to them must have shot straight.

> It was the first Field of Glory I had seen in my May of life, and the first time that Glory sickened me with its repulsive aspect, and made me suspect it was all a glittering lie ....

Carnage at Shiloh

Panic shot through Pittsburg Landing as surely and as violently as Confederate bullets. Many of the disorganized Union troops sought places to hide rather than fight. For its opening 12 hours, the battle was a one-sided pounding of Confederates against Federals, and by the end of Sunday, the army in gray had captured the key position of Shiloh Chapel and nearly pushed the Federal lines into the river.

This map of the Shiloh battlefield suggests the rough, swampy character of the landscape.

(Harper's Pictorial History of the Civil War, *1866)*

Sherman Emerges

Union defeat seemed certain, but William Tecumseh Sherman rallied and regrouped his forces, who had received the first full brunt of the attack, broken, and run.

Sherman, as Grant later recalled, inspired "confidence in officers and men that enabled them to render services on that bloody battlefield worthy of the best of veterans."

Grant had admired Sherman ever since Sherman had been transferred to his Army of the Tennessee in February. But many others had their doubts; after First Bull Run, Sherman served as commanding general of the Department of the Cumberland in Kentucky and was vigorously outspoken in his criticism of strategic policy. He feuded savagely with his superiors and the press, protesting that they did not understand that this war would assume a terrible magnitude. Sherman was so vehement that he was accused of insanity. Shiloh and subsequent battles proved him all too sane and his appraisal chillingly accurate. His conduct at Shiloh and throughout the rest of the war revealed Sherman as among the nation's fiercest and most skillful warriors.

Others also fought heroically to save the day for the Union. Gen. Benjamin M. Prentiss made an extraordinary stand on a wooded elevation in the heart of the Union's position. The Confederate attackers called it the Hornet's Nest because of its stubborn resistance. Although the stand was costly—and the press later scapegoated Prentiss for it—it bought time until the arrival of Union general Don Carlos Buell's Army of the Ohio and a division under Lew Wallace (who in 1880 would win fame as the author of the popular novel *Ben-Hur*).

Despite their initial triumph, the Confederates suffered one loss more damaging than all the others. About 2:30 on Sunday afternoon, Albert Sidney Johnston sustained a wound in the leg. He ignored it at first. Then his aide saw him reel in the saddle.

"General, are you hurt?"

"Yes, and I fear seriously," Johnston replied.

The aide saw that his right boot had filled with blood. A bullet had severed his femoral artery. Albert Sidney Johnston bled to death from a wound that needn't have been fatal had a tourniquet been applied in timely fashion.

Sunday night, General Beauregard was left alone to telegraph the devastating news of Johnston's death, albeit tempered with a report of Southern victory at Shiloh.

That report proved premature. Unlike most Union generals at the time, Grant did not give up. As darkness fell, William Tecumseh Sherman observed, "Well, General, we've had

---

Sites and Sights

Shiloh National Military Park, located 22 miles northeast of Corinth, Mississippi, on TN 22, is a beautiful spot. All the major sites are well marked, and the Shiloh Methodist Church has been reconstructed. The park is adjacent to the Shiloh National Cemetery.

The park is open every day except Christmas. For information, call 1-901-689-5275.

the Devil's own day," to which Grant responded, "Yes. Lick 'em tomorrow, though." The reinforced Union army counterattacked on Monday morning, and Beauregard, after a 10-hour fight, withdrew his army to Corinth.

The Battle of Island 10

Shiloh was either a narrow Union victory or a draw. In either case, it was a bloodbath without precedent on the North American continent. Yet, in the broader context of its impact on Confederate operations in the western theater, Shiloh began the defeat of the Southern cause in that region.

In part, this was because of the ingenuity and initiative of another of Halleck's generals, the surly and arrogant John Pope. He had begun methodically attacking the Mississippi River defenses in March. The toughest of these was Island No. 10, at the extreme northwestern edge of Tennessee at the Kentucky line, which bristled with 50 guns and occupied a seemingly unassailable double-hairpin turn of the river. Flag Officer Foote thought it suicide to run past Island No. 10's batteries with ironclad gunboats, let alone with unarmored troop transports.

Pope was not stymied for long, however. He had his engineers dig a shallow canal connecting the Mississippi to a Kentucky stream called Wilson's Bayou, which joined the river *below* Island No. 10. This enabled Pope's transports simply to bypass the Confederate defenses, which they did on April 7. The canal was too shallow for the ironclad gunboats Pope still needed as artillery support for his land force, but on April 4, under cover of night, one of Foote's captains, Henry Walker, succeeded in a harrowing run past the island. On April 6, another vessel made it past. Pope managed to cut off the Confederate line of retreat from Shiloh at Tiptonville, Tennessee, resulting in the capture of 3,500 men. By neutralizing the Mississippi defenses, he also opened the river clear downstream to Ft. Pillow, destined to fall in June. General Halleck sent Pope a telegram: "I congratulate you and your command on your splendid achievement."

Count Off!

Of 62,682 Union soldiers engaged at Shiloh, 1,754 were killed, 8,408 wounded, and 2,885 went missing. Confederate losses were 723 killed, 8,012 wounded, and 959 missing out of 40,335 men engaged.

He Fights

The success of the Battle of Island 10 notwithstanding, Shiloh had been the bloodiest battle fought to that date in North America, and Abraham Lincoln was pressed by many to remove Grant from command. The president, burdened with generals who moved slowly and failed to pursue the enemy, resisted. Yes, the losses under Grant were terrible. But, Lincoln realized, Grant had caused terrible Confederate losses as well, and he realized further that the Union, so much larger than the Confederacy, could afford to lose more men than the South. To calls for Grant's dismissal, Abraham Lincoln replied, "I can't spare this man; he fights."

The Least You Need to Know

♦ The Union, depressed by defeat at Bull Run, looked to George B. McClellan, a dashing young general, as the commander who would win the war.

♦ Lee and Grant, destined to emerge as the central military figures of the war, began the war obscurely and inauspiciously with defeat and near disaster.

♦ Grant's capture of forts on the Tennessee, Cumberland, and Mississippi rivers began the ultimate defeat of the Southern cause in the war's western theater.

♦ At the time it was fought, Shiloh, a narrow Union victory, was the largest and bloodiest battle ever seen on the North American continent.

Ocean, Valley, and River

In This Chapter

- ◆ McClellan's failure to act
- ◆ Clash of the *Monitor* and the *Merrimac*
- ◆ Stonewall Jackson's Shenandoah Valley campaign
- ◆ Farragut takes New Orleans for the Union
- ◆ "Beast" Butler occupies New Orleans

"I can do it all," McClellan had assured Lincoln when the president named him general-in-chief of the Union armies. Never a shrinking violet, the "Young Napoleon" then wrote to his wife: "Who would have thought, when we were married, that I should so soon be called upon to save my country?"

It was a tall order. And, as weeks dragged into months without a decisive campaign from McClellan, Lincoln's hopes for his general turned to impatience and doubt. On March 11, 1862, Lincoln formally relieved McClellan as general-in-chief of the armies, returning him to command of the Army of the Potomac only. But when the president urged him to lead this now drilled and polished force from Washington to Richmond, McClellan proposed a much more ambitious plan and Lincoln, grudgingly, agreed.

This chapter begins at this point, with McClellan's hesitations, and then focuses on more decisive action at sea, in the Shenandoah Valley, and on the great Mississippi River leading to the Crescent City, New Orleans.

"What Are You Waiting For, Tardy George?"

A song lyric of the day said—or sang—it all. By early 1862, the vaunted "Young Napoleon" had for many become the comical "Tardy George." "What are you wait-ing for?" the song asked. Lincoln asked, too, as did congressmen and senators—some of whom began to suspect McClellan of Southern sympathies. The situation went from bad to worse when McClellan's roundabout route to Richmond met reality.

Instead of driving directly overland from Washing-ton to the rebel capital, McClellan proposed to transport his army by ship down the Chesapeake Bay to the James River, to a position below Gen. Joseph E. Johnston's lines, thus outflanking him by sea, forcing the Confederates to pull back, and, in the process, avoiding a major battle. However, by the time McClellan got under way, Johnston had left his position at Manassas (site of the First Bull Run battle) and moved south to the Rappahannock River, closer to Richmond.

This not only required McClellan to rethink his plan, but also when Union forces inspected the abandoned Confederate trenches at Manassas, they discovered that what they had thought were cannons were nothing more than logs painted black to simu-late cannons. The press called them *Quaker guns*, a wry reference to that denomination's pacifist beliefs. "Our enemies," one reporter wrote, "like the Chinese, have frightened us by the sound of gongs and the wearing of devils' masks."

Words of War

A **Quaker gun** was a log positioned and painted to look like a cannon barrel. The Confederates used them to deceive Union commanders into inflating estimates of their strength.

Quaker guns weren't the half of it. McClellan had delayed his advance because he believed that the Confederate army outnumbered him. In part, his grossly exagger-ated estimate of enemy troop strength was a product of his own overcautious nature, but intelligence reports from Allan J. Pinkerton's detectives turned spies were also wildly inflated, furnishing McClellan with figures too large by factors of two, three, and even more.

Oh, well. If the enemy moved south, so would McClellan. He decided to ferry his troops down to Fort Monroe, near Newport News and Hampton Roads, in the southeastern corner of Virginia, well below the rebel capital. His plan was to land and proceed north toward Richmond via the peninsula separating the York and James rivers. That geographical feature gave the operation its name: the Peninsula Campaign. It was the largest amphibious operation in American history to that time, and, although skillfully planned, would produce tragically disappointing results.

Voices

In March 1862, journalist George H. Boker published satirical verses about McClellan, which became a popular song, "Tardy George."

> What are you waiting for, George, I pray?—
> To scour your cross-belts with fresh pipe-clay?
> To burnish your buttons, to brighten your guns;
> Or wait you for May-day and warm spring suns?
>
> Are you blowing your fingers because they are cold,
> Or catching your breath ere you take a hold?
> Is the mud knee-deep in valley and gorge?
> What are you waiting for, tardy George?
>
> Are you waiting for your hair to turn,
> Your heart to soften, your bowels to yearn
> A little more towards "our Southern friends,"
> As at home and abroad they work their ends?
>
> "Our Southern friends!" whom you hold so dear
> That you do no harm and give no fear,
> As you tenderly take them by the gorge?
> What are you waiting for, tardy George?
>
> Now that you've marshaled your whole command,
> Planned what you would, and changed what you planned;
> Practiced with shot and practiced with shell,
> Know to a hair where every one fell,
>
> Made signs by day and signals by night;
> Was it all done to keep out of a fight?
> Is the whole matter too heavy a charge?
> What are you waiting for, tardy George?

Flesh and Iron

The Army of the Potomac landed on April 4 under rainy, miserable conditions. Some 90,000 men slogged through a soupy, low-lying coastal mud flat as Johnston's Confederates withdrew up the Peninsula, and then, instead of immediately attacking the Confederate entrenchments at Yorktown—where George Washington and the Comte de Rochambeau had won *the* decisive battle of the American Revolution—set up a static siege. On April 9, a disgusted Abraham Lincoln penned a sneering note he never sent: "If McClellan is not using the army, I should like to borrow it for a while."

Just a few weeks earlier, nearby Hampton Roads had seen something a lot more dramatic than a mass of soldiers bogged down in the mud. There, a new kind of warfare had been born: ironclad, relentless, and ugly.

Tweaking the Anaconda

In the West, Grant was taking forts and doing very bloody work at Shiloh. In the East, McClellan was merely jockeying for position. At sea, Confederate blockade runners were very active. Thinly spread, the Union's "Anaconda" blockade succeeded in capturing perhaps one in ten rebel vessels. (By the conclusion of the war, the numbers were closer to one in three.)

But the embryonic Confederate Navy was not content with merely *running* the blockade. Its officers wanted to destroy it.

A Resurrection

On the south shore of Hampton Roads was the Gosport Navy Yard, evacuated by Union forces at the beginning of the war. Before they left, they scuttled the frigate *Merrimac* rather than let it fall into rebel hands. Not that Northern naval officials thought the Confederates could do much with the USS *Merrimac* anyway because vessels of the Union fleet were blockading the Roads, thereby sealing off the water route to Richmond.

Words of War

In the mid-nineteenth century, a **frigate** was any high-speed, medium-sized warship.

Perhaps most Northerners shared the opinion William Tecumseh Sherman had voiced back in December 1860: That Southerners were neither technologically inclined nor technologically capable. Although it was true that the South's industrial capacity was dwarfed by that of the North, factories such as the Tredegar Iron Works in Richmond, employing slave labor, steadily turned out cannon and other weaponry. The works could also produce iron plates, with which Confederate engineers clad the hull of the USS *Merrimac* after they refloated it and rechristened it the CSS *Virginia*.

The prospect of an ironclad was terrifying. In the 1860s, the world's navies were making a slow transition from sail to steam-powered craft. Most modern ships were hybrids, rigged for sail, but also equipped with steam engines driving side wheels or aft screws (propellers). But even these hybrids were based on *wooden* hulls, which were vulnerable to naval artillery and to being rammed by vessels equipped with special iron ramming gear mounted on their prows. An ironclad vessel could withstand bombardment while delivering a lethal pounding.

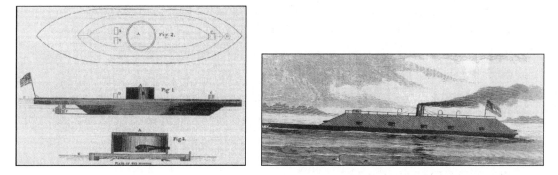

The USS Monitor *is illustrated in plan and elevation: a "cheesebox on a raft." The CSS* Virginia—*born the USS* Merrimac—*didn't look much prettier. Together, they changed the course of naval warfare forever.*

(Harper's Pictorial History of the Civil War, *1866*)

Tin Can on a Shingle

Fortunately for the Union navy, word of the *Merrimac*'s resurrection and conversion did leak out. In response, a contract was let to John Ericsson, a Swedish-born New Yorker, to design and build a ship capable of killing an ironclad. Ericsson designed an ugly, flat raft of a vessel, equipped with his own invention, a *revolving* armored turret sporting two 11-inch guns. Importantly, unlike the *Merrimac* conversion, the USS *Monitor* (as Ericsson's ship was called), was not merely clad in iron and steel, it was built of it, through and through, from keel to superstructure.

Construction was put on a 100-day rush schedule, which Ericsson failed to meet. But when

Words of War

The name **monitor** was soon applied generically to all steel-built or ironclad vessels with gun turrets, especially those designed for coastal bombardment.

news came (from a Union sympathizer resident in Norfolk) that the *Merrimac/Virginia* was nearing completion, Ericsson redoubled his efforts, and the *Monitor* was launched on March 6.

Clumsy and barely seaworthy, likely to be swamped by anything resembling high seas, she looked, with her protruding turret, like a "tin can on a shingle" or a "cheesebox on a raft."

At about this time, Franklin Buchanan, the former commandant of the Brooklyn Navy Yard, was now made skipper of the *Merrimac/Virginia*. On March 8, he took her out to meet the wooden-hulled Union fleet blockading Hampton Roads.

CSS *Virginia* was no more attractive than the USS *Monitor*, looking (according to one Union sailor) "like the roof of a very big barn belching … smoke," and, to another, like "a huge half-submerged crocodile." She had no turret; instead, her guns were fixed in rows poking out through narrow ports cut into her sloping ironclad sides. Mounted on her prow was a stout iron ram.

War News

"Brother against brother" is the hoariest cliché associated with the Civil War. Nevertheless it was often all too true. On board the USS *Congress* was McKean Buchanan, brother of the CSS *Virginia*'s skipper, Franklin Buchanan.

Sites and Sights

Artifacts relating to the *Merrimac/Virginia* are housed in the Portsmouth Naval Shipyard Museum (2 High Street, Portsmouth, Virginia; 1-804-393-8591) and the Hampton Roads Naval Museum (333 Waterside Drive, Norfolk; 1-804-444-8971). USS *Monitor* artifacts are exhibited at the Mariners' Museum (100 Museum Drive, Newport News, Virginia; 1-804-595-0368).

The blockading vessels and the Union shore batteries opened fire on the *Virginia*, but, as the USS *Cumberland*'s pilot, A.B. Smith, recalled, the cannonballs bounced "upon her mailed sides like India-rubber." The Confederate craft opened up on the *Cumberland*, killing five marines, and then rammed the ship, sending her to the shallow bottom just outside the Roads. The masts protruded from the water, the Stars and Stripes still flying.

The USS *Congress*, which had run aground and was immobilized, was the next to take *Virginia*'s fire. After the Union vessel burst into flame, it struck colors and surrendered. Chivalrously, Franklin Buchanan dispatched a boarding party from another Confederate ship to rescue the Union's wounded, but when the Union shore batteries fired on the rescuers, an enraged Buchanan seized a rifle and shot back. Sustaining a bad leg wound in this exchange, he turned over command of the *Virginia* to Lt. Catesby ap Jones.

Jones broke off the engagement at the end of the day, having forced the USS *Minnesota* and two smaller Union frigates aground. He intended to finish these off the next day.

In the meantime, as word of the battle traveled north, panic shot through Washington. It was reported that the invincible *Virginia* would now sail up the Potomac and train her guns on the capital. Lincoln's cabinet convened for an emergency meeting and could think of nothing better to do than pray.

Duel at Hampton Roads

Perhaps that was for the best. For, on March 9, the brand-new *Monitor*, having barely managed to avoid being swamped by ocean waves, arrived at the Roads and took up a position athwart the disabled *Minnesota*.

At 9:00 in the morning, the *Virginia* opened up on the *Monitor*, and the two vessels pounded one another for the next three hours. As difficult to manage as the *Monitor* was, it readily outmaneuvered the slower and even more unwieldy *Virginia*. While both vessels dumbly endured the ceaseless pounding, the toll on their crews was far more brutal. Cannonballs might bounce off either ship like "India-rubber," but to the human beings onboard, each impact was a mighty blow. The sound and shock of iron against iron was terrifying and maddening. Knees buckled, and the soles of the men's feet bled—as did many men's ears whose eardrums burst from the incessant concussions.

On the deck of the Monitor, *some of the tough men who sailed the new iron and steel warships—black as well as white, for the Navy was the only integrated service at the time. The Navy also recruited tough boys: at left is a "powder-monkey"—a gunner's assistant, who hauled gunpowder, water, and other necessities— aboard a conventional wooden vessel.*

(Library of Congress)

Encased within the *Monitor*'s iron pilot house was the ship's skipper, Lt. John L. Worden, who, at about noon, put his face to one of the narrow observation slits in the pilot house wall. At that moment, a shot exploded against the pilot house, temporarily blinding Worden. The *Monitor* suddenly drifted out of control, and Jones, on the *Virginia*, assumed that his adversary was withdrawing. His own vessel damaged, taking on water, his crew exhausted, and his supply of powder almost gone, Jones also withdrew.

Sails Furled

On balance, the duel of the ironclads at Hampton Roads was a draw—though the *Monitor* had saved the *Minnesota*, had prevented the Confederates from breaking the blockade of Richmond, and had averted yet another Union military disaster. More important, however, the battle changed naval warfare forever, bringing to a close the great age of wooden ships. In the short term, the battle persuaded both the Union and Confederate navies to concentrate on building more ironclads and *Monitor*-class vessels rather than wooden sail craft. With its far more developed industrial base, the North could—and would—build far more *Monitor*-class ships than the Confederacy.

War News

Neither of the original iron ships enjoyed long careers. *Virginia* ran aground on May 11, 1862, and was set ablaze by its own crew to prevent capture. The *Monitor*, which rode a mere *18 inches* above her waterline, foundered in heavy seas while being towed off Cape Hatteras, North Carolina, on December 31, 1862. Sixteen crew members perished. On August 5, 2002, a salvage team under the auspices of the National Oceanic and Atmospheric Administration (NOAA) recovered the *Monitor*'s turret from the bottom of waters off Cape Hatteras. The turret was sent to the Mariners' Museum for preservation work.

Blue Light in the Valley

George B. McClellan's mud-soaked soldiers laid siege against Yorktown, Virginia, on April 5. Lincoln deemed it nothing more than inaction and pleaded with his general to attack the Confederate defenses.

No, McClellan insisted. He would attack only after his big guns had softened up the enemy. His spymaster Pinkerton had reported that Yorktown was very heavily defended and that he was outnumbered. McClellan blamed Lincoln for having insisted that he leave behind, to defend Washington, a significant number of the 130,000 men he had originally intended to take with him up the Virginia peninsula.

The fact was that Confederate General Joseph E. Johnston had pulled most of his army back, closer to Richmond, leaving only about 15,000 men under Gen. John B. Magruder at Yorktown. McClellan commanded nearly six times that number. By digging in instead of attacking, McClellan gave Robert E. Lee, trained as a military engineer, valuable time to create elaborate permanent defenses around Richmond. Handed shovels instead of rifles, rebel soldiers groused that they hadn't joined up to dig ditches, and they cursed Lee as the "King of Spades," but the work they did made the Confederate capital a formidable objective.

Retreat at Kernstown

Robert E. Lee and the other top Confederate military commanders understood Lincoln's intense concern to defend Washington, and they saw in this an opportunity to leverage their relatively small numbers against the superior Union forces. "Old Blue Light," as the intensely blue-eyed Thomas J. "Stonewall" Jackson was reverently called, would sweep through Virginia's Shenandoah Valley as if it were Washington's vast backyard, to persuade the North that an invasion of the capital, from the west, was imminent. Since classical times, victorious generals had devised strategies to "divide and conquer" their enemies. Jackson's Shenandoah Valley campaign was aimed at just such an objective: to compel the Union to divide its comparatively numerous forces, which could then be attacked and defeated in detail.

The first battle of the campaign was fought on March 23, at Kernstown, near Winchester. Jackson thought he was attacking the four-regiment rear guard of Union general Nathaniel Banks (former Speaker of the House of Representatives), but found himself up against an entire 9,000-man division. Suffering a sharp defeat, Jackson retreated.

Yet this tactical defeat was quickly translated into a strategic triumph: The battle persuaded Northern leaders that an invasion was indeed afoot, and 35,000 men under General Irvin McDowell were detached from McClellan's peninsula command and dispatched to reinforce the defense of Washington. McClellan was left with 90,000 men, which he (mistakenly) thought insufficient.

Victory at McDowell

On May 8, Jackson fought another tactically undistinguished battle, managing to repulse Federal forces at McDowell, Virginia, but suffering in the process twice the casualties (498 versus 256) incurred by the attackers.

This likeness of Thomas J. "Stonewall" Jackson, one of the Confederacy's greatest tacticians, was probably made well before the Civil War, when Jackson was a young U.S. Army officer.

(Harper's Pictorial History of the Civil War, 1866)

Front Royal

From his costly but effective victory at McDowell, Jackson deployed his cavalry under Col. Turner Ashby to deceive Banks into thinking he was moving west, toward Strasburg. However, after picking up reinforcements, Jackson marched the main body of his army, now about 17,000 men, to the Federal outpost at Front Royal, Virginia, which he attacked on May 23.

Words of War

In the military jargon of the period, a **commissary** was a store from which rations and supplies were drawn, as well as the officer in charge of provisions and supplies.

Jackson easily outfought Banks, netting 904 prisoners and, even more important, two cannon and a cache of arms. The Confederates appropriated so much in the way of supplies from Banks's army that they dubbed him "Commissary Banks."

Attack at Winchester

Banks sent his army into retreat toward Winchester, Virginia, having divided his forces on May 24, when Jackson hit one of his columns at Middletown. It was a reduced army that Jackson attacked at Winchester on May 25, quickly overwhelming Banks and sending his army in full retreat back across the Potomac. Jackson pursued Banks to Harpers Ferry, and then tweaked Union commanders and politicians alike by feigning a Potomac crossing before turning southward.

Cross Keys

Banks's army was not the only Union force in the Shenandoah Valley. Some 16,000 men under Gen. John Charles Frémont attacked a Confederate bivouac (temporary camp) at Cross Keys, Virginia, on June 8. Frémont has been accurately described (by T. Harry Williams, in *Lincoln and His Generals*) as a "sincere and attractive person, but a giddy and fumbling general," who surrounded himself with ornately uniformed and totally useless staff officers. His attack on Maj. Gen. Richard Ewell's bivouac was typically uncoordinated and therefore readily beaten back.

Words of War

A **bivouac** is a temporary encampment.

Port Republic

One of Frémont's abler subordinates, Irish-born Brig. Gen. James Shields, dispatched his vanguard under Col. Samuel S. Carroll to raid Jackson's position at Port Republic on June 8. The Confederate general narrowly escaped capture by driving Carroll off with artillery and an infantry regiment. The next day, Jackson attacked Brig. Gen. Erastus Tyler, who had reinforced Carroll to the northeast, at Port Republic. At first Tyler's men seemed to prevail, but, after hand-to-hand combat (a rare occurrence in this war), the rebels captured an important Federal artillery position, while Frémont and his troops, stranded on the opposite bank of the flood-swollen South Fork, could only watch helplessly.

Despite his victory, Jackson realized that the columns of Shields and Frémont would unite, and he pulled back, as did the Union forces. Jackson's Shenandoah Valley campaign, perhaps the most spectacular and brilliant military maneuvering of the entire war, had come to an end. Jackson had used some 17,000 men to occupy and immobilize 50,000 Union soldiers, frightening the politicians in Washington, who feared an attack on the capital, thereby denying to McClellan the overwhelming numbers he felt necessary to attack Richmond. The Confederate capital was spared.

New Orleans Falls

Richmond, capital of the Confederacy, may have been saved, but the South's largest city and its most important port would not be so fortunate.

David Dixon Porter, one of the U.S. Navy's senior commanders, worked in secret to plan the assault, invasion, and capture of New Orleans. To lead the assault, he recommended David Glasgow Farragut, 60 years old and without doubt the Navy's most experienced sailor. Farragut had served from age nine as a midshipman aboard USS *Essex* during the War of 1812. His captain, mentor, and adoptive father was David Porter, father of David Dixon Porter. Farragut was no older than any number of other military men serving the Union, and he was in better shape than most. He made it a practice to turn a handspring on each birthday, remarking that he'd know he was getting old if the stunt ever proved difficult.

At age 60, David Glasgow Farragut, U.S.N., planned and executed naval operations that made the capture of New Orleans possible.

(Harper's Pictorial History of the Civil War, *1866*)

Words of War

A **screw sloop** was a small armed vessel powered by a steam-driven propeller (screw). A **gunboat** was a small, shallow-draft vessel designed especially for use in coastal waters, lakes, or rivers. A **schooner** was (and is) a fore-and-aft-rigged sailing vessel. A **mortar** was a short, thick-walled artillery piece designed to lob a heavy projectile in a steep, high trajectory; it was most often used against high-walled forts.

Farragut assembled a fleet of two steam frigates, seven *screw sloops*, and nine *gunboats*, plus 20 *schooners* converted to carry *mortars*, artillery pieces designed to fire very heavy 13-inch projectiles in a high trajectory—devastating against walled forts. The mortar boats were commanded by David Dixon Porter.

Farragut took his fleet into the mouth of the Mississippi and, in mid-April, commenced a week-long bombardment of Forts Jackson and St. Philip, guarding the approach to New Orleans. Then, at 2:00 A.M. on April 24, having sufficiently reduced the forts, the Union fleet steamed upriver, successfully dodging the blazing unmanned fire rafts the Confederates launched against it. Other Confederate vessels offered combat, but were quickly disposed of. Soon,

Farragut's fleet broke through all opposition and steamed past the forts, which, now cut off, surrendered.

Union General Ben Butler marched his troops in to take possession of the fallen forts and the now-defenseless city. New Orleans and, with it, the mouth of the Mississippi, belonged to the Union again. The defeat of the Confederacy in the West, which had begun with Grant's capture of Forts Henry and Donaldson, had progressed another giant step.

Count Off!

Farragut took New Orleans and its forts at the cost of a single Union ship sunk and the loss of 37 men killed and 147 wounded.

"Beast" Butler in the Crescent City

Benjamin Butler was not a tolerant man. At the start of the war, he had quelled rioters in Baltimore, and he now brought harsh martial law to New Orleans. When a mob tore down the Stars and Stripes newly raised over the Mint, Butler responded by taking into custody a citizen found wearing a fragment of the flag in his buttonhole and boasting about helping to tear it down, summarily tried him for treason, sentenced him to death by hanging, and hanged him in front of the Mint. That put an end to anti-Union demonstrating in New Orleans.

The "Woman Order" and the Will to Fight

At least, the *men* of New Orleans were sobered into submission by the execution. The city's *women*, in contrast, missed no opportunity to demonstrate their contempt for the "invaders" and took particular pleasure in wearing Confederate insignia on their dresses, holding their noses when Yankees passed, and forcing soldiers off the city's "banquettes" (sidewalks) into the mud by refusing to step to the right when passed.

When one New Orleans belle allegedly took careful aim from her window and emptied a chamber pot on Flag Officer Farragut's head, Butler responded with General Order 28 on May 15, 1862:

> As the Officers and Soldiers of the United States have been subject to repeated insults from the women calling themselves ladies of New Orleans, in return for the most scrupulous non-interference and courtesy on our part, it is ordered that hereafter when any Female shall, by word, gesture, or movement, insult or show contempt for any officer of the United States, she shall be regarded and held liable to be treated as a woman of the town plying her avocation.

For this infamous "Woman Order," citizens and the press of New Orleans dubbed the general "Beast" Butler, and General Beauregard used the outrage as means of renewing the resolve of his troops: "Men of the South! shall our mothers, our wives, our daughters and our sisters, be thus outraged by the ruffianly soldiers of the North, to whom is given the right to treat, at their pleasure, the ladies of the South as common harlots? Arouse, friends, and drive back from our soil, those infamous invaders of our homes and disturbers of our family ties."

War News
Even after the Civil War ended, chamber pots featuring the face of Benjamin Butler on the inside bottom were popular items in many Southern homes.

Mary Boykin Miller Chesnut, daughter of a prominent South Carolina political leader and wife of a Confederate army staff officer, kept an extraordinarily insightful and detailed diary of the war years. She understood that the loss of New Orleans meant much more than an affront to Southern womanhood: "New Orleans is gone," she wrote, "and with it the Confederacy. Are we not cut in two? The Mississippi ruins us if it is lost … "

Hollow Victory

While the Union enjoyed victory on the Mississippi, and as Stonewall Jackson in the Shenandoah occupied (and thereby effectively neutralized) Union troops either detached from McClellan's command or intended to reinforce it, the "Young Napoleon" was finally ready to move against Yorktown.

To his acute embarrassment, the Confederates, under Gen. John Bankhead Magruder (nicknamed "Prince John," for his regal manner), had by this time withdrawn from that position and moved closer to Richmond. Cavalry commanded by Gen. Jeb Stuart covered the withdrawal, and, on May 4 and 5, McClellan's subordinates Gen. Edwin V. Sumner and Gen. Joseph Hooker engaged Johnston's rear guard at Williamsburg, the colonial capital of Virginia, but now no more than a sleepy little village.

The battle was inconclusive, but McClellan claimed victory. He had *chased* Magruder out of Yorktown, hadn't he? Then he had *chased* Stuart out of Williamsburg, right?

The Northern press bought Little Mac's interpretation and congratulated him. Lincoln, however, fretted. And McClellan himself would soon reap the harshest reality of his Peninsula Campaign in a series of meatgrinder battles that would be remembered simply as The Seven Days.

The Least You Need to Know

♦ George McClellan was a brilliant administrator and organizer, but he lacked the initiative and resolve to be an effective military leader.

♦ The duel of the USS *Monitor* and *Merrimac/Virginia*, although inconclusive, ushered in a new era in naval warfare.

♦ Stonewall Jackson's Shenandoah campaign was one of the most sweeping and brilliant shows of military maneuvering of the entire war.

♦ David Farragut's triumph at New Orleans was a brilliant coup that deprived the Confederacy of its most important port city.

Chapter 9

Blue, Gray, and Red

In This Chapter

- Drain of soldiers from the West to the East
- Guerrilla warfare in Missouri
- The "Gettysburg of the West"
- The fight for Texas
- Indian warfare

As you read in Chapter 7, when Civil War soldiers and politicians talked about the "war in the west," they usually meant the action in Kentucky, Tennessee, and elsewhere along the Mississippi River. But the Civil War was also fought in what most of us, today, think of as the American West: in Missouri (and Arkansas), Kansas, Texas, New Mexico, and Arizona.

To be sure, the character of the war in the West was markedly different from that east of the Mississippi. Out West, no great cities were lost or won, and few decisive strategic ends were achieved. In one important respect, though, the two theaters *were* the same: Men fought, and men died.

Many who died were Indians. In some places, especially the Far Southwest, withdrawal of federal troops to eastern battlegrounds gave Indians license to raid. Elsewhere, white settlers took advantage of unsettled local conditions to make war on Indians. Out West, the Civil War joined seamlessly with the Indian wars that did not end until Wounded Knee in 1890.

This chapter turns from the East to the far-flung, small-scale, intensely bitter combat in the West.

An Army Without Officers

The first shots of the Civil War might have been fired on the Carolina coast, but their impact was felt—hard—in the West. By Sumter's fall, 313 officers, one third of the Army's officer corps, had left their commands to join the Confederate forces. "We are practically an army without officers," one Federal soldier in the West complained. And of the few soldiers and officers who remained at their posts, many would be transferred to the East, where most of the war's action was unfolding.

Missouri's Misery

If the U.S. Army in the West was swept into chaos at the beginning of the war, Missouri, like its neighbor Kansas, had been wallowing in it since the 1850s. We saw in Chapter 6 how the state was torn between its pro-Confederate governor and its mostly pro-Union legislature, and how the impetuous Union firebrand captain-turned-general Nathaniel Lyon attacked Confederate forces encamped at Wilson's Creek on August 10, 1861.

The ambitious but inept Union general John Charles Frémont had been involved in the Wilson's Creek debacle. Because Gen. William A. Harney lacked aggressiveness, Abraham Lincoln relieved him of command in Missouri on May 29 and temporarily elevated Lyon to his post. On July 3, Lincoln put Frémont in "permanent" command of a newly created Western Department. He arrived in St. Louis on July 25, 1861, and promptly found himself overwhelmed by the complex military situation in Missouri. When Lyon asked for reinforcements to fight Confederate general Sterling Price at Wilson's Creek, Frémont ordered him to *avoid* combat. Lyon ignored the order, lost the battle, and was killed.

Despite this defeat, on August 30, Frémont declared martial law in Missouri and proclaimed the emancipation of Missouri's slaves—something Lincoln had not yet even contemplated and Frémont had no authority to do. Frémont also began confiscating property of known Confederate sympathizers. These actions drove many undecided Missourians off the fence and straight into the Confederate camp. Guerrilla war, always simmering in Missouri, now boiled over. Gen. Sterling Price won another victory at Lexington, Missouri, on September 13, and Frémont's brief reign as commander of the Western Department came to an end. He was transferred to West Virginia.

Pea Ridge

In the afterglow of Confederate victories in Missouri and Frémont's outrageous emancipations and confiscations, a pro-South *rump* minority of the Missouri legislature convened in October 1861 at Neosho and voted to secede. Although the Neosho group was not the legally constituted legislature, Jefferson Davis quickly welcomed the state into the Confederacy.

But now it was Davis's turn to suffer a lapse in judgment. The Confederate president was suspicious of Gen. Sterling Price, who had been a close personal friend of the former Union commander Harney. Davis, therefore, declined to commit troops to Price, who was now confronted by forces under Brig. Gen. Samuel R. Curtis. Curtis had been ordered by the new commander of the Western Department, "Old Brains" Halleck, to drive the Confederates out of the state. Without support, Price had no choice but to withdraw into Arkansas.

Words of War

In political terms, a **rump** is a legislature having only a small part of its original membership; it has no legal authority, but acts as if it did.

War News

Stand Watie (1806–1871) was a mixed-blood Cherokee tribal leader from Georgia who became a Confederate general. At Pea Ridge, his troops captured vital Union artillery positions, and then effectively covered the retreat of Confederate forces. At the end of the war, Gen. Stand Watie was the last Confederate general to surrender his troops, in June 1865.

Henry Wager Halleck, called (none too affectionately) "Old Brains," was commander of the U.S. Army's Western Department at the time of Pea Ridge.

(Harper's Pictorial History of the Civil War, 1866)

Sites and Sights

The 4,300-acre Pea Ridge National Military Park preserves the site of the March 1862 battle that saved Missouri for the Union. The park is located near the town of Pea Ridge, Arkansas, off U.S. Route 62. For information, e-mail PERI Interpretation@nps.gov or write to Pea Ridge National Military Park; P.O. Box 700; Pea Ridge, AR 72751-0700 (phone 1-479-451-8122).

Count Off!

Of 11,250 Union troops engaged at Pea Ridge, 1,384 were killed, wounded, or missing. Of some 14,000 Confederates, 800 were casualties.

Words of War

Jayhawkers were self-appointed abolitionist guerrillas active in the Kansas-Missouri border region. The most aggressive of them were called "Red Legs," after the red leggings they often wore as their only uniform. **Bushwhacker** was the generic term for pro-Confederate guerrillas active in the same area.

He wanted to join forces there with a contingent under Gen. Ben McCulloch, but Gen. Earl Van Dorn intercepted Price and McCulloch and joined them to reinforcements that included several thousand Indians led by the Cherokee general Stand Watie. With a combined, albeit motley, army of 17,000 men, Van Dorn proposed to attack Curtis, whose forces numbered only about 11,000.

Curtis was alerted to the Confederate buildup by one James Butler Hickok, a 25-year-old abolitionist employed by the army as a civilian scout. As "Wild Bill" Hickok, he would, after the war, become one of the West's legendary gunfighters, gamblers, and lawmen.

Curtis decided to take up a strong defensive position at Pea Ridge, on high ground overlooking Little Sugar Creek. He formed his line of battle by March 6, and, in the cold, clear dawn of the 7th, skirmishing broke out near Elk Horn Tavern. This soon developed into heavy fighting.

The Federals held their ground against Van Dorn on the 7th, but the Confederate general renewed his attack on the 8th, whereupon the Union forces were able to seize the initiative and drive Van Dorn's forces from the field in complete disarray. Ordered to assist in the doomed defense of the Mississippi River, Van Dorn left Arkansas.

Guerrillas and Young Guns

After Pea Ridge, the rump legislature hightailed it out of the state, and the fighting in Missouri became a sporadic and bloody contest between *Jayhawkers* (pro-Union raiders), and pro-Confederate guerrillas called *bushwhackers*. This combat continued throughout the war.

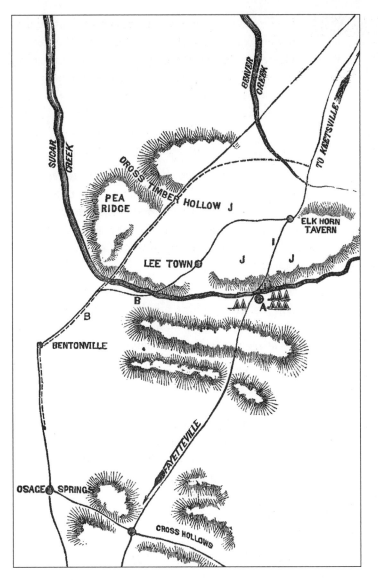

Map of Pea Ridge, Arkansas, and vicinity. The fighting centered near the Elk Horn Tavern. (The Confederates called Pea Ridge the Battle of Elk Horn Tavern.)

(Harper's Pictorial History of the Civil War, *1866*)

Most notorious of the Confederate bushwhackers was 24-year-old William Clarke Quantrill (1837–1865). Son of a schoolmaster and himself a former teacher, Quantrill had been an abolitionist, but unaccountably changed sides once war broke out. He was commissioned a captain in the Confederate army and, with William C. "Bloody Bill" Anderson, wreaked havoc on Kansas border patrols and Missouri's Union militia. Among Quantrill's and Anderson's men were Frank and Jesse James and the Younger brothers, Bob and Thomas Coleman, better known as Cole.

For the James and Younger brothers, "guerrilla" work was an internship in thievery and mayhem. Doubtless these "young guns" sided with the Confederates because their families held slaves; but once the war was over and lost, they readily transferred their guerrilla skills and attitudes to a life of looting banks in Missouri and surrounding states.

On August 14, 1862, Union general John M. Schofield, who had replaced Halleck, approved a plan to "remove" everyone in Missouri known to have aided or abetted Quantrill and company. The wives, mothers, and sisters of suspected bushwhackers were rounded up and deposited under lock and key in a tumble-down three-story building in Kansas City. The improvised prison collapsed from overloading, severely injuring a number of the women and killing five, including Quantrill's sister.

For this outrage, Quantrill swore revenge, and, with 450 men, attacked much-beleaguered Lawrence, Kansas, on August 21. The raiders killed more than 150 unarmed civilians and put the town to the torch.

Indeed, Quantrill recognized no morality in guerrilla warfare. At Baxter Springs, Kansas, on October 6, 1863, he and his men donned Union uniforms to deceive a detachment of Federal troops into ambush. Sixty-five men in a troop of 100 soldiers were gunned down, many of them disarmed prisoners who were simply and summarily executed.

Schofield's subordinate, Gen. Thomas Ewing Jr. next issued the notorious General Order Number 11, giving everyone living within one mile of Union military posts in Jackson, Cass, Bates, and the northern half of Vernon counties 15 days to leave their homes. The order also required them to take all grain and hay from their farms to the local military post. Any other crops and foodstuffs would be destroyed.

Count Off!

The legends surrounding him notwithstanding, Jesse James killed only one man in the course of nine post-Civil War gunfights, though he might have assisted in killing three more. Cole Younger killed three men in four gunfights and might have assisted in killing another two. Neither Frank James nor Bob Younger is "credited" with any murders during their criminal careers.

War News

Bushwhacker William Clarke Quantrill was killed by Union guerrillas on May 10, 1865, as he traveled through Kentucky, supposedly on a self-assigned mission to Washington, D.C., where he had planned to assassinate President Lincoln. By that time, John Wilkes Booth had beaten him to it.

Federal troops then swept through the Missouri-Kansas border country, burning everything in their path. For decades after the war, this area would be called the "Burnt District."

The Yankees' depredations garnered renewed support for Gen. Sterling Price, who, in January 1864, led a last invasion of Missouri. He ordered "Bloody Bill" Anderson and other bushwhackers into action. Anderson raided Centralia, and while he presided over the torture and murder of a number of civilians, a train happened through town. The raiders intercepted it, robbed the passengers, and, finding 25 unarmed Union soldiers headed home to Iowa on furlough, ordered them to strip off their uniforms. Each was executed at point-blank range.

The Centralia Massacre was the last major guerrilla action in Missouri.

Count Off!

Counting all the guerrilla actions and skirmishes, 1,162 engagements took place in Missouri, 11 percent of all the engagements in the Civil War, the third highest number in the war-torn nation.

Confederate Arizona

"We are practically an army without officers," went the Union lament in the far Southwest, and Confederate Lt. Col. John Robert Baylor took advantage of the Federal army's weakness to sweep through the southern New Mexico Territory—all the way from the Rio Grande to California.

Fort Bliss in El Paso, Texas, fell to him in July 1862, and he marched into the Mesilla Valley of New Mexico, taking Forts Fillmore and Stanton. This accomplished, Baylor grandly proclaimed the Confederate Territory of Arizona, which encompassed all of present-day Arizona and New Mexico south of the 34th parallel. He also named himself territorial governor.

Sibley's Invasion

Baylor's almost-unopposed advance was followed during the winter of 1861–1862 by a larger Confederate invasion led by Gen. Henry Hopkins Sibley (no relation to Union general Henry *Hastings* Sibley). The Confederate Sibley's mission was to take the rest of New Mexico and to seize the silver mines of Colorado, which would greatly enrich the Southern war chest. If possible, Sibley was to press the invasion all the way to Southern California.

Sibley advanced up the Rio Grande. His first objective was Fort Union, along the strategically vital Santa Fe Trail. The best-provisioned Union post in the Southwest, it was the headquarters of Col. Edward R.S. Canby, commander of the Department of New Mexico.

Even as Sibley's invaders menaced, Canby had his hands full fighting Navajo raids in New Mexico and dealing with unauthorized citizen counterraids, which only made the Indian violence worse. Although the Confederates had their own Indian troubles, Sibley pressed the attack on Canby, engaging him at Valverde, New Mexico, on February 21, 1862, and emerging victorious. From here, he was able to take Santa Fe, and then he advanced to Fort Union.

The Battle of La Glorietta Pass

The route to Fort Union lay through La Glorietta Pass, at the apex of the climb through the Sangre de Cristo Mountains. There, on March 26, 1862, Union troops under Col. John Slough, reinforced by Colorado volunteers commanded by Maj. John M. Chivington, opened battle with Sibley's Texans. For the next two days, through the 28th, they fought it out on harsh desert mountain terrain.

By Eastern standards, the Battle of La Glorietta Pass was a mere skirmish, and both sides, exhausted, declared victory. But the advantage was clearly with the North. The Confederates lost 121 men to the Union's 31, and Sibley retreated back to Texas. After the war, some would call this encounter the "Gettysburg of the West" because it turned the tide against the Confederates in the Southwest.

Arizona Rangers

If Union general Canby had to fight Indians as well as Confederates, Confederate colonel Baylor also had his own problems with the Indians. Chiricahua and Mimbreño Apaches freely raided the newly proclaimed Confederate Territory of Arizona. Baylor responded by creating units of Arizona Rangers and Arizona Guards. When this failed to halt the raids, Baylor sent the Guards commander a letter announcing,

> The Congress of the Confederate States has passed a law declaring extermination of all hostile Indians. You will therefore use all means to persuade the Apaches or any tribe to come in for the purpose of making peace, and when you get them together, kill all the grown Indians and take the children prisoners and sell them [as slaves] to defray the expense of killing the Indians.

Leaked to the public, Baylor's ghastly letter torpedoed Southern efforts to win allies among the tribes.

California Column

At about the time Slough and Chivington were battling Sibley, Col. James H. Carleton, having raised for the Union the First California Regiment of Infantry, led this so-called "California Column" into New Mexico Territory. Carleton was promoted to brigadier general and proceeded to push the Confederates out of the present-day state of Arizona. The culminating battle of Carleton's sweep was fought on April 15, 1862, at Picacho Peak in New Mexico. It was the westernmost action of the Civil War—all but ending the brief existence of the Confederate Territory of Arizona. By the end of the year, the last vestiges of the Confederate presence in the territory would be gone.

Texas Troubles

At the outbreak of the war, Texas was another western trouble spot for the Union. Gov. Sam Houston, the mastermind and hero of Texas independence, confounded his fellow Texans by supporting the federal government and resisting secession. In February 1861, however, his state seceded out from under him, and he resigned office. Gen. David E. Twiggs, commander of the U.S. Army's Department of Texas, surrendered all federal property to the Confederates—promptly, ignominiously, and without firing a shot.

In October 1862, the U.S. Navy took the important Texas port city of Galveston, which was occupied by Union troops in December. After converting a pair of riverboat steamers, the *Neptune* and *Bayou City*, to gunboats, the Confederates retook Galveston on January 1, 1863, after a four-hour fight. Nevertheless, the Union kept up a sometimes effective naval blockade of Galveston, though the city did not surrender until June 2, 1865, a month after Lee's capitulation at Appomattox.

By late 1863, the Mississippi River was firmly in Union hands, and Texas was cut off from the rest of the South. But there was still fighting to be done. President Lincoln understood that, perhaps ironically, the North needed cotton for its war effort. For that reason, he winked at a certain limited Northern trade with Southern cotton planters. When this got out of hand, leading to outrageous gouging by Northern speculators, Lincoln ordered Gen. Nathaniel Banks to raid Texas for the cotton the Union needed.

Banks's Red River campaign spanned March to May 1864. The objective was the capture of Shreveport, Louisiana, which would give the Union control of East Texas. A joint U.S. Army-Navy action ran afoul of treacherous river waters, giving Confederate general Edmund Kirby Smith's troops time to evade the Northern pursuers and to set fire to their cotton stores rather than let them fall into Yankee hands.

Worse, Kirby Smith's troops routed Banks's forces at the battles of Sabine Cross Roads (April 8, 1864) and Pleasant Hill (April 12). The Union troops piled into their riverborne transports and beat a hasty retreat.

The Real Conflict

The late action in Texas hardly mattered to the fate of the Confederacy in the West. With the loss of New Mexico and Arizona by the end of 1862 and the loss of the Mississippi River by late 1863, the entire West was lost to the Confederate cause.

This does not mean that war wasn't raging in the West. Union supporters in the West worried that the Confederates would cajole or even buy Indian allies, and it is true that the Confederacy recruited from among the Caddos, Wichitas, Osages, Shawnees, Delawares, Senecas, and Quapaws. Both the North and the South also recruited from other tribes that had been "removed" by act of Congress to Indian Territory (present-day Oklahoma) during the 1830s and 1840s. These included Cherokees, Chickasaws, Choctaws, Creeks, and Seminoles. Finally, it is a fact that Confederates did not *recruit* but did *arm* Comanches and Kiowas on the southern plains.

For the most part, however, the Western Indians who fought during the Civil War sided with neither the white North nor the white South. They fought against both sides.

The Rage of Cochise

Cochise, the tall, handsome chief of the Chiricahua Apaches, got on well with his white neighbors, even enjoying a profitable contract with the Butterfield Overland Mail to supply wood to the station at Apache Pass. A dozen miles from Fort Buchanan, Arizona, lived a thoroughly disreputable rancher named John Ward. His common-law wife, Jesusa Martinez, had been captured by Pinal Apaches and, during her captivity, had conceived and borne a son. She was subsequently released, but late in 1860, a Pinal band raided Ward's place and recaptured the child.

Ward had been too drunk to offer resistance or even to identify the raiders correctly. He told Fort Buchanan's commander that *Chiricahua* Apaches, led by Cochise, had taken his stepson as well as some cattle. Three months later, in February 1861, the fort commander dispatched 2nd Lt. George N. Bascom with 60 men to recover the boy and the stock. Cochise, together with his brother, two nephews, and a woman and child, came voluntarily to talk with Bascom. (Some say that Cochise was accompanied by six or seven others.)

With all the bluster he could summon, Bascom told Cochise that he and his party would be held until Ward's boy and property were returned. Cochise responded by drawing his knife, slitting the canvas of the conference tent, and making a run, leaving the other five behind. (Some report that one warrior followed his chief, but was killed.)

Enraged, Cochise raided the Butterfield station, killing one employee and taking another prisoner. When a small wagon train passed by the station, Cochise captured it, along with the eight Mexicans and two Americans riding with it. The Mexicans he ordered bound to the wagon wheels and burned alive. The Americans he offered to exchange for the Bascom's captives.

Bascom refused and called for reinforcements, which arrived on February 14, only to find that Cochise and his braves had vanished, leaving behind the bodies of the three American hostages, pierced by lances and mutilated. Bascom responded by hanging the hostages he held. And, in turn, Cochise vowed to exterminate all Americans in the Arizona Territory.

The result was what the army, drained of manpower by the Civil War, called the "Apache Uprising" of 1861–1863. In fact, the violence triggered by the wrongful accusations of a drunk rancher would span the next quarter-century.

A Lost Horse Race

In white-Indian relations, bloody tragedy often sprung from trivial things. When he learned that most New Mexicans were loyal to the Union, E.R.S. Canby quickly organized the First and Second Regiments of New Mexican Volunteers. But it took more than an official name to bring these ranchers and cowboys under military discipline and control. Lt. Col. Manuel Chaves, second in command of the Second Regiment, was put in charge of Fort Fauntleroy (soon renamed Fort Lyon because its namesake, Col. Thomas T. Fauntleroy, defected to the Confederacy) at Ojo del Oso, New Mexico, on August 9, 1861. The fort housed 210 officers and men.

In a bid to keep the Indians peaceful, Canby had agreed by treaty to distribute rations to the Navajos in August and September. As life at the frontier fort was dull, the officers and men of the Second Regiment also provided booze and set up a series of horse races. The featured event was a race between the celebrated Chief Manuelito on a Navajo pony and an army lieutenant on a quarter horse.

Betting was heavy. So heavy that somebody on the army side decided to hedge his bet by slashing the reins and bridle of Manuelito's mount. The chief lost control, and his pony ran off the track. Against the Indians' protests, the "judges" (soldiers all) declared the army quarter horse and rider victorious.

The troops formed a victory parade into the fort. When the Navajos, their fury heightened by drink, followed, the stockade gates were shut in their faces. One brave tried to force his way in and was cut down by gunfire.

Then Colonel Chaves unleashed all his troops on the 500 or so Navajos gathered outside the fort. Indian men, women, and children were butchered. Although Canby rushed to make amends, the Navajo War was underway.

Apache Uprising and Navajo War

With the help of the redoubtable scout and Indian fighter Christopher "Kit" Carson, Gen. James H. Carleton and his California Column managed to subdue the Apaches and the Navajos, at least for a time.

Desiring to secure *permanent* peace with the Indians, Carleton proposed to consign all Apaches and Navajos to a 40-square-mile reservation at the Bosque Redondo on the Pecos River in New Mexico. It was a place so desolate that the threat of being sent there actually renewed warfare, and those who did submit to confinement at the Bosque suffered disease and starvation at the hands of a government that had promised to feed, clothe, and shelter them. It was one more obscenity in the dark record of Indian-U.S. relations.

Massacre at Sand Creek

John M. Chivington had performed boldly against the Confederates at La Glorietta Pass and, promoted to colonel of volunteers, was named military commander of the Colorado territory. The victory at La Glorietta ended the rebel threat in his territory, but it had also served to release the dogs of war. When Colorado governor John Evans failed in negotiations for mineral-rich Cheyenne and Arapaho hunting grounds, he turned to Chivington and asked him to use his military resources to remove the Indians by force. It did not matter that, of all the Plains tribes, the Cheyenne and Arapaho had given the white settlers very little excuse for a fight, and Chivington, a confirmed Indian hater, needed little prompting. In an 1864 speech made in Denver, he called for nothing less than genocide. Indian children as well as adults should be exterminated, he argued, because "Nits make lice!"

Seizing on the hostile actions of a small faction of Cheyennes, the Hotamitainio, or Dog Soldier Society, Chivington launched a number of attacks in 1864, which provoked Indian counterraids in response. Having manufactured an Indian war, Evans and Chivington formed the Third Colorado Cavalry. In response, Black Kettle, an old and respected Cheyenne chief, sued for peace. Evans and Chivington met with the Cheyennes as well as Arapahos, and, as a gesture of submission to military authority, the Indians left the meeting and marched to Sand Creek, about 40 miles northeast of Fort Lyon. Instead of acknowledging this gesture, Chivington ordered a reduction of the Indians' government-mandated rations and demanded the surrender of their weapons. He then marched the Third Colorado Regiment into Fort Lyon, and, on November 28, 1864, deployed his 700-man force around the Sand Creek camp of Black Kettle's people.

Without provocation, Chivington's men rushed the camp and committed a catalog of atrocities in which all 200 Cheyennes present, two thirds of them women and children, were killed. Although nine chiefs were among the slain, Black Kettle escaped.

Outrage over the "Sand Creek Massacre" united the Southern Sioux, Northern Arapaho, and Cheyenne in a series of retaliatory raids during late 1864 and early 1865, the so-called Cheyenne-Arapaho War, one of the many white-Indian outbreaks the Civil War indirectly spawned in the West.

"Necessity Knows No Law"

The Southwest was not the only scene of white-Indian conflict. The remote village of New Ulm, in south-central Minnesota, seemed distant indeed from the ravages of the Civil War; nevertheless, like the other states of the Union, Minnesota was obliged to send its quota of recruits into the army.

But then crisis descended on New Ulm.

The Santee Sioux (a division of the Sioux often called the Dakota, consisting of the Mdewakantons, Wahpekutes, Sissetons, and Wahpetons) at first accepted the policy of "concentration" that the Apaches and Navajos in the Southwest had so vigorously resisted. But resentment smoldered among them as they suffered crop failures and were increasingly hemmed in by growing numbers of Scandinavian and German immigrants.

Worst of all, the corrupt federal Indian agency system consistently diverted the funds and supplies promised by treaty. During the summer of 1862, Santees repeatedly petitioned for the release of their rations and funds. Repeatedly, they were rebuffed.

Little Crow, chief of the Mdewakanton villages, put his case to those in charge of the local Indian agency: "We have no food, but here are these stores, filled with food. We ask that you, the agent, make some arrangements by which we can get food from the stores, or else we may take our own way to keep ourselves from starving. When men are hungry they help themselves."

To this, a local trader, Andrew J. Myrick, replied, "So far as I am concerned, if they are hungry, let them eat grass."

Shortly after this encounter, on August 17, four young Mdewakanton men were returning from an all too typically fruitless hunting trip. One of them stopped to steal eggs from the nest of a hen belonging to a white man. When another of the young hunters cautioned against the theft, the others called him a coward. He declared that he was not afraid to kill a white man, whereupon the four impulsively murdered the farmer and his family.

Andrew Myrick was the very next white to die. Attacked in his store on August 18, he tried to run and was shot down. Into his dead mouth, the Indians stuffed a tuft of grass.

Then war spread throughout a region very short on soldiers. The immigrant village of New Ulm fell under siege on the afternoon of August 20 and, again, on the 23rd. Thirty-six townspeople died, and another 23 were wounded. Most of the town lay in ruins, and its 2,000 citizens evacuated to Mankato.

They were not alone in their flight. By August 27, it was clear that the entire Sioux nation in Minnesota was on the warpath. Between 350 and 800 settlers had been killed, horrible atrocities were committed, and about half the state's population were refugees from Indian wrath. Unfounded rumor held that the Indians had been provoked by Confederates.

If abuse and starvation, not the Confederacy, was the real cause of the Santee Sioux Uprising, the bloody episode did indirectly benefit the South. Minnesota governor Alexander Ramsey asked President Lincoln for permission to delay sending his state's quota of enlistees to fight the Civil War in the East. Lincoln replied by telegraph: "Attend to the Indians. If the draft cannot proceed of course it will not proceed. Necessity knows no law."

The orgy of raiding ended on September 23, 1862, at the Battle of Wood Lake. Little Crow fled west and did not return to Minnesota until the following year. On July 3, 1863, he was picking raspberries with his 16-year-old son when he was ambushed and killed by settlers seeking to collect a $25 bounty on Sioux scalps.

The Least You Need to Know

◆ Although no great battles were fought in the far West, chronic guerrilla and Indian warfare affected the war effort of both sides by draining manpower that might have been used elsewhere.

♦ Of all states, Missouri suffered the ravages of guerrilla warfare most severely.

♦ For a short time during 1861–1862, the Confederacy maintained the Confederate Territory of Arizona in the Southwest until the Battle of La Glorietta Pass (the "Gettysburg of the West") turned the tide toward the Union.

♦ The demands of the Civil War greatly reduced the military presence in the West and gave rise to widespread Indian hostilities, most notably the Apache Uprising and Navajo War in the Southwest and the Santee Sioux Uprising in Minnesota.

Chapter 10

Seven Days and Another Bull Run

In This Chapter

- Jeb Stuart's ride around McClellan
- The Seven Days' Battles
- McClellan temporarily loses command
- The Second Battle of Bull Run
- Civil War nursing

Alas for George McClellan, still believing he was outnumbered when his numbers were actually far superior to the enemy's; at the end of June, he found himself with a divided army. More than a quarter of his strength, about 25,000 men, remained isolated north of Virginia's Chickahominy River, having been dispatched to cope—unsuccessfully—with Stonewall Jackson's Shenandoah Valley campaign. With the broad flank of the Federal army thus exposed and vulnerable, McClellan was about to reap the consequences of his faulty troop dispositions. He would face a new adversary, Robert E. Lee, leading some 65,000 troops. McClellan's worst fears were about to become reality.

This chapter chronicles some hard times for the Union's Army of the Potomac and its commander.

Fair Oaks Prelude

Let's go back, briefly, to the *beginning* of June. At that point, most of McClellan's army was north of the Chickahominy, except for a corps commanded by Gen. Erasmus Darwin Keyes. Confederate general Joseph E. Johnston was quick to recognize the vulnerability of Keyes's isolated position, and he decided to attack. On May 31, 1862, he hit Keyes at Fair Oaks and Seven Pines.

Map of Richmond, Virginia, and vicinity. The Chickahominy River is east of Richmond, and Mechanicsville (focus of one of the early Seven Days' Battles) may be seen to the northeast.

(Harper's Pictorial History of the Civil War, *1866*)

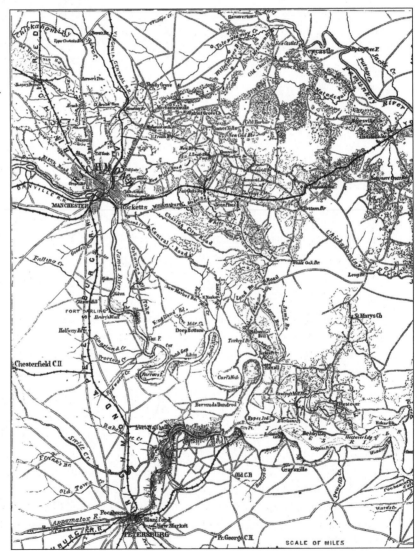

A series of Confederate errors and misunderstandings followed, resulting in delays that protracted the battle over two days and gave other elements of McClellan's forces time to join the fray. The result was an inconclusive and bloody two-day battle, one of the costliest of the war thus far (only Shiloh was bloodier), fought between almost equally matched forces.

An inconclusive battle, but not one without consequence.

In the course of the fight, Gen. Johnston was severely wounded and would have to drop out of the war for a time. His replacement was Robert E. Lee.

Count Off!

Of 41,797 Union troops engaged at Fair Oaks and Seven Pines, 5,031 were casualties; of 41,816 Confederates, 6,134 became casualties.

Jeb and the Gray Ghost

Thus far in the war, Lee's career had lacked luster. He had fared poorly in western Virginia, saddled with badly trained and undisciplined troops and laboring among a hostile populace. He had performed important but not very exciting work improving coastal fortifications, and he had served behind the lines as President Jefferson Davis's personal military advisor. In this capacity, he had given Stonewall Jackson the idea and impetus for his Shenandoah Valley campaign. But it *was* Jackson's campaign, and Jackson got the glory for it.

Other Confederate commanders were getting glory at this time, too. There was James Ewell Brown Stuart—Jeb Stuart—who, not yet 30, was a brigadier general cavalry commander decked out in an ostrich-plumed hat, a cape lined in red, and gold spurs at his heels. Come evening, he busied himself writing dispatches—not to Confederate headquarters, but to the London newspapers, which made him an international celebrity.

In military tactics of the mid-nineteenth century, the cavalry was the "eyes" of the army. Its chief function was rapid reconnaissance. For all his preening, Jeb Stuart was a highly skilled and daring tactician, and, between June 12 and 15, 1862, he demonstrated just how skilled and how daring. With 1,200 cavalrymen, he performed a reconnaissance that completely circled the Union positions in Virginia—he rode around the army. He was guided in this by his scout, 1st Lt. John Singleton Mosby. Mosby would soon gain renown equal to Stuart's as the "Gray Ghost of the Confederacy," the leader of the Partisan Rangers, a remarkably bold, stealthy, and effective band of guerrillas.

James Ewell Brown "Jeb" Stuart (left) and John Singleton Mosby, with his "Partisan Rangers" (right), were the two great raiders of the Civil War. As Confederate cavalry commanders, their tactics were swift, shrewd, and stealthy. Mosby, known as the "Gray Ghost of the Confederacy," is second from left.

(Image of Stuart from Harper's Pictorial History of the Civil War, *1866; image of Mosby courtesy Library of Congress.)*

Seven-Day Duel

Stuart's ride made the young brigadier a legend. For McClellan, it was just one more embarrassment. But it was also a wake-up call. The Federal commander realized that, by shifting north to link up with the expected reinforcements, he had put his army in a vulnerable position. He began to move it, except for a single corps, south of the Chickahominy. He was at last determined to stop delaying and to begin his drive to Richmond in earnest.

Words of War

Canister shot, or just canister, was a type of artillery shell designed to explode upon firing, spraying out the lead or iron shot that was packed within the canister. It was a cruelly effective antipersonnel weapon, generally used at close range.

Resistance at Oak Grove

On June 25, at Oak Grove, near Mechanicsville, right along the Chickahominy River, McClellan's forces met stiff resistance. At first driven back, McClellan was able to bring up reinforcements, who used *canister shot* to drive back the Confederate troops. This accomplished, the Union forces were able to occupy positions around Oak Grove. But, as night began to fall, operations were halted.

Mechanicsville

As it turned out, Oak Grove was just a curtain-raiser to seven days of intense combat. Lee's strategy was to bring the bulk of his army—65,000 troops—to the north bank of the Chickahominy and overwhelm the 25,000 Union troops under Gen. Fitz-John Porter, who were left on that side of the river. It was a bold and risky plan; Lee could afford to leave only a very thin line to defend Richmond, south of the river. Had the plan worked, Porter's corps would have been cut to ribbons.

But it didn't work. Jackson, so dazzling in the Valley, inexplicably decided to bivouac (make a temporary camp) on June 26 instead of attacking Porter. Confederate general A.P. Hill, impatient with Jackson's failure to arrive, attacked alone and without Lee's orders.

The result: Mechanicsville was a bloody repulse for the Confederates, but, yet again, an inconclusive battle. Jackson's failure allowed Porter to withdraw to the south bank of the Chickahominy.

But it was now McClellan's turn to err. Once again believing inflated estimates of the size of the Confederate army—and apparently intimidated by Lee's skill and initiative—McClellan ordered the withdrawal of his army to a new supply base on the James River, below and *away from* Richmond. His subordinate officers protested this, but to no avail.

Count Off!

Armies were the largest operational units and contained several corps, each consisting of two or more divisions and commanded by a major general. A Union division consisted of about 6,200 officers and men; a Confederate division, 8,700. A division was two or more brigades. Union brigades averaged 2,000 men; Confederate brigades averaged 1,850. A brigade comprised two or more regiments, which was two or more battalions. A battalion consisted of two or more companies or (in the case of an artillery battalion) batteries.

Gaines's Mill

But Lee wasn't about to let McClellan off so easily. He hounded and attacked mercilessly throughout the remaining seven days. While McClellan was rarely personally present to supervise his troops, his corps commanders executed skillful rear-guard actions and counterattacks that made McClellan's retreat costly for Lee as well.

For Lee had his problems, too. After Jackson's brilliance in the Shenandoah Valley, Lee put much faith and reliance in "Old Blue Light." Uncharacteristically, however,

Jackson disappointed him, failing to attack on time not only on June 26, but also on three more occasions during the series of the Seven Days' Battles. Another problem was Lee's *staff officers*, whose job it was to coordinate field operations. Lee hatched superb plans to isolate and defeat in detail the elements of McClellan's vulnerably positioned army, but poor staff work made effective coordination impossible. Lee's brilliant plans often failed in the execution.

Words of War

A commander's **staff officers** assist in performing planning and administrative functions. They often see to it that the commander's decisions are implemented by the line officers, the actual subordinate commanders in the field.

Count Off!

At Gaines's Mill, the bloodiest of the Seven Days' Battles, 34,214 Union troops were engaged—of whom 893 died, 3,107 were wounded, and 2,836 were reported missing. Although the Confederates forced a Union retreat, their casualties were heavier, numbering 8,751 killed and wounded.

At the Battle of Gaines's Mill, on June 27, Jackson was again tardy, which gave the beleaguered Union corps commander, Fitz-John Porter, time to reinforce his outnumbered position. The fighting, when it finally began in earnest, was severe. The Federal line held until shortly before dark, but once the Confederates at last fully coordinated their attack, the Union began a bloody retreat.

Savage's Station

McClellan's order to withdraw to the James River was issued to the corps commanders immediately following the retreat from Gaines's Mill. Lee, eager to renew the attack on the retreating Union army, nevertheless bided his time until he was certain of McClellan's direction. Lee's plan of attack was complex, however, and beyond the ability of his corps commanders to carry out effectively. The attack came late on June 29 and was highly spirited, but not well coordinated. Confederate corps commander "Prince John" Magruder unleashed only two and a half of his six available brigades, while, once again, Jackson arrived late—3:00 in the morning of the 30th.

War News

The Union typically named its armies after rivers: the Army of the Potomac, the Army of the Mississippi, and so on. The Confederacy typically named its armies after states or regions. Sometimes, this could be confusing; the Union had an Army of *the* Tennessee (the river), while the Confederacy had an Army of Tennessee (the state). The most famous Confederate army was the Army of Northern Virginia, led by Robert E. Lee.

Once again, Lee had missed an opportunity to deal a decisive, damaging blow to the Army of the Potomac. Federal rear-guard actions and counterattacks cost him heavily, but it was the breaking of a violent thunderstorm that finally cut the battle short and saved the Union rearguard from ultimate defeat. Still, the withdrawing Union forces left behind a large quantity of supplies, as well as 2,500 wounded men (victims of Savage's Station and previous battles) in a field hospital.

Count Off!

Losses in the engagement at Savage's Station were 1,590 killed and wounded on the Union side and 626 on the Confederate side.

Frayser's Farm

Having withdrawn from Savage's Station, McClellan concentrated his forces behind White Oak Swamp and in a line to Malvern Hill to protect the Union supply trains on their way to Harrison's Landing on the James River.

Lee again formulated a plan for a coordinated attack designed to pummel McClellan's army, but, yet again, the coordination failed in execution. Lee did succeed in pushing McClellan back, but the Confederates sustained heavier losses than the Federals.

Count Off!

At Frayser's Farm (also called Glendale), Union casualties were 2,853 killed and wounded; Confederate losses were 3,615 killed and wounded.

Malvern Hill

After Frayser's Farm, McClellan withdrew his entire army to Malvern Hill, a low, two-mile-wide ridge alongside the James River. Having reached Malvern Hill meant the failure of McClellan's Peninsula Campaign. At great cost, McClellan had failed to take Richmond and, at the end of the Seven Days, was farther from the rebel capital than he had been at the start.

Yet McClellan had positioned his army on the high ground and could not be *flanked* (attacked on a vulnerable side), which put Lee at a great disadvantage. Nevertheless, recognizing that this was his last opportunity to destroy the Army of the Potomac, Lee attacked Malvern Hill on July 1.

Words of War

As a noun, **flank** refers to the right or left elements of a body of troops. As a verb, it means to attack from a vulnerable side, usually a lightly defended side.

By now, the results were all too predictable. Poor coordination combined with terrain that made it impossible to bring more than a fraction of the Confederate artillery up to support the piecemeal attacks. By deadly accurate Union artillery fire—massed cannons almost wheel to wheel—Lee was repulsed, and two of McClellan's field officers, Porter and Col. Henry J. Hunt, urged their commander to seize the initiative now, hold Malvern Hill, and order a counterattack. But McClellan was thoroughly intimidated by his adversary. He completed the withdrawal to Harrison's Landing.

Success and Glory; Disaster and Shame

With the completion of McClellan's retreat, the vaunted Peninsula Campaign was over, though McClellan's army remained at Harrison's Landing, and thus a potential threat to Richmond, until mid-August. Tactically, perhaps, McClellan had been successful. Commanding the larger army, he had sustained during the Seven Days a total of about 16,000 casualties (killed and wounded), whereas Lee's smaller force suffered nearly 20,000 casualties. Yet, strategically, Lee clearly won. He had kept McClellan from taking Richmond.

War News
Among the units encamped at Harrison's Landing was the 3rd Brigade of the I Corps, 1st Division, commanded by Brig. Gen. Daniel Butterfield. Butterfield was dissatisfied with the regulation bugle call that signaled lights out at night. He found it neither musical nor, as he thought it should be, soothing. Working with the brigade bugler, he composed the call that became "Taps." Soon the entire Army of the Potomac had adopted "Taps," which spread to the whole of the Union army and has endured ever since.

Pope Takes Command

One victim of the Seven Days wasn't on any casualty rolls. George Brinton McClellan, entrenched at Harrison's Landing, protesting that Lee's army numbered near 200,000 (a wild overestimate due to McClellan's overcaution and spymaster Pinkerton's miscalculation), appealed for reinforcements. Lincoln had had enough. He called on Gen. John Pope, who had shown such leadership as commander of the Army of the Mississippi, to take command of the new Army of Virginia (a consolidation of several forces and a confusing designation that didn't stick). The Army of the Potomac marched back down the Peninsula and boarded steamers to take them up the Chesapeake Bay to join Pope. The Peninsula Campaign was over, and McClellan was a general without a command.

Lincoln also called on Henry Wager "Old Brains" Halleck to become general-in-chief of the Union armies.

Union General John Pope, victorious in the West, was summoned to take command in the East. His arrogance earned him hatred from the South and resentment from the North.

(Harper's Pictorial History of the Civil War, *1866)*

Though ambitious and full of bravado, Pope lacked what we might today call "people skills." In a word, he was obnoxious. Successful in relatively minor actions in the Western theater, his first address to his new troops was to disparage and scold them, and he treated the citizens of Virginia as a conquered people, freely seizing their food when he needed it and threatening to execute as traitors Southern civilians and soldiers alike. Robert E. Lee was a consummately professional soldier, but above all a "gentleman," and Pope's treatment of the citizens of his native state aroused in him a personal animosity. "The miscreant Pope," Lee said, "should be suppressed."

At the beginning of August, Pope was in northern Virginia, harassing the Virginians and attending to the defense of Washington while McClellan remained dug in on the Peninsula. Halleck, convinced that McClellan would never advance, ordered him off the peninsula and back to northern Virginia to join his army to Pope's.

For the Union, this move would cost valuable time, and Lee took advantage of it, directing Jackson to attack part of Pope's army at Cedar Mountain, near Culpeper, Virginia, on August 9. In itself, this battle was of slight consequence, but it was only the opening move in what would prove Pope's undoing.

Lee maneuvered Pope into retreat north of the Rappahannock River. With the object of defeating Pope before all of McClellan's troops arrived, Lee boldly violated a cornerstone of military tactics: He divided his army in the presence of the enemy.

Separated from Pope by only the shallow Rappahannock, Lee put half his forces under the command of Maj. Gen. James Longstreet to occupy Pope while he sent the other half under Stonewall Jackson on a roundabout march to the northwest—to make a surprise attack on the rear of Pope's army.

In the meantime, in a quick raid, some of Pope's troops captured Jeb Stuart's adjutant and, Stuart and others having fled in a hail of bullets, snatched Stuart's fancy plumed hat and scarlet-lined cloak. Outraged, Stuart secured permission to raid the railroad behind Pope's lines. On August 22, he overran Pope's headquarters camp at Catlett's Station and made off with $35,000 in payroll greenbacks, Pope's personal baggage (including *his* dress uniform coat), 300 prisoners, and papers that gave Lee critical information about Pope's battle plans.

To add to Pope's consternation, Jackson destroyed his supply depot at Manassas Junction, Virginia—near the site of the Bull Run battle—on August 26, cutting off Pope's rail and telegraph communications. Pope turned to pursue Jackson, but was unable to find him until Jackson fought Brig. Gen. Rufus King at Groveton on August 28. It was a fierce battle—in which both Confederate division commanders were wounded and the Union's "Black Hat Brigade" (or "Iron Brigade," as it was later called) demonstrated incredible heroism and suffered a 33 percent casualty rate.

The fight at last alerted Pope to Jackson's position, and he ordered his forces to concentrate near Groveton in order to destroy Jackson once and for all. The *Second Battle of Bull Run* was about to begin.

Slow March to Freedom

While Jackson and Lee were (often literally) running rings around Union commanders, the U.S. government marched slowly toward making emancipation and abolition issues of the war. On July 17, 1862, Congress passed a second Confiscation Act, which freed the slaves owned by those who supported the "rebellion." This was a stronger, broader, and more forthright measure than the first Confiscation Act, of August 1861, which merely conferred "contraband" status on slaves whose labor had been used directly in the war effort; that is, such slaves could be "confiscated" by Union officers and, effectively, liberated.

On July 22, 1862, Lincoln showed his first draft of an emancipation proclamation to the cabinet. He heeded their advice, however, to keep it under wraps until the Union army had achieved a significant victory. To proclaim emancipation now (the cabinet argued), in the shadow of defeat, would at worst appear to the North, South, and the world like an act of desperation and, at best, would be a hollow gesture.

Second Bull Run

Pope faced the culmination of the Second Bull Run campaign with confidence. No longer fighting rearguard actions, it was he who launched the attack on August 29, 1862, boasting that he would "bag the whole crowd."

The Union did seize and hold the initiative on the first day of the battle, hammering at Jackson's Confederates, who refused to yield. Having repulsed Pope's repeated attacks, however, Jackson withdrew from the positions he had reached during the repulse. Pope, confused or falling victim to wishful thinking, interpreted this as a retreat. Declaring himself victorious, he vowed a hot pursuit the next day.

What Pope did not realize is that the second half of Lee's divided army, under General Longstreet, had arrived about 11:00, but hadn't joined the battle. Longstreet did not fail to fight the next day, August 30, and, instead of a hot pursuit, Pope faced a battle even hotter than the day before. Five rebel divisions under Longstreet stormed into the Union flank along a two-mile front.

Pope suffered a very costly tactical defeat, and again a shattered Union army was humiliated at Bull Run. However, the exhausted Confederates didn't press on in immediate pursuit, costing Lee a truly decisive strategic victory. Beaten, Pope's troops were at least able to retreat intact.

Just three days after Second Bull Run, boastful John Pope was relieved of command in the East and was exiled to the U.S. Army's Department of the Northwest to fight the Sioux in Minnesota. McClellan had never been officially

> ## War News
>
> When General Pope came east to take command, a newspaper reporter asked him where his headquarters would be. "In the saddle," Pope pretentiously replied. Reading this, Robert E. Lee, who rarely made jokes at anyone's expense, quipped that this was precisely Pope's problem: he "had his headquarters where his hindquarters should be."

Count Off!

At Second Bull Run, Pope commanded 75,696 Union troops against the Confederates' 48,527. The Union lost 1,724 killed, 8,372 wounded, and 5,958 missing—a staggering 21 percent casualty rate. The Confederates lost 1,481 killed, 7,627 wounded, and 89 missing—an almost equally devastating 19 percent casualty rate.

relieved of command of the Army of the Potomac; Pope had just been appointed over him. Now General McClellan was once again in charge.

Dragon Dix and the Angel of the Battlefield

A Civil War soldier was far more likely to be wounded than killed. Unfortunately, as Union surgeon general William A. Hammond remarked years after the war, "the Civil War was fought at the end of the medical Middle Ages." This meant that a wounded soldier was eight times more likely to die from his wounds than a World War I doughboy, who fought 60 years later. He was even more likely to succumb to disease than to be wounded or killed in battle.

It was not just that medical science was far less advanced in the 1860s than in the 1910s, but that so few resources were devoted to even the most basic care of the wounded and the most fundamental issues of sanitation. A handful of dedicated men—and especially women—sought to improve this horrific situation.

Dorothea Lynde Dix was born in 1802 in Hampden, Maine. She left her school-teacher's position in 1836, traveled, and became a passionate advocate for the improvement of conditions in American prisons and institutions for the mentally ill. She earned an international reputation as a reformer, and soon after the commencement of the Civil War in 1861, she was appointed Superintendent of Women Nurses for the Union army.

Enter the Nurses

Dix created the foundation of what would become the Army Nursing Corps, and, more immediately, introduced a level of basic sanitation and humanity into the care of those wounded in a war that had taken weaponry to a new level of destructiveness.

In the days of high Victorian morality, female nurses, whose work brought them into intimate contact with any number of men, were typically regarded as little better than prostitutes. Understandably, therefore, male nurses outnumbered female nurses. Dix set about recruiting women of impeccable moral character, strength of mind, and strength of will. Determined and deliberately overbearing, she ruled her nursing corps with an iron hand—"Dragon Dix," they called her—but she made the profession respectable for women, eased unspeakable suffering, and saved untold lives.

But relief for the wounded was never solely the work of the government or the army. The U.S. Sanitary Commission was formed by prominent private citizens to improve conditions for the sick and wounded, and Clara Barton (1821–1912), for 18 years a schoolteacher in Massachusetts and New Jersey and then a clerk in the U.S. Patent

Office in Washington, D.C., almost single-handedly organized an agency to obtain and distribute supplies for wounded soldiers. She personally visited the battlefields and field hospitals, carrying supplies in a wagon she drove herself, and her kind demeanor, the opposite of Dix's steely sternness, won her the soldiers' grateful affection.

Called the "Angel of the Battlefield," Clara Barton was a former teacher and patent clerk who took it upon herself to bring supplies and comfort to the Union wounded. Some years after the war, she founded the American Red Cross.

(Library of Congress)

They called Barton the "Angel of the Battlefield." Later in the war, she would set up a bureau of records to try to identify the unknown dead on both sides, and, after the war, in 1881, she established the American National Red Cross.

Walt Whitman Among the Wounded

Dix, Barton, and the professional woman associated with them were not the only nurses in the war. Relatives of soldiers and concerned volunteers also pitched in. One such was Walt Whitman, a self-published poet from Long Island, New York, who, in 1862, went to Fredericksburg, Virginia, to tend to his wounded brother, a soldier in the Union army. Whitman remained in camp for a time, caring for his brother and other wounded soldiers, and then he took a temporary job in the paymaster's office in Washington. In his off-hours, he visited the wounded and dying in the Washington hospitals. He spent his meager salary on treats for the young men, to whom he read or with whom he spoke, always in an effort to cheer them as best he could.

Best known for such poems as *Song of Myself* and "When Lilacs Last in the Dooryard Bloom'd," Whitman also wrote unblinking prose descriptions of his work among the wounded (in *Specimen Days*, 1882) and fine, honest war verse (in *Drum-Taps*, 1865, and *Sequel to Drum-Taps*, 1866). These lines are from "The Dresser" of 1865:

> Returning, resuming, I thread my way through the hospitals;
> The hurt and wounded I pacify with soothing hand,
> I sit by the restless all the dark night—some are so young;
> Some suffer so much—I recall the experience sweet and sad;
> (Many a soldier's loving arms about this neck have cross'd and rested,
> Many a soldier's kiss dwells on these bearded lips.)

The Least You Need to Know

- ◆ McClellan's chronic hesitation caused him to bungle the Peninsula Campaign, greatly prolonging the war.

- ◆ Robert E. Lee was a brilliant strategist, but some of his officers—particularly those in staff positions—were unable to execute his elaborately choreographed plans.

- ◆ The Seven Days' Battles were tremendously costly. Although McClellan was the tactical victor, Lee won the all-important strategic objective of fending off an invasion of Richmond, the Confederate capital.

- ◆ The Union defeat at the Second Battle of Bull Run was even more disastrous than the defeat suffered at the First Battle of Bull Run.

- ◆ Dorothea Dix, Clara Barton, and Walt Whitman were among the sympathetic civilians who provided nursing care for wounded soldiers.

Part 3

Die to Make Men Free

In this part, you'll understand how the war took on a deeper moral dimension for the North after Lincoln's preliminary Emancipation Proclamation. But this didn't lead immediately to victory, as you'll see when you read about the Union disasters at Fredericksburg and at Chancellorsville.

The Confederate triumphs came, but always at great cost, and Southern civilians suffered from shortages of food, goods, and cash.

In this part, you'll see the increasing toll the war exacted on both the North and South.

Chapter 11

In Blood Proclaimed

In This Chapter

♦ Lincoln and emancipation

♦ Lee invades Maryland

♦ The Battle of Antietam

♦ The true effects of the Emancipation Proclamation

When Ronald Reagan was dubbed "the Great Communicator" during the 1980s, it was hardly the first time a president had been given a public nickname. George Washington was the "Father of His Country," Andrew Jackson was "Old Hickory," and, as generations of schoolchildren were taught, Abraham Lincoln was "the Great Emancipator." Yet when Gen. John Charles Frémont took it upon himself to liberate Missouri's slaves, Lincoln promptly annulled the order. When Gen. David Hunter—commanding the U.S. Army's Department of the South—took Fort Pulaski, Georgia, in April 1862, and first declared free all slaves who were now in Union hands and then freed all slaves living within the reach of his military jurisdiction, Lincoln again annulled the orders.

This chapter explains Lincoln's delicate position on slavery and how the Civil War finally did become a fight "to make men free."

The Prayer of Twenty Million

Doubtless Abraham Lincoln did not relish annulling the emancipation orders his generals had issued. He was anything but a lover of slavery. However, in 1862, he understood that most men were *not* fighting the war in order to end slavery, and he

Words of War

To **emancipate** is to free from bondage or involuntary servitude.

feared that defining *emancipation* (the freeing of slaves) as the purpose of the war would alienate the soldiers and turn volunteers away. He feared, too, that the border states—which permitted slavery but remained loyal to the Union—would fly to the cause of the South if he suddenly acknowledged that the war was to end slavery and thus deprive citizens of their human property.

Yet, in the North, especially in New England, the voices calling for emancipation grew louder, more numerous, and more strident. On August 19, 1862, Horace Greeley, the eloquent and influential editor of the *New York Tribune*, published in his paper an open letter to Abraham Lincoln on behalf (he said) of the 20 million citizens of the loyal states. He took the president to task for annulling his generals' orders of emancipation, for failing vigorously to enforce the Confiscation Acts (discussed in Chapter 10), and, in short, for not recognizing that "no loyal person [could be] rightfully held in Slavery by a traitor." Greeley called for immediate emancipation.

The president replied, by letter, just three days later:

> … My paramount object in this struggle is to save the Union, and is not either to save or destroy Slavery. If I could save the Union without freeing any slave, I would do it; and if I could save it by freeing all the slaves, I would do it; and if I could do it by freeing some and leaving others alone, I would also do that. What I do about Slavery and the colored race, I do because I believe it helps to save this Union; and what I forbear, I forbear because I do not believe it would help to save the Union ….

Yet quietly, Lincoln continued to hone and polish a draft of an emancipation proclamation, waiting for the right time to make it public.

"Again I Have Been Called Upon to Save the Country"

That time was not now. Not after the disastrous defeat of Pope and the Union forces at Second Bull Run (see Chapter 10), which produced Union casualties *five times* what they had been at the first humiliating Bull Run defeat. In desperation, Lincoln again

turned over command of the Army of the Potomac—now augmented by the troops
Pope had led—to George McClellan, realizing that, for all his faults, McClellan had
an unsurpassed ability to boost the morale of the troops.

"Again I have been called upon to save the country," McClellan wrote to his wife.
He told her that, as he rode among them, his men called to him: "George, don't leave
us again."

Invasion Plans

On September 5, 1862, Robert E. Lee dramatically changed the conduct of the war.
He led his Army of Northern Virginia across the Potomac into Maryland. He invaded
the North with about 60,000 men.

It was yet another of Lee's astoundingly bold moves—the army he led looked like
anything but an army of invasion. Ragtag and exhausted, many of his men lacked
ammunition, not to mention shoes. Yet Lee understood that the South could not win
a long war of attrition. The North, with far more men, money, and munitions, would
surely prevail if the struggle went on long enough. Lee saw that the best hope for the
South was to win over the border states—of which Maryland was the most important—
gain international credibility, and, in the process, destroy the North's will to fight.

Voices

On entering Maryland, Robert E. Lee published a secession invitation to that state's citizens on September 8, 1862:

> The government of your chief city has been usurped by armed strangers—your
> Legislature has been dissolved and by the unlawful arrest of its members—freedom
> of the press and of speech has been suppressed—words have been declared
> offenses by an arbitrary decree of the Federal Executive—and citizens ordered to
> be tried by military commissions for what they may dare to speak.

> Believing that the people of Maryland possess a spirit too lofty to submit to such a
> government, the people of the South have long wished to aid you in throwing off
> this foreign yoke, to enable you again to enjoy the inalienable rights of freemen,
> and restore the independence and sovereignty of your state.

> In obedience to this wish our army has come among you, and is prepared to assist
> you ...

> Marylanders shall once more enjoy their ancient freedom of thought and speech ....

> It is for you to decide your destiny ....

The Lost Order

Then something incredible happened. Lee drew up Special Order No. 191, which detailed his plan for opening the invasion of the North. Lee distributed copies of the document to his chief generals. Stonewall Jackson copied a set for Gen. Daniel Harvey Hill, who, having already been sent the orders by Lee, apparently discarded the copy, although some recent scholarship suggests it may not have been deliberately discarded, but accidentally dropped by one of Jackson's staff. On September 13, Union troops occupied the campground Hill had just vacated. There, Union Private W.B. Mitchell, 27th Indiana, found the discarded or dropped document wrapped around some cigars. Mitchell coveted the cigars, but he also realized that he had something more important, and he passed the paper to his superiors, who sent it to McClellan.

McClellan saw that Lee's plan was a hazardous one: He would split his forces in two, with Jackson heading toward Harpers Ferry and Longstreet toward Hagerstown. McClellan must have rubbed his hands together with glee: "Here is a paper with which, if I cannot whip Bobby Lee, I will be willing to go home."

Yet McClellan again hesitated, believing Lee had twice the number of men he actually commanded and (prompted by a fretful Henry Wager Halleck) fearing that the "lost order" might be a ruse to a snare. On September 14, McClellan's troops fought their way through three gaps in South Mountain. The heights were bravely defended by badly outnumbered Confederates under D.H. Hill in a desperate battle that bought crucial time for Lee to regroup his army west of Antietam Creek.

The Battle of Antietam

After Shiloh and the Seven Days, no one would have thought that fighting could be harder or more fierce. But Antietam would be the scene of the hardest fighting yet.

The Blast of a Thousand Bugles

McClellan seems to have planned an attack to strike at both of Lee's flanks, and then attack the center with his reserves. However, when it came on April 17, the attack was an uncoordinated series of piecemeal assaults. Union general Joseph "Fighting Joe" Hooker drove back Stonewall Jackson's corps so far, so quickly, that Lee was forced to order up reserves. Daniel Harvey Hill's and James Longstreet's rebels joined the battle in the East and West Woods, in Farmer Miller's cornfield, and around a church belonging to a German pacifist sect called the Dunkards.

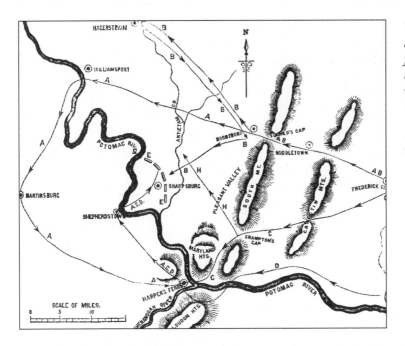

The Antietam battlefield and vicinity. Sharpsburg, the focal point of the fighting, is between the Potomac (to the west) and Antietam Creek (to the east).

(Harper's Pictorial History of the Civil War, 1866)

Sites and Sights

Antietam National Battlefield and National Cemetery are located along MD65 and MD34 immediately to the north and northeast of Sharpsburg, Maryland. The park includes a visitor center and offers many driving and hiking opportunities. Clearly marked are the infamous sites of major combat: the East, North, and West Woods; the Corn Field (Miller's Cornfield); Bloody Lane; and Burnside Bridge. Although the Dunkard (or Dunker) Church was destroyed in the 1920s by a wind storm, it was reconstructed and restored in the 1960s. For more information, contact 1-301-432-5124.

Bloody Lane

By midday, the fighting shifted to the center, along a sunken farm road ever after called "Bloody Lane," held by Confederate General D.H. Hill. Three divisions of Union Major General Edwin "Bull" Sumner's corps managed to drive Hill out in a five-hour battle.

By midafternoon, the left wing of the Federal army under Gen. Ambrose Burnside, after repeated delays (caused in large part by Burnside's refusal simply to give up on the bridge and ford the stream), forced a crossing of the stone bridge that still bears his name. He broke through the Confederate line, only to be repulsed by a surprise counterattack from A.P. Hill, whose troops had just arrived from Harpers Ferry.

Before the Battle of Antietam, this was a sunken road. During the battle, it became infamous as "Bloody Lane."

(Library of Congress)

"McClellan's … infantry fell upon the left of Lee's lines with the crushing weight of a landslide," Confederate Brig. Gen. John Brown Gordon recalled. But when Lee approached the line, the troops "re-formed … and with a shout as piercing as the blast of a thousand bugles, rushed in countercharge upon the exulting Federals [and] hurled them back in confusion."

Burnside Bridge—the crossing of which was paid for with many lives.

(National Archives and Records Administration)

Despite McClellan's erroneous intelligence reports, his troops far outnumbered the Confederates, and the sheer weight of this superiority, coupled with the grit of the fighting men, finally drove the rebels back to the outskirts of Sharpsburg. Yet McClellan persistently refused to accept that he indeed held the advantage. In the days following the battle, he did not pursue the withdrawing Confederates, who escaped back across the Potomac and into Virginia. Once again, an opportunity to destroy a Confederate army had been lost.

Slow Road to Emancipation

Historians call Antietam the "single bloodiest day of the war." Union casualties numbered about 12,000, while Confederate losses may have been close to 14,000, if the missing are included.

Tactically, the battle was a draw. Strategically, it was both a Union victory and tragedy. McClellan drove Lee out of Maryland, but he missed an opportunity to destroy the Army of Northern Virginia and, quite probably, end the war. Although McClellan allowed Lee to escape with what was left of his army, it was clear to Lee that the Confederacy could not afford the kind of losses suffered at Antietam. The Maryland campaign had failed. Nevertheless, the war would go on.

Count Off!

The Union threw 75,316 young men into the Antietam meatgrinder. Of these, 2,108 were killed, 9,549 were wounded, and 753 went missing. The Confederates engaged 51,844, losing some 2,700 killed, 9,024 wounded, and approximately 2,000 missing.

Voices

Lincoln's secretary of the treasury, Salmon P. Chase, recorded the president's words at a cabinet meeting of September 22, 1862:

> Gentlemen, I have, as you are aware, thought a great deal about the relation of this war to slavery, and you all remember that, several weeks ago, I read to you an order I had prepared upon the subject, which, on account of objections made by some of you, was not issued. Ever since then my mind has been much occupied with this subject, and I have thought all along that the time for acting on it might probably come. I think the time has come now. I wish it was a better time. I wish that we were in a better condition. The action of the army against the Rebels has not been quite what I should have liked best. But they have been driven out of Maryland, and Pennsylvania is no longer in danger of invasion. ... I have got you together to hear what I have written down. I do not wish your advice about the main matter, for that I have determined for myself. ... What I have written is that which my reflections have determined me to say ....

Preliminary Proclamation

Whatever was and was not accomplished at Antietam, Lincoln judged it enough of a victory to issue a preliminary Emancipation Proclamation on September 23, 1862. In hindsight, this seems a timid document, its rhetoric more legalistic than inspiring. It did not free a single slave, but, rather, warned slave owners living in states "still in rebellion on January 1, 1863" that their living property would be declared "forever free."

Voices

The Emancipation Proclamation, January 1, 1863:

Whereas, on the twenty-second day of September, in the year of our Lord one thousand eight hundred and sixty-two, a proclamation issued by the President of the United States containing among other things the following to wit:

"That on the first day of January in the year of our Lord one thousand eight hundred and sixty-three, all persons held as slaves within any State, or designated part of a State, the people whereof shall then be in rebellion against the United States, shall be then, thenceforth and forever free, and the Executive Government of the United States, including the military and naval authorities thereof, will recognize and maintain the freedom of such persons, and will do no act or acts to repress such persons, or any of them, in any efforts they may make for their actual freedom ...."

Now, therefore, I, Abraham Lincoln, President of the United States ... do order and declare that all persons held as slaves within the said designated States and parts of States are, and henceforward shall be free; and that the Executive Government of the United States, including the Military and Naval authorities, thereof, will recognize and maintain the freedom of said persons.

And I hereby enjoin upon the people so declared to be free, to abstain from all violence, unless in necessary self-defense, and I recommend to them, that in all cases, when allowed, they labor faithfully for reasonable wages.

And I further declare and make known that such persons of suitable condition will be received into the armed service of the United States to garrison forts, positions, stations, and other places, and man vessels of all sorts in said service.

And upon this, sincerely believed to be an act of justice, warranted by the Constitution, upon military necessity, I invoke the considerate judgment of mankind and the gracious favor of Almighty God ....

Forever Free

Only after the January 1 deadline had come and gone did President Lincoln issue the "final" Emancipation Proclamation. But even that document liberated only those slaves in areas still "in rebellion," that is, in parts of the Confederacy that were not under the control of the Union army. It was reasoned that areas now under Union control were no longer, strictly speaking, in rebellion. Lincoln also still couldn't afford to drive the border states into the Confederacy by freeing their slaves. With bitter irony, then, this meant that ...

♦ Slavery was alive and well where the Union army had been victorious.

♦ No slave was set free in the border states—Delaware, Kentucky, Maryland, and Missouri. (West Virginia, already broken away from Virginia, was not admitted to the Union until June 20, 1863, and then on the condition that its slaves would be gradually emancipated.)

♦ In the states where the slaves *were* declared free, the law could not, of course, be enforced until the war was won.

Congress Acts

Timorous and tentative as the Emancipation Proclamation might seem from our perspective, it was a momentous document and probably just right for its time and circumstances. It gave the war new moral force. For those who chose to see the Civil War as a war to make men free, the document officially made it such a struggle. Yet the proclamation was also sufficiently cautious to avoid inflaming the occupied South and the border states.

Before the war ended, Congress would take action beyond the proclamation. The 13th Amendment to the U.S. Constitution was passed by the Senate on April 8, 1864, and by the House (after a fight) on January 31, 1865. Within a year, by December 18, 1865, the measure was ratified by the states. The amendment is brief: "Neither slavery nor involuntary servitude, except as a punishment for crime whereof the party shall have been duly convicted, shall exist within the United States, or any place subject to their jurisdiction."

The Least You Need to Know

♦ Lincoln moved cautiously on the issue of emancipation, to avoid alienating his soldiers and officers (most of whom were not abolitionists), and to avoid losing the tenuous loyalty of the border states.

♦ Because of Gen. John Pope's terrible defeat at the Second Battle of Bull Run, Lincoln reinstated Gen. George B. McClellan to command of the Army of the Potomac.

- Antietam saw the "bloodiest single day of the Civil War." While McClellan achieved a narrow victory for the Union, he tragically missed an opportunity to destroy Lee's Army of Northern Virginia and bring the war to an end.

- The victory at Antietam, slim and incomplete though it was, provided Lincoln with the opportunity to issue his preliminary Emancipation Proclamation.

- The Emancipation Proclamation freed only those slaves in parts of the country that were still "in rebellion." Slaves living in areas of the Confederacy under Union control and in the border states were not liberated by law until the 13th Amendment was ratified in December 1865.

Chapter 12

A Worse Place Than Hell

In This Chapter

- ◆ McClellan is permanently relieved of command
- ◆ Burnside assumes command
- ◆ Burnside's blunders
- ◆ Gen. Joseph Hooker takes command

Before Antietam, the Confederacy had reached what historians call its "high-water mark." It had invaded the North, Great Britain was on the verge of recognizing it as a sovereign nation, and the Union seemed incapable of doing anything about either of these things. But the narrow Federal victory at Antietam began the ebbing of that Southern tide. Lee blamed his defeat on the loss of Special Order 191, but for failing to pursue and crush Lee, George McClellan had no one to blame other than himself. (Nevertheless, he blamed Lincoln for having failed to give him the endless reinforcements he craved.)

The president's patience was growing short. To friends and colleagues, he complained that McClellan suffered from a bad case of the "slows." In contrast, Lee, strategically defeated at Antietam, simply refused to act as if he had been beaten. This chapter chronicles the next step in Lincoln's desperate search for a commander to match the Confederacy's greatest general.

A Second Ride Around

Abraham Lincoln was a patient man, but the blood of Antietam weighed heavily on him. What had McClellan purchased with all that carnage? The battle was over on September 17. The rest of that month passed without action from McClellan. Lincoln personally visited Antietam to see the situation there for himself. After his return to Washington, on October 1, he ordered McClellan to "cross the Potomac and give battle to the enemy."

McClellan did nothing.

When, a week later, Lincoln wrote his general demanding to know why he had not attacked, McClellan replied that his cavalry was exhausted, broken down. The horses were fatigued and sick, he wrote, with hoof-rot. At this the president's patience finally snapped: "Will you pardon me for asking," he wrote in reply, "what the horses of your army have done since the battle of Antietam that fatigues anything?"

Lee, in the meantime, sent Stuart back into the North. This time, it was not into Maryland, a contested border state, but into Pennsylvania, a solid nonslavery state of the Union. Jeb Stuart, who had infamously ridden around McClellan's army before the Battle of Mechanicsville at the start of the Seven Days (see Chapter 10), rode around him a *second* time, during October 9–12, 1862, to raid the Pennsylvania town of Chambersburg.

The raid was of no great military significance—500 horses were captured and a machine shop was wrecked, along with several stores—but it tweaked the collective noses of the North. Stuart's cavalry troopers had camped openly in the very streets of a Union town in a Union state!

On October 26, McClellan finally began to march south, to Warrenton, Virginia, but so slowly that Lee was able to interpose his army between the Federal forces and Richmond. On November 7, 1862, the Young Napoleon received a telegram from General Halleck:

> General: On receipt of the order of the President, sent herewith, you will immediately turn over your command to Major General Burnside, and repair to Trenton, N.J., reporting your arrival at that place, by telegraph, for further orders.

George Brinton McClellan had been fired. After an emotional farewell to the troops, who still loved "Little Mac," the general left the Army.

Popular, Reluctant, Hapless: Burnside

A native of Liberty, Indiana, and a West Point graduate, Ambrose Everett Burnside (1824–1881) cut a handsome military figure. His trademark mutton-chop whiskers became a popular fashion and have been known by a kind of inversion of his name ever since: *sideburns*. Like McClellan, he was popular with his troops, whose affection and respect he readily returned.

Ambrose E. Burnside (seated, arms folded), pictured here with some of his Rhode Island regimental staff, reluctantly accepted command of the Army of the Potomac.

(Library of Congress)

In sharp contrast to McClellan, Burnside was modest and self-effacing, with little confidence in his own capacity for leadership. He twice declined Lincoln's offer of command of the Army of the Potomac before accepting, with great reluctance, the president's third entreaty. Long after the war, in his memoirs, Ulysses S. Grant would describe Burnside as "an officer who was generally liked and respected. He was not, however, fitted to command an army." Grant added, "No one knew this better than himself."

Even before he ordered a shot fired, Burnside blundered. He reorganized the structure of the army into three grandiose, two-corps divisions, commanded by Generals

Edwin V. Sumner, Joseph Hooker, and William B. Franklin. This gave the Army of the Potomac an impressively streamlined appearance on paper, but it made movement in the field unwieldy.

Slaughter at Fredericksburg

Burnside positioned his army just north of the Rappahannock River at Warrenton, Virginia, 30 miles from Lee's army, which consisted of just two corps, commanded by Stonewall Jackson and James Longstreet. Burnside might have attacked between the separated wings of Lee's army, a sound tactic that could have *defeated* Lee *in detail;* instead, pressured by officials in Washington demanding a quick, decisive victory, he decided to continue an advance on Richmond and attack well south of Warrenton, at Fredericksburg.

General Sumner's Grand division arrived at a position across the Rappahannock from Fredericksburg on November 17. Confederate general Longstreet would not reach the town until the next day. Burnside should have ordered Sumner to cross the river immediately, but he insisted instead on waiting for the arrival of five *pontoon bridges* (transportable temporary bridges) that had somehow gone astray, and ordered Sumner's troops to make camp on the river's north bank. This gave Longstreet ample time to entrench defensively in the hills south and west of Fredericksburg.

Words of War

To **defeat in detail** is the time-honored tactic of attacking the spread-out elements of an enemy force one by one before they have time to unite in a single, more powerful unit. A **pontoon bridge** is a transportable temporary bridge resting on floating pontoons or pontoon boats rather than permanent piers or pilings.

Burnside's delay stretched into days, and each day, Lee fortified his defensive positions even more strongly. On December 11, 78,000 Confederates were securely dug in on the south bank of the Rappahannock, with the town between their positions and the river. At last, on December 11, Burnside's bridges were in place, and the Union crossing began. Yet, with Lee entrenched, the conditions necessary for Union success had vanished many days earlier. The crossing was senseless, and the attack doomed.

Confederates destroyed the bridges across the Rappahannock, photographed in April 1863 by Union captain A.J. Russell. The figures on the far side are soldiers of Barksdale's Mississippi Brigade. It is believed that this is the only photograph of active Confederate soldiers taken by a Union photographer.

(Library of Congress)

With Stonewall Jackson, Gen. James Longstreet was a principal Confederate commander at Fredericksburg.

(Harper's Pictorial History of the Civil War, *1866*)

This map shows Fredericks-burg's strategic position between Washington, to the north, and Richmond, to the south.

(Harper's Pictorial History of the Civil War, 1866)

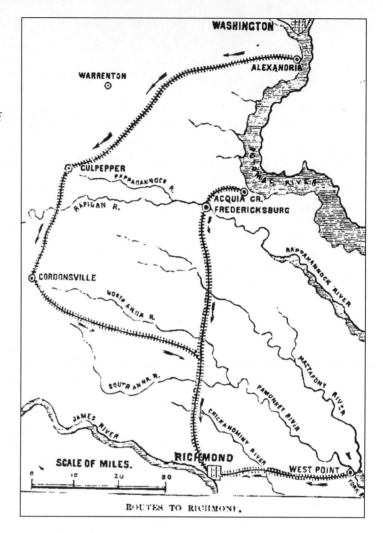

ROUTES TO RICHMOND.

Tragic, too, was the artillery barrage Burnside ordered just before the crossing. Confederate snipers were firing on the Union troops, and, presumably, the artillery attack was intended to stop them. It did nothing, however, but ravage the town. And what the cannonade left standing, Burnside's soldiers looted when they entered Fredericksburg.

A Chicken Could Not Live

The Battle of Fredericksburg proper took place on December 13, 1862. Despite some success against Jackson on the Confederate left, the Union effort fell apart when

Burnside made a series of hopeless assaults on the Confederates' impregnable hilltop positions. Even as the Federal dead piled up before a stone wall in front of a sunken road below the Confederates' chief position at Marye's Heights, Burnside continued to order one assault after another.

One Federal officer described the battle as "murder, not warfare," and an artillery officer of Longstreet's corps remarked, "a chicken could not live on that field when we open[ed] on it."

"I Am Responsible"

Burnside ordered 14 charges, each of them a virtual suicide mission. At dusk, weeping, he announced that he would lead a final attack personally. Instead, he at last allowed himself to be persuaded to withdraw back across the Rappahannock. He heard his aide call for three cheers as he rode past his men. There was a silence as dead as the dead below Marye's Heights.

Burnside reported to his superior, Henry Wager Halleck:

> To the brave officers and soldiers who accomplished the feat of … recrossing the river in the face of the enemy, I owe everything. For the failure in the attack I am responsible …. To the families and friends of the dead I can offer my heartfelt sympathies, but for the wounded I can offer my earnest prayers for their comfortable and final recovery.

> **War News**
>
> After the Battle of Fredericksburg, Stonewall Jackson and his staff surveyed the devastation of the town. Shaking his head, one of Jackson's officers wondered aloud what could be done about this. Jackson, whose martial skill was matched only by his deep religious piety and sense of honor, gave an answer as uncharacteristic as it was terrible: "Kill 'em. Kill 'em all."

> **Count Off!**
>
> The Battle of Fredericksburg stands as one of the worst defeats in the history of the U. S. Army. It is estimated that 106,000 Union soldiers participated in the attacks; 12,700 were killed or wounded. Confederate losses were 5,300 killed or wounded out of some 72,500 engaged.

"Heartfelt Sympathies … Earnest Prayers"

To be killed in battle was the hard fate that awaited many young men of the North and the South, but to be wounded was often an even harder fate. "Earnest prayers" were typically about all that could be offered a wounded soldier.

Military historians have often observed that the Civil War was the world's first modern war. It would be more accurate to say that it was poised at the threshold of the new and the old. *New* because burgeoning technology turned out firearms in staggering quantities, and fashioned bigger and more destructive artillery. *Old* because most of the actual fighting consisted of blasting away with musket-rifles at very close range.

Modern Weapons, Medieval Medicine

If fighting techniques lagged behind weapons technology, medical practices dragged even farther back. Weaponry could do far more damage than doctors could repair.

For abdominal or head wounds, next to nothing could be done, and the best a surgeon might offer a man wounded in the leg or arm was a quick amputation. Chloroform, the only anesthetic, was widely used. The practice of *antisepsis*—the destruction of infection-causing bacteria—would not emerge until the British physician Joseph Lister discovered the work of Louis Pasteur in 1865, the closing year of the American Civil War.

In field hospitals, wounds were often poorly cleaned, and dressings were not sterile. To stanch the flow of blood, wounds were packed with lint, material obtained from scraping linen cloth. Surgeons did perform complex operations, but even if an operation or procedure was successful, relatively minor wounds routinely became infected, causing fever, illness, and often death. Physicians greeted the suppuration of wounds as natural and normal, and spoke of the appearance of "laudable pus" as a positive sign, yet weren't surprised when a patient exhibiting such symptoms sickened and died.

Of course, one didn't have to be wounded to contract a dread disease: More men died of disease in the Civil War than of wounds sustained on the battlefield. In the filthy conditions of military camps containing thousands of men, typhoid, dysentery—the "Tennessee Two-Step," it was called—cholera, malaria, and pneumonia were endemic and sometimes epidemic. Physicians and commanders learned from experience to dump the camp's waste downstream from the supply of drinking water, but, if the water didn't actually stink and wasn't visibly contaminated, they assumed it was fit to drink. They also didn't understand that mosquitoes carried malaria. If men still got sick, well, it was because the air was bad—"miasmatic," they called it—and there was simply nothing to be done but endure as best they could.

Mary Edwards Walker, M.D.

As we saw in Chapter 10, such tireless reformers as Dorothea Dix and Clara Barton struggled to bring skilled nursing care and a decent level of sanitation to the battlefield. If female nurses were accepted grudgingly by the military medical establishment, women doctors were all but unheard of.

Mary Edwards Walker, born in Oswego, New York, on November 26, 1832, bucked the male-dominated medical establishment by winning admission to and graduation from Syracuse Medical College. During the 1840s and 1850s, she struggled to survive in her Cincinnati, Ohio, practice, gaining little professional acceptance from either sex.

Mary Edwards Walker, M.D., was finally allowed to practice field surgery in 1864, and was the first woman awarded the Medal of Honor.

(National Archives and Records Administration)

With the outbreak of the war, Walker volunteered her medical services in the only capacity the Union army would allow: as a nurse. Early in 1864, however, an Ohio regiment hired her as a "contract surgeon" for six months, and, in October of that year, the Union army at last commissioned her as an assistant surgeon. During her tour of duty, she saw service not only as a physician, but also as a spy. Walker, who was known for looking after wounded on both sides, was captured by Confederates when she stopped to treat a wounded rebel. She spent four months in a Southern prison camp.

Walker was the first woman to be awarded the Medal of Honor. In 1919, however, the Board of Medals revoked the award because she was not an official member of the armed forces. "You can have it over my dead body," the 87-year-old physician told federal authorities. Six days later, she died. The medal was not officially restored to her until 1977.

Shoddy Goods: A Soldier's Life

It was not only the sick and wounded soldier who suffered during the Civil War. Weather and exposure are ever-present adversaries that take no sides and give no quarter, especially to men who are ill equipped. And Civil War soldiers, both North and South, were about as ill equipped as any troops of the nineteenth century. *Quartermasters*, officers in charge of procuring and distributing clothing, tents, and other nonfood supplies, were inefficient and, very often, thoroughly corrupt.

Words of War

A **quartermaster** was the officer in charge of procurement and supply of clothing, supplies, tents, and so on, for army units. The **commissary** was the officer responsible for food. The word **shoddy** is derived from the Civil War, meaning a kind of cloth made from scraps of material compounded and glued rather than woven together and, therefore, subject to disintegration. Today, it's an adjective applied to anything cheap or poorly made.

Corruption and war profiteering were rampant in the North. The soldiers' rations, poor at best, were sometimes downright deadly, as purveyors foisted condemned meat on military *commissaries*.

Even the proud blue uniforms fell apart as government contractors started making of them of what came to be called *shoddy*, a kind of felted rather than woven cloth, made up of waste fabric that was not woven but, rather, compounded and glued together. It looked good enough when brand new, but would disintegrate and dissolve on exposure to the weather.

As corruption touched the lives of the lowliest private in the Union army, it went to the very top of Union government. Lincoln's secretary of war, Simon Cameron, was up to his elbows in dirty deals with military supply contractors and was so bold in this regard that the U.S. House of Representatives voted an official censure. In January 1862, Lincoln "promoted" him out of the cabinet by naming him minister (ambassador) to Russia, a posting as far from the United States as possible. ("Ugh!" remarked a senator. "Send word to the czar to bring in his things at night!") Edwin Stanton took his place at the helm of the War Department.

Bad as all this was, conditions were even worse for the Confederates. True, they had won a great victory at Fredericksburg, but the men faced the onset of winter even more poorly clothed and meagerly fed than the Northern soldiers. This was not due to corruption and profiteering, but to lack of money. Scott's Anaconda—the naval blockade of the South so roundly mocked at the beginning of the war (see Chapter 6)—was gaining in effectiveness with each passing week. Worse, recognition by the great European powers was not forthcoming. Despite the Southern victory at Fredericksburg, the failure of the Confederate invasion of the North at Antietam, coupled with the moral high ground seized by the Union with the Emancipation Proclamation, turned France and Britain away from any thought of active alliance with the Confederacy.

North *and* South, soldiers shivered miserably around their campfires during the dreary winter of 1862–1863.

The Mud March

In contrast to George B. McClellan, Ambrose Burnside desperately wanted to please the administration in Washington and act against the enemy. Unfortunately, the action he proposed was desperate indeed. After the useless bloodshed of Fredericksburg, he was determined to cross the Rappahannock again. He started to turn back to cross the river downstream from Lee's strong position, but some of Burnside's alarmed subordinates alerted President Lincoln, who vetoed this movement.

So the Army of the Potomac huddled in winter quarters until January 20, 1863, when Burnside began to execute what looked like a much sounder strategy. He would envelop Lee's army via a river crossing called Banks's Ford. But a two-day torrent of icy rain transformed the scarred landscape into a quagmire, and the movement became the "Mud March."

The all-too-symbolic spectacle of an entire army bogged down in impassable mud, its morale at rock-bottom, was too much for the Union and for Abraham Lincoln to bear. On January 26, 1863, the president relieved Ambrose Burnside as commander of the Army of the Potomac and replaced him with Joseph "Fighting Joe" Hooker.

> ### War News
>
> Relieved of command in November 1862, George B. McClellan permanently retired and, in 1864, ran against Lincoln as the Democratic candidate for president. In contrast, Burnside accepted responsibility for Fredericksburg and selflessly volunteered for a series of subordinate commands. He proved himself an able subordinate until the Battle of the Crater (see Chapter 19), when his mismanagement contributed to a bad defeat. Found culpable by a court of inquiry, he resigned from the army in April 1865.

Give Us Victories

Fredericksburg had been hell for the *Billy Yanks* (Union soldiers) who fought there. For Abraham Lincoln, unable to find a winning general and beset by disintegrating morale, it was even worse: "If there is a worse place than hell, I am in it."

To Hooker, Lincoln wrote a letter well known to students of the Civil War. The president began by citing to Hooker all his reasons for having made him commander

Words of War

Billy Yank is what Union soldiers were called and called themselves. Johnny Reb was the Confederate equivalent. Yanks and Rebs were the Civil War version of World War II's "G.I. Joes" as names for the common soldier.

of the Army of the Potomac. He then went on to express all his doubts and reservations as well, criticizing Hooker for having failed to support Burnside when he was that hapless commander's subordinate and chiding him for his remark that "both the Army and the Government needed a dictator."

Lincoln wrote: "Only those generals who gain success can set up dictators. What I now ask of you is military success, and I will risk the dictatorship. … Beware of rashness, but with energy and sleepless vigilance go forward and give us victories."

Fighting Joe

Joseph Hooker (1814–1879) was born in Hadley, Massachusetts, and graduated from West Point in 1837. He served in the Second Seminole War (1835–1843) and in the Mexican War, fighting alongside Robert E. Lee and Thomas J. Jackson (long before anyone called him "Stonewall"). Hooker fought well and bravely, but even then he had a tendency to be disloyal to his commander. During the Mexican War, there was a dispute between Gen. Gideon Pillow and Gen. Winfield Scott. Hooker took Pillow's side, and Scott never forgave him. When the Civil War broke out, Scott snubbed Hooker, who had resigned from the army, when he sought an officer's commission.

"Fighting Joe" Hooker, hard-drinking and full of bluff and bluster, always ready to speak ill of a superior officer, replaced Burnside after Fredericksburg.

(Harper's Pictorial History of the Civil War, *1866)*

That was just fine with Henry Wager Halleck, who, at the beginning of the war, was Scott's chief of staff. Hooker had welched on gambling debts owed to Halleck when the two of them were in San Francisco during the 1850s. At the First Battle of Bull Run, therefore, Hooker was just one of the many civilians who watched the fighting. He pestered Lincoln with unsolicited advice, and when he finally obtained an audience with the president, he told him: "I was at … Bull Run … and it is neither vanity nor boasting in me to declare that I am a damned sight better general than you, sir, had on that field."

Lincoln personally gave Hooker a commission as brigadier general of volunteers, and he fought well under McClellan, but, his disloyal streak surfacing yet again, mocked his commander as an "infant among soldiers." Little wonder, then, that the army's senior officer corps did not welcome Hooker's appointment as commander of the Army of the Potomac. General Hooker hated his nickname, "Fighting Joe," which had become attached to him by a copyediting error. A series of quick reports issued by the Associated Press covering Hooker during the Seven Days' Battles was headed "Fighting—Joe Hooker." Newspapers all over the country printed the articles without the dash: "Fighting Joe Hooker."

Camp Followers

Folklore holds that Hooker lent his name to practitioners of the world's oldest profession. The story goes like this: The general's troops were quartered in a Washington, D.C., neighborhood rife with saloons and brothels. The area came to be called "Hooker's Division," and the prostitutes (it was said) were dubbed "hookers." Like most folk etymologies, however, this is wrong. *Hooker* was a synonym for prostitute well before General Hooker and the Civil War; however, it is abundantly true that prostitutes were hardly strangers in the vicinity of military camps.

Soldiers freely indulged in what were termed "horizontal refreshments." By 1862, Washington, D.C., had 450 bordellos and at least 7,500 full-time prostitutes. The Confederate capital, Richmond, harbored at least an equal number. About 8 percent of the soldiers in the Union army sought medical treatment for venereal disease during the war. Presumably, figures were about the same for the Confederacy.

Prostitutes plying their trade among troops were often termed "camp followers"; however, the phrase was also applied to sutlers, civilian purveyors of goods not issued by the army, including candy, tobacco, tinned meats, newspapers, and so on. Sutlers did not scruple to gouge troops hankering for a host of minor comforts.

Of Cavalry and Balloons

Whatever senior officers thought, the common soldier greeted the advent of Joseph Hooker with great excitement. He roused the Army of the Potomac out of its despair and restored its morale. Undoing Burnside's unwieldy reorganization, he made the army supple and manageable. He greatly upgraded the quality of rations and clothing, insisting fresh-baked bread be issued instead of the hated hardtack, and he mercilessly pursued and prosecuted corrupt commissary officers.

Hooker also gave the Army of the Potomac something the Confederates had long used effectively: a revised and expanded role for the cavalry. Whereas McClellan had employed infantry at cavalry's expense, Hooker saw the cavalry as a vitally important instrument of reconnaissance. Nor was Hooker content with men on horses to perform the reconnaissance mission. He also liked the idea of men in balloons.

Since the fall of Sumter, a handful of balloonists had tried to interest the army in their services. The army purchased a single balloon for observation use at the First Battle of Bull Run, but it was wrecked before reaching the battlefield. By January 1862, the army had seven balloons—the nucleus of the first air arm of the United States military—and, in contrast to the overwhelming majority of his military contemporaries, Hooker was enthusiastic about the possibilities of the balloon in reconnaissance, in artillery spotting, and even for directing battles from aloft. He personally made an ascent in a tethered balloon.

"The Finest Army on the Planet"

By the early spring of 1863, Hooker was in high spirits, and not just because he had been up in a balloon. His troops were better fed, better clothed, better armed, and better trained than they had ever been before. Declaring that he was now in possession of the "finest army on the planet," he swore: "May God have mercy on General Lee, for I will have none."

The Least You Need to Know

- Lincoln replaced George McClellan with Ambrose Burnside as commander of the Army of the Potomac, over Burnside's own self-doubts.

- Burnside conducted his first campaign, at Fredericksburg, disastrously, bringing, on December 13, 1862, the U.S. Army the worst single defeat in its history.

- Whereas the Confederate army was short on food and supplies because it was strapped for cash, the Union army, well funded, was plagued by corrupt and inefficient suppliers as well as supply officers.

- Burnside was replaced by Gen. Joseph "Fighting Joe" Hooker. He did much to restore and improve the battered Army of the Potomac, and he faced confidently the prospect of battle against Robert E. Lee.

Chapter 13

Bread and Bullets

In This Chapter

- ◆ Trouble on the Confederate home front
- ◆ Wartime inflation
- ◆ The problem of desertion
- ◆ The Confederates invade Kentucky
- ◆ The Vicksburg campaign

If New Year's 1863 was not happy for the North, it was downright miserable for the South. True, Southern commanders had out-generaled Northerners everywhere but in the West; *yet the South wasn't winning the war*. But, then, neither was the North. If anything, both sides were losing.

In the North, morale and confidence were on the wane. "Gone are the proud hopes," a Union soldier named William Thompson Lusk wrote to his mother after Fredericksburg. "Once more unsuccessful, and only a bloody record to show our men were brave …. [The army] has strong limbs to march and meet the foe, stout arms to strike heavy blows, brave hearts to dare—but the brains, the brains! Have we no brains to use the arms and limbs and eager hearts … ?"

In the South, the people admired their commanders, but saw that their soldiers were going without enough food and decent clothing. And now civilians were feeling the pinch. Rich and poor, many went hungry.

This chapter looks at the home front in the South and the suffering of the Southern civilian. After a few words on reporting the Civil War, the discussion returns, too, to combat west of the Appalachians.

"Bread! Bread!"

At the outbreak of the war, Richmond was neither a sleepy little Southern village nor a great metropolis, but a middling city. When the town was suddenly proclaimed the capital of the Confederacy, its population doubled almost overnight. In the best of times, such instant growth would have put a strain on the food supply and other necessities. But these, of course, were hardly the best of times. The Union blockade was increasingly effective, and although McClellan and Burnside had both failed to invade Richmond, the major fighting in Virginia had taken place on the outskirts of the city—on the farms and fields that were supposed to supply Richmond with food.

If there is a popular image of the Southern home front, it is of a homogenous people fiercely loyal to their land and thoroughly convinced that their way of life was worth fighting for. The truth is that although the South was generally more unified than the North in its commitment to the war, there was nevertheless a wide spectrum of commitment—from total devotion to those who wanted a negotiated settlement with the North, to others favoring immediate unconditional surrender and reunification, and to those who were pro-Union in the first place. Under the pressure of privation, even the most loyal Confederates were liable to snap.

Count Off!

In 1863, a Richmond newspaper estimated that the cost of feeding a small family in the city was $68.25 per week. During the year before the war, that cost had been only $6.55. This was at a time when an unskilled laborer could expect to earn a little more than a dollar a day.

On April 2, 1863, a mob of Richmond women started a bread riot. With shouts of "Bread! Bread!" they smashed store windows and looted all the food, as well as jewelry, clothing, and whatever other goods they could find. Richmond's mayor called out the militia, ordering them to fire on the rioters (never mind that they were *Southern women*) if they failed to disperse.

That's when Jefferson Davis himself appeared. As his wife, Varina, tells it (and the story is otherwise uncorroborated), Davis mounted a wagon and, after scolding the rioters for stealing trinkets and finery while crying for bread, he called out: "You say you are hungry and have no money—here is all I have!" With that, he dug into his pockets and threw out money. Neither history nor Varina Davis records whether this was gold and silver coins (worth something) or Confederate notes (worth almost nothing).

Having distributed his largesse, Davis pulled out his pocket watch and declared that he would order the militia to open fire on the crowd if it failed to disperse in five minutes.

Paper War

Paper. By 1862, that's pretty much all Confederate money was. The "Anaconda" naval blockade (see Chapter 6) reduced the flow of goods in and out of the South, which was bad enough, but the Davis government made the situation even worse by imposing an *embargo* (export ban) on cotton. By purposely curtailing exports of the South's most important crop, Confederate leaders hoped to force France and England to intervene in the war on the side of the South.

It didn't happen.

And yet the government had to finance the war somehow. It offered bonds paying 8 percent interest, but as early as the end of 1861, inflation in the Southern states topped 12 percent—*a month*. Stiff taxes were also imposed on everything manufactured or grown, but few could afford to buy much, so the levies generated little revenue.

Nothing was left for the government to do but print more Treasury notes. The predictable result was inflation so severe that Confederate money was practically worthless as soon as it was issued.

Words of War

An **embargo** is a government-imposed ban on the export or import of certain goods or on trade with certain other countries.

Count Off!

A Confederate paper dollar was worth

80 cents	December 1, 1861
60 cents	February 1, 1862
20 cents	February 1, 1863
8 cents	June 1863
4.5 cents	November 1864
2.5 cents	January 1865
1.5 cents	April 1, 1865

After this, up until the surrender at Appomattox on April 9, it took approximately $1,000 in Confederate currency to buy a gold dollar.

The Draft and Desertion

Southerners liked to believe that the Confederate fighting man was superior to the Union common soldier. There can be little question that, for most of the war, the Confederate army was led by more daring, enterprising, and skilled officers, but the enlisted men on both sides, although sometimes poorly disciplined and inadequately trained, showed equally remarkable courage, endurance, and resourcefulness.

The Confederate "Johnny Reb" did have the morale-lifting advantage of defending his homeland rather than fighting on "foreign" soil, but as the families of these warriors suffered, it became increasingly clear to many of them that fighting and dying had less to do with protecting their wives, mothers, sisters, and children than it did with preserving the feudal world of the South's wealthy landowners—the 1,800 or so planters wealthy enough to own more than a hundred slaves.

Significant numbers of Southern men always chose to join the Union army, and, as the war ground on, these numbers increased. More important, however, were problems with enlistment and desertion.

Fighting, it claimed, to end the tyranny of a government that trampled the rights of states and individuals, the Confederacy enacted a conscription law on April 16, 1862, almost a full year before the Union did so. All white males between 18 and 35 who were not legally exempt were conscripted for three years' service. In September 1862, the upper age limit was raised to 45, and in February 1864, to 50 (with the lower limit pushed down to 17).

As explained in Chapter 5, Confederate conscription laws, like those later enacted in the North, were grossly unjust. Anyone with enough money could pay a commutation fee or hire a substitute to avoid being drafted. In the South, men who owned or oversaw 20 or more slaves were automatically exempt.

Draft evasion was common, and those who did serve were often resentful. Desertion was epidemic. After the simultaneous Confederate defeats at Gettysburg and Vicksburg in July 1863, 50,000 to 100,000 Confederate soldiers deserted.

> ### War News
>
> In February 1864, the Confederate Congress authorized conscription of free blacks and slaves for auxiliary (noncombat) military service. Despite resistance, on March 13, 1865, the "Negro Soldier Law" permitted the recruitment (not conscription) of slaves for combat. Such soldiers could remain slaves or, with the "consent of the owners and of the States," could be emancipated. A few companies of African American Confederate soldiers were enrolled, but the war ended before any saw combat.

> ### War News
>
> The Richmond *Enquirer* for October 6, 1864, reported President Davis's announcement that "two-thirds of the Army are absent from the ranks." Thus, at this time, there were more deserters than fighting men.

Diary of a Southern Lady

Mary Boykin Miller was born in Pleasant Hill, South Carolina, on March 31, 1823, the daughter of Stephen Miller, governor of South Carolina. In 1840, she married James Chesnut. Owner of a large plantation in Mulberry, South Carolina, James Chesnut was elected to the Senate in 1858, but, at the start of the war, Chesnut joined the Confederate Army and became military aide to Gen. P.G.T. Beauregard. Promoted to general himself, Chesnut was appointed advisor to President Jefferson Davis.

Accompanying her husband on his various assignments, Mary Chesnut lived in wartime Charleston, Montgomery, Columbia, and Richmond. Between February 1861 and July 1865, she kept a 400,000-word diary. Unpublished during her lifetime (she died on November 22, 1886), the work appeared as *A Diary from Dixie* in 1905 and is now regarded as a classic of both Civil War and women's literature.

Chesnut personally abhorred slavery, but believed in states' rights. Loyal to the Confederacy, she nevertheless refrained from glorifying the "great cause" in her diary. Instead, she meticulously recorded the pleasures, heartbreaks, and hardships of daily life.

> "My husband bought yesterday at the Commissary's one barrel of flour, one bushel of potatoes, one peck [a dry volume equal to two gallons] of rice, five pounds of salt beef, and one peck of salt—all for sixty dollars," she noted on December 4, 1863. "In the street a barrel of flour sells for one hundred and fifteen dollars." Then she continued, "Today, a poor woman threw herself on her dead husband's coffin and kissed it. She was weeping bitterly. So did I in sympathy."

War News

The writings of those who, like Chesnut, kept Civil War diaries and journals are today invaluable to historians and anyone else who wants to experience the impact of the war at ground level. During the conflict, however, people turned to newspapers and illustrated weekly magazines for information about the war. The weeklies were illustrated by engravings made from on-the-spot drawings—the great American painter Winslow Homer worked as a combat artist—or from photographs.

Journalists and Artists

Every major newspaper, North and South, sent reporters and correspondents into the field to cover battles. They also often reported on general troop movements—much to the chagrin of commanders, who wanted to keep such things secret.

For the most part, reportage in the daily newspapers was undistinguished and, more often than not, grossly inaccurate. Given the relatively slow pace of communications during the period, the illustrated weeklies had an advantage over the daily papers. Not only did the weekly format allow writers to gain a degree of perspective on the events reported, but also there was sufficient time to prepare often elaborate engravings of battle scenes. The leading illustrated weeklies were *Harper's*, founded by Fletcher Harper in 1857, *Frank Leslie's Illustrated News*, established in 1855, and *New York Illustrated News*, begun in 1859 by John King. In the South, the *Southern Illustrated News*, founded in 1862, portrayed the war from a Confederate perspective.

The weeklies employed a small legion of artists and artist-correspondents. *Harper's* leading artist-correspondent was Theodore Davis (1840–1894), who covered the war from beginning to end on many fronts, from the Potomac to Sherman's "March to the Sea." *Leslie's* employed, among others, Edwin Forbes (1839–1895), who covered the Virginia theater and was present at Second Bull Run, Antietam, Chancellorsville, Gettysburg, the Wilderness, and more. The most famous of the Civil War artist-correspondents was Winslow Homer (1816–1910), who worked for *Harper's* and became celebrated for his depictions of ordinary soldiers in battle and in camp. He also worked behind the scenes—for example, portraying the grim work of Union surgeons. After the war, Homer went on to a brilliant career as a fine artist and is considered one of the very greatest of America's late nineteenth- and early twentieth-century painters.

The Photographers

At the outbreak of the Civil War in 1861, the art and science of photography was less than three decades old. Louis Nicéphore Niepce and Louis Jacques Mandé Daguerre created the Daguerreotype process in France in the 1830s, and, by the 1860s, photography was sufficiently advanced to enable both studio portraiture and on-the-scene coverage. Cameras, photographic plates, and the necessary on-the-spot processing equipment were too cumbersome and photographic emulsions too "slow" (insufficiently light sensitive) to enable genuine battle-action photography, but scenes of encampments, marches, and aftermaths were within the state of the art, and Civil War photographers made an estimated one million wartime images.

Although the technology for directly reproducing photographs in illustrated newspapers did not exist in the 1860s, photographs were used as the basis of many widely reproduced engravings. However, much Civil War photography was sold directly to the public, and even more was intended strictly for personal use. Soldiers visited photo studios to have portraits made for their mothers, fathers, and sweethearts. Those images that survive are among the most compelling and emotionally powerful artifacts of the war.

By far the most celebrated Civil War photographer was Mathew B. Brady (c. 1823–1896), who opened a New York City photo studio in 1844 and was very well established by the time of the war. With Scotch-born Alexander Gardner (1821–1882), whom he hired in 1856, and who ran for him a Washington, D.C.–based studio and gallery, Brady organized an army of more than 100 photographers to cover every aspect of the Civil War, on the battlefield and on the home front. So well respected was Brady that the U.S. government and army gave him an unprecedented degree of support, cutting through red tape to furnish necessary permits and even supplying special transport.

Another notable photographer of the era was Timothy O'Sullivan (1840–1882), a protégé of Brady's, who specialized in portraying war-ravaged landscapes and battlefields—most notably the famous "Harvest of Death," an image of Gettysburg.

The Confederacy had four prominent photographers. James M. Osborn and F. W. Durbec, Charlestonians, portrayed the aftermath of the surrender of Fort Sumter, and Julian Vannerson, a Virginian, photographed the South's most important military leaders. Unique not only among the Southerners but also all Civil War photographers was A. J. Lytle of Baton Rouge, Louisiana, who worked for the Confederate Secret Service, covertly photographing Federal forces deployed in and around Baton Rouge during the occupation of that city.

Foreign Affairs

Early in the war, both the British and the French seriously considered recognizing the Confederate States of America as a sovereign nation and even, perhaps, concluding an alliance with it. But the narrow Union victory at Antietam convinced these governments that the Confederate invasion of the Union would fail, and the Emancipation Proclamation proved so popular with the people of England and France that neither government would dare risk recognition of the Confederacy, let alone an alliance.

This did not mean, however, that all Confederate-European diplomacy was dead. Just after the fall of Fort Sumter, James D. Bulloch called on Confederate Secretary of the Navy Stephen R. Mallory, offering his services as a naval officer. Georgia-born Bulloch had been a sailor since age 16, when he joined the U. S. Navy as a midshipman. Since 1853, he had been skipper of a commercial mail steamer plying the waters between New York and New Orleans. But Secretary Mallory was less interested in Bulloch's seamanship than in his business sense, knowledge of naval architecture, and discretion. He sent Bulloch to England to buy or commission to be built six commerce raiders, arm them, and recruit the crews to man them.

During the opening months of the Civil War, visitors to the industrial and shipbuilding city of Liverpool reported seeing as many Confederate flags as British Union Jacks flying. Despite this show of popular support, Britain was officially neutral. Bulloch, therefore, hired a prominent attorney to find a loophole in Britain's Foreign Enlistments Act, which, among other provisions, prohibited the arming of ships to be used by foreign combatants. The lawyer declared that the act did not forbid the building of *unarmed* ships in Great Britain that might be *armed* elsewhere. Having found his loophole, Bulloch crawled through it and negotiated for the construction of vessels in England to be fitted elsewhere with guns.

This was the beginning of an international cat-and-mouse game played out in England and other parts of Europe between Bulloch and U.S. diplomats.

But warships weren't the only armaments produced in England for export to the Confederacy. For example, Bulloch purchased the *Fingal*, a blockade runner, which he loaded with "1,000 short rifles, with cutlass bayonets, and 1,000 rounds of ammunition per rifle; 500 revolvers, with suitable ammunition; two $4\frac{1}{2}$-inch muzzle-loading rifled guns, with traversing carriages, all necessary gear, and 200 made-up cartridges, shot and shell, per gun; two breech-loading $2\frac{1}{2}$-inch steel-rifled guns for boats or field service, with 200 rounds of ammunition per gun; 400 barrels of coarse cannon powder, and a large quantity of made-up clothing for seamen." In addition, as many as 14,000 Enfield rifles might have been onboard.

This was typical, and while United States officials worked through diplomatic channels to stem the flow of munitions, Union secret agents worked behind-the-scenes to intercept and purchase the supplies out from under the Confederates. Sometimes the Union agents were successful, and sometimes they were not. The most famous Southern warship built in England and successfully delivered to the Confederate Navy was the CSS *Alabama*, which left Liverpool on July 29, 1862, and embarked on a most destructive career (covered in Chapter 20) against Union shipping.

Old Kentucky Home

While McClellan was entrenching on Virginia's James River after the failure of his Peninsula Campaign, and after Ulysses S. Grant had won his victories over the rebel forts on the Mississippi, Confederate major general Edmund Kirby Smith left Knoxville, Tennessee, to invade central Kentucky on August 14, 1862. Two weeks later, Confederate general Braxton Bragg left Chattanooga to join Kirby Smith in Kentucky. On August 30, Union general Don Carlos Buell ordered the pursuit of these Confederate invaders.

Gen. Braxton Bragg, CSA, boldly invaded Kentucky, but was chased out of the state by Gen. Don Carlos Buell.

(Author's collection)

Friendly Advice

The little town of Munfordville, Kentucky, was hotly contested during September 14–17, 1862. A premature Confederate assault on the town was repulsed with heavy losses on the 14th. Then, as the Federals reinforced the town, Bragg mounted a much larger attack and, by the 16th, had surrounded the Union garrison there. Confederate general Simon Bolivar Buckner formally demanded surrender.

Now, the 4,133 men of the Union garrison were led by a Col. J.T. Wilder, an industrialist from Indiana, who had no military experience whatsoever. He knew surrender didn't appeal to him, but he didn't know what else to do. So he responded to Buckner's demand by visiting the Confederate general's headquarters under a flag of truce. Explaining that he was ignorant of military matters, he told Buckner that he understood him to be an officer and a gentleman, who would not deceive him. He then asked *Buckner* what he should do.

The Confederate commander, taken aback, politely declined to advise his enemy on how to respond to the surrender demand. Wilder replied that he understood, but then asked if he might be permitted to inspect Buckner's forces so that he could count the cannon. To this Buckner consented, and, after his tour, Wilder turned to the general: "I believe I'll surrender."

Curtain Down: Iuka, Corinth, Perryville

The fall of Munfordville temporarily cut Buell's communications with Louisville, but Bragg did not press this advantage and sought instead to avoid further battle until he united with Kirby Smith. Meaning to occupy Kentucky, he wanted to recruit troops in this border state and to establish supply depots before he engaged in large-scale combat.

In the meantime, however, on September 19, Union general William S. Rosecrans, under Grant, had defeated some 17,000 Confederate troops commanded by Gen. Sterling Price at Iuka, Mississippi. Price withdrew southward and Confederate general Earl Van Dorn moved to join him. Believing, however, that Corinth, Mississippi, was lightly defended by a handful of Union troops, Van Dorn attacked the town on October 3. To Van Dorn's surprise, the town was actually held by 23,000 of Rosecrans's troops (versus Van Dorn's 22,000), and Grant quickly reinforced it. Fighting was heaviest on October 4, resulting in a bloody Confederate repulse and Van Dorn's withdrawal to Holly Springs.

Gen. William S. Rosecrans defeated Confederate forces under Gen. Sterling Price at Iuka, Mississippi.

(Harper's Pictorial History of the Civil War, *1866*)

The defeat of Van Dorn cut off Bragg in Kentucky from any hope of reinforcement, and Buell maneuvered the now vulnerable Bragg into battle at Perryville, Kentucky, on October 8.

With Buell's combined forces amounting to 36,940 men, and Bragg having only about 16,000 available at Perryville, a glorious Union victory should have followed.

A victory it was, but hardly glorious. Buell was unable to bring all of his forces to bear, and although he did push Bragg and Kirby Smith out of Kentucky and into eastern Tennessee, he failed to pursue the retreating Confederates. The opportunity for a truly decisive Union victory was again lost, and Buell was replaced as commander of the Department of the Ohio by Rosecrans.

Count Off!

Union losses at Corinth were 2,520 killed, wounded, and missing; Confederate losses were 2,470 killed and wounded, with an additional 1,763 missing in action.

Assault at Vicksburg

Yet again the Union found itself victorious, but indecisively so. Following Grant's initial victories against the rebel forts on the Mississippi River, Gen. Henry Wager "Old Brains" Halleck, in overall charge of operations in this theater of the war, had made the mistake of dispersing his forces in order to occupy enemy territory. The effect of this was to forfeit the initiative to the Confederates and to assume a defensive posture. Had Halleck instead consolidated his forces—about 100,000 strong—he could have mounted a powerful offensive deep into Southern territory. Doubtless, the war would have been shortened.

As it was, by the middle of October, the Union had at least beaten back the Confederate invasion of Kentucky, and Grant could turn his attention once again to the drive down the Mississippi. He understood that complete control of the river—and with it, the final isolation of the western from the eastern Confederate states—required the capture of Vicksburg. As his superior officer Halleck declared, "In my opinion, the opening of the Mississippi River will be to us more advantage than the capture of forty Richmonds."

But the Confederacy was also well aware of the strategic importance of Vicksburg. It was a fortress town, heavily defended by artillery, occupying a high bluff overlooking the river, which made it virtually impregnable. With guns positioned to sweep the river, direct naval assault was impossible. Grant proposed an all-out combined water and land assault.

Holly Springs and Chickasaw Bluffs

In December, Grant established an advance base at Holly Springs, Mississippi, preparatory to a planned movement of some 40,000 troops down the Mississippi Central Railroad to link up with 32,000 riverborne troops led by William Tecumseh Sherman. Confederate cavalry under General Van Dorn raided Holly Springs on

December 20, catching Col. R.C. Murphy's 8th Wisconsin Regiment asleep in their tents. After destroying $1,500,000 worth of supplies at Holly Springs, Van Dorn raided one Union outpost after another. In the meantime, the remarkable Confederate general Nathan Bedford Forrest led his cavalry against the railroad, destroying 60 miles of it.

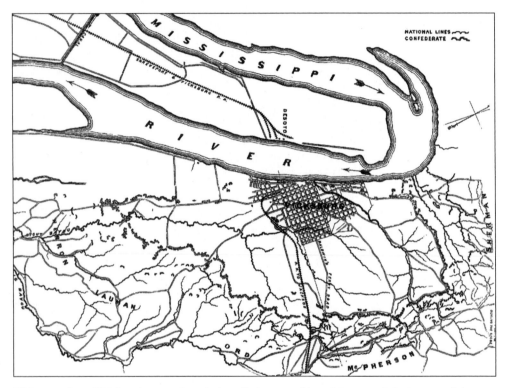

This map shows Vicksburg's strategic and virtually impregnable position on a hairpin turn of the Mississippi.

(Harper's Pictorial History of the Civil War, *1866*)

The actions of Van Dorn and Forrest stopped Grant's advance, and Sherman, without Grant's support at Chickasaw Bluffs (just a few miles north of Vicksburg), failed as well. Sherman summed up the action of December 27–29, 1862, succinctly: "I reached Vicksburg at the time appointed, landed, assaulted, and failed."

Try, Try Again

Grant next took a leaf from John Pope's book and decided to dig a canal to avoid the guns of Vicksburg, as Pope had done to get behind the guns of Island Number 10 (see Chapter 7). But heavy rains and high water during February 1863 prompted Grant to drop the project in March. Shortly after this, Grant tried a more ambitious canal at Duckport, and did manage to get a small steamer through the canal-connected bayous, but it soon became clear that the canal approach was impractical on any meaningful scale.

African American laborers did most of the digging of the canals Grant planned to use to get around the guns at Vicksburg.

(Harper's Pictorial History of the Civil War, *1866*)

Grant next ordered Gen. James B. McPherson to open up a 400-mile route through Louisiana swamps, lakes, and bayous to a point on the Mississippi below Vicksburg. This incredibly laborious process was successfully underway when, in March, it was abandoned in favor of a more roundabout water route through the so-called Yazoo Pass. The Confederates built a fort to block the pass 90 miles north of Vicksburg, and, on March 11, the Yazoo Pass expedition was also abandoned.

Sites and Sights

Vicksburg National Military Park is one of the largest such parks in the nation. It includes an extensive visitor center, as well as a section of reconstructed earthworks and an artillery exhibit. In addition to the park, the town of Vicksburg has many historical buildings to visit. Contact the park at 1-601-636-0583.

Yet another water route, through Steele's Bayou, was attempted. Adm. David Porter led 11 Union vessels through the difficult waterways, with Sherman's infantry following. On March 19, at Rolling Fork, Mississippi, due north of Vicksburg, Confederate forces stopped Porter's boats and might have destroyed the fleet had Sherman not arrived in the proverbial nick of time. Although the Steele's Bayou expedition was yet another failure, Sherman's rescue was brilliant and daring, his entire unit marching through the swampland at night, their path lighted only by candles inserted in their rifle barrels.

Victory, Slow and Bold

Grant probably had little hope that the preliminary expeditions against Vicksburg would succeed, but he understood the importance of keeping the offensive alive and keeping the enemy guessing. However, he kept his own superiors guessing as well. Grant had been ordered to move south once he had crossed the Mississippi to link up with forces under Gen. Nathaniel Banks for a joint assault on Port Hudson, Louisiana. Learning that Banks was bogged down in his fruitless Red River campaign, Grant boldly decided instead to move immediately against Jackson, Mississippi, where, he knew, Confederate reinforcements were being assembled.

Count Off!

Fighting at Champion's Hill was the most severe of the Vicksburg campaign. Of 29,373 Union troops engaged, 410 were killed, 1,844 wounded, and 187 went missing. Of some 20,000 Confederates, 381 died, about 1,800 were wounded, and 1,670 went missing.

On May 14, 1863, Grant used corps under McPherson and Sherman to take Jackson. This paved the way for the bloody Battle of Champion's Hill on May 16, which fell to the Union after heavy losses on both sides.

Total War

The hard-won victories at Jackson and Champion's Hill put Grant in position for an attack on Vicksburg. He ordered a frontal assault on the city on May 19, but was repulsed. He tried again on the 22nd, and was again repulsed with some 3,200 casualties.

Grant settled in for a prolonged siege. From late May through the beginning of July, 200 heavy Union artillery pieces and siege mortars continuously pounded Vicksburg.

Vicksburg was more than a military fortress, the South's "Gibraltar of the West." It was also a city populated by men, women, and children. Grant, like many of his professional military contemporaries, was probably familiar with the magnum opus of the world's most famous military theorist, Karl von Clausewitz (1780–1831). *On War*, published shortly after Clausewitz's death, presented (among many other things) the concept of "total war," combat waged against the civilian population as well as military targets, with the object of reducing a people's will to fight. The siege of Vicksburg, like Sherman's infamous "March to the Sea" later in the war (see Chapter 21), and like the hardships faced by the citizens of Richmond and other places in the South, was an exercise in total war.

A Union artillery position in the long siege of Vicksburg.

(Harper's Pictorial History of the Civil War, *1866*)

Voices

 An unknown lady, a Northern woman who lived in Vicksburg, kept a diary of life during the siege:

> May 28— ... We are utterly cut off from the world, surrounded by a circle of fire. Would it be wise like the scorpion to sting ourselves to death? The fiery shower of shells goes on day and night .... People do nothing but eat what they can get, sleep when they can, and dodge the shells .... I watched the soldiers cooking on the green opposite. The half-spent balls ... were flying so thick that they were obliged to dodge at every turn. At all the caves I could see ... people ... sitting, eating their poor suppers at the cave doors, ready to plunge in again. As the first shell again flew they dived, and not a human being was visible. The sharp crackle of the musketry-firing was a strong contrast to the scream of the bombs. I think all the dogs and rats must be killed or starved: we don't see any more pitiful animals prowling around ....

The citizens of Vicksburg responded to the siege heroically. They dug caves into the yellow-clay hillsides, and then furnished them with finery dragged out of their ruined houses. Weeks crawled by under the pounding shells. The cave dwellers fought lice, rats, disease, boredom, and despair, eating their emaciated mules, horses, and dogs when all the food ran out.

Surrender came on July 4, 1863, a day after the Union's victory at Gettysburg (see Chapter 15). With Gettysburg, Vicksburg was the most important victory of the war. The Mississippi River was now in Union hands, and the backbone of the Confederacy was broken.

For the next 81 years, the citizens of Vicksburg would refuse to celebrate Independence Day.

The Least You Need to Know

- Southern civilians were plagued by food and other shortages and by runaway inflation.

- Draft dodging and desertion were major problems in the Confederate army. At times, deserters outnumbered those on active duty.

- The Civil War was covered by a legion of journalists, artist-correspondents, and photographers.

- Although Gen. Don Carlos Buell managed to turn back the Confederate invasion of Kentucky, his failure to pursue the army of Braxton Bragg was yet another missed opportunity for a decisive Union victory.

- Vicksburg, the most arduous campaign of the war, ended on July 4, 1863, after the Confederacy's "Gibraltar of the West" surrendered, thereby yielding the strategically vital Mississippi River to Union control.

Chapter 14

Thunderstorm from a Cloudless Sky

In This Chapter

- Hooker rebuilds the Army of the Potomac
- Lee defeats Hooker at Chancellorsville
- "Stonewall" Jackson dies
- Lee advances to invade Pennsylvania
- Meade replaces Hooker as commander of the Army of the Potomac

In plans and on paper, the position of the North always looked so good, whereas that of the South appeared just about hopeless. The North had so many more men, so much more money, so many more factories, and many, many more miles of railroad. The South, in contrast, was starving; its soldiers dressed in rags, often going without so much as shoes. The Emancipation Proclamation had injected new moral vigor into the war and had won, for the North, as much popular approval as it could expect from Europe.

Yet plenty of Northerners either didn't care about emancipation or downright resented it. The North, for all its advantages, was experiencing war weariness, frustration, and despair at the seemingly endless "effusion of blood" (to use a phrase often repeated at the time). Finally, the South was fighting to defend its home against a very real invading army; the North had to be convinced to fight for concepts, albeit powerful ones: first "union," then "emancipation." The will to fight could not be sustained on hopes and wishes alone. Lincoln needed results. He desperately needed Hooker to win.

This chapter shows how Hooker tried, and how he failed.

"May God Have Mercy on General Lee ..."

Under Gen. Joseph Hooker, the Army of the Potomac was restored in spirit and strength. Hooker had reorganized the army, trained it, and grown it to 130,000 men. With this magnificent instrument, Hooker decided to strike Robert E. Lee's Army of Northern Virginia at Fredericksburg—scene of Burnside's defeat—and at Chancellorsville. Lee commanded 60,000 men, less than half the number available to Hooker.

"May God have mercy on General Lee," Hooker said, "for I will have none."

Hooker's Plan

Hooker enjoyed the numerical advantage McClellan had always craved, but mistakenly believed he lacked. Hooker also enjoyed a key advantage over his immediate predecessor, Ambrose Burnside: He was a better strategist and tactician, and he was determined to learn from Burnside's chief mistake.

Unlike the ill-fated Burnside, Hooker would not hurl his massive army head-on against the formidable Fredericksburg defenses. Instead, he would deploy about one third of his forces under Gen. John Sedgwick, a capable corps commander, to make a diversionary attack across the Rappahannock above Lee's Fredericksburg entrenchments, while he personally led another third of the army in a long swing up the Rappahannock, coming around to attack Lee on his vulnerable left flank and rear. Except for about 10,000 cavalry troopers under Gen. George Stoneman, who would disrupt Lee's lines of communication to Richmond, the remainder of the Army of the Potomac would be prudently held in reserve at Chancellorsville, ready for use to reinforce either Sedgwick's or Hooker's wings, as needed.

It was an excellent plan, and it seemed certain to send Lee falling back to Richmond in defeat.

Union soldiers lay a pontoon bridge across the Rappahannock in preparation for General Sedgwick's advance during the Chancellorsville campaign.

(Harper's Pictorial History of the Civil War, *1866*)

Outgeneraled on a Cracker Barrel

The first part of the grand plan unfolded beautifully. By April 30, 1863, Hooker had established about 70,000 men in Chancellorsville and had set up headquarters in a plantation home outside of town called Chancellor House. Hooker then dispatched his cavalry to cut the Richmond, Fredericksburg, and Potomac Railroad.

The trouble with Hooker's plan is that Robert E. Lee immediately grasped it and understood it as well as Hooker did. Maybe even better.

Lee did not direct his attention to Hooker's cavalry. Instead, he used his own, under Jeb Stuart, to control the roads in and out of Chancellorsville. Unable to send patrols out, Hooker was effectively blinded. He couldn't tell where the Confederates were. Worried and confused, he deployed his men defensively in hastily erected *breastworks* close to Chancellorsville, instead of advancing to his chosen battlefield about 12 miles east of town.

Words of War

Breastworks are temporary, improvised defensive barriers, made of earth, stone, wood—whatever materials are available—usually affording protection that is breast high.

In the meantime, having concluded from Stuart's reconnaissance that Hooker intended to attack him from the flank and rear through a thicket known as "the Wilderness," Lee sent 10,000 men under Jubal Early to delay the Union troops at Fredericksburg, while he led the remainder of his army against Hooker at Chancellorsville.

Words of War

Civil War **crackers** were not the saltines of today, but were synonymous with hardtack, an extremely hard biscuit made with flour and water. Crackers were stored in crates or barrels—in either case called **cracker barrels**.

Then General Lee hit on an even bolder and riskier plan. As he had done against Pope at the Second Battle of Bull Run (see Chapter 10), Lee flouted accepted military doctrine by dividing his army in the presence of the enemy. On the night of May 1, he found a scout who could lead Stonewall Jackson's corps through the confusion of the Wilderness to strike at Hooker's exposed flank. Around midnight, Lee invited Jackson to pull up an empty cracker barrel, sit down, and listen to his plan.

A map of the Chancellorsville area.

(Harper's Pictorial History of the Civil War, *1866*)

Lee proposed to divide his army yet again, giving 26,000 men to Jackson for the surprise attack against Hooker's flank, and retaining 17,000 to hold attacks against Hooker's front. Early's portion would continue to hold the Union troops at Fredericksburg.

Lee's Masterpiece

Even with Hooker in a state of worried confusion, Jackson's maneuver was very dangerous. In broad daylight, he had to move 26,000 men across the Federal front, no more than two-and-a-half miles away. Indeed, even with Jeb Stuart in control of the roads, pickets with the Union XI Corps under Gen. O.O. Howard saw Jackson's movement. Nevertheless, they were unable to persuade Howard or Hooker that this represented any great danger.

Just two hours before dusk on May 2, Jackson attacked Howard, in command of Hooker's right flank. Most Federals were relaxing, playing cards, and talking, their rifles stacked. One Union soldier recalled that the surprise attack came "like a clap of thunderstorm from a cloudless sky."

The results were devastating. One entire Federal corps panicked and was routed, and then Hooker's entire army was knocked out of its prepared positions.

This was just the beginning of a battle so brilliantly planned that military historians have dubbed it "Lee's Masterpiece." Fighting went on through May 4, by which time Hooker, in full retreat, had withdrawn all of his troops north of the Rappahannock.

"... And Rest Under the Shade of the Trees"

The cost to Hooker was staggering. He had faced an army less than half the size of his—a ragtag army at that: tired, ill-fed, and poorly equipped. Against this force, he lost 17,000 men, as well as, yet again, the chance for a decisive Union victory. But Robert E. Lee also paid a terrible price. He lost 13,000 men—almost one quarter of his strength—at Chancellorsville. And, perhaps even worse, he lost Thomas J. "Stonewall" Jackson.

> **War News**
>
> "Lee's Masterpiece" ranks with the great campaigns of such ancient commanders as Alexander and Caesar, as well as those of Napoleon, as one of the most intensively studied of all history's momentous battles.

Count Off!

The Union's 17,000 casualties at Chancellorsville represented 17 percent of the numbers engaged. Lee's 13,000 casualties amounted to a quarter of his forces.

Jackson's assault on Hooker's right flank had begun too late in the day for him to finish it satisfactorily before nightfall. On the night of May 2, Jackson and his staff were in the Wilderness, scouting for a possible night assault. Confusion reigned in that dark thicket, and as Jackson returned to the Confederate lines, one of his own pickets opened fire on him. The general was wounded in the right hand, left wrist and hand, and left arm. By themselves, none of the wounds were mortal. But this was pre-antisepsis, pre-antibiotic 1863. Infection quickly followed, and then pneumonia set in. Stonewall Jackson died on May 10.

Voices

Stonewall Jackson's physician, Dr. Hunter McGuire, recalled the great commander's death:

> His mind ... began to ... wander, and he frequently talked as if in command upon the field ...
>
> About half-past one he was told that he had but two hours to live, and he answered ... feebly but firmly, "Very good; it is all right."
>
> A few moments before he died he cried out in his delirium, "Order A.P. Hill to prepare for action! Pass the infantry to the front rapidly. Tell Major Hawks—" then stopped, leaving the sentence unfinished.
>
> Presently a smile ... spread itself over his pale face, and he said quietly, and with an expression as if of relief, "Let us cross over the river and rest under the shade of the trees."

"What Will the Country Say?"

Jefferson Davis told his countrymen on May 10, 1863, "Our loss was much less killed and wounded than that of the enemy, but of the number was one, a host in himself, Lieutenant General Jackson ... war has seldom shown his equal."

Robert E. Lee had once, in a letter, described Jackson as a man "of contrasts so complete that he appears one day a Presbyterian deacon who delights in theological discussion and, the next, a reincarnated Joshua. He lives by the New Testament and fights by the Old." Now Lee said simply, "I have lost my right arm."

Abraham Lincoln had his own words in the aftermath of Hooker's shocking and total defeat at Chancellorsville: "My God! My God! What will the country say? What will the country say?"

And Hooker, having failed in his confusion to use even half of his forces at Chancellorsville—and having used the rest (as one officer described it) like a "disjointed army"—analyzed his failure straightforwardly: "Well, to tell the truth, I just lost confidence in Joe Hooker."

Lee's Bold Offensive

What the country said—what *Lincoln's* country said—was contained in a phrase often repeated in Union newspapers: "Abraham Lincoln, give us a man!"

Jefferson Davis's nation said that Robert E. Lee had won a great victory—never mind the loss of Jackson and a quarter of the forces engaged. Lee heard and heeded the acclaim. He saw that Chancellorsville had raised the spirits of the South, even as they continued to lose food, money, and men. He saw, too, that Chancellorsville had appalled and disheartened the well-fed, populous North. It was, he decided, now or never. He had gambled at Second Bull Run and at Chancellorsville by doing what the textbooks said one must never do, and he had won. Now he embarked on a gamble with even bigger stakes. He would again invade the North.

> ### Sites and Sights
>
> The Chancellorsville Battlefield Unit of the Fredericksburg and Spotsylvania Memorial National Military Park includes a Visitor Center located just north of State Route 3 on Bullock Road. Points of interest are well marked throughout the park.

Lee Heads Northward

Lee had no illusions about "conquering" the Union states. The Confederacy certainly lacked the resources to do that. But if he could stage a swift, massive, and punishing raid well into Northern territory, perhaps he could demolish the Union's will to continue the fight and thereby force a favorably negotiated peace. True, fighting a defensive war held many tactical advantages for the Confederacy, but it also had a major strategic liability. If—*if*—any hope of English or French intervention in this American civil war lingered, it could be revived only by aggressive *offensive* action. No European power would ally itself with a would-be nation fighting a defensive war. Moreover, Lee understood all too clearly that generals do not win wars defensively. Sooner or later, successful offensive action is required.

But if Lee's gamble failed?

At worst, the Confederacy would lose its principal army and, with it, the war. Yet that could also happen without an invasion of the North. Southerners could *hope* the

North would quit, but that was unlikely. Lincoln would find himself yet another general, who would, yet again, refit the battered Army of the Potomac, and, in the space of a month or two, launch another attack into Virginia. Maybe that one would succeed. But, even if it failed as the others had, its failure would surely come at great cost to the Confederacy. Lee could not afford another *Pyrrhic victory*, beating the Union while losing—proportionately—more men than the enemy.

Words of War

A **Pyrrhic victory** is one that comes at a self-defeating cost. The word derives from Pyrrhus (319–272 B.C.E.), king of Epirus, who defeated a Roman army at the Battle of Heraclea (280 B.C.E.), but lost so many men in the triumph that he remarked, "One more such victory and I shall be lost."

One more factor was pushing Lee to an invasion of Pennsylvania. The general's grasp of strategy extended far beyond the borders of his home state. He recognized the significance of what Grant was accomplishing along the Mississippi. It was now almost June, and Lee understood that Vicksburg, last of the Confederate citadels on the great river, would, in the fullness of time, fall (see Chapter 13). Lee knew that, soon after it fell, many of those western-based Federal troops would be moved east.

So Lee moved north, beginning on June 3, and with that move, the entire pattern of the war shifted.

The Confederate commander divided his army into three corps. Leading the movement was a corps commanded by James Longstreet, who, of Lee's three lieutenants, was the only one to raise objections to the invasion. He thought it far better to launch offensives within Virginia, while reinforcing Bragg in the menaced area of Chattanooga, Tennessee, and sending troops west in an effort to turn the tables on Grant. But he swallowed his doubts and marched in obedience to Lee's command, pausing with his corps at Culpeper Court House, Virginia, while another corps, under Richard S. Ewell (a sour-tempered man nicknamed "Old Baldy"), advanced against piecemeal Union detachments still in the lower Shenandoah Valley. The third corps, commanded by A.P. Hill, remained at Fredericksburg, eye to eye with the Yankees there.

Hooker had a plan for responding to these movements. Stopping his ears to the clamor for his removal as commander of the Army of the Potomac (he had friends in high places, particularly Secretary of the Treasury Salmon P. Chase, willing to take his side), Hooker proposed to ignore Lee's move and advance against Richmond. He reasoned that this would soon bring Lee marching back southward.

But the administration that had pleaded with McClellan to march to Richmond now refused to approve Hooker's proposed offensive against the rebel capital. Badly shaken by his performance at Chancellorsville, Lincoln and his advisors ordered Hooker to pursue a defensive course only and follow Lee.

Brandy Station

On June 5, obediently and doggedly following Lee, Hooker ordered Gen. John Sedgwick to make a reconnaissance to determine if the Confederates had left Fredericksburg. The result was a skirmish at Franklin's Crossing, Virginia, after which Hooker ordered a full-scale cavalry reconnaissance under Alfred Pleasonton to ascertain the extent and significance of Lee's movements.

The result, on June 9, was the Battle of Brandy Station. Forces under the overall command of Pleasonton surprised the Confederate cavalry under Jeb Stuart, whose own reconnaissance failed to alert him to the Union cavalry's presence. It was the first real cavalry engagement of the Civil War—the largest ever fought in North America, and doubtless an extraordinary spectacle. It was reported that the First New Jersey Cavalry alone made six full regimental charges—the kind of action, full of gallantry and glory, that quickens the hearts of soldiers and civilians alike, but that rarely occurred in a war mostly about muddy foot soldiers ingloriously shooting other muddy foot soldiers.

In terms of losses, and because Confederate general Jeb Stuart remained in possession of the field after the battle, Brandy Station must be counted a Union defeat. Yet, in an important sense, it was a Union victory. For the first time in the war, the Federal cavalry, neglected by McClellan but brushed up and bolstered by Hooker, more than stood its own against Stuart, who was by now legendary and believed unbeatable. Although he had driven the Federals from the field, Stuart had been badly surprised and hadn't prevented them from accomplishing their reconnaissance. Hooker now knew that Lee was leaving Fredericksburg and was heading north. For the first time in his career, Stuart came under stinging criticism from his military superiors and, worse, from the Southern press. As for the Union cavalry, it had at last come of age, finding a new confidence in itself.

Count Off!

Some 20,000 horsemen were engaged at Brandy Station, charging and countercharging for a full 12 hours of battle. Union casualties numbered 936 killed, wounded, and captured; Confederate casualties were 523.

Disaster at Winchester

But Brandy Station also alerted Lee to the fact that Hooker knew of his movements. With his usual strategic acuity, Lee concluded that Hooker might now turn to advance on Richmond—the very plan Hooker had, in fact, proposed, but which had been overruled. On June 10, Lee dispatched Ewell to attack the remaining Union garrisons in the Shenandoah Valley, which would (Lee hoped) force Lincoln to recall the Army of the Potomac for the defense of the capital.

Ewell's forces clashed with Union troops at Berryville (June 13) and Martinsburg (June 14). Most of the Union soldiers managed to evade capture in these two places, but Ewell's attack on Winchester (June 13–15) was a Union disaster. The Confederates bottled up the Union garrison in the forts just west of the town— with the result that 4,443 soldiers became casualties, of whom 3,538 were taken prisoner. Ewell's losses were a mere 269.

Words of War

If cavalry could be used for **reconnaissance**, an exploration to ascertain military information, it could also be used in **counterreconnaissance**, an effort to foil the enemy's attempt to carry out a reconnaissance mission.

Crossing the Potomac

The first units of the Army of Northern Virginia crossed the Potomac into Maryland on June 15. Stuart's cavalry created a *counterreconnaissance* screen to prevent Pleasanton's Union cavalry from discovering Lee's objective—Washington or Pennsylvania. This resulted in a series of cavalry duels at Aldie, Virginia (June 17); Middleburg, Virginia (June 19); and Upperville, Virginia (June 21).

Stuart's Raid

Following these engagements, Stuart, still smarting from his partial humiliation at Brandy Station, hit on a way to redeem himself. While the main body of Lee's army joined the advance detachments in crossing the Potomac, wheeling toward the east, Stuart was to serve as Lee's "eyes," moving along the army's right flank and front to report on the whereabouts of Hooker's forces. Stuart had a choice of taking a short, direct route across the Potomac or a longer route clear around Hooker's rear and flank. He secured Lee's permission to take the longer way around, which, he argued, would give him an opportunity to raid Hooker's supply depots and lines. One cannot help suspecting, however, that Stuart, as vainglorious as he was skilled, wanted yet a third opportunity to make a dashing and spectacular ride around the Union army.

Stuart's "Gettysburg Raid" did allow the cavalryman to cut across and disrupt Hooker's supply lines, and he was also able to capture 125 U.S. Army wagons at Rockville, Maryland, as well as 400 prisoners in skirmishes at Fairfax Courthouse, Virginia (June 27); Westminster, Maryland (June 29); Hanover, Pennsylvania (June 30); and Carlisle, Pennsylvania (July 1). But the Union army proved to be much more spread out and active than had been expected. The ride around the army took much longer than Stuart had anticipated, and, for 10 critical days, he was out of touch with Lee. Because Stuart's cavalry was Lee's "eyes," this meant that Lee advanced into Pennsylvania blind.

Surprise!

Robert E. Lee rarely allowed himself to be surprised, but without reports from Stuart, he could only assume that Hooker had not yet followed him across the Potomac. Lee, therefore, dispersed his forces in a long line, with the rear at Chambersburg, Pennsylvania, and the front of the army at York, some 50 miles to the east.

The fact was that Hooker *had* crossed the Potomac during June 25–26, and not until June 28 did Lee learn that the entire Army of the Potomac was concentrated around Frederick, Maryland, directly south of the 50-mile-long and highly vulnerable flank of the Army of Northern Virginia.

A Used Up Man

Lee learned another thing, too. The Army of the Potomac was no longer under the command of Joseph Hooker. Despite opposition from Chase and others, Lincoln relieved him with Maj. Gen. George Gordon Meade. Certainly, Meade was a competent general, "brave and conscientious," Grant recalled in his memoirs, and commanding "the respect of all who knew him." But, Grant continued, he "was unfortunately of a temper that would get beyond his control …. This made it unpleasant … for those around him to approach him even with information."

An irascible temperament is one thing when it is accompanied by genius. But Meade was no genius. He was not a bad choice as commander of the Army of the Potomac, but a better general was available. John Fulton Reynolds, courageous, self-reliant, and resourceful, was both more charismatic and more temperamentally suited to independent command than Meade. If President Lincoln wanted a hero to lead the Army of the Potomac ("Abraham Lincoln, give us a man!"), surely John Reynolds was it.

George Meade, however, possessed one qualification that Reynolds lacked. He had been born in Cadiz, Spain, the son of an American naval agent. Although his parents were Americans, his foreign birth prevented his ever running for president. Military heroes win elections, and Lincoln already had George B. McClellan breathing down his neck as a prospective rival in the upcoming 1864 presidential contest. If the Army of the Potomac was to produce a hero, Lincoln must have thought, let him be an unelectable one.

Gen. George Gordon Meade (1815–1872) was a solid, if uninspired, military man. Although the tough, popular Gen. John Reynolds was more qualified to command the Army of the Potomac, Meade, foreign-born and therefore ineligible to become president, made for a politically harmless military hero.

(Harper's Pictorial History of the Civil War, *1866*)

As for "Fighting Joe" Hooker, he would yet see much action and perform capably, but in subordinate roles. Nevertheless, within a year of Hooker's failure at Chancellorsville, Theodore Lyman, an aide to Meade, described him as "red-faced … with a lack-luster eye and an uncertainty of gait and carriage that suggested a used up man."

The Least You Need to Know

♦ General Hooker revitalized and rebuilt the Army of the Potomac, and formulated an excellent plan of battle against Lee; nevertheless, Lee outgeneraled Hooker and defeated him at Chancellorsville.

♦ Chancellorsville was a shocking defeat for the Union, but it was also a very costly (albeit tactically brilliant) victory for Robert E. Lee.

♦ Lee's decision to invade Pennsylvania was a high-stakes gamble ventured in the hope that it would break the North's will to continue the war.

Part 4

That the Nation Might Live

This section begins with the Battle of Gettysburg, July 1–3, 1863—one of the most fiercely contested battles in the history of warfare. Along with the fall of Vicksburg, Gettysburg spelled the beginning of the end for the Confederacy. However, victory did not bring uniform harmony to the North, which was torn by draft riots and dissension from a Southern-sympathizing faction called the Copperheads.

Chapter **15**

Gettysburg

In This Chapter

- ◆ Lee hopes to win the war at Gettysburg
- ◆ How Jeb Stuart failed Lee
- ◆ General Buford seizes the high ground for the Union
- ◆ "A great battlefield"
- ◆ The Gettysburg Address

One of the host of clichés people use either to comfort or prod themselves is the well-worn line about *a* battle and *the* war. A salesman who fails to make a sale will say, "I've lost a battle, but not the war." Or a stern sales director will caution that same salesman when he does succeed: "Look, just because you've won a battle doesn't mean you've won the war."

Yet history is full of single battles that have turned the tide of entire wars. The very first battle history records, at Megiddo in Palestine, brought Egypt to the height of its power in 1469 B.C.E. The Battle of Hastings in 1066 ended Saxon rule in England and established the Normans there. The Battle of Yorktown in 1781 heralded America's victory in the Revolution. The Battle of Waterloo, 1815, ended forever Napoleon's dream of dominating Europe. And the Battle of Gettysburg—July 1–3, 1863—was the certain beginning of the certain end of the Confederate States of America. This chapter tells the story of the horrific battle on which the Civil War turned.

Legend of the Shoes

The Battle of Gettysburg begins with a legend. Picture a barefoot army in need of shoes. By 1863, Confederate soldiers were chronically in need of everything: food, clothing, and—always—shoes. It is said that, on June 30, 1863, shoeless Confederates of Gen. A.P. Hill's division were foraging in the Pennsylvania town of Gettysburg in search of footgear.

Such a homely task certainly appeals to the imagination as the reason for a momentous battle, just as Gettysburg itself is appealing as the site of that battle. Seat of a Lutheran Theological Seminary and Pennsylvania College (now Gettysburg College), just north of the Maryland state line, home to 3,500, Gettysburg was a genteel, pastoral village, the kind of tranquil place popular printmakers Currier and Ives were already offering as a nostalgic image of American peace and plenty.

But the truth is, barefoot or shod, Hill's men were primarily on a mission of reconnaissance, not shoe hunting, a mission made necessary by the absence of cavalry intelligence; for Jeb Stuart, still riding around the Union army, was long out of touch with Lee (see Chapter 14). When the detachment reported that Gettysburg was occupied by Union cavalry, Gen. Henry Heth (pronounced *Heath*) secured Hill's permission to take a brigade into town to clear it out.

The cavalrymen in Gettysburg were a division under Brig. Gen. John Buford—the advance guard of the main body of the Army of the Potomac. Yet Robert E. Lee, out of touch with the errant Stuart, was only just now learning how close the Army of the Potomac was. Some weeks earlier, Maj. Gen. James Longstreet had hired a spy, a bearded Mississippian with pale hazel eyes, an actor, it was said, known to Longstreet—and to history—only as Harrison. He now revealed to Lee that the Army of the Potomac was approaching, quickly, and that George Gordon Meade was now at its head. Lee hesitated momentarily, bewildered that he had not heard of this from Stuart, then decided that he must concentrate his army here, at Gettysburg.

Although named James, General Longstreet was known affectionately as "Pete" and, even more indulgently, as "Gloomy Old Pete." Lee called him "My Old War Horse." While no one ever questioned his courage—a commodity he had in abundance—Longstreet habitually took the pessimist's, or perhaps the realist's, view. He had tried to talk Lee out of invading Pennsylvania to begin with, and now he advised against tangling with the Army of the Potomac at Gettysburg.

The Union's Brig. Gen. John Buford led a cavalry division into Gettysburg in advance of Meade's army. Thanks to him, Confederate forces were deprived of the high ground surrounding the town, and thus Gettysburg was not for the Union a repeat of the Fredericksburg massacre.

(Harper's Pictorial History of the Civil War, *1866*)

It was true, Lee conceded, that Gettysburg was not strategically the ideal place for so important a battle, but he believed that he had been presented with the proverbial golden opportunity. Meade's army was spread out. If Lee could quickly concentrate at Gettysburg, he could attack and destroy it in detail. With the Army of the Potomac battered on its own soil, the Northern will to fight might well collapse. Almost certainly, defeat at Gettysburg would mean disgrace for the Lincoln administration, and perhaps the election of a Democrat in 1864, someone like George McClellan, who might be receptive to a negotiated peace. In any case, defeating the Union army here would open a road to Washington.

As if all this weren't sufficient reason for concentrating at Gettysburg, Lee realized that his army, like Meade's, was spread out. If he didn't seize the initiative and concentrate now, *Meade* would have the opportunity to defeat *Lee* in detail.

Of "Gods and Generals"

Both the North and the South would recognize Gettysburg as a momentous battle as soon as it had been fought, and certainly generations of historians have treated it as such. But it probably wasn't until the publication, in 1974, of a novel called *The Killer Angels*, by Michael Shaara, that anyone fully presented the human dimension of the historically momentous battle. For Shaara told the story from the points of view of some of the principal commanders involved, focusing most closely on Lee and Longstreet. The novel, deservedly, was a bestseller, and it was later made into a movie, *Gettysburg* (1993).

When it was fought, the Civil War united some families and tore apart many others. In the after-years, interest in the war has created uncanny bonds between one generation and the next—what Lincoln would have recognized as the "mystic chords of memory"—and in 1996, Michael Shaara's son, Jeff, published *Gods and Generals* (also released as a movie, in 2003). Described as a "prequel" to his father's book, the novel tells the story of the years and months leading up to Gettysburg—from the points of view of Lee and Stonewall Jackson of the Confederacy and Winfield Scott Hancock and Joshua Lawrence Chamberlain on the Union side.

Anyone interested in the Civil War, American history, or even in history itself as human drama would do well to read both *The Killer Angels* and *Gods and Generals*. Together, they reveal the full dimension of Gettysburg—and some of the war's other great battles— as the violent meeting place not just of arms and tactics, but of minds, hearts, loyalties, and imaginations. Lee was one of history's most brilliant tacticians and charismatic generals, yet, as Gettysburg revealed, beset by fatal leadership flaws. Jackson, a fierce warrior, was both guided and misguided by what he took as divine inspiration. Hancock was a straightforward military hero whom all, North and South, admired, yet he was never given top command. And Chamberlain, a professor of rhetoric from little Bowdoin College in Maine, discovered in battle the fire in his belly that made him instrumental in saving the day, the Army of the Potomac, and, quite possibly, the entire Union cause.

Day One: July 1, 1863

Brig. Gen. John Buford was a tough-as-nails Kentuckian who had already shown himself to be an outstanding cavalry commander under Pope and Hooker. When he reached Gettysburg, he immediately grasped the importance of holding the *high ground* called McPherson's Ridge, just west of town. Buford had fought at Fredericksburg and had seen how the Confederates, secure on the heights around that town, had rained down slaughter upon the Union army of Ambrose Burnside (see Chapter 12). At Gettysburg, he knew that he would be badly outnumbered, but he also knew that he would have the advantage of fighting from the high ground and that his men would be fighting with breech-loading carbines, the shorter and lighter rifle favored by cavalrymen, which would allow them to load and fire much faster than the Confederates, who were armed with traditional muzzle-loading muskets.

Words of War

Soldiers and strategists frequently speak of the **high ground**. This is any elevated ground, such as a hill, on which troops can be placed so as to command clear fields of vision and fire over the ground below. Occupying the high ground always confers a tactical advantage.

The fighting began at 9:00 on the morning of July 1.

The High Ground

Buford's dismounted cavalry held off the first waves of Heth's and William Pender's Confederate infantry divisions while General Reynolds's I Corps and Gen. O.O. Howard's XI Corps rushed to reinforce Buford. Reynolds's troops began to arrive by 10:30, but by this time the Confederates were massing and had built up superior strength. Union I Corps commander John Reynolds took personal command of the celebrated 1,800-man "Iron Brigade" in McPherson's Woods, to the west of the ridge. Within minutes, the gallant major general, the man many thought should have been in Meade's place, was shot through the head. He died instantly.

Maj. Gen. John F. Reynolds commanded the Union's I Corps at Gettysburg and personally led the famed "Iron Brigade" in the field. Cut down early in the battle, he was the highest-ranking officer to die at Gettysburg.

(Harper's Pictorial History of the Civil War, *1866*)

When O.O. Howard and his XI Corps arrived, shortly before noon, the situation had become terribly confused. Union forces were repeatedly pushed back, only to rally and counterattack, but when Howard, who assumed overall command in the field following the death of Reynolds, tried to join a division commanded by Maj. Gen. Carl Schurz to the beleaguered brigades of I Corps, the units failed to meet, and the combined strength of Confederate units under generals Robert Rodes, Jubal Early, and A.P. Hill at last drove the Federals off McPherson's Ridge and their other positions west and north of Gettysburg. The blue-coated soldiers *retreated* into the town,

Words of War

A **retreat** is an orderly withdrawal of troops from battle.

fighting hand-to-hand near Pennsylvania College and, ultimately, retreating southeast of the town down the Baltimore Pike. Meade, not yet on the field, sent his most trusted subordinate—Gen. Winfield Scott Hancock—to take charge of the battered defense.

This battle map of Gettysburg shows the principal Confederate stronghold at Seminary Ridge, southwest of town, and the fishhook-shaped deployment of the Union army, directly south of town (at Culp's Hill, Cemetery Hill, Cemetery Ridge, and, to the far south, at Little Round Top and Big Round Top).

(Harper's Pictorial History of the Civil War, *1866*)

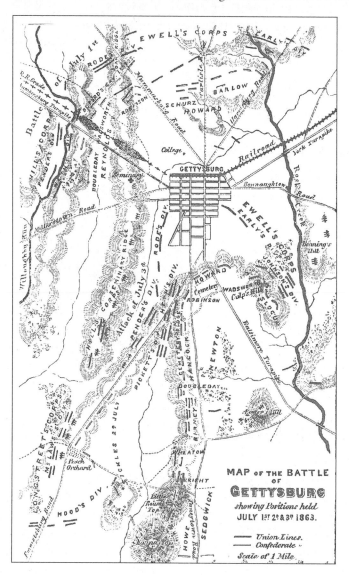

MAP of the BATTLE
of
GETTYSBURG
showing Positions held
JULY 1ST 2D & 3D 1863.

—— *Union Lines.*
—— *Confederate "*

Scale of 1 Mile.

Retreat to a Cemetery

The first day's fighting ended in a Southern victory, but the battle was not over. The high ground of McPherson's Ridge was lost to the Union, but a *rout* of the Federal forces had been stemmed, and, what is more, it had been stemmed on *other* high ground: East Cemetery Hill, Cemetery Ridge, and Culp's Hill, running from due south to southeast of town. The Confederates occupied some high ground, too: Oak Hill, northwest of town, and Seminary Ridge, due west of Gettysburg.

Words of War

A **rout** is a withdrawal in panic and disorder, typically accompanied by a high rate of casualties.

Thus, toward the end of July 1, the armies were in place on hills separated by a mile of the fields and woods that lay to the southwest of town.

"If I Had Stonewall Jackson ..."

It was not like Robert E. Lee to leave a situation in such a static state, and, indeed, he had ordered General Ewell to follow up on his initial and incomplete rout of the Union army—"if he found it practicable." Following up meant an attack, on Day One, against Cemetery Hill. But Lee's order, the order of one Southern gentleman officer to another, was couched in ambiguous and indirect language, the phrase *"if he found it practicable."* Richard Stoddart Ewell did not find it practicable. As he saw it, his men needed a rest.

Well after the war, it is said, Lee bemoaned Ewell's decision: "If I had Stonewall Jackson at Gettysburg, I would have won that fight." And, having won that fight, he might have won the war. The point is, however, that the decision should never have been Ewell's to make. The excessive latitude Lee offered his subordinate was a fatal lapse in leadership.

Day Two: Union Holds the High Ground

Dawn of July 2 found Robert E. Lee exhausted and sick with the diarrhea that was as routine a feature of camp life as rising, drilling, and sleeping. (Some historians believe that Lee, a chronic sufferer from heart disease, had actually sustained a mild heart attack.) But, sick or not, his mood was bold, and he met with his corps commanders to give detailed orders for an offensive he hoped would crush the enemy army. Stuart was still absent, and Lee was not fully aware of how many more Union troops were massing at Gettysburg, though he knew they *were* massing, and that made him all the more eager to strike, strike now, and strike vigorously, to finish what had been started the day before.

Longstreet Advises

As usual, it was Longstreet who dissented. He believed—rightly, as it turned out— that almost the entire Army of the Potomac would be massing against the Confederates on this day. He feared that the Army of Northern Virginia would be overrun and overwhelmed. His advice was to pursue a policy of what he called "strategic offense—tactical defense"; that is, to manipulate the Union army into attacking the Confederate army where and when it was strategically advantageous to the Confederacy and, when attacked, to defend, inflicting great losses on the Federals. Longstreet pointed out that this approach had worked well at the two Bull Runs, at Antietam, and at Fredericksburg—all of which had resulted in costly repulse of the Federals (although Antietam ended as a very narrow Union victory).

Longstreet proposed a withdrawal to the south and a move against Meade from the rear.

No, Lee responded. He could not *withdraw* his army after it had *won* a victory! To do so, he argued, would demoralize the men and, most likely, result in losing this opportunity to win a decisive victory.

The Fishhook

Everyone who has written about the opening of this second fateful day at Gettysburg has observed that the Union line was deployed in a giant, upside-down fishhook. The hook's barb was just south of Culp's Hill, its turn was at Cemetery Hill, and the end of its shaft—its tie-end—at two hills, well to the south of town, known as Little Round Top and Big Round Top. Lee directed Longstreet to attack the Union left, the shaft of the fishhook running along Cemetery Ridge and terminating at the Little and Big Round Tops. Lee was northwest of the fishhook, where the curve met the shaft.

Ewell, to the north and northeast, above the curve of the fishhook, was to be prepared to swing down and smash the Union's right.

Sites and Sights

Gettysburg National Military Park encompasses 3,850 acres, with 35 miles of park roads, 1,300 monuments, and some 400 cannon. A visitor's center at 97 Taneytown Road contains many exhibits. The Gettysburg National Cemetery is adjacent to the park. Contact the park at 1-717-334-1124.

Quick, Bold, Cheerful, and Hopeful

Despite the defeat on July 1, George Gordon Meade was (as an aide described him) "quick, bold, cheerful, and hopeful" on the morning of July 2. Certainly, he was no wild-eyed optimist. When the Confederate officers assembled at Gettysburg heard that Lincoln had replaced Hooker with Meade, most of them were overjoyed. For although Meade had a reputation for competence and was certainly thought to be as skilled as Hooker, he was known to lack Hooker's boldness.

But Lee had served with Meade in the old, prewar army. Like himself, Meade was trained as an engineer. "General Meade will commit no blunder on my front," Lee declared to his staff, "and if I make one he will make haste to take advantage of it."

Yet what reason did Meade have for optimism? After all, to look at the situation on a flat map would suggest to anyone that the Union was in grave trouble—surrounded on three sides. But battles are not fought in two dimensions. In fact, what Meade must have seen is that the Federal position was strong—possessed of the high ground—and that it commanded clear fields of observation and clear fields of fire. Moreover, Meade now had almost 90,000 men at Gettysburg, opposing 75,000 Confederates, and the Union army's central position, surrounded by the rebels, actually leveraged or magnified this numerical superiority.

War News

Johnny Reb and Billy Yank fought fiercely at Gettysburg. But both were often terrified—so scared that many of them simply *forgot* to shoot. Some 27,500 muskets were recovered on the field after the battle. Of these, more than 12,000 contained 2 charges. They had been loaded, but not fired, and loaded again. Another 6,000 contained 3 to 10 charges and balls, and one musket was found stuffed with 23 rounds.

Temporary Insanity

The southernmost Union corps, the tie-end of the fishhook terminating at the Round Tops, was commanded by Maj. Gen. Daniel Sickles. A "political general," Sickles nevertheless had more military acumen than other such commanders, having fought well at the Seven Days, Antietam, Fredericksburg, and Chancellorsville. Yet he also carried into battle a very heavy freight of controversy.

Two years before the war, in Washington's Lafayette Park, just across Pennsylvania Avenue from the White House, Sickles shot and killed the son of Francis Scott Key, author of "The Star-Spangled Banner." It seems that Philip Barton Key had been sleeping with Sickles's wife. Sickles was tried for a murder he certainly committed, but his lawyer, none other than the future secretary of war, Edwin M. Stanton, pleaded him not guilty. For the first time in legal history, that plea was based on a claim of "temporary insanity." Sickles's subsequent acquittal was scandalous enough, but he created further shock waves by taking his errant wife back.

Maj. Gen. Daniel Sickles's impulsive and imprudent advance west of the Round Tops triggered a nearly disastrous attack by troops from Longstreet's corps. Hit in the leg during the battle, Sickles was carried from the field smoking a cigar. His injured limb was amputated and he donated it to a medical museum, in later life frequently paying visits to it.

(Library of Congress)

When Abraham Lincoln, a close friend, nominated Sickles as a brigadier general in September 1861, the Senate rejected the nomination. Only by twisting arms was a second nomination approved.

For many, it was most disquieting to serve under or alongside a commander judged insane, temporarily or otherwise. And now Sickles gave ample justification for that unease. Without orders from Meade, he inexplicably advanced his III Corps about a half-mile from the Union line, where he stuck out, one combatant said, "like a sore thumb," exposing the Union's left flank to Longstreet's offensive.

But Longstreet was as reluctant as Sickles was impulsive. It was four in the afternoon before the Confederate commander attacked. One of his subordinates, Maj. Gen. John Bell Hood, hit Sickles in the Peach Orchard northwest of the Round Tops, pushing him back toward Little Round Top through a rocky area later called the Devil's Den for the ferocity of the fighting there.

The Professor

Battles begin with plans and require much skill and courage to maneuver and fight, but, in the end, they are also subject to random chance. Just before Hood's men attacked Sickles, Brig. Gen. Gouverneur K. Warren, Meade's chief engineer, noticed that Little Round Top was undefended, save for a few signalmen. He realized in an instant that Hood's division would seize that high ground and thereby be in position to crush the Union's flank, traveling right up the shaft of the Federal fishhook.

Warren's staff officers hurriedly rounded up a brigade led by Col. Strong Vincent and sent it to occupy Little Round Top. Vincent was soon fatally wounded in the action. A brigade under Brig. Gen. Stephen Weed also fought Hood, and at the extreme south end of the Federal flank was the 20th Maine, a battle-battered regiment, commanded by Col. Joshua Lawrence Chamberlain.

Chamberlain was not a professional soldier. A professor of rhetoric at Bowdoin College, he took a sabbatical in 1862 intending to study in Europe, but joined the Union army instead. Now, with his regiment at less than half strength—under 500 men, including some mutinous soldiers who had been put under his guard—he held off attack after attack from a superior force of Alabama troops. Finally, in one of the battle's greatest moments of extraordinary achievement, he *defeated* them. His ammunition was all but exhausted, a circumstance that would have prompted—*forced*—just about anyone else to surrender, but, realizing the grave importance of holding his position and preventing the Confederates from turning the Union flank, he led a fierce downhill charge, exclusively using bayonets, with which he scattered the rebels.

> **War News**
>
> Joshua Lawrence Chamberlain (1828–1914) was wounded at Gettysburg and on three other occasions. He was given the honor of receiving the Confederate surrender at Appomattox Court House on April 9, 1865, and, after the war, served several terms as governor of Maine. In 1893, he received the Medal of Honor for his actions at Little Round Top.

Devil's Den, Peach Orchard, and Wheatfield

The Confederates still held Devil's Den, below Little Round Top, and fired on the reinforced defenders of that hill from behind boulders. Action was hot, too, in the Peach Orchard and Wheatfield, to the northwest of Little Round Top. In the Wheatfield, no fewer than six Confederate attacks were met by six Union counterattacks, leaving casualties and corpses thicker than any wheat harvest.

Sickles's impulsive advance might have meant Union defeat, but Longstreet was never able to coordinate his attacks—devastating as they were—to decisive effect, and Meade as well as Maj. Gen. Winfield Scott Hancock, now leading II and III Corps, repaired Sickles's error by skillfully redeploying forces as needed to check each major Confederate attempt at a breakthrough.

At sundown, the Confederates attacked Cemetery, East Cemetery, and Culp's Hills. The Federals held on to all their positions except at Culp's Hill, but then counterattacked there at 4:30 on the morning of July 3 and, after seven hours of fighting, turned back the Confederates.

Day Three: Massive Assault

As July 2 melted into July 3, the Union army continued to hold its high ground, but, as Robert E. Lee saw it, tenuously. For Lee, it was a tempting situation. He had won significant victories on the 1st, and while he had failed to crush the Union army on the 2nd, he believed that he had worn it down sufficiently to destroy it on the 3rd.

Voices

Longstreet later recalled his feelings about Lee's proposed attack:

My heart was heavy. I could see the desperate and hopeless nature of the charge and the hopeless slaughter it would cause. That day at Gettysburg was one of the saddest of my life.

Longstreet Advises Again

As Lee saw it, he had been repulsed on July 2, repeatedly, but each time just barely. He now proposed an all-out attack. As usual, Longstreet protested the plan, but Lee insisted that too much blood had been invested to withdraw now.

Meade's forces had hardly been idle during the night and early morning. In addition to retaking Culp's Hill, they greatly improved their defenses and positioned final reinforcements, bracing for the attack.

Both sides were tired, bone tired, as the warm morning of July 3 simmered into an oppressively sultry midday.

Pickett's Charge

The massive assault Lee had in mind was destined to be perhaps the single most celebrated operation of the war. It was also destined to be misnamed after the general Longstreet had assigned to form the brigades in preparation for the assault. Maj. Gen. George Pickett was a courageous and high-spirited Virginian, but hardly the most skilled of Lee's commanders, and he commanded just three of the nine brigades—nine brigades, a total of 12,500 men—massed for the attack. James Johnston Pettigrew and Isaac Ridgeway Trimble led the others.

By noon, they were arrayed: disciplined veteran soldiers perfectly aligned in battle ranks across an open field, facing the Union soldiers dug in on Cemetery Ridge a mile away. In preparation for the operation that came to be called "Pickett's Charge," 150 Confederate cannon pounded the ridge, only to be answered by equally devastating fire from Union artillery. Such a duel of cannon was unprecedented in war up to this time.

Maj. Gen. George Pickett, CSA, forever regretted the desperate charge on July 3 that bears his name.

(Library of Congress)

At 1:45 in the afternoon, 12,500 men, in closely formed ranks, advanced. The Union artillerists replaced their solid ammunition with canister, shot consisting of iron balls packed into cans, which burst apart, spraying the field of fire with hundreds of deadly projectiles.

Still, the gray-uniformed men—those who did not fall—advanced. When they were close enough, the Union infantry, from cover and from the high ground, opened up with musket fire.

"A Sob—A Gasp"

A Federal soldier described the rebel advance as "an overwhelming relentless tide of an ocean of armed men sweeping upon us! On they move, as with one soul in perfect order … magnificent, grim, irresistible."

But fated to fail and to die.

Two of Pickett's three brigadier generals were cut down in the charge, and the third was gravely wounded. All 15 regimental commanders engaged were killed or wounded. At a place called the Angle, 150 men led by Brig. Gen. Lewis Armistead actually succeeded in raising the Confederate colors above Cemetery Ridge, but they were soon killed or captured.

Voices

The night of July 3, Pickett wrote to his fiancée:

> My brave boys were so full of hope and confident of victory as I led them forth! Over on Cemetery Ridge the Federals beheld a scene which has never previously been enacted—an army forming in line of battle in full view, under their very eyes—charging across a space nearly a mile in length, pride and glory soon to be crushed by an overwhelming heartbreak.
>
> Well, it is all over now. The awful rain of shot and shell was a sob—a gasp.
>
> I can still hear them cheering as I gave the order, "Forward!" the thrill of their joyous voices as they called out, "We'll follow you, Marse George, we'll follow you!" On, how faithfully they followed me on—on—to their death, and I led them on—on—on—Oh God!
>
> I can't write you a love letter today, my Sally. But for you, my darling, I would rather, a million times rather, sleep in an unknown grave.

Never Forget

Some 12,500 men had charged Cemetery Ridge. Five thousand returned to Seminary Ridge.

 Count Off!

The Union fielded 88,289 men at Gettysburg, of whom 3,155 were killed and another 14,529 were wounded, mortally wounded, or captured; 5,365 went missing. Of 75,000 Confederates engaged, 3,903 were killed, 18,735 were wounded, mortally wounded, or captured, and 5,425 were reported missing in action. Combined Union and Confederate casualties: 51,112.

Pickett, an ebullient, even superficial officer before July 3, 1862, was forever sorrowful after that day. "That old man," he said after the war, referring to Lee, "had my division massacred."

But no one was harder on Robert E. Lee than Lee himself. Organizing the retreat from Gettysburg, he said to Longstreet, "It was all my fault; get together, and let us do the best we can toward saving which is left us."

"My God, Is That All?"

Meade had won a great victory—"great" in that to have lost at Gettysburg might well have meant the downfall of Lincoln, an attack on Washington, and a negotiated settlement with an independent

Confederate States of America. Yet, like McClellan after Antietam, Meade lacked the will to press his weary, battered army to pursue Lee's even wearier, more badly battered, and more severely reduced forces. On July 4, 1863, the anniversary of American independence ("four score and seven years ago"), there was no more fighting at Gettysburg.

"My God," Lincoln exclaimed when he heard that Meade had allowed Lee to retreat back across the Potomac and into Virginia. "My God, is that all?"

These Honored Dead

Yet Lincoln knew that, with the simultaneous collapse of Vicksburg in the West (see Chapter 13), Gettysburg was the irrevocable turning point of the war. On November 19, 1863, the president delivered a speech at the dedication of the Soldiers' National Cemetery at Gettysburg.

Voices

The Gettysburg Address

Four score and seven years ago our fathers brought forth on this continent a new nation, conceived in Liberty, and dedicated to the proposition that all men are created equal.

Now we are engaged in a great civil war, testing whether that nation or any nation so conceived and so dedicated, can long endure. We are met on a great battlefield of that war. We have come to dedicate a portion of that field, as a final resting place for those who here gave their lives that that nation might live. It is altogether fitting and proper that we should do this.

But, in a larger sense, we can not dedicate—we can not consecrate—we can not hallow—this ground. The brave men, living and dead, who struggled here, have consecrated it, far above our poor power to add or detract. The world will little note, nor long remember what we say here, but it can never forget what they did here. It is for us the living, rather, to be dedicated here to the unfinished work which they who fought here have thus far so nobly advanced. It is rather for us to be here dedicated to the great task remaining before us—that from these honored dead we take increased devotion to that cause for which they gave the last full measure of devotion—that we here highly resolve that these dead shall not have died in vain—that this nation, under God, shall have a new birth of freedom—and that government of the people, by the people, for the people, shall not perish from the earth.

Gettysburg: Impact and Heritage

Lincoln had been invited to speak at Gettysburg at the last minute. His appearance was an afterthought. The *featured* speaker was the great orator Edward Everett, whose remarks consumed two hours. But Lincoln's speech, concluded in two minutes, is one of the most profound oratorical monuments ever erected to military achievement and human sacrifice.

The president understood that this battle, fought to save the Union, *had* saved the Union, and he wanted others to know this as well.

For later generations of Americans, no battle, not even Yorktown, the culminating triumph of the Revolution, has carried greater symbolic weight than Gettysburg. Bringing together some of the divided nation's best and most valiant military figures, it was the scene of both gallantry and slaughter, and more than any other battle of the war, it proved the limits of Confederate prowess of arms and the full extent of the Union's resolve and capacity to preserve the nation as a nation, indivisible.

The Least You Need to Know

- ◆ Robert E. Lee saw Gettysburg as his opportunity to crush the Army of the Potomac on Northern territory and thereby force the North to agree to a negotiated peace with an independent Confederate States of America.

- ◆ By seizing and holding the high ground around Gettysburg, Union forces obtained a decisive advantage against Lee's army.

- ◆ In a battle full of heroism, two of the most extraordinary actions were the defense of Little Round Top led by Col. Joshua Lawrence Chamberlain of Maine on July 2 and "Pickett's Charge," a massive, gallant, and ultimately suicidal attack by the Confederates on July 3.

- ◆ By defeating Lee at Gettysburg, the Army of the Potomac turned the tide of war irrevocably against the South; however, by allowing Lee's survivors to escape, Union general George Gordon Meade also prolonged the war.

Chapter 16

"Not for Uncle Sambo"

In This Chapter

- The draft triggers a race riot in New York
- Attempts to create a rebellion in the North
- The role of African American soldiers in the war
- The 54th Massachusetts wins glory

For many of us in this twenty-first century, it is almost impossible to imagine an *American* civil war: a political and psychological scenario in which the country splits itself along a certain line and neighboring states suddenly become a foreign and hostile nation.

Yet the fact is that the nation was even *more* divided in the 1860s than neatly between North and South. Within the two regions, there were many sharp divisions as well, and none were sharper, more bitter, or more ugly than the division between blacks and whites. So deep were *these* divisions that, although the wound gashed between North and South has, after many years, healed, the hurts that afflict the races still burn. This chapter is about race, hate, treachery, and the glory that was born despite it all.

The Draft Riots

This book, like every other history of the Civil War, tells you that the Union victories at Vicksburg and Gettysburg were the turning points in the war. That a Northern triumph was now inevitable may be apparent in hindsight, but, in July 1863, it was by no means clear to either North or South. War weariness gripped much of the North even as its armies approached the threshold of victory. In what should have been the triumphant afterglow of Vicksburg and Gettysburg, that despair, fanned by racial fear and hatred, burst into flames during one violent week in New York City.

Even before the fall of Sumter, many New Yorkers failed to rally round the flag. Mayor Fernando Wood proposed the secession of the city—and Long Island, too—as early as January 1861. The wealth of New York was bound to the South by the stout cords of trade, and Wood proposed that the city declare itself an independent, neutral nation and a free port trading equally with North and South.

Although the city did not pursue this radical course, it was, throughout the war, guided more by a spirit of commerce than by the stated principles on which the rest of the North prosecuted the war. To some New Yorkers, however, one of those proclaimed principles was downright repugnant.

Racial Rage

To most of the struggling immigrants who called the city home, the prospect of a tidal wave of even more downtrodden immigrants, newly emancipated slaves coming up from the South, was terrifying and enraging. In no immigrant group were such feelings stronger than among the 200,000 Irish New Yorkers, many of whom had fled the great Potato Famine that had starved their native land in 1848. Most of the midcentury Irish immigrants endured discrimination and persecution and earned their living mainly by supplying cheap common labor.

Freed black slaves, they figured, would supply that labor for even less. A new famine was on the horizon, and, worst of all, Lincoln's new draft law, the Conscription Act passed by Congress in March, would force the Irish to fight and die to free the very slaves who would take their jobs.

Aside, perhaps, from the beleaguered Irish, few Northerners objected to a draft. They realized that the army needed the troops, and passage of the

Count Off!

Despite the draft, the Union army was a largely volunteer force. The number of draftees actually held to service during the war was a mere 52,068; 86,724 men paid the $300 commutation fee to receive exemption, and 42,581 men enlisted as substitutes for draftees.

Conscription Act even prompted a good many young men to enlist; they felt it would be shameful to wait to fight until the law compelled them.

But what a grossly unfair law it was! A conscript could avoid service by hiring a substitute or by paying a $300 "commutation fee." In 1863, only the well-to-do could afford such a sum. Immigrant laborers, who earned about a dollar a day, hadn't a prayer of scraping together a year's pay.

There were rumblings and violent demonstrations in Iowa, Illinois, Indiana, and Ohio, but the worst violence broke out in New York City.

A Ragged, Coatless Army

The draft commenced in the city on Saturday, July 11. On Monday the 13th, in the words of journalist Joel T. Headley,

> … a ragged, coatless, heterogeneously weaponed army heaved tumultuously along toward Third Avenue. Tearing down the telegraph poles as it crossed the Harlem & New Haven Railroad track, it surged angrily up around the building where the drafting was going on …. The mob seized the [draft-lottery] wheel in which were the names, and what books, papers, and lists were left, and tore them up.

When the rioters were unable to break open a safe, they set fire to the building. They overran and looted the Second Avenue armory, and pillaged jewelry and liquor stores as well.

Then they loosed their rage upon the race they scorned and feared. Knots of rioters ran down blacks, beating some, hanging others from lampposts. On Tuesday, as the rioting and looting continued unabated, the Colored Orphan Asylum was set ablaze. The rioters cheered the flames.

By Wednesday, the rioters were tearing down the houses of blacks by hand. But Wednesday evening, a detachment of General Meade's weary Gettysburg veterans marched into the city to restore order. "There was some terrific fighting," a witness recalled. "Streets were swept again and again by *grape[shot]*; houses were stormed at the point of

War News
Filmmaker Martin Scorsese's much anticipated *Gangs of New York* was released at the end of 2002 and portrays the intense ethnic violence of New York City during the Civil War years. A spectacular dramatization of the ethnic and racial aspects of the Draft Riots concludes this wonderful movie.

Words of War

Grape or **grapeshot** was a type of ammunition consisting of a cluster of small iron balls used mostly on ships as a cannon charge. Like **canister** ammunition, grapeshot was intended to spray out and kill personnel.

the bayonet; rioters were picked off by sharpshooters as they fired on the troops from housetops; men were hurled, dying or dead, into the streets."

The New York Draft Riots (July 13–16, 1863) were racially motivated. White rioters, mostly Irish immigrants, lynched blacks and burned the Colored Orphan Asylum.

(Harper's Pictorial History of the Civil War, 1866)

Count Off! _____

No accurate count was ever made of New York City's Draft Riot victims. Estimates range from 300 to over 1,000 killed on all sides.

Words of War _____

Sambo was one of the many demeaning names whites applied to African Americans during the nineteenth century. Some linguists have suggested that the term might be derived from the Fulani (Senegalese) word for uncle.

Northern Rebellion?

Meade's men quickly quelled the New York City Draft Riot, but sporadic violence flared in nearby Brooklyn, Jamaica, Staten Island, Jersey City, Newark, and farther afield in Albany and Troy, New York. Boston and Portsmouth, New Hampshire, as well as Columbia and Bucks counties, Pennsylvania, all saw rioting, as did parts of Kentucky. In Wisconsin, the governor called out the militia to put down disturbances in Milwaukee and Ozaukee County.

A Pennsylvania newspaper headline summed up the "rebellion" in an ugly but accurate headline:

WILLING TO FIGHT FOR UNCLE SAM BUT NOT FOR UNCLE SAMBO

Rebellion? The South hoped so. J.B. Jones, a clerk in the Confederate War Department, Richmond, noted gleefully in his diary for July 17: " ... *awfully* good news from New York: an INSURRECTION, the loss of many lives, extensive pillage and burning."

Copperheads: Snakes in the Grass?

If Southerners were thrilled by the prospect of riots growing into out-and-out rebellion in the North, many Northerners attributed the riots to a conspiracy of Confederate *agents provocateurs*.

In truth, all the ingredients necessary to start a riot were amply present in the Conscription Act and what it meant to the Irish and other white workingmen. No outside agitators were required. Yet there were those, in the North as well as the South, who saw the Draft Riots as visible evidence of disloyalty simmering in the Union states, and certain people were eager to exploit it.

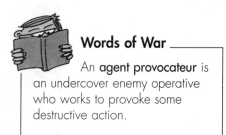

Words of War

An **agent provocateur** is an undercover enemy operative who works to provoke some destructive action.

Knights and Castles: Secret Societies

The polite name for any Northerner who advocated restoration of the Union through a negotiated settlement with the South was *Peace Democrat*, but such people were more commonly called Copperheads. The term was first used by the *New York Tribune* on July 20, 1861, which compared the Peace Democrats to the venomous snake in the grass, which strikes without warning.

Words of War

A **Peace Democrat** was any Northerner who advocated a negotiated settlement of the war, with concessions to the South. **Copperhead** was the disparaging term applied to Peace Democrats, evoking the image of a venomous snake. Copperhead was a pejorative term, but many Peace Democrats embraced the title and even fashioned badges by cutting the goddess Liberty out of copper pennies. (Historians debate whether the badges came before or after the label was applied to Peace Democrats.)

The Copperheads opposed the Conscription Act as well as the Emancipation Proclamation, which, they argued, changed the Civil War from a struggle to preserve the Union to a "war for the Negro." They also opposed the Radical Republican view, as expressed by Pennsylvania Congressman Thaddeus Stevens, that, following victory, the North should "treat those states outside of the Union as conquered provinces and settle them with new men."

Who would these "new men" be? Well, they would *not* be Democrats, which meant that Northern Democrats were being asked to fight a war that might restore the Union but would certainly destroy their party.

Words of War

Radical Republicans were Northerners who advocated continuation of the war to absolute, total victory, and they further proposed severe punishment for the South following its defeat.

The most determined Copperheads organized secret societies either modeled on, or actual outgrowths of, so-called Southern Rights clubs, which had sprouted up during the Nullification Crisis of the 1830s (discussed in Chapter 2). In 1854, a physician of dubious medical credentials, George W.L. Bickley, founded the Knights of the Golden Circle. Headquartered in Cincinnati and full of elaborate rituals, the society—later called the Order of the American Knights and the Sons of Liberty—spawned satellite lodges ("castles," they were called) throughout Kentucky, Missouri, Iowa, Illinois, Indiana, and Ohio.

A Man Named Vallandigham

If the Copperheads and Knights rallied around any one leader, it was Clement Vallandigham, a prodigy who knew the alphabet at age 2, spoke Greek and Latin at 12, became principal of Union Academy in Maryland at 19, and was editor of the *Western Empire*, a radical Democratic newspaper, at 20. Vallandigham gained renown in Ohio as an unbeatable defense attorney.

Clement Vallandigham was the leading figure among Ohio Copperheads. He survived the Civil War, but in 1870, while practicing law in Ohio, he accidentally shot and killed himself by demonstrating a firearm that was an exhibit in a murder trial.

(Harper's Pictorial History of the Civil War, 1866)

After a term as lieutenant governor of Ohio, Vallandigham was elected to Congress as an anti-Abolitionist Democrat, but was defeated in 1862. His last speech before Congress, just after passage of the Conscription Act, urged his countrymen to stop fighting. Republicans called the speech treason; Copperheads heard it as a rallying cry.

The Great Northwest Conspiracy

Governor Oliver Morton of Indiana, fearing the spread of Copperhead influence in his state, appealed to Secretary of War Edwin Stanton to send Brig. Gen. Henry B. Carrington to Indianapolis for the purpose of organizing a squad of undercover agents to infiltrate Copperhead secret societies.

Although Carrington soon discovered widespread Copperhead activity, the administration in Washington dismissed groups such as the Knights of the Golden Circle as harmless fanatics. Carrington learned that certain Copperheads had graduated from preaching mere defeatism to actively aiding and abetting John Hunt Morgan, a Confederate guerrilla leader whose "Morgan's Raiders" were famed and feared in the Old Northwest and Kentucky.

John Hunt Morgan was a famed and much-feared Confederate guerrilla leader. His July 1863 raids into Indiana and Ohio were the farthest north any Confederate force penetrated during the Civil War. Morgan was killed by Union forces on September 4, 1864, in Greenville, Tennessee.

(Harper's Pictorial History of the Civil War, *1866*)

Morgan Rides and Raids

On March 19, 1863, Carrington wired Lincoln that Morgan intended to "raise the standard of revolt in Indiana. Thousands believe this and his photograph is hung in many homes. In some counties his name is daily praised."

Carrington did not know the full extent of the charismatic Morgan's plans. Early in the summer of 1863, he was working with Confederate Captain Thomas Henry Hines, who intended to coordinate Morgan's planned Ohio Raid—a cavalry incursion into Ohio and the vicinity of Cincinnati—with an uprising of "Bowles's Army," some 10,000 men led by Dr. William A. Bowles, an Indiana Copperhead leader. Bowles proposed to take over state and local government and seize arsenals, assassinating whoever got in the way.

Morgan's Raid did take place, during July 2–26, 1863, and was the longest cavalry raid of the war: over 700 miles in 25 days of virtually continuous combat. Although his commanding officer, Braxton Bragg, had ordered him to stay south of the Ohio River, the impetuous Morgan believed that only by bringing the war into the North, and thereby winning Copperhead support, could action in the region be truly effective. However, Morgan did not attempt to distinguish between loyal Northerners and Copperheads in the course of the raid. His men indiscriminately plundered homes and businesses, wrecked railroads and bridges, and generally looted whatever of value they found.

Although Morgan's Raid was therefore impressive, it was strategically without value because it did nothing to win support in the Ohio and Indiana region. Dr. Bowles's Copperhead "army" never materialized. As for Morgan, half his men were eventually run to ground, at Buffington Island on July 19, and he himself was captured at Lisbon, Ohio, eight days later, after an exhausting pursuit by some 120,000 militiamen. Treated as common criminals, he and his men were sent to the Ohio State Penitentiary—from which they soon escaped.

Another Riot

The collapse of Bowles's planned insurrection and the capture of Morgan might have persuaded top Northern leaders that the Copperhead threat was of no great consequence, but Maj. Gen. Ambrose Burnside, who had been named Commander of the Army of the Ohio after his removal as head of the Army of the Potomac following the disaster at Fredericksburg (see Chapter 12), continued to take the Copperheads seriously. On April 13, 1863, he issued Order No. 38, which authorized the death penalty for couriers carrying secret mails, for enemy agents operating behind Union lines, and for "recruiting officers of secret societies."

Clement Vallandigham responded during a May Day address to Democrats assembled at Mount Vernon, Ohio. Spitting on a copy of the order, he decried Burnside as a tyrant and accused the Republicans of prolonging the war for the purely political purpose of destroying the Democratic Party.

Burnside, no more adroit as a politician than as a military tactician, imperiously ordered Vallandigham's arrest, which touched off riots in Dayton and elsewhere across the country. Even newspapers opposed to the radical Democratic Party line rose to defend Vallandigham's right of free speech, and the Ohio politician, whom few outside his own state and party took seriously, was now catapulted into national prominence.

With the North drawing as close to widespread insurrection as it ever would, Lincoln wisely intervened to defuse the crisis. Although Vallandigham was tried and sentenced to imprisonment for the duration of the war, the president commuted the sentence to banishment to the South.

Confederate authorities, however, informed Vallandigham that he could not remain in the South if he still considered himself loyal to the Union. Declaring himself loyal, he sailed for the West Indies and, from there, made his way to Nova Scotia. Despite his banishment, the Ohio Democratic Party defiantly nominated him as its candidate for governor. On July 15, 1863, he opened his campaign—in exile—by directing an address to the people of Ohio from the Canadian side of Niagara Falls.

The Northern Revolt Sputters and Dies

Vallandigham was not elected, and, with his removal, the so-called Great Northwest Conspiracy—the South's poorly coordinated effort to collaborate with Northern Copperheads in order to bring about a revolution in Ohio, Indiana, Kentucky, and Illinois—sputtered. Yet, through the late summer of 1864, Copperhead activity persisted, and talk continued to buzz about raising Copperhead armies and of liberating Confederate POWs in a large prison camp outside of Chicago.

It was all just talk. The flames of Northern revolt died into embers and cooled as each passing month after Vicksburg and Gettysburg further dimmed the Confederate prospects.

Glory

Doubtless some Copperheads were moved by a sincere desire to see the end of bloodshed, but most were *politically* motivated by a desire to block the Radical Republican destruction of their party. *Emotionally*, their motives were uglier: They did not want to fight a "war for the Negro." They did not want to die to free the slaves.

Oddly, something akin to this sentiment was also shared by a growing number of African Americans—freed slaves, runaway slaves, and Northern blacks who had never been slaves. These men did not wish to stand by while *white* men died for their freedom. In increasing numbers, African Americans agitated and petitioned for the privilege of fighting—and dying—to secure their own freedom. As early as August 1861, Frederick Douglass had spoken eloquently for the enrollment of black soldiers (see Chapter 5), but Northern resistance to the proposal was at first unyielding.

The reasons for the resistance were *mostly* racist. Many in the white military establishment believed that blacks were inferior, untrainable, cowardly, and utterly unfit to be soldiers. Others just didn't trust African Americans with firearms. Still others thought putting blacks in the uniform of the United States of America was just plain wrong.

There was another reason for resistance. Military men feared that the presence of African American soldiers in the Union army would actually boost Confederate morale and incite Southern soldiers to renewed effort fueled by outrage. Lincoln worried that recruiting black soldiers would also turn the tenuous Border States against the Union.

Voices

> I don't believe you could make soldiers of these men [freed slaves] at all,—they are afraid, and they know it.
>
> Negroes—plantation negroes, at least—will never make soldiers in one generation. Five white men could put a regiment to flight.
>
> —White missionaries, South Carolina Sea Islands, spring 1862
>
> To arm the negroes would turn 50,000 bayonets from the loyal Border States against us that were for us.
>
> … if we were to arm [the Negroes], I fear that in a few weeks the arms would be in the hands of the Rebels.
>
> —Abraham Lincoln, summer and fall 1862

Corps d'Afrique

In the spring of 1862, a group of free blacks who had formed a (never activated) Confederate regiment in 1861 offered their services to Gen. Ben Butler after New Orleans fell to the Union. Butler declined the offer, until he was threatened with a Confederate attack in August, whereupon he recruited three black regiments as the Louisiana Native Guard, or Corps d'Afrique. The troops took to the field in November 1862, even though the War Department refused officially to muster them in.

In the meantime, also during the spring of 1862, on the Union-occupied Sea Islands of South Carolina, Maj. Gen. David Hunter raised a black regiment, which consisted of volunteers as well as men he drafted. The War Department refused to sanction the regiment, and Hunter disbanded all but a single company of troops by August.

Out west, in Kansas, James H. Lane, a major general of militia, raised two regiments of fugitive slaves and free blacks, which actually saw some action early in the war *before* they were officially recognized by the War Department in 1863.

Congress Acts

President Lincoln and the War Department vetoed the actions of Hunter and Butler, but as Union defeats weighed more and more heavily on public opinion, popular resistance to the recruitment of blacks began to thaw. The Confiscation Act of July 17, 1862, authorized the president to "employ as many persons of African descent as he may deem necessary and proper for the suppression of this rebellion." Another law enacted on this date repealed a 1792 law barring African Americans from serving in the armed forces and explicitly authorized the recruitment of free blacks and freedmen.

On August 25, 1862, the War Department authorized the military governor of the South Carolina Sea Islands to raise five regiments of black troops on the island. All officers were to be white. Although volunteers trickled in at first, by the fall the trickle had become a flood, and the unit was mustered in on November 7 as the First South Carolina Volunteers.

After the final Emancipation Proclamation was issued on January 1, 1863, President Lincoln personally called for four black regiments. By war's end, approximately 178,985 African Americans were serving in 166 regiments. This represented about 10 percent of the Union army.

> **War News**
>
> In contrast to the U.S. Army, the U.S. Navy did employ black sailors, even before the Civil War, albeit generally in menial capacities. During the Civil War, 15 percent of the U.S. Navy was African American.

> **War News**
>
> On May 1, 1863, the Confederate Congress authorized President Davis to "put to death or ... otherwise [punish]" any black soldiers taken as prisoners of war. President Lincoln responded on July 30 with a warning that "for every soldier of the United States killed in violation of the laws of war, a Rebel soldier shall be executed; and for every one enslaved by the enemy or sold into Slavery, a Rebel soldier shall be placed at hard labor on public works."

> **War News**
>
> Although all black military units were commanded by white officers, a handful of African Americans (fewer than 100) *were* eventually commissioned as officers before the war ended. This included eight army surgeons commissioned as majors.

Civil War photographs of African American troops are extremely rare. This one shows the members of Company E, 4th U.S. Colored Troops, a unit formed in Baltimore during the summer of 1863.

(U.S. Army Military History Institute, Carlisle, Pennsylvania)

Muskets or Shovels?

Many African Americans were gratified and proud to serve in the Union army, and two of Frederick Douglass's own sons joined the 54th Massachusetts. But the mass of white soldiers and officers did not greet the troops' arrival with open arms. The soldiers were wholly segregated in all-black regiments commanded by white officers. They were often subject to physical and verbal abuse. They were the very last in line to receive equipment and proper uniforms. For a time, they were paid less than white soldiers.

Words of War

Fatigue duty is military jargon for manual labor.

For many African American soldiers, eager to prove themselves, the worst thing was not being allowed to fight. Most black regiments were initially assigned *fatigue duty* (common labor) and *garrison duty* (minding the fort). But eventually the need for soldiers at the front saw many blacks on the battlefield.

War News

Segregation prevailed in the U.S. armed forces until July 26, 1948, when President Harry S Truman signed Executive Order 9981 mandating "equality of treatment and opportunity to all persons in the Armed Services without regard to race." The order did not use the word *integration*, but when Truman was asked by a reporter if that's what the order meant, his reply was characteristically direct: "Yes."

The 54th Massachusetts Regiment

Although many African American soldiers were relegated to laboring assignments, black units did fight in 449 engagements, including 39 major battles. The most celebrated black regiment was the 54th Massachusetts Infantry. It drew attention as the first African American regiment raised in the North (previous black units were all recruited from occupied Southern states), and it was led by the earnest, handsome, and dashing 25-year-old Col. Robert Gould Shaw, son of a prominent Boston abolitionist family. But it was thrust into truly national prominence by its performance on July 18, 1863, in a desperate assault on Battery Wagner, a Confederate fort protecting the entrance to Charleston Harbor.

War News

The achievements and sacrifices of Robert Gould Shaw and the men of the 54th Massachusetts Regiment were commemorated in a magnificent bronze bas-relief sculpture by Augustus Saint-Gaudens dedicated in Boston in 1897. The sculpture is on display at the Saint-Gaudens National Historic Site on Boston Commons, and a plaster cast of the original is on long-term loan to the National Gallery of Art in Washington, D.C. In 1990, the excellent film *Glory* movingly celebrated Shaw and the men of the 54th for a new generation.

Col. Robert Gould Shaw was commander of the 54th Massachusetts Regiment, the black unit depicted in the 1990 film Glory.

(Harper's Pictorial History of the Civil War, *1866)*

Spearheading the attack by two brigades, the 54th took on a suicidal assignment—one soldier called it "the most fatal and fruitless campaign of the war"—but Gould

Count Off!

Approximately 37,300 African American soldiers died in the Civil War.

and his men accepted it cheerfully. They failed to take the fort, losing 281 of the 600 men engaged, including Shaw, whom the rebels sought to dishonor by throwing into a common grave with the bodies of the black soldiers he had led. Hearing of this, the young hero's father spoke for his family: "We can imagine no holier place than in which he is."

A 54th Massachusetts man, Sgt. William H. Carney, became the first African American to receive the Medal of Honor, for his service against Battery Wagner (16 other black soldiers and four sailors would also receive the medal during the war), and President Lincoln, for so long reluctant to recruit black troops and then to commit them to battle, later called the "use of colored troops … the heaviest blow yet dealt to the rebellion."

The Least You Need to Know

♦ The Union's unfair Conscription Act, combined with the resentment some whites felt about fighting a war to free black slaves, touched off Draft Riots in New York City and elsewhere.

♦ Northern "Peace Democrats," popularly called Copperheads, agitated for a negotiated end to the war and concessions to the South.

♦ Some Copperhead secret societies collaborated with Confederate guerrillas to foment general insurrection in the North.

♦ The U.S. government long resisted recruiting African American soldiers, but began officially to recruit them after the Emancipation Proclamation was issued.

♦ Despite discrimination, persecution, and (often) relegation to menial labor, African American regiments performed with distinction.

Chapter 17

From Chickamauga Mud to a Battle Above the Clouds

In This Chapter

- ◆ Bloodless win at Chattanooga
- ◆ Counterattack at Chickamauga
- ◆ A costly Confederate victory
- ◆ Battles of Lookout Mountain and Missionary Ridge
- ◆ The Confederates lose the West

In the aftermath of the Union victories at Vicksburg and Gettysburg, the pace of the war slowed to an exhausted crawl. Confederate guerrilla John Hunt Morgan's 700-mile, 25-day cavalry raid across Ohio accomplished nothing of strategic value.

New York City, as we saw in Chapter 16, erupted into three days of draft and race riot, but that, too, was quickly extinguished. And Lee, finding the Potomac flooded, entrenched his Gettysburg-battered soldiers at Williamsport, Maryland. Meade, exhausted as well, did not attack, and by July 14, the Army of Northern Virginia had crossed the Potomac back into Virginia, with Maj. Gen. Henry Heth successfully fighting a rear-guard action against Union forces at Falling Waters, Maryland.

Slowly, slowly, the main battle action shifted from Mississippi and Pennsylvania to central Tennessee and northern Georgia.

By the Book

Ulysses S. Grant and his men might have been tired and worn after the fall of Vicksburg, but Grant was all for pushing on through southern Mississippi and Alabama. He could take Mobile, and that would bring Confederate general Braxton Bragg running down from Chattanooga, leaving that key city along the Moccasin Bend of the Tennessee River firmly in Union hands. Grant wanted to push on because, well, who was there to stop him? Certainly no one the Confederates could field against him.

But Henry Wager "Old Brains" Halleck *could* and *did* stop Grant. He was a by-the-book general, and the book said that it was important for a victorious army to occupy the territory it took. This meant dispersing Grant's forces to various places in Louisiana (for an invasion of Texas), to Missouri, to Arkansas, and to garrisons in occupied Tennessee and Mississippi.

"Old Rosy" Gets a Kick in the Pants

The action, then, moved east from Mississippi and west from Virginia, concentrating in middle Tennessee. There Union general William Starke Rosecrans, West Point Class of 1842, was at the head of the Army of the Cumberland. His opponent was Braxton Bragg, general in command of the Confederate Army of Tennessee.

"Old Rosy," as his troops called Rosecrans, had been sparring with Bragg since the end of October 1862 without taking the initiative. It is true that Rosecrans avoided disaster during the Battle of Stones River, Tennessee, during December 30, 1862–January 3, 1863, but he had lost ground to Bragg. Tennessee, Lincoln was well aware, harbored strong Union interests, and by seizing Chattanooga, it would be possible to take Knoxville and thereby gain control of the entire eastern portion of the state. Rosecrans was popular with his troops, but by spring of 1863 Lincoln was making noises about relieving him.

Thus kicked, Old Rosy at last decided he'd better move, and he got underway, if slowly. After Grant crossed the Mississippi below Vicksburg on May 1, 1863, Union strategists realized that Bragg would most likely want to send reinforcements to the beleaguered river stronghold. Rosecrans's mission was to bottle up Bragg in Tennessee to prevent any troops from going to Vicksburg, but the Union general didn't get going until mid-June. Still, his deliberation proved effective, for he maneuvered skillfully and in such a way as to force Bragg to withdraw south of the Tennessee River.

The city of Chattanooga during the war. Note the army tents in the foreground and Lookout Mountain in the background.

(National Archives and Records Administration)

Through a series of brilliant feints and deceptions—all carried out during 17 consecutive days of miserable, driving rain—Rosecrans moved his troops behind Bragg's right flank near Tullahoma. By July 4, after another flanking movement, Rosecrans forced Bragg, outnumbered, to retreat from Tullahoma and withdraw to Chattanooga.

At this point, Rosecrans begged for reinforcements in order to take Chattanooga. When none were forthcoming, Rosecrans decided to keep maneuvering, and he executed a surprise crossing of the Tennessee River 30 miles west of Chattanooga. Were Rosecrans a Burnside, he probably would have launched a desperate frontal assault on Bragg's defensive positions in Chattanooga. And, like Burnside, he would have gotten his men slaughtered. Instead, he marched through a series of gaps in Lookout Mountain, the long ridge south-southwest of Chattanooga, and targeted the Western and Atlantic Railroad. This was Bragg's supply and communications line to Atlanta. With it severed, Bragg had no choice but to evacuate Chattanooga.

War News

The Civil War was the first war that ran on rails. Of the 31,000 miles of railroad networking the nation in 1860, only 9,000 miles were in the South. Northern railroads tended to run east and west, Southern routes from inland terminals to seaports, mostly north and south. The result was poor rail interconnection that put the South at a decided disadvantage for moving large numbers of troops.

Counterattack at Chickamauga

Up to this point, slow, deliberate "Rosy" Rosecrans had pulled off one of the most brilliant and remarkable campaigns of the war. After two-and-a-half years of combat in which each small gain was paid for by a torrent of blood, Rosecrans had taken the prize of Chattanooga almost without shedding any blood at all.

Inertia: the tendency of a body at rest to remain at rest, or—if in motion—to *stay* in motion. If one quality dominated the strategic thinking of William S. Rosecrans, it was *inertia*. He was slow to start his campaign, reluctant to accelerate his campaign, and, now that it was in full swing, he was not about to *stop* his campaign.

But he should have. He held Chattanooga now. He could concentrate his forces there, rest them, and resupply them, and *then* resume the offensive against Bragg. Instead, Rosecrans kept going, his three tired corps becoming separated from one another in the mountain passes.

Bragg, in the meantime, halted at LaFayette, Georgia, 25 miles south of Chattanooga, where he was met by substantial reinforcements, including two divisions commanded by James Longstreet. Reinforced, Bragg moved in for a counterattack. The place was Chickamauga Creek, in Georgia, just 12 miles south of Chattanooga, Tennessee. The date was September 19.

Sites and Sights

The place where the fighting at Chickamauga started still stands. The recently restored Lee and Gordon's Mill, a half-mile south of the Chickamauga and Chattanooga National Military Park (profiled later in this chapter) can be reached by taking Exit 350 (Battlefield Parkway or Highway 2) off I-75 west to Three Notches Road. Turn left and drive 10 miles (the road becomes Burning Bush Road) to the mill. The mansion of mill owner James Gordon, The Gordon-Lee Mansion, briefly used by Rosecrans as his headquarters, is located in the town of Chickamauga. Today, it is a functioning inn. Contact: 1-706-375-4728.

In the Thick of It

The night before the battle, both sides shifted and moved troops. In the thick woods, neither side knew the other's position. Worse, neither side was fully aware of the disposition of its own troops. With daybreak, Union general George Henry Thomas ordered a reconnaissance near Lee and Gordon's Mill, a local landmark on Chickamauga Creek. These troops, led by Brig. Gen. John Brannan, encountered and drove back the dismounted cavalry of Nathan Bedford Forrest.

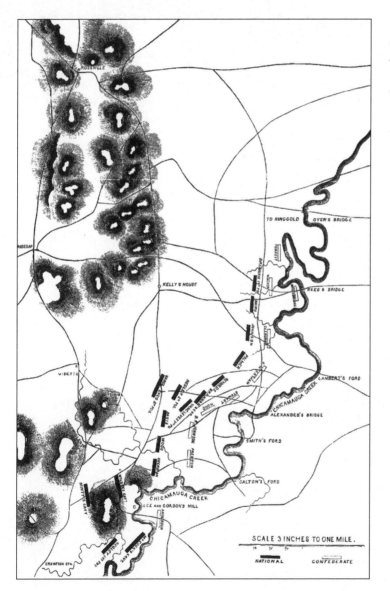

The Chickamauga battlefield on September 19, 1863. The solid rectangles represent Union troop positions, the open rectangles Confederate.

(Harper's Pictorial History of the Civil War, *1866)*

Forrest called on nearby infantry units for help, and, suddenly, an all-out battle exploded. Every division of the three Union corps was engaged, and, of the Confederates, only two divisions were held in reserve.

The fighting—it lasted all day—was some of the bloodiest in the war's western theater, more than making up for Rosecrans's relatively pacific capture of Chattanooga. Yet, for all the bloodshed, neither side had gained an advantage by day's end.

Voices

Wounded Union private Arthur van Lisle recalled an act of kindness at the end of the first day of battle at Chickamauga:

> … The day is waning. What a terrible day it has been! Night approaches. What horrors will it bring forth? Surely if my comrades cannot help me I must die; and I must die here, with no friend to soothe my last moments or tell the story of my death to the loved ones at home. I am growing weaker and weaker from the loss of blood, which is now drying upon my body and stiffening my clothing. Fever is in my veins, and I am perishing from thirst. Oh for a drink! Water, water, WATER! …

> … a Confederate soldier, standing over me, bravely fighting, seeing my bloody side and parched lips, stooped down and, throwing the strap of his canteen over his head, put the nozzle to my mouth, saying as he did so, "Drink, Yank, I reckon you're powerful dry." …

> I drank … [then] offered to return the [canteen], feebly raising [it] above my head with outstretched arm.

> "Jest you keep it," I heard him shout that as he retired, loading his gun.

A "Gap" That Wasn't

Applied to the site of the contest at Chickamauga, the word "battlefield" was a misnomer. A *field* it was not, but heavily forested and difficult terrain that had been turned into muddy soup by heavy rains. On the first night, both sides hastily tried to improve their positions, and Rosecrans's men dug in as best they could. That night, too, Bragg received reinforcements in the form of Longstreet's divisions.

At 9:00 on Sunday morning, September 20, the Confederates attacked, and for the next two hours, the Federals held them off.

Rosecrans was nothing if not a careful planner. But the terrain of Chickamauga could confuse any commander and confound any plan. The fact was, General Rosecrans did not have an accurate understanding of just how his own units were deployed. His object, by midmorning of this second day of battle, was to fill what he thought was a gap in his right flank. Accordingly, he ordered troops from what he thought was the left to plug the gap in the right.

But there was no gap. Worse, thinking he was moving troops from the left to the right, Rosecrans actually moved them out of the right flank, thereby *creating* the very gap he had meant to plug. At 11:30, Longstreet attacked at precisely the gap Rosecrans had inadvertently made, hitting divisions commanded by Maj. Gen. Philip Sheridan and by Brig. Gen. Jefferson Columbus Davis, shattering them, and driving the Union right onto its left.

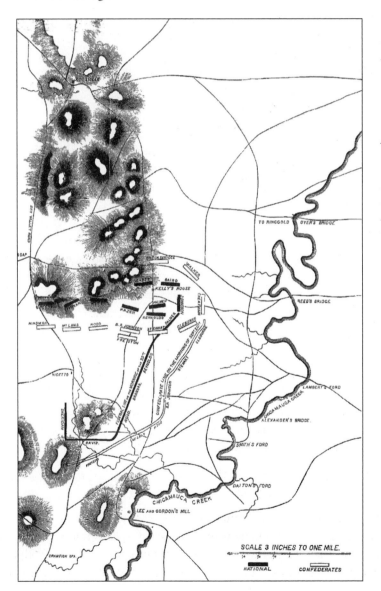

The Chickamauga battlefield on September 20, 1863. The solid rectangles represent Union troop positions, the open rectangles Confederate. The map shows how the Union lines were broken and pushed back against the thickly wooded hills. The Confederate line engulfed the Federal troops, leading Rosecrans to assume the Army of the Cumberland was done for.

(Harper's Pictorial History of the Civil War, *1866*)

Rock of Chickamauga

The Battle of Chickamauga was rapidly disintegrating into a military disaster as terrible as any that had ever befallen the Union army. Rosecrans and two of his corps commanders, Thomas Leonidas Crittenden and Alexander McDowell McCook, unable to rally their routed forces, believed that the entire army was being destroyed. They joined the chaotic retreat to Chattanooga.

War News
Thomas Leonidas Crittenden was one of two sons of Kentucky Senator John Jordan Crittenden, whose Crittenden Compromise of 1860 was a last-ditch effort to avert civil war (see Chapter 4). Crittenden's other warrior son, George, became a *Confederate* general. For Alexander McDowell McCook, the Civil War was also a family affair. He was one of the 17 "Fighting McCooks of Ohio," which included six generals, an army surgeon, and a naval officer, in addition to other officers and enlisted men.

Count Off!

The name Chickamauga is derived from a Cherokee word meaning "river of death." Of 58,222 Union troops engaged, 1,657 were killed, 9,756 wounded, and 4,757 went missing. Confederate losses were 2,312 killed, 14,674 wounded, and 1,468 missing out of 66,326 engaged. Chickamauga was the costliest battle of the war's western theater.

But Maj. Gen. George Henry Thomas did not run. He rallied units under Brig. Gen. Thomas John Wood and Brig. Gen. John Brannan to block Longstreet on the south. Because Bragg had not held any men in reserve, he had nobody to send in to exploit Longstreet's initial breakthrough. In the meantime, Union general Gordon Granger deliberately violated his orders to remain in place to protect the army's flank and, instead, rushed to the aid of Thomas with two brigades. This action proved a splendid example of initiative on the field. Thomas—later hailed as the "Rock of Chickamauga"—was able to hold the field until nightfall and thereby save the Army of the Cumberland from destruction.

The Good Dog

The Battle of Chickamauga was a tactical victory for Braxton Bragg. He had driven Rosecrans from the field. However, Confederate losses were greater than those of the Union and, even worse, Bragg had coordinated the attack poorly. Even after Longstreet found the nearly fatal gap in the Union line, the Confederate assaults were piecemeal, and without a reserve the Confederates could not exploit their gains to provide a strategically decisive victory.

"Bragg's a good dog," William S. Rosecrans had said after he withstood the Confederate's attacks at Stones River on December 31, 1862, "but Hold Fast's a better." "Hold Fast"—the name Rosecrans slapped on himself after Stones River—was swept away in the rout at Chickamauga and, for that, would be relieved of command. The reputations of his subordinates A.M. McCook, T.L. Crittenden, and Maj. Gen. James Scott Negley would be ruined or badly damaged.

As to Bragg, he took it upon himself to relieve three of *his* subordinates, Leonidas Polk, Daniel Harvey Hill, and Thomas C. Hindman—all of whom were subsequently reinstated. Bragg, the "good dog" himself, would be relieved as commander of the Army of Tennessee at the end of December 1863; he became military advisor to Jefferson Davis in Richmond.

Sites and Sights

The Chickamauga and Chattanooga National Military Park is the largest Civil War battlefield park in the National Park system. The scene of much confusion and carnage during the fall of 1863, it is beautiful and tranquil today. There is a visitor's center, three period cabins (two reconstructions and one original structure), and Wilder Tower, which affords a breathtaking view of the battlefield. Near the summit of Lookout Mountain is a spectacular overlook and the Adolph S. Ochs Museum. A bit farther down is the restored Cravens House, scene of the climactic action of the Lookout Mountain battle.

The park's address is P.O. Box 2128, Fort Oglethorpe, GA 30742, but it extends into Chattanooga. Contact: 1-706-866-9241.

Yankees Under Siege

But much more was at stake than the reputations of a handful of officers. The Union's Army of the Cumberland was holed up in Chattanooga, to which Bragg's Confederates were laying siege. Starvation and capture were the grim prospects staring the Union forces in their gaunt faces.

Yet, in a sense, this desperate situation was a boon to the Union cause. It suddenly riveted Washington's focus on this neglected theater of the war. Two entire army corps were detached from Meade and sent west under Joe Hooker. In the war's most dramatic demonstration of the strategic importance of rail transportation, they were transferred from the banks of eastern Virginia's Rappahannock River to Bridgeport,

War News

Remember, the Union named its armies after the major river in the unit's region of operations, while the Confederates named theirs after states or regions; thus Sherman led the Army of *the* Tennessee, and Bragg commanded the Army of Tennessee.

Alabama, in the space of eight days, arriving on October 2. In the meantime, Sherman led part of the Union's Army of the Tennessee east from Memphis, and Ulysses S. Grant was given command of all military operations west of the Alleghenies (save Nathaniel Banks's hapless campaign along the Louisiana-Texas border).

Cracker Line

Grant took charge as only Grant could. Through a series of complex operations planned and executed with great vigor and precision, the new commander efficiently punched through a Confederate outpost on the Tennessee River west of Lookout Mountain and opened up a supply route to beleaguered Chattanooga. By this time, Maj. Gen. Thomas had taken over command of the Army of the Cumberland from Rosecrans, and Thomas's miserable, hungry, lice-infested troops gratefully dubbed the new stream of supplies that flowed to them the "Cracker Line." The line, 60 miles long, was cobbled together with steamboats and *scows* (flat-bottomed boats), a pontoon bridge, and wagons.

Words of War

A **scow** is a large flat-bottomed boat with square ends fore and aft. It is used for transporting freight.

A Visit from the President

Braxton Bragg's plan had been to starve Rosecrans out. When that didn't seem to work, he ordered raiding operations against the Union lines of communication (Wheeler's Raid of October 1–9 and Roddey's Raid of October 7–14), but these actions, although disruptive, were not decisive.

Bragg, a dour and cantankerous man, was intensely disliked by the officers and men of his command. Both Longstreet and Brig. Gen. Nathan Bedford Forrest reviled him for his failures at Chickamauga and for his long inaction at Chattanooga. Those now laying siege against Chattanooga were almost as hungry as the city's Union defenders. The situation was deteriorating, and President Jefferson Davis paid a personal battlefield visit.

"Send us something to eat, Massa Jeff. I'm hungry," Private Sam Watkins called out to his commander-in-chief as he reviewed the ragtag troops.

Davis backed his old friend and commander, telling Longstreet and Forrest during his visit that Bragg had his full support. Only after the big battles at Lookout Mountain and Missionary Ridge would Davis replace Bragg with Joe Johnston.

A Battle Above the Clouds and a Soldier's Battle

Sherman did not reach the Union rallying point at Bridgeport, Alabama, until November 15, having been delayed by Maj. Gen. Halleck's frustrating insistence that he pause to repair rail lines into Nashville. It was perhaps just as well; for now the defenders of Chattanooga, fed by the Cracker Line, were refreshed and ready to fight. Grant, too, was in position, and, after a delay imposed by heavy rains, Sherman was ready to attack as well. The fight was set for November 24.

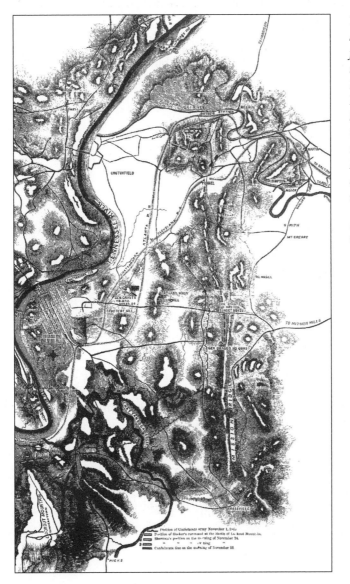

This map shows Chattanooga and the sites of the two most famous battles associated with its defense on November 24–25, 1863. The Tennessee River runs through the upper left quadrant of the map; Chattanooga is halfway up the map at the left; Lookout Mountain is in the lower left corner; and Missionary Ridge is in the lower right quadrant.

(Harper's Pictorial History of the Civil War, *1866*)

Fighting Joe

November 24, 1863, dawned heavily overcast and foggy. Maj. Gen. Joseph Hooker, a failure in command at Chancellorsville (see Chapter 14), was now subordinate to Grant. Ordered to take Lookout Mountain, the 1,100-foot prominence guarding the Tennessee River just outside Chattanooga, Hooker commenced what was literally an uphill battle at eight in the morning. It would continue until well after midnight. Then, early on the morning of the 25th, soldiers from the 8th Kentucky Regiment scrambled up to the summit and planted the Stars and Stripes.

The sun had come out by then, and the spectacularly dramatic effect was not lost on war correspondents, who dubbed the Battle of Lookout Mountain the "Battle Above the Clouds." And Joe Hooker? He was "Fighting Joe" again, a national hero.

Sherman

William Tecumseh Sherman did not fare as gloriously. He took his units upstream on the Tennessee and hit the Confederates' right wing, but made little headway against it. Finally, on the afternoon of November 25, Grant ordered Thomas to lead the men of the Army of the Cumberland forward to take the Confederate *rifle pits* (dug-out emplacements) at the base of Missionary Ridge south of Chattanooga and just to the east of Lookout Mountain. Grant's object was to put enough pressure on Bragg to force him to recall troops from Sherman's front and possibly allow Sherman to break through.

Words of War

Rifle pits were the Civil War equivalent of World War II's foxholes: hastily dug shallow trenches that afforded riflemen a degree of protection.

"You Scaled the Mountain!"

The men of the Army of the Cumberland had been bottled up in Chattanooga for a long while, and they had been given a hard time by the soldiers of Hooker and Sherman, who took every available opportunity to remind them that because they lost at Chickamauga, they had been in sore and sorry need of a rescue.

Clearly feeling that it had something to prove, the Army of the Cumberland advanced, took the rifle pits, thereby accomplishing the mission Grant had assigned them; then, with no orders from Grant or Thomas, they kept right on going, charging up the steep slope of Missionary Ridge and sweeping all before them. Incredibly, the Army of the Cumberland broke Bragg's line where it was the strongest, sending the Confederates into full retreat.

"Who ordered those men up the hill?" Grant turned to an aide.

"No one," came the answer.

Voices

Confederate private Sam Watkins recalled what it was like retreating down the mountainside:

> The Yankees were cutting and slashing, and the cannoneers were running in every direction. I saw [one] brigade throw down their guns and break like quarter horses. Bragg was trying to rally them. I heard him say, "Here is your commander," and the soldiers hallooed back, "Here is your mule."

A Union war correspondent heard General Granger declare to the victorious men of his command: "You ought to be court-martialed, every man of you. I ordered you to take the rifle pits, and you scaled the mountain!" "His cheeks," according to the reporter, "were wet with tears as honest as the blood that reddened all the route."

Thus the Chattanooga Campaign came to a victorious conclusion for the Union. The assault on Missionary Ridge was a *soldier's battle*, an explosion of fury, frustration, and a burning desire to avenge defeat at Chickamauga, not because the "Rock of Chickamauga" or even U.S. Grant himself had given a command, but because *it was what the soldiers themselves needed to do.*

Words of War

The Army of the Cumberland's assault on Missionary Ridge was a classic **soldier's battle**—a battle in which the outcome is determined more by the action of the soldiers and the junior officers than by the leadership of principal commanders.

Sunset in the West

The sun, as everyone knows, sets in the west. With the loss of the Chattanooga Campaign, the sun set as well on any hopes the Confederacy had in the West.

For the Union, however, this victory was the dawn of a new day. As Navy Secretary Gideon Welles wrote in his diary on December 31, 1863, "The year closes more satisfactorily than it commenced …. There have been errors and misfortunes … but the heart of the nation is sounder and its hopes brighter."

The Least You Need to Know

- ◆ Major General Rosecrans took Chattanooga in a campaign of brilliant maneuver with little cost, only to blunder into the Battle of Chickamauga and suffer a tactical defeat.

- ◆ Although tactically victorious at Chickamauga, Braxton Bragg failed to gain any strategic objectives and certainly failed to destroy the Army of the Cumberland.

- ◆ Relieving the Confederate siege of Chattanooga revealed Ulysses S. Grant at his most skillful, brilliant, and effective.

- ◆ The Union victory in the Chattanooga Campaign permanently ended the Confederate threat west of the Allegheny Mountains.

Part 5

The Last Full Measure

In this section, the principal commanders are Ulysses S. Grant, Robert E. Lee, and William Tecumseh Sherman. Grant, the new general-in-chief of all Union armies, personally leads the Army of the Potomac in its final thrust toward Richmond, but pays an unspeakably heavy price. Sherman decides to turn away from the enemy *army* and attack the enemy *people*, leaving a swath of destruction in his wake.

Grant finally breaks through at Petersburg, takes Richmond, and pursues Lee and his broken army to a place called Appomattox Court House. There, on April 9, 1865, Lee surrenders to Grant. Within days, the other Confederate commanders also surrender, and the war is over.

Chapter 18

Mr. Lincoln's General

In This Chapter

- ◆ Grant emerges as a Union leader
- ◆ "That devil Forrest"
- ◆ The Fort Pillow Massacre
- ◆ The fate of the Civil War POW

Military men, as well as historians, often speak of the "art of war," a phrase that might strike our ears as strange. Armies are about killing people and breaking things. What has this to do with "art"?

Yet this ambiguous word, *art*, is valuable for thinking about war in general and about the Civil War in particular. On the one hand, *art* suggests beauty, the beauty of planning and pattern, and to look at a great commander's battle plan is to behold a work of art: a dynamic pattern. But, on the other hand, *art* suggests a contrast with *science*. Whereas science deals in orderly fact, art embraces *disorder*, inventiveness, improvisation, brilliance of inspiration, and reliance on gut instinct.

Over and over again, in the American Civil War, this second connotation proved to be the chief feature of the art of war. Lincoln hired and fired one general after another in search of a commander to lead the Union's forces and, in particular, the Army of the Potomac. Plan after plan and man after man failed in the disordered reality of war. After Winfield Scott retired, the president turned to George B. McClellan, then John Pope, Henry Wager Halleck, and Ambrose Burnside, then "Fighting Joe" Hooker, then George Meade, and finally, on March 9, 1864, he found Ulysses Simpson Grant. This chapter is about Grant's hard choices in a very hard war.

He Fights

If war were an orderly science, Lincoln would have put Robert E. Lee at the head of his nation's army. The president offered the post to Lee, but geography and politics refused to cooperate with Lincoln's desires, and Lee went off to fight for the Confederacy instead.

Of Lincoln's commanders, McClellan certainly showed evidence of understanding the art of war. He built the Army of the Potomac into a well-organized and disciplined body—but it seemed he was *forever* ordering and organizing rather than using the well-oiled machine he'd created. Halleck had written a book about war, and he had an academician's understanding of strategy and tactics. But the realities of combat showed this to be as much a liability as it was an asset. Burnside was well liked and brave, but he proved sorely deficient in strategic and tactical sense; as you remember from Chapter 12, Fredericksburg was "murder, not war." Hooker was an able strategist and tactician, but Lee was abler, and at Chancellorsville, by his own admission, Hooker simply lost his nerve.

Of all the men who had commanded the Army of the Potomac, George Meade was probably the most satisfactory. Almost immediately after assuming command from Hooker, he led the army to victory at Gettysburg, one of the great turning-point battles of the war. Yet he, too, fell short, allowing Lee and the Army of Northern Virginia to limp away from what should have been total defeat.

Only after three full years of war did Ulysses S. Grant emerge as the most adept practitioner of its "art." When the cost of Grant's victory at Shiloh (see Chapter 7) in April 1862—13,047 Union soldiers killed, wounded, or missing—was made public, calls came for Grant's dismissal. He was rumored to be a hard drinker, and stories circulated that he was drunk during the battle. Disgusted by these accusations and even more by the nation's refusal to accept what he grimly accepted—that war means hurt and hurting and death and killing—Grant almost resigned. Lincoln, however, gave him his vote of confidence: "I can't spare this man," the president said. "He fights."

Grant's Will

It was a bold position for the president to take. Of all his generals, Grant *seemed* one of the least likely to succeed in independent command. For one thing, there were the rumors of his drinking. Lincoln brushed that issue aside after Vicksburg by asking (according to the *New York Tribune*), "By the way, can you tell me where he gets his whiskey? … I should like to send a barrel of the same brand to every general in the field."

And then there was his mediocre record at West Point (21st out of a class of 39 in 1843) and his repeated failures in civilian life after he resigned his commission in 1854. There was failure as a farmer, as a real estate speculator, and as a merchant, which compelled him to take a job as clerk in the small-town tannery owned by his father and brother. Most of the army's other generals either enjoyed military careers of uninterrupted success or were captains of industry, like McClellan, who had been president of the Illinois Central Railroad. Grant entered the Civil War not as a regular army officer or even as a politician important enough to merit a patronage commission, but as the drillmaster of the patriotic but provincial Galena, Illinois, militia company.

Words of War

Independent command, as contrasted with **subordinate command,** is the label applied to the highest military ranks, in which commanders must determine overall strategy as well as specific tactics.

If war proceeded by orderly plan, Grant would have remained an obscure failure. But war, especially *this* war, killed plans as prodigiously as it killed men. And as the war killed men and their plans, exposing the weaknesses of one commander after another, war brought out in Ulysses Grant a genius for combat on a scale unprecedented on the American continent.

From the beginning, Grant grasped the terrible common denominator at the root of this war. The South had fewer men, less money, and fewer resources than the North. The South could not afford to lose what little it had. The North *could* afford to lose more of what it had because it had so much more. It was a simple equation, the terrible calculus of attrition, written in flesh and blood.

Grant understood this equation and, even more important, had the will to accept it. Importantly, Grant had time to learn from his mistakes, to mature as a soldier, and to apply what he learned, away from the scrutiny of Washington that so many Eastern commanders were subjected to.

Grant's Strategy

Summoned to Washington on March 9, 1864, to receive his commission as lieutenant general and supreme commander of all the Union armies, Grant was also prepared with a strategy as deadly simple as the equation that drove this war.

Henry Wager "Old Brains" Halleck, until now Grant's commanding officer, was a conventional man who understood the art of war in conventional terms. He believed an army should hold and occupy the "strategic points," the cities and towns, of the territory it captured. The result of this thinking was the repeated dispersal and dilution of forces west of the Alleghenies, much to the frustration of Grant. In particular, an expedition to invade Texas via Louisiana, the Red River campaign of 1864 (March 10–22), led to nothing but wasted effort, a congressional investigation, and the dismissal from command of expedition leader Maj. Gen. Nathaniel Prentiss Banks.

Now Grant would do things differently. He saw that the taking of cities and strategic points and the occupation of Southern territory meant nothing as long as the principal Confederate armies remained in the field. Not with the occupation of land and the subjugation of cities would victory come, but only with the death of the Confederate armies. The only reason to attack a city, Grant reasoned, was to force the enemy army to fight so that the army could be destroyed. As for the city itself, it was nearly an irrelevant objective.

Two main armies needed to be destroyed: Robert E. Lee's Army of Northern Virginia and the Army of Tennessee, now under the command of Joseph E. Johnston, who had replaced Bragg after the loss of Chattanooga.

Focus was one of Grant's strongest points. To be sure, other Confederate forces were west of the Mississippi River. But Grant, in contrast to Halleck, understood that his own victories in that region had severed those forces from the rest of the Confederacy. They were there, true enough, but they hardly mattered now. The important fight was against Lee and Johnston.

A New Army of Veterans

Grant commanded an army with a high proportion of veterans; yet, as he reorganized its command, it also became a new, reinvigorated army. The armies of 1864 also had many drafted men, as well as those induced to enlist through the payment of bounties. With great good judgment, Grant turned over command of the western theater to a general who had earned his most profound respect, William Tecumseh Sherman.

Like Grant, Sherman did not possess a distinguished record of achievement, military or otherwise. He had been stationed in California as an administrative officer during the Mexican War, and so missed the fighting and the glory. When he resigned his commission in 1853, he started a banking and building firm, which went belly up four years later. He practiced law briefly in Leavenworth, Kansas, and then became superintendent of the Alexandria Military Academy in Louisiana.

We have seen (in Chapter 7) that Sherman's early record in the Civil War was disappointing. But, like Grant, he had an unflinching vision of just what this war would be. When he spoke frankly about what he saw as the conflict's likely cost in lives, he was branded insane by the press, and his career was nearly ended. Subsequent bloody months would prove Sherman all too sane (and, conversely, perhaps the rest of America mad).

Sherman performed brilliantly and heroically at Shiloh and in all subsequent operations under Grant, and, like Grant, he learned from his past mistakes. With Grant's elevation to commander in chief of the Union army, Sherman took his place as commander of the Military Division of the Mississippi, in charge of action in the West. He was to move down the route of the Western and Atlantic Railroad, advancing inexorably against Atlanta—and, more to the point, doing battle with the Army of Tennessee.

"I was to go for Joe Johnston," Sherman laconically observed of the role Grant had assigned him.

While Grant had overall command of the forces "going for" Robert E. Lee, he asked General Meade to remain in command of the Army of the Potomac, although Grant himself exercised much personal control of that army. He saw the Army of the Potomac for what it was: a remarkable fighting force that had been poorly and inconsistently led, its tremendous exertions and sacrifices having therefore yielded disappointing results.

Grant brought one more officer into top command of the Army of the Potomac. Philip Sheridan—Little Phil, his men affectionately called him—was a scrappy, no-nonsense fighter and a resourceful, courageous infantry commander, whom Grant now tapped to lead the cavalry.

As Sherman would advance on Atlanta, forcing Johnston to fight him in order to defend the city, Grant would advance on Richmond, less with the object of taking the Confederate capital than with the purpose of fighting the Army

> ## War News
>
> Sheridan was as blunt-spoken as Sherman. After the war, in 1867, he was named military commander of Louisiana and Texas, but he was so harsh in administering the stringent and punitive Reconstruction measures that President Andrew Johnson soon removed him. "If I owned both Hell and Texas," Sheridan declared, "I'd rent out Texas and live in Hell."

of Northern Virginia, which would rush to the capital's defense. In addition to the main body of the Army of the Potomac, Grant aimed two other armies at Richmond: the Army of the James, 33,000 men under Ben Butler, and a force in the Shenandoah Valley, led by Franz Sigel. For the very first time in this three-year-old war, the Union army would make a truly coordinated movement: one army against Atlanta and three against Richmond. The grand operation began on May 4, 1864.

Short, scrappy Philip Sheridan was trained as an infantry commander, but Grant put him in charge of the Army of the Potomac's cavalry. He performed brilliantly.

(Harper's Pictorial History of the Civil War, *1866*)

"And Fightin' Means Killin'"

Who were the great antagonists of the Civil War? "Grant and Lee" is a good answer, although they became adversaries only during the climactic months of the war. Although it is true that Grant was *the* great Union general, and Lee was *the* great Confederate general, perhaps Grant's truer opposite number was not Robert E. Lee, but Nathan Bedford Forrest.

A Tale of Two Generals

We first met Forrest in Chapter 7, when he indignantly refused to join generals Simon Bolivar Buckner and Gideon Pillow in surrendering Fort Donelson. He deftly escaped the fort, saving from surrender his own command and hundreds of additional volunteers.

That was only one of the many remarkable things this officer did. He had been raised in poverty in Tennessee with almost no formal education, but nevertheless made a fortune as a cotton planter in Mississippi. He enlisted in the Confederate army as a private one month before his fortieth birthday in 1861; then, in October of that year, raised a battalion at his own expense and was commissioned a lieutenant colonel to command it. Forrest fought a brilliant rear-guard action at Shiloh, thereby preserving the battered Confederate army after that costly battle. Severely wounded in that action, he narrowly escaped paralysis from a bullet lodged near his spine.

Nathan Bedford Forrest was deemed by Union general Sherman the most brilliant commander of the war. His philosophy: "War means fightin', and fightin' means killin'." His strategy: "Get there first with the most men." After the war, he helped start the Ku Klux Klan.

(Harper's Pictorial History of the Civil War, *1866*)

Promoted to brigadier general, Forrest conducted raids in 1864 throughout Mississippi, Tennessee, and Alabama so brilliant and destructive that Sherman, calling him "that devil Forrest," declared that he must be "hunted down and killed if it costs ten thousand lives and bankrupts the Federal treasury." Sherman continued: "There will never be peace in Tennessee till Forrest is dead."

After the war, both Sherman and Confederate general Joe Johnston named Forrest the most remarkable soldier of the entire conflict. Johnston declared that, if Forrest "had had the advantages of a thorough military education and training, [he] would have been the great central figure of the Civil War." Forrest himself

War News

Forrest was wounded on and off the battlefield. On June 14, 1863, a subordinate picked a fight with him and shot him. In the scuffle that followed, the wounded Forrest held the subordinate's gun hand while prying open a penknife with his teeth, and then used it to deliver a fatal wound to his opponent's gut.

summed up his theory of battle in a single sentence: "Get there first with the most men," a maxim popularly misquoted as "Git thar fustest with the mostest."

The Fort Pillow Massacre

And Forrest had another saying. "War," he said, "means fightin', and fightin' means killin'." U.S. Grant never put it quite this way, but he might have. Like Grant, Forrest had no patience with romantic concepts of chivalry and "civilized" rules of engagement. Victory meant defeating one's enemy, and usually defeating him meant killing him, or killing more of him than he killed of you.

Grant and Forrest, had they ever met, would have understood one another, and yet, for all his willingness to kill, and to suffer casualties in order to kill, Grant remained a soldier. Forrest, apparently, crossed the line and became something else.

It happened on April 12, 1864. Forrest sent a Confederate division under Brig. Gen. James R. Chalmers to Fort Pillow, an earthwork fort and trading post on a high bluff overlooking the Mississippi, originally built by Confederate general Gideon Pillow, but now occupied by a Union garrison. Its mission was to defend Union supply lines.

Forrest's mission was to disrupt Union supply lines. Taking Fort Pillow would allow him to do just that. The fort was garrisoned by 262 black soldiers and 295 whites—many of them Tennesseans loyal to the Union. After Chalmers had driven in the fort's pickets and surrounded the garrison, Forrest arrived to take personal command. He made a surrender demand, which was refused. Then the Confederates swarmed into the fort.

At this point, Southern and Northern accounts differ. What is certain is that some 231 members of the garrison were killed and another 100 grievously wounded; in addition, 168 whites and 58 blacks were captured. Southern losses were disproportionately slight: 14 killed, 86 wounded. Southerners explained that the Federal losses were the result of resistance to surrender, whereas Northern sources claimed that the garrison surrendered as soon as the fort had been breached. The rebels (Northern survivors said) shouted, "No quarter! No quarter! Kill the damned niggers; shoot them down!"

And, over it all presided Nathan Bedford Forrest.

A Congressional Committee on the Conduct of the War concluded that Forrest and his troops were guilty of atrocities: murdering most of the garrison *after* it had surrendered, burying some black troops alive, and putting to the torch tents sheltering the Federal wounded. Most historians believe that atrocities were in fact committed—although some Southern historians dissent from this view, calling the massacre story Northern propaganda.

After the war, Nathan Bedford Forrest rebuilt his fortune, becoming a plantation owner again as well as president of the Selma, Marion, and Memphis Railroad. He was also a founder of the original Ku Klux Klan and served as its Grand Wizard.

Prisoners of War

Civil War atrocity came in many forms. For Grant, it was a willingness to spend lives; because that expenditure eventually bought victory, it was called "strategy" rather than "atrocity." For Forrest at Fort Pillow, atrocity was not strategy, but the unleashing of pent-up racial and political hatred.

And then there was another kind of atrocity, which the world first saw on a large scale in the American Civil War and would not see again until the mid-twentieth century brought World War II: atrocities against prisoners of war.

Exchange and Parole

By the nineteenth century, most Western nations had made some attempt to treat prisoners of war humanely. Sometimes nations even signed formal treaties to guarantee decent treatment. At the very least, diplomats and generals had *gentlemen's agreements* (diplomatic letters) on the subject.

The most humane way to handle POWs was to exchange them. That's the way it usually worked in nineteenth-century Europe. There were no large POW camps; instead, prisoners were exchanged on a regular, one-for-one basis. But President Lincoln declined to set up a formal exchange system because he did not want to make any treaty with the Confederacy. To do so, he argued, would be implicitly to recognize the Confederate States of America as a sovereign foreign power (only such powers have legitimate treaty-making authority) rather than an illegal collection of rebellious citizens.

Words of War

As used in diplomacy, a **gentlemen's agreement** is an understanding between two nations, usually drawn up in the form of a diplomatic letter rather than a fully binding treaty.

Nevertheless, he allowed his generals to make informal exchanges under flags of truce. By 1862, this casual arrangement was formalized by an agreement, the Dix-Hill Cartel of July 22, between the opposing *armies*—not the *governments*—whereby prisoners were to be exchanged within 10 days of capture. They even agreed on an exchange rate: one private for one private, but two privates for one noncommissioned officer, all the way up to 60 privates for a lieutenant general. (A major general merited 40 privates.) The cartel applied similarly to sailors and naval officers.

The relatively complex arithmetic of the exchange system quickly broke down, however, and each side's prisons filled with POWs awaiting exchange. From the very beginning of the war, civilians suspected of disloyalty—or caught out-and-out spying for the enemy—were not imprisoned or executed (that form of punishment came later in the war), but were merely "paroled." That is, a man caught spying in the North was sent to the South in return for his pledge not to come North again. Unable to make the Dix-Hill Cartel work, the military decided to try this system as well. POWs awaiting exchange were not housed in prison camps, but returned to their lines in exchange for their pledge that they would not return to duty until they had been formally exchanged.

Words of War

Parole comes from the French word for *word* or *promise* and, during the Civil War, meant the act of releasing a POW to his own lines on the condition that he give his word of honor not to fight until he was officially exchanged for a prisoner held by the enemy.

Grant's Grim Decision

Taking prisoners was a good thing because it removed enemy soldiers from action. Prisoners, however, were also a burden on the manpower and supplies of the victor, who had to use resources to guard, transport, feed, house, and (if they were wounded) care for the prisoners. After his victory at Vicksburg (see Chapter 13), Grant captured more than 31,000 rebel POWs. Faced with the prospect of transporting and guarding them, he decided to parole them instead.

Then, during the Chattanooga Campaign (see Chapter 17), Grant discovered that an alarmingly high proportion of the prisoners he now took were the very men he had paroled at Vicksburg. After Grant was given overall command of the Union armies, he called a halt to all prisoner exchange on April 17, 1864.

In part, his motives sprang from frustration over Confederate violations of parole and from the Confederacy's refusal to exchange black POWs and the white officers of black regiments. But an even more important consideration was Grant's realization that prisoner exchange was of far more benefit to the manpower-poor Confederacy than it was to the relatively manpower-rich Union. The South desperately needed its prisoners returned; the North could afford to lose some prisoners. Moreover, Northern prisoners in Southern POW camps put an added burden on a government so strained that, as Grant and anyone else could see, it was hard pressed to clothe and feed its own army properly.

It was a grim decision. Grant must have known that conditions in Confederate POW camps were unspeakably filthy and cruel, that starvation rations and rampant disease were the norm, and that a refusal to exchange prisoners was, for many of his soldiers, a death warrant and a guarantee that conditions would only worsen. But the grim decision was typical of Ulysses S. Grant. He knew this: However hard the consequences were on his own side, they were far harder on the other. It was yet one more equation of war, and nothing short of victory could change it.

Andersonville and Other Horrors

Early in the war, prison camps were fairly civilized places. Not only did the military on both sides treat its prisoners well (they were usually only short-term "guests," after all), but also local ladies, out of a sense of "Christian charity," typically visited the prisons and brought the inmates bundles of fresh food and other small comforts.

These Confederate prisoners (captured at Gettysburg) strike casually defiant poses for a Union photographer.

(Library of Congress)

Then, as the war ground on, life, it seemed, grew cheaper, bitterness grew sharper, supplies grew scarcer, and the desire for retribution and revenge grew ever more powerful. In Richmond, the warehouse of Libby & Sons Ship Chandlers and Grocers was converted into a prison for Union officers. The floor plan of the three-story building measured only 100 by 150 feet, but into it were jammed 1,200 men. Ostensibly to prevent escapes—and there *were* escapes—jailer Dick Turner gave his guards leave to shoot anyone who ventured to a window, say, to catch the sound of birdsong, a glimpse of sunlight, or even a breath of air.

As bad as conditions were in Richmond-area prisons, they were far worse at the place officially called Camp Sumter, but better known by the name of the adjacent town: Andersonville.

Set in the sweltering heart of Georgia, the Andersonville stockade was built to accommodate 10,000 POWs. Tents provided the only shelter, medical care was nonexistent, food was next to nil, and water came from Stockade Creek, which also served as the prison latrine and sewer. At the height of its operation, prisoners poured in at the rate of 400 a day. By August 1864, Andersonville harbored 33,000 POWs.

The camp was first run by Brig. Gen. John Henry Winder, provost marshal general of the Confederate army. After he was transferred to Richmond (where he collapsed and died from fatigue in February 1865), Capt. Henry Wirz was put in charge of the prison.

Wirz soon earned a reputation for extravagant cruelty. He reportedly took pride in the knowledge that (as one prisoner heard him declare) he "was killing more damned Yankees with his treatment than they were with powder and lead in the army." Among the most notorious of his actions was his establishment of a perimeter within the stockade. He called it the "dead line," and any prisoner who ventured beyond it was shot down without warning.

After the war, Henry Wirz was tried by a Union tribunal, which found him guilty of unjustly causing at least 10,000 deaths, mostly from neglect and starvation. He became the only Confederate soldier executed by the United States for his actions during the war. The Daughters of the Confederacy, maintaining that all prisoner deaths were caused by unavoidable food shortages, declared Wirz a victim of "judicial murder" and erected a memorial to the captain at the town of Andersonville in 1909. It still stands.

Sites and Sights

The Andersonville National Historic Site, along State Route 49, 10 miles northeast of Americus, Georgia, features reconstructions of various prison structures and is a moving memorial not only to Civil War POWs, but to all the prisoners of war in America's history. Contact: 1-912-924-0343.

Words of War

A **provost marshal** is, in effect, the chief of the military police. His job is to maintain both security and order.

Count Off!

Of 45,000 prisoners confined at Andersonville during 1864–1865, 13,000 died and were buried in proper graves; the actual death toll was probably significantly higher. Nevertheless, at minimum, mortality at Andersonville ran to 29 percent. Only one Confederate prison, the much smaller 10,000-man camp at Salisbury, North Carolina, had a higher mortality rate: 34 percent.

Andersonville might have been the worst and most notorious of Civil War prison camps, but it wasn't the only scene of inhumane prisoner treatment. The North, which, unlike the South, had plenty of food and other supplies to go around, also treated its POWs with little charity and less conscience. At the POW camp in Elmira, New York, for example, the death rate among some 12,000 prisoners ran to 25 percent—the result of poor rations, disease, and perhaps most of all, exposure to the Upstate winter. Eventually, Secretary of War Edwin Stanton ordered the already inadequate rations *cut* to the levels Confederates supplied Union prisoners. The secretary declared this to be fair play. Others, in both North and South, saw it as raw revenge.

Prison camps like Andersonville and "Hellmira" (as rebel POWs called the Elmira facility) lifted the veil, exposing this war for what all war finally is. *Death*. Patriotism, glory, gallantry, courage, strategy, loyalty, and all the rest were ultimately side issues. It was the terrible genius of such commanders as Ulysses S. Grant and Nathan Bedford Forrest to effectively and consistently divorce such side issues from the only issue that finally mattered. In men like Grant and Forrest and at places like Andersonville and Elmira, the United States cruelly came of age and lost its innocence.

The Least You Need to Know

- Ulysses S. Grant emerged as the man to command the Union armies only after trial by three years of war.

- Grant understood the most important basic truth about this war: Men would die, and the North could afford to lose more men than the South.

- Grant's victory strategy was simple: Don't worry about taking cities and occupying territory; just destroy the enemy armies.

- After Grant halted prisoner exchange on April 17, 1864, POWs on both sides suffered under great inhumanity; many died of disease, starvation, abuse, and neglect.

Chapter 19

The Butcher

In This Chapter

- ◆ Why Lee kept fighting
- ◆ Battle of the Wilderness
- ◆ South to Spotsylvania
- ◆ Jeb Stuart dies at Yellow Tavern
- ◆ Grant's ill-fated assault on Cold Harbor
- ◆ Missed opportunity at Petersburg

Chewing on a cigar, his short, dark beard rough rather than gentlemanly, his uniform somehow always rumpled, Ulysses S. Grant bore the name of an epic hero, but didn't much look the part. Nevertheless, Lincoln and the nation embraced him eagerly as he ascended to overall command of the Union forces. On March 9, 1864, the day he was promoted to lieutenant general, they had faith in him and placed their hopes in him. But, soon, many would call Grant "the Butcher."

Down in the Confederate states, faith and hope were as scarce as food and clothing by March 1864. Manpower dwindled daily, through death, disability, and desertion. Conscription was extended to include boys (age 17) and middle-aged men (age 50). In the cities, many talked surrender, but, in the armies, despite epidemic desertion, officers were still able to lead, and many men were willing to follow. As hopes brightened in the North and dimmed in the South, the war in its final 12 months would be more violent than ever.

Lee's Hope

Friend and foe alike acknowledged Robert E. Lee a great general. He was a bold and daring commander, but his judgment was always tempered by an engineer's eye for the realities of the situation. Why, then, did he fight on?

For one thing, it is much harder to stop a war than to start one. Blood, blood beyond imagining, had been spilled, and to stop now would be to say that it had been spilled in vain. There is also the sheer momentum of killing, which a phrase spoken by Shakespeare's mass murderer Macbeth describes vividly:

> … I am in blood
> Step'd in so far that, should I wade no more,
> Returning were as tedious as go o'er.
> (*Macbeth*, act 3, scene 4)

But Lee also had one specific, rational hope to cling to. No question that the North would win this war—*if* it preserved the will to continue the fight.

That *if* was Lee's hope. Abraham Lincoln was up for reelection in November 1864 and was opposed by others, chiefly George B. McClellan, who, although he personally wanted victory in the war, had powerful supporters who wanted, above all else, an end to the fighting—an armistice and a negotiated peace. Before Grant, Union generals had targeted the territory and towns of the Confederacy, not the army itself. Thus, although much of the South was in ruins, the army, though reduced, was intact. The fighting *could* go on; therefore, as Lee saw it, it *would* go on, and if he could make the battles costly enough for the North, even though *their* cities and farms would come to little or no harm, perhaps the North would simply quit.

Lost in the Wilderness

Now the focus of the war would shift, with the sharpness of a saber, from west of the Alleghenies back to Virginia, where it had begun. On May 4, 1864, Grant led the 120,000-man Army of the Potomac across the Rapidan River with the objective of reaching open country south of the river and fighting what he knew to be Lee's badly outnumbered Army of Northern Virginia.

Grant was certainly right about Lee's being outnumbered—he could field no more than 66,000 men—but he was wrong in assuming that Lee would fight where he wanted him to. That was not the Confederate general's style. With his customary boldness, apparently not blunted by defeat at Gettysburg, Lee attacked the Federal columns as they passed through the tangled and densely forested area known as the Wilderness—the same Wilderness that had brought such disastrous confusion to "Fighting Joe" Hooker at Chancellorsville almost a year to the day earlier (see Chapter 14).

Two Days and 17,666 Men

By the conventional standards of warfare, the Wilderness was what commanders called "bad ground"—no place to fight a battle. Most of the country was wooded, overgrown with thick underbrush, thoroughly veined with creeks, streams, and ravines, and short on roads (what roads existed were narrow and deeply rutted). In country like this, the only thing more difficult than moving your army was *seeing* the opposing army.

That's just the way Lee wanted it. Outnumbered almost two to one, he needed an ally, and that ally would be the Wilderness itself. The difficult terrain meant that Grant could not readily deploy his troops to meet Lee's attacks; therefore, his great superiority of numbers meant far less than it would have on an open battlefield. Moreover, the lack of visibility rendered Grant's formidable artillery all but totally useless. What's more, Grant seems to have allowed Meade, the Army of the Potomac commander, to direct the tactical situation. And Meade fell short.

The fighting began on May 5 and went on through the 6th. It was confusing combat, even more hellish than the many hells of the past three years, because the men were fighting blind and were choked by smoke. The intense gunfire touched off innumerable brush fires, and soon the Wilderness was ablaze. Although both sides periodically called off the fight to retrieve the wounded, at least 200 men would suffocate or burn to death during the night of May 7–8.

Count Off!

Federal losses were 17,666 (of which 2,246 were killed, 12,073 wounded, and the rest missing) out of 101,895 engaged in the battle. Two Union generals were killed, two wounded, and two captured. Confederate records are sketchy, but estimates are that, of 61,025 engaged, losses amounted to 7,500 killed, wounded, or missing. Three generals were killed and four more were wounded but recovered, including James Longstreet, accidentally shot by his own men on almost the same spot where Stonewall Jackson was fatally wounded by friendly fire a year earlier.

This map shows the area of the Wilderness, Spotsylvania, and Cold Harbor relative to Richmond. Culpeper is at upper left, the Wilderness is to its southeast, Spotsylvania is to the southeast of the Wilderness, and Richmond, southeast of that. Cold Harbor (misspelled on this map as Coal Harbor) *is just to the northeast of Richmond.*

(Harper's *Pictorial History of the Civil War,* 1866)

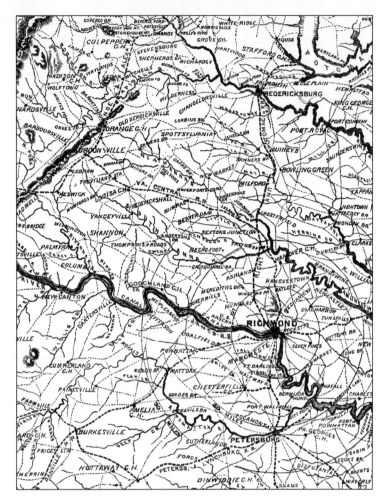

The fighting on the 5th was bloody, but indecisive. On the 6th, however, the arrival of Confederate general James Longstreet turned the tide, and the Confederates drove in the two flanks of the Union army. With nightfall, Grant and Meade began to withdraw.

Spotsylvania

The Wilderness was almost as heavy a setback as the one Hooker had suffered the year before. But Grant kept uppermost in his mind the grim equation he knew would determine the outcome of the war. *He* could afford to lose men. *Lee* could not. Instead of doing what a defeated army is supposed to do, retreat, Grant advanced, south to Spotsylvania Court House, at a crossroads on the way to Richmond. The morale of his exhausted soldiers revived at the realization that they were moving on. Grant would force Lee to fight and fight again. Lee might win the next battle and even the next, but he would lose men with each fight, even in victory, and because of this, Grant knew that Robert E. Lee would ultimately lose the Army of Northern Virginia.

Voices

The poet Walt Whitman, who served as an unofficial volunteer nurse during the war, recorded, in *Specimen Days* (1882), vivid and touching scenes of the human cost of combat:

> Steward C. Clover, company E, 5th Wisconsin—was wounded May 5, in one of those fierce tussles of the Wilderness—died May 21—aged about twenty. He was a small and beardless young man—a splendid soldier—in fact almost an ideal American, of his age. He had serv'd nearly three years, and would have been entitled to his discharge in a few days. He was in Hancock's corps. The fighting had about ceas'd for the day, and the general commanding the brigade rode by and called for volunteers to bring in the wounded. Clover responded among the first—went out gaily—but while in the act of bearing in a wounded sergeant to our lines, was shot in the knee by a rebel sharpshooter; consequence, amputation and death. He had resided with his father, John Clover, an aged and feeble man, in Batavia, Genesee county, N.Y., but was at school in Wisconsin, after the war broke out, and there enlisted—soon took to soldier life, liked it, was very manly, was belov'd by officers and comrades. He kept a little diary, like so many of the soldiers. On the day of his death he wrote the following in it, "Today the doctor says I must die—all is over with me—ah, so young to die." On another blank leaf he penciled to his brother, "Dear brother Thomas, I have been brave but wicked—pray for me."

The trouble was that Lee didn't yield to the logic of the equation. With his customary genius for reading his opponent's mind, he grasped Grant's strategy in moving to Spotsylvania, and beat him to the crossroads. A skirmish developed on May 8, and then blossomed like some monstrous, fatal flower into combat lasting through the 19th.

Every day, for 11 days, there was fighting—some of it the most desperate of the Civil War, and therefore the most violent and bitter combat ever seen on the American continent. As the two armies clashed, Grant kept shifting his troops to the left, always probing for Lee's flank, the most vulnerable aspect of an army, but Lee always succeeded in covering his flank, his troops fiercely defending their positions from hastily dug rifle pits, the Civil War equivalent of the World War II foxhole.

This rare photograph shows a strongly built Confederate rifle pit on the Spotsylvania battlefield.

(U.S. Army Military Institute)

Yellow Tavern

With the opposing armies quite literally *locked* in combat, Phil Sheridan, commander of the Army of the Potomac's 10,000-man cavalry, proposed a cavalry breakout onto Richmond, which would draw Jeb Stuart and the Confederate cavalry, about 4,500 troopers, into a fight. Sheridan was confident that he could "whip Stuart out of his boots."

Sheridan could hardly conceal the massed movement of 10,000 troopers, whose line, even riding four abreast, stretched for 13 miles. Seeing the advance, Stuart placed his

4,500 cavalrymen squarely between the Union column and Richmond, at an abandoned wayside inn called Yellow Tavern, only six miles north of the city.

On May 11, the two cavalry forces dueled. Stuart had secured a formidable defensive position, and his soldiers, defending their capital, were determined to stop the Union advance. After three hours, Sheridan withdrew, but not before one of his troopers, spying an ostentatiously uniformed rebel officer some 30 feet off, shot him.

It was Jeb Stuart, and he died the following day.

For Lee, it was a blow second only to the loss of Stonewall Jackson at Chancellorsville (see Chapter 14).

The Mule Shoe

Having probed for a weak spot since the fighting began, Grant, on May 11, ordered Maj. Gen. Winfield Scott Hancock to make a massed attack—with 20,000 men—against Confederate general Richard Ewell's corps. Because Ewell had deployed his men in entrenchments shaped like an inverted "U," the *salient* (concentration of troops) was called the Mule Shoe. After a day of hand-to-hand combat here, the "Mule Shoe" became known as "Bloody Angle."

Hancock, one of the central heroes of Gettysburg, was a superb and determined field commander. He unleashed the attack at 4:30 on the morning of May 12, and, within a quarter-hour, his men were pouring through gaps they had punched in the Confederate lines. During the next 45 minutes, they captured at least 2,000 prisoners (some sources say 4,000), including two generals, and 20 artillery pieces.

But then the Union advance was stopped, and for the rest of the day and into the night, combat was at close quarters, hand to hand, and unremitting, as a rainfall that had begun on the 11th became increasingly heavy.

Words of War

A **salient** is any strong or strongly fortified position or concentration of troops.

Mule Shoe/Bloody Angle was the last heavy fighting at Spotsylvania, as Grant again moved the Army of the Potomac south, always toward Richmond. Each day there was a skirmish or minor battle, such as those at the North Anna River (May 24), where Lee's defensive positions proved too strong to overrun, and, farther south, at Totopotomoy Creek (May 26–30). None of these exchanges was decisive. The Confederates refused to yield, and Grant could achieve no breakthrough, but each engagement cost the Southern army blood it could ill afford to shed, and each engagement was fought closer to the Confederate capital.

> **" " Voices** _____
>
> Grant's aide Horace Porter recalled "Bloody Angle" as
>
> … probably the most desperate engagement in the history of modern warfare. … The opposing flags were in places thrust against each other, and muskets were fired with muzzle against muzzle. Skulls were crushed with clubbed muskets [muskets held by the barrels and wielded as clubs], and men stabbed to death with swords and bayonets thrust between the logs in the parapet which separated the combatants. Wild cheers, savage yells, and frantic shrieks rose above the sighing of the wind and the pattering of the rain, and formed a demoniacal accompaniment to the booming of the guns as they hurled their missiles of death into the contending ranks. Even the darkness of night and the pitiless storm failed to stop the fierce contest, and the deadly strife did not cease till after midnight.

Sigel Struggles, Butler Beaten

During this time, other elements of the Union army were flailing and wallowing elsewhere in Virginia. Maj. Gen. Franz Sigel, a German immigrant who had served in the German military and then fled to the United States after participating in the ill-fated revolution of 1848, performed a great service to the Union by rallying fellow Germans to the Union cause. ("I fights mit Sigel" was their battle slogan.) His political weight brought Sigel promotion, but as a commander he was inept, as evidenced by his defeat on May 15 at New Market, in the Shenandoah Valley, at the hands of Maj. Gen. John C. Breckinridge, who was gallantly assisted by 247 youths from the Virginia Military Institute. (Ten VMI boys died, and 47 were wounded.) Sigel was soon relieved of command.

Benjamin Butler's Army of the James advanced up the river for which it was named, only to be defeated at Bermuda Hundred late in May. Like Sigel, Butler was "a political general"—a powerful Democrat who supported the war. Butler foolishly made camp on the Bermuda Hundred peninsula, thereby putting his forces in a cul de sac.

Words of War _____

Earthworks are entrenchments and/or mounded earth parapets used as defensive positions.

The Confederates built a line of fortified earthworks (mounded parapets) across the base of the little peninsula, efficiently corking the bottle that contained "Beast" Butler and his army. Not only were these forces put out of action, but also, without them to worry about, Lee was able to draw badly needed reinforcements from that front to use against Grant.

"To Fight It Out on This Line"

In a May 11 telegram to the War Department in Washington, Grant reported his losses at Spotsylvania as heavy, but "I think the loss of the enemy must be greater." He concluded, "I propose to fight it out on this line, if it takes all summer."

And so Grant fought on, not from victory to victory, but from heartbreak to heartbreak, on a line always southward. When repulsed, he did not retreat, but sidestepped and jumped even farther south.

Cold Harbor

On the night of June 1, Grant and Lee both raced toward a crossroads called Cold Harbor, a half-dozen miles northeast of Richmond. Lee got there first and dug in. During June 1–2, Grant lost 5,000 men knocking against the entrenched Confederate positions. Determined as ever, Grant decided to mount a massed assault. His buglers blew the charge at 4:30 A.M. on June 3. Sixty thousand Federal soldiers moved against an army that was all but invisible within its entrenchments. Confederate artillery roared into action, and entire Union regiments dissolved in eruptions of earth, rock, and metal.

During the month of nonstop fighting that had begun at Spotsylvania and culminated now at Cold Harbor, the new commander of the Union armies, Ulysses S. Grant, had lost more than 50,000 men, killed or wounded. About 7,000 of these fell in a single hour in the attack at Cold Harbor. It is believed that, of this number, most were hit in the first eight minutes of battle.

"I have always regretted that the last assault at Cold Harbor was ever made," Grant wrote in his *Personal Memoirs* years later.

Military historians write that Union and Confederate lines "stabilized" within 100 yards of each other after the last assault. *Stabilized?* The fact was that Grant called off further attack, and for three days and nights the armies sat in position, stunned, paralyzed, and exhausted. Not until June 7 was a truce called to pick up the wounded and bury the dead. Some five acres were heaped with the dead and those unlucky enough to still be dying. By the time litter bearers were allowed onto the Cold Harbor battleground, only two of the thousands of unrecovered Union wounded were still alive.

Among the crowds who had cheered Grant's promotion to lieutenant general and his elevation to command of the Union armies back in March were now many who decried him as "Butcher Grant."

Voices

Daniel Chisholm, Company K, 116th Pennsylvania Infantry, kept a diary:

Tuesday, June 7th—Cold Harbor

… At daylight this morning all was quiet. The enemy advanced a white Flag, asking permission to bury their dead, which was granted. We had an armistice of two hours. The quietness was really oppressive. It positively made us feel lonesome, after a continual racket day and night for so long. We sit on the works and let our legs dangle over on the front and watch the Johnnies carry off their dead comrades in silence, but in a great hurry. Some of them lay dead within twenty feet of our works—the live Rebel looks bad enough in his old torn, ragged Butternut suit, but a dead Rebel looks horrible all swelled up and black in the face. After they were through there was nothing left but stains of Blood, broken and twisted guns, old hats, canteens, every one of them reminders of the death and carnage that reigned a few short hours before. When the 2 hours was up we got back in our holes and they did the same ….

Abraham Lincoln was not one of these. To be sure, Cold Harbor seemed manifestly a terrible failure of generalship. Yet Lincoln understood that whereas 50,000 Union casualties represented a staggering 41 percent of Grant's original strength, the 32,000 casualties incurred by Lee amounted to 46 percent of his forces. Lincoln knew, too, that the Union's losses would be replaced in a matter of weeks, whereas the South could never restore the manpower it had lost.

Petersburg

Grant did not lick his wounds for long. He slipped his army out of Cold Harbor under cover of darkness and crossed the Chickahominy. Lee naturally assumed that he was heading toward Richmond and hurriedly dispatched most of his troops to the outskirts of the city. But Grant's objective was Petersburg, a rail junction vital to the supply of Richmond. Take and control this, and Richmond—starved, cut off from the rest of the Confederacy—would fall as surely as Vicksburg had fallen.

For once, Lee had missed his guess, and, when the first 16,000 Federals arrived at Petersburg on June 15, only 3,000 Confederates, commanded by the redoubtable P.G.T. Beauregard, were there to defend it.

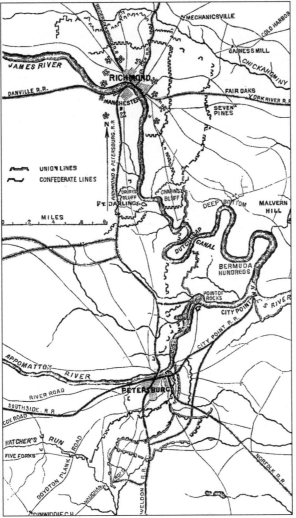

Map of the Petersburg area.

(Harper's Pictorial History of the Civil War, *1866)*

But Petersburg would prove yet another missed Union opportunity. The Federal troops under Maj. Gen. William Farrar "Baldy" Smith were battle worn and slow to attack. In truth, so was Smith. His assault against Petersburg on June 15 was bungled, and Beauregard gained time to reinforce his position. Smith was relieved of field command, and Grant personally led two more assaults, on the 16th and 18th, which failed. As at Vicksburg, Grant settled in for a long siege.

The Crater Catastrophe

One of Grant's subordinates besieging Petersburg was Ambrose Burnside. To him came Col. Henry Pleasants, a mining engineer now in command of a Pennsylvania regiment made up almost entirely of coal miners. Pleasants proposed to effect a break through the rebel fortifications by digging a tunnel under them and blowing them up.

Count Off!

The Petersburg mine tunnel was 510.8 feet, ending behind the Confederate lines and directly under a Confederate strong point. The longest military tunnel ever excavated, it was dug by the hand labor of 400 men at the rate of 40 to 50 feet a day. They moved some 18,000 cubic feet of earth. The tunnel was packed with 320 kegs of black powder explosive.

Persuaded, Burnside approved the plan, and the miners commenced digging on June 25. By July 27, the tunnel, a most impressive piece of military engineering, was completed, and the miners transported four tons of black powder to its end, returned to the Union lines, and then plugged up the Union end of the tunnel so that the blast would not backfire.

In the wee hours of the morning of July 30, Burnside prepared his assault force, which would rush through the gap blown in the fortifications. At 3:15 A.M., Pleasants lit a 98-foot fuse and ran out of the tunnel to await the explosion.

After three quarters of an hour, there was still no blast.

At last, two volunteers scampered into the five-foot-high tunnel, relit the fuse, and, after only a few minutes, 175 feet of Confederate entrenchments exploded spectacularly, sending men and debris hundreds of feet into the air, destroying an artillery battery then burying virtually an entire regiment.

Once again, however, Union commanders managed to snatch defeat from the jaws of victory. Burnside had planned to use a "colored" division to make the initial attack through the gap. Beginning on July 18, these soldiers were specially trained for the mission. They were ready and eager to serve. But on the day before the planned assault, Maj. Gen. George Meade had second thoughts. He told Burnside that using black troops for such an unconventional and hazardous mission was unacceptable. If they suffered severe losses, the army would be criticized for sacrificing black lives as if they were of inferior value to those of white soldiers. Now, at the eleventh hour, Meade ordered Burnside to find a white division to lead the assault.

The exhausted Burnside refused to make a command decision and instead had his division commanders draw straws for the dangerous work. The short straw was drawn by a unit under one James H. Ledlie—by the consensus of contemporaries and historians alike the very worst of the "political generals." The evidence suggests that his chief distinction was a prodigious capacity for hard liquor.

The Petersburg mine blast: stage one of the disastrous assault on "The Crater," which Grant called "the saddest affair I have witnessed in the war."

(Harper's Pictorial History of the Civil War, *1866)*

When the time came for the attack, Burnside, who had clearly lost focus on the operation, forgot to order the preparation of passages through his own fortifications to make it easier for the troops to sally forth without being cut down by rebel sharpshooters. This, coupled with the fact that the attacking division had not been trained for the mission, led to fatal confusion. After an hour's delay, they charged *into* the blast hole—175 feet across, 34 feet deep—rather than *around* it. They hadn't even thought to bring ladders. As a result, three Union divisions were pathetically trapped, proverbial fish in a barrel, and made easy targets for Confederate muskets. Union casualties in the assault topped 4,000.

As for Ledlie, in the words of historian Bruce Catton, he "was snugly tucked away in a bomb-proof [shelter] 400 yards behind the line, plying himself with rum borrowed from a brigade surgeon."

"It was," Grant later remarked, "the saddest affair I have witnessed in the war."

Another New Kind of War

The Civil War had brought a host of innovations to combat: rail transportation for troops and supplies, ironclad warships with revolving gun turrets, the submarine, new forms of artillery and artillery projectiles, improved breech-loading rifles for rapid fire, and so on. In some places, it also introduced a new landscape to warfare.

For the next eight months, while Petersburg lay under siege, the countryside was networked with trenches. Christened Fort Sedgwick, these siege lines—filthy, miserable ditches shored up with lumber and straw—provided the most modern-looking images to emerge from the Civil War, anticipating images that would become all too familiar in the next century when similar trenches scarred the face of Europe in World War I. In that "Great War," as in the Civil War, these images bespoke the terrible futility of much modern combat, in which glory died as men dug ditches and sat in the mud, waiting to slaughter one another.

The entrenchments of the Petersburg siege.

(Library of Congress)

The Least You Need to Know

◆ Robert E. Lee knew well that the Union would win the war *if* it kept fighting. His objective was to make the fight so costly that the North would lose the will to continue and would then negotiate a peace favorable to the South.

◆ Union losses at the Wilderness, Spotsylvania, and Cold Harbor far surpassed Confederate losses in number; nevertheless, the Confederates lost a greater proportion of their forces, and, unlike the North, could not draw on a large pool of manpower to replace their dead, wounded, and captured.

◆ Through the bungling of a subordinate commander (W.F. "Baldy" Smith), Ulysses S. Grant narrowly missed an opportunity to take Petersburg, the principal rail junction supplying Richmond. After two unsuccessful assaults by Grant, the armies settled into a long and costly siege here.

Chapter 20

Damn the Torpedoes

In This Chapter

- ◆ Rebel commerce raiders
- ◆ Career of the CSS *Alabama*
- ◆ Farragut's victory at Mobile Bay
- ◆ The submarine *Hunley*
- ◆ Lincoln reelected

Walt Whitman once described the face of Abraham Lincoln, "much worn and tired; the lines, indeed, of vast responsibilities, intricate questions, and demands of life and death, cut deeper than ever upon his dark brown face; yet all the old goodness, tenderness, sadness, and canny shrewdness, underneath the furrows." Whitman continued: "I never see that man without feeling that he is one to become personally attach'd to, for his combination of purest, heartiest tenderness, and native western form of manliness."

Goodness? Tenderness? President Lincoln understood and *approved of* what "Butcher Grant" was doing in his blood-soaked advance on Richmond. But would the nation? Would the *nation* continue to accept the equation by which Grant proposed to redeem the Union, spending, if necessary, more lives than the rebels could afford to spend?

Lincoln often doubted the nation's willingness to accept the terrible calculus. As the elections of 1864 drew nearer, he more than half expected to lose to a candidate whose party promised to *negotiate* an immediate end to the war. This chapter shows how a Union admiral and a Union general helped Lincoln retain the White House and continue the fight.

Pirate Navy

Almost by definition, a civil war is chiefly a land war. The combatants, after all, live on the same continent, the same large piece of land. But we have already seen that the U.S. Navy played a crucial role in the capture of New Orleans and in the reduction of the Confederate forts on the Mississippi (see Chapters 7, 8, and 13). Even more important, though far less glamorous, was the navy's role in making Winfield Scott's "Anaconda Plan" a reality. As the strength of the Union fleet grew from 42 vessels (of which only three were steam powered) in 1861 to 641 modern ships by 1865, the blockade of Southern imports and exports became increasingly effective.

This did not stop Southern vessels from trying to "run" the blockade, and many daring sailors succeeded in doing just that. But the Confederate naval strategy was not limited to such evasive and defensive measures. Jefferson Davis's government knew that it could never hope to match the Union navy ship for ship. It didn't have the money, it didn't have the shipyards, it didn't have the personnel, and it didn't have the time.

Instead, the Confederate Navy, under Davis's naval secretary Stephen R. Mallory, pitted its few vessels (many skippered by private citizens rather than naval personnel) not against those of the U.S. Navy, but against Union vessels of commerce—privately owned ships carrying goods. This was in essence common piracy, but when a government employs pirates, it is called *privateering*, and by the 1860s it had many precedents. Britain's Captain Henry Morgan (1635–1688), for example, plundered Spain's Caribbean colonies during the late seventeenth century with the crown's blessing. During the American Revolution, more than a thousand privateers preyed on British shipping. In the War of 1812, the privately owned U.S. brig *Yankee* alone seized or destroyed $5,000,000 worth of English property.

Words of War

A **privateer** is a privately owned armed vessel commissioned by a warring state to attack enemy vessels of commerce. The word can also be applied to the captain of the privateer vessel. Captains and crews were generally not paid by the government, but were entitled to claim captured ships as prizes for their own profit.

From *Enrica* to *Alabama*

The single most famous Confederate raiding vessel was not a privateer, however, but a craft commissioned and paid for by the Confederate Navy and built in ostensibly neutral England.

The CSS *Alabama* was clandestinely ordered by the Confederate agent in charge of procuring European arms, James D. Bulloch, from Laird Shipyards in 1861. Despite the protests of the U.S. *minister* (ambassador) to England, Charles Francis Adams, the ship was launched (as the *Enrica*) on May 15, 1862. The British government might have been officially neutral, but plenty of members of Parliament favored the Confederate cause and were willing to turn a blind eye toward profitable trade in arms.

Words of War

In the eighteenth and nineteenth centuries, U.S. ambassadors were generally called **ministers**. Charles Francis Adams was officially the United States minister to the Court of St. James's.

In the British government, the **foreign secretary** is the equivalent of the secretary of state in the government of the United States.

Although frustrated, Adams knew that, before it could set out on the high seas, the ship had to be fitted with masts and engines at a *graving dock* (dry dock) in Liverpool. Adams worked quickly, hiring famed barrister Robert R. Collier, who presented Lord Russell, the British *foreign secretary*, with a legal opinion that, if the *Enrica* were allowed to sail, the United States would have a valid claim against Great Britain for any and all damages she might cause to American shipping.

Words of War

A **graving dock** is a dry dock where major work is done on ships.

Russell summoned Sir John Harding, a Queen's Law Officer, and asked for an immediate opinion. As fate would have it, Harding was in the process of a nervous breakdown, a condition his wife had covered up so well that no one in the Law Offices was aware of it. In the delay and confusion caused by Harding's incapacity, word leaked to Bulloch that *Enrica* was in danger. He rushed it to completion, and she was launched for what Bulloch announced as "sea trials" on July 29.

Enrica never returned to Liverpool, however. Instead, she headed for the Welsh coast, where Bulloch planned to board her, steal out of English waters, sail beyond the influence of U.S. diplomatic pressure, and then, after fitting her guns in the Azores, take command of her as the CSS *Alabama*.

But Confederate navy secretary Mallory had a different commander in mind. *Enrica* evaded a Federal sloop and braved a bad storm in the Irish Sea to rendezvous with the *Agrippina*, from which Capt. Raphael Semmes, a 53-year-old Maryland-born Alabamian, boarded her and took command.

Raphael Semmes was the justly legendary captain of the CSS Alabama, *which captured or sank 69 vessels before it was sunk by the USS* Kearsarge.

(Library of Congress)

Adventures of the *Alabama*

On February 15, 1861, Semmes resigned his commission as a commander in the U.S. Navy and joined the Confederate service as a buyer of arms and as head of the "lighthouse bureau" (the government agency in charge of lighthouses). Later, Semmes was given command of the cruiser *Sumter*, with which he sliced through the Anaconda blockade out of New Orleans, sailed for six months, and took 18 *prizes* (captured vessels). He then abandoned *Sumter* in Gibraltar, boarded *Agrippina*, and took command of the *Alabama*.

From September 1862 until June 1864, Semmes was the terror of the high seas. He preyed upon the commercial shipping lanes, capturing or destroying 69 vessels and, in the process, monopolized the resources of a significant portion of the Union navy in vain pursuit of himself.

Words of War

In naval jargon, a **prize** is a captured vessel and any and all cargo it carries.

Duel at Sea

On Sunday, June 12, 1864, the USS *Kearsarge*, an eight-gun, 1,083-ton sloop with a crew of 162, was lying at anchor off the Dutch coast when Capt. John A. Winslow received word that the *Alabama*, which he had been chasing fruitlessly for the better part of a year, had steamed into the French port of Cherbourg to discharge prisoners and take on coal. Winslow set sail immediately, reaching Cherbourg two days later. In deference to international law, Winslow assumed a position in the English Channel, just beyond the three-mile territorial waters limit. And he waited.

Semmes was determined to fight his way out even though the *Kearsarge* outgunned his vessel, and by the time he sailed, at 9:45 on Sunday morning, June 19, crowds of French onlookers were on hand to watch the battle. Word had spread of the impending battle, and there wasn't a vacant hotel room to be found in all Cherbourg.

Winslow was reading the Sabbath service to his crew when the watchman announced: "She's coming out and she's headed straight for us!"

With that, the captain hastily concluded services, *beat to quarters* (summoned all hands to battle stations), and headed for more open waters, so that the *Alabama*, if crippled, could not find easy refuge. Winslow wanted a fight to the finish.

At 10:57, with the two vessels a mile apart, *Alabama* opened fire with a 100-pounder. Semmes fired again and again, but Winslow was closing so fast that *Alabama*'s shots were all too high; the gunners could not adjust their trajectories quickly enough. Only after he had closed to half a mile did Winslow return fire.

Words of War

To **beat to quarters** is to order the crew to prepare for battle and assume their battle stations. In the eighteenth and nineteenth centuries, the signal was a continuous drum roll—hence the term *beat* to quarters.

The two commanders and crews were a study in contrast. Semmes and his gunners fired rapidly and wildly, whereas Winslow and his men were methodical in pacing and aiming their shots. Winslow fired about 173 volleys—half what the *Alabama* got off—in the course of little over an hour, but far more of them found their mark.

As noon approached, the *Alabama* began to sink—fast. As Semmes and his crew abandoned ship, Winslow launched his only two boats that had not been smashed by Confederate shells. Realizing that these would never hold the *Alabama*'s entire crew, Winslow called out to a British yacht that had sailed out to watch the battle: "For God's sake, do what you can to save them!"

Outgunned by the USS Kearsarge, *CSS* Alabama *sinks near Cherbourg, France.*

(Harper's Pictorial History of the Civil War, *1866)*

At 12:24, CSS *Alabama* disappeared under the waves. *Kearsarge* took aboard 70 men, French boats picked up a dozen more, and the British yacht *Deerhound* saved 42, including Semmes, who thereby evaded capture. About 20 men lost their lives. After a gentlemanly tour of the Continent, Semmes returned to the Confederacy as commander of the James River squadron.

The *Alabama* Claims

The sinking of the *Alabama* was not quite the end of its story. After the Civil War, relations between the United States and Great Britain deteriorated, in part because the United States held England responsible for the destruction caused by the *Alabama*. A joint high commission was set up to adjudicate the matter, and, on May 8, 1871, the Treaty of Washington established a system of arbitration to settle the "*Alabama* Claims" and other disputes. On September 14, 1872, the tribunal found Britain legally liable for direct losses caused by the *Alabama* and other ships and awarded the United States damages of $15,500,000 in gold.

Count Off!

The United States had demanded payment of $19,021,000 for damage done by 11 Confederate craft (including the *Alabama*) built in England. Pursuant to the 1871 Treaty of Washington, a high commission of five representatives each from the United States, England, Italy, Switzerland, and Brazil awarded the United States $15,500,000, which was duly paid in 1873.

Impatient Admiral

Having been the prime force in the capture of New Orleans in 1862 (see Chapter 8), Rear Adm. David Glasgow Farragut was running out of patience as commander of the squadron blockading the Gulf coast. With New Orleans gone, the Confederates' principal Gulf port was now Mobile, Alabama, and, despite the blockade, plenty of shipping still made it in and out of the harbor.

The only way to bottle up Mobile Bay was to take it. But that would not be easy. Thirty miles long, the bay was defended by three forts, three gunboats, and a mighty *ram* (a vessel built for deliberate collision with other ships) named the *Tennessee*. Moreover, the channel that gave passage into the harbor was mined with what were then called *torpedoes*. These were tethered kegs (sometimes they were nothing more than beer barrels) that bobbed just at the surface of the water, packed with black powder and rigged to explode on contact with a vessel. The entire network of Confederate defenses was commanded

Words of War

A **ram** is a vessel expressly built, with a specially reinforced iron prow (or "beak"), for deliberate collision with other ships. A ram sinks enemy vessels by punching through the enemy's hull at or below the water line.

At the time of the Civil War, a **torpedo** was not a projectile, but a stationary mine, often a beer barrel made watertight and packed with explosive black powder. The torpedo would explode when struck by a vessel.

by Franklin Buchanan, skipper of the *Virginia/Merrimack* and a man who had, before the war, served with Farragut. They knew one another well.

Mobile Bay, August 5, 1864: 6:00 A.M.

The odds, certainly, were against the success of the Union flotilla, but that was just fine with Farragut. He liked to make his own odds.

He scoped out the situation and decided to run the gauntlet of the bay with a flotilla of 4 ironclad monitors and 14 conventional wooden vessels. The latter he lashed together in pairs so that they could better endure the pounding they would get from the forts. At six in the morning on August 5, Farragut led the flotilla from the deck of his flagship, *Hartford*. When the firing became intense and visibility was reduced to a minimum, the 63-year-old admiral climbed the rigging and ordered a sailor to lash him to the mast, so he wouldn't fall if wounded. When the smoke of battle grew too thick for him to see at all, he untied himself, climbed even higher, then lashed himself to the rigging again.

Tecumseh Sinks

The do-or-die moment came when one of the Union's monitors, the *Tecumseh*, struck a torpedo and sank. This gave the other captains pause, and the advance through the bay slowed, even as the rebel bombardment continued.

That's when Farragut shouted down to his flag captain, Percival Drayton, a phrase that has echoed through history to become a permanent part of the English language: "Damn the torpedoes! Full speed ahead, Drayton!"

With that, *Hartford* poured it on, and the rest of the flotilla followed. One of the Confederate gunboats was captured, and two more were damaged beyond use. Only the *Tennessee*, with Franklin Buchanan commanding, remained in the fight.

Tennessee Strikes Her Colors

Buchanan decided to use his ship for the purpose it was intended. He built up a head of steam and aimed his ram directly for the *Hartford*. Surprisingly, the collision caused little damage, and now the Union vessels *Monongahela*, *Lackawanna*, and *Hartford* exacted their vengeance, ramming the *Tennessee* repeatedly, by turns, at five-minute intervals. The *Tennessee* withstood this, and, at one point, the Union's choreography became so confused that the *Lackawanna* accidentally rammed the *Hartford*—at almost exactly the point where Farragut was standing. The admiral narrowly escaped death.

Voices

Captain James D. Johnson of the *Tennessee* recalled that a Union shot "struck the edge of the [gun]port cover immediately over the spot where [a] machinist [was repairing the jammed gun port]." His body was instantly reduced to fragments. Iron splinters killed another seaman and broke Admiral Buchanan's leg below the knee. Fleet Surgeon D.B. Conrad rushed to Buchanan's aid and later recalled:

> All of the gun's crew and the admiral were covered from head to foot with [the machinist's] blood, flesh, and viscera .... I ... asked, "Admiral, are you badly hurt?"

> "Don't know," ... but I saw one of his legs crushed up under his body, and ... I ... carried him on my back down the ladder to the cockpit, his broken leg slapping against me as we moved slowly along.

> After applying a temporary bandage, he sat up on the deck and received reports .... "Well, [Captain] Johnston, they have got me again. You'll have to look out for her now; it is your fight."

> "All right, answered the captain, "I'll do the best I know how."

Although the *Tennessee* endured pounding from the wooden ships, it could not live long under fire from the ironclads. By 10:00, the vessel was out of control, Buchanan had been badly wounded, his leg shattered, and *Tennessee*'s skipper, J.D. Johnston, struck her colors (surrendered).

Within the next two days, two of the Mobile Bay forts fell to the Union, and the last fort, Fort Morgan, surrendered on August 23.

Silent Service

Since World War II, American submariners have called their profession the "Silent Service," and few twentieth-century weapons have had more impact on the nature of war than the stealthy submarine. Yet although the submarine is a cutting-edge weapon, its technology continually refined, the idea of a submersible vessel was discussed at least as early as 1578 by William Bourne, a British mathematician and writer on naval subjects. Cornelis Drebbel (or Cornelius van Drebel), a Dutch inventor, built the first actual submarine vessel, of greased leather stretched over a wooden frame, in about 1620, and a submarine was first used as a naval weapon during the American Revolution. Yale student David Bushnell's *Turtle*, however, failed to do any real damage in that war—but it did submerge and resurface successfully. In 1800, Robert Fulton, pioneer steamboat builder, created the *Nautilus* for Napoleon Bonaparte, but the invention met with little interest, and while he later obtained Congressional funding for an American version of the submarine, Fulton died before completing it, and the project languished. A copy of the *Turtle* was built during the War of 1812, but, like its prototype, it didn't sink anything.

A Man Named Hunley

Horace L. Hunley was born in Summer County, Tennessee, in 1823 and went on to serve in the Louisiana State Legislature and to practice law in New Orleans. In 1861, after the outbreak of war, he joined James R. McClintok and Baxter Watson in building a submarine for the Confederacy with the express purpose of providing a means of overcoming Scott's "Anaconda" blockade. The *Pioneer*, however, had to be scuttled in 1862 to prevent its capture. The three partners later financed construction of the *American Diver*, which was soon lost in Mobile Bay, and another vessel, launched in July 1863 and known by various names, including *Fish Boat*, but ultimately called the *H. L. Hunley*.

Anatomy of a Submarine

Just under 40 feet long, the *Hunley* resembled a large steam boiler. Its hull was constructed of wrought-iron plates onto which were affixed two conning towers, sets of dive planes for maneuverability underwater, and, on top of the hull, five sets of portholes. A bellows was connected to a snorkel to draw fresh air into the vessel, and although, during one test, the *Hunley* remained submerged for 2 hours, 35 minutes, the pump and snorkel proved troublesome and unreliable. In practice, the boat could remain underwater as long as the available air held out. For the eight or nine crewmembers, that meant at most two more or less suffocating hours.

A crankshaft ran the length of the submarine. Seven or eight seated crewmembers turned the shaft, which drove a single screw (propeller). The commander steered—using rods and cables connected to a rudder—and controlled depth with a lever attached to the dive planes and by pumping ballast water in or out using a hand-powered pump.

H. L. Hunley was fitted with a single weapon: a "torpedo," packed with 90 pounds of black powder and affixed to a long spar that projected from the bow. The planned method of attack was to aim for the broadside of the target vessel, crank like mad, and then ram the vessel with sufficient force to penetrate the hull with the spar and its torpedo. This accomplished, the crew would crank—again, fiercely—in reverse, leaving the torpedo in the target vessel's hull. At a safe distance from the enemy ship—about 200 feet—a crewmember would tug at a lanyard attached to the torpedo, which would detonate, destroying the enemy.

Brave Men, Doomed Men

The *Hunley* was transported to Charleston, South Carolina, by rail, and tests were begun.

The boat submerged beautifully, but getting her back to the surface often proved problematic. While on the surface, Hunley was barely seaworthy, and, during one test, while she was riding with her hatches open, a steamer passed by, flooding *Hunley* with her wake water. The submarine sank with the loss of six crewmen—two men and the skipper were able to jump overboard before she went under.

Hunley was refloated, and H.L. Hunley personally took command of his namesake for some practice dives. On October 15, 1863, she dived in a burst of air bubbles. She did not resurface. A hatch had sprung a leak, and all hands, including Hunley, drowned.

Refloated yet again, sailors opened her hatch, revealing the doomed crew. Gen. Beauregard, commanding officer at Charleston, a soldier accustomed to battlefield deaths, was wholly unprepared for the sight of what he described as men "contorted into all sorts of horrible attitudes, some clutching candles … others lying in the bottom tightly grappled together."

Death of the *Housatonic*

The stunned Beauregard issued an order forbidding further tests. However, *Hunley* skipper Lt. George Dixon persuaded Beauregard to allow an attack. The general reluctantly agreed, provided that the boat submerge only partially.

On February 17, 1864, at 8:45 P.M., *Hunley* rammed the nine-gun Federal sloop *Housatonic* in Charleston Harbor. Union crewmembers sighted a dark object in the water, but they had no idea what it was. Pierced through to her powder magazine, *Housatonic* was rocked by an explosion, heeled to port, and sank stern first. Five crew members were drowned, but the water in this part of the harbor was so shallow that most of the crew saved themselves simply by clinging to the masts and rigging, which remained above the surface as the shattered vessel hit bottom.

According to eyewitnesses on the *Housatonic*, the *Hunley* pulled back. But it was not seen again. It was generally assumed that the submarine was too close to the blast and was lost with its victim.

Yet there is a U.S. Navy record of a report of light signals exchanged, after the attack, between the shore and "some object" at sea. In August 1994, preservationists exploring under the auspices of the privately funded National Underwater and Marine Agency detected a metal object roughly matching the dimensions of the *Hunley* about 1,000 feet southeast of the boiler of the *Housatonic*, which still rested at the bottom of Charleston Harbor, near Sullivan's Island. A diving expedition confirmed the discovery of the *Hunley* in May 1995, and on August 8, 2000, a massive salvage operation raised and recovered the boat.

Sites and Sights

As of 2003, the *Hunley* is under restoration at the Warren Lasch Conservation Center in Charleston, South Carolina. Public tours are available on weekends; call 1-877-448-6539 for information and tickets or order online at www.etix.com. The site is closed to the public during the week while archaeologists do their work. The most complete source of current information on the *Hunley* and conservation efforts may be obtained from the Friends of the *Hunley* website at www.hunley.org.

Why had *Hunley* sunk, apparently after the successful completion of its mission? Perhaps the blast had damaged the vessel. Assuming that the *Hunley* did send a light signal, perhaps an excited crewman had failed to secure the porthole from which he had signaled. Who knows?

Welcome Victory

While the development of the submarine would have a profound effect on twentieth-century naval warfare, the single, fatal mission of the *Hunley* had negligible effect on the course of the Civil War. Far more consequential was David Farragut's great victory in Mobile Bay, which cut off a major source of supply to the Confederacy. But of even greater consequence is what Farragut's triumph did to improve Abraham Lincoln's prospects for reelection.

Lincoln versus McClellan

Within his own cabinet, the president was opposed by Secretary of the Treasury Salmon P. Chase, who worked behind the scenes to steal the Republican nomination from Lincoln. Although he had won many influential backers, his disloyalty, once it was exposed, clearly crossed the line, and Chase bowed to pressure for his resignation. He left the Cabinet in June 1864. (Never one to hold a grudge, Lincoln nominated Chase to the post of chief justice of the Supreme Court after Roger Taney died in October 1864.)

Although some Radical Republicans pressed for the nomination of uncompromising abolitionist Maj. Gen. John C. Frémont (who had been relieved of command on June 28, 1862, and had been "awaiting orders" in New York ever since), the nod went to Lincoln, albeit with a new running mate, Tennessee governor Andrew Johnson, replacing Vice President Hannibal Hamlin.

In August, as the victory at Mobile Bay unfolded, the Democratic Party convention in Chicago nominated George B. McClellan. The party's platform included a pledge that "efforts be made for a cessation of hostilities"—in other words, a negotiated peace as opposed to unconditional surrender. Many expected McClellan to run on this platform, but he soon repudiated it. Nevertheless, the politician Lincoln was content to ensure that McClellan was tarred with the defeatist Democrat brush, and he campaigned for reelection by drawing a simple contrast between "the Democrats" and himself: *They* would throw away the great sacrifices that had been made, while *he*, Abraham Lincoln, would honor those sacrifices by fighting through to nothing short of total victory.

Voices

Abraham Lincoln was capable of eloquence both lofty—as in the Gettysburg Address and the Second Inaugural Address—and homely. He advised voters "it was not best to swap horses while crossing the stream, and … I am not so poor a horse that they might not make a botch of it in trying to swap." This simple metaphor appealed to a population all too familiar with the experience of riding horses along bad roads cut by streams. The president's point was made, and the world had a new figure of speech: *Don't change horses in midstream.*

Sherman Enters Georgia

With the fall of Mobile Bay, Lincoln's political prospects brightened. On May 6, 1864, while Grant fought his costly series of battles against Lee on the way to Richmond, William Tecumseh Sherman began his advance on Atlanta, fighting Joe Johnston's Army of Tennessee. As we shall see in the first part of the next chapter, it would be a four-month fight through Georgia. But when Sherman finally marched into Atlanta on September 2, 1864, the sun shone fully on the president. His reelection was assured. Election day was November 8, 1864, and when the votes were tallied, Lincoln's total was 2,216,067 popular votes (212 electoral), while McClellan had garnered 1,808,725 (21 electoral) votes. The soldiers of the Union army had cast their ballots overwhelmingly in Lincoln's favor.

The Least You Need to Know

◆ The diminutive Confederate Navy did not attempt to fight the Union navy ship for ship, but relied on a strategy of commerce raiding to disrupt Union shipping.

◆ The most famous—and destructive—Confederate raider was CSS *Alabama*, which captured or sank 69 vessels before being sunk itself by USS *Kearsarge*.

◆ The British, ostensibly a neutral power in the Civil War, illegally allowed English shipyards to build ships for the Confederacy; this led to the settlement of the "*Alabama* Claims" for damages caused by these vessels.

◆ The Confederate *H. L. Hunley* was the first submarine actually used in combat.

◆ Admiral Farragut's daring victory at Mobile Bay not only tightened the stranglehold around the throat of the Confederacy, but also helped propel Abraham Lincoln to a second term.

Chapter 21

"I Almost Tremble"

In This Chapter

- ◆ Sherman and the concept of "total war"
- ◆ Evacuation, occupation, and destruction of Atlanta
- ◆ Sherman's "March to the Sea"
- ◆ Capture of Savannah, Charleston, and Fort Sumter

On June 19, 1879, William Tecumseh Sherman, now filling Grant's place as commanding general of the army, addressed the graduating class of the Michigan Military Academy. "War," he said, "is at best barbarism .... Its glory is all moonshine. It is only those who have neither fired a shot, nor heard the shrieks and groans of wounded who cry aloud for blood, more vengeance, more desolation. War is hell."

This was not the opinion of a pacifist. With Grant, Sherman was probably the nation's fiercest warrior. It was the conclusion of a realist, and, what is more important, a realist willing to *embrace* the reality he saw—and the reality he created. War is hell? Yes, and for the citizens of Georgia and South Carolina, General Sherman was the very devil.

This chapter explains what Sherman did to bring the war home to the people he believed had made the war in the first place.

The Atlanta Campaign

On the surface, Grant's orders to Sherman were simple: "To move against Johnston's army, to break it up, and to get into the interior of the enemy's country as far as you can, inflicting all the damage you can against their war resources." Indeed, the first part of the mission required little analysis. As Sherman later explained, "I was to go for Johnston."

But the second part of the orders left vast latitude for interpretation. To inflict damage against "war resources" is, of course, a crucial objective in any major war. But just what constitutes "war resources"?

Most important towns and cities develop near great rivers or other bodies of water, but not landlocked Atlanta. It owed its existence to the railroads. Situated at the southern end of the Appalachian Mountains, Atlanta developed as the gateway through which overland traffic passed from the Southern coast to the West. In 1837, the Atlanta downtown neighborhood now called Five Points was chosen for the southern terminus of a railroad to be built north to Chattanooga. By the Civil War years, several other key Southern rail lines converged on Atlanta. Certainly, then, the city and its railroads qualified as "war resources," and Atlanta became Sherman's objective.

> **War News**
>
> How important were the railroads to Atlanta? Before the city was named Atlanta in 1845, it was called, simply, Terminus.

> **Words of War**
>
> **Total war** is combat waged against civilian as well as military targets with the object not only of destroying the enemy's capacity to fight, but also his will to fight.

But Sherman did not interpret his mission so narrowly. He might have read the writings of Karl Maria von Clausewitz, a Prussian officer who served in the French Revolutionary Wars and the Napoleonic Wars. When von Clausewitz wasn't fighting wars, he was writing about them, and his masterpiece, *Vom Kriege* (*On War*), was published after his death in 1831. For much of the rest of the nineteenth century (and well into the twentieth), it was a tremendously influential book on the art of war.

Whether or not Sherman read Clausewitz, he would have agreed with him on the subject of *total war*. For his part, Clausewitz would have agreed with Grant that victory requires the destruction of the enemy's army, but he would have added that victory was also a matter of destroying the *will* of the enemy to fight. That meant waging war against the civilian population and their property as well as against military targets, hence *total* war.

A modern edition of *On War* runs to more than 700 pages. William Tecumseh Sherman needed just three words to explain how he would wage total war in the Atlanta campaign and in the March to the Sea that would follow it. He would, he pledged, "make Georgia howl."

William Tecumseh Sherman (1820–1891) convinced General Grant to let him wage "total war" on the people of the South, not only hitting military objectives, but cities, farms, and other civilian property as well.

(Author's collection)

Sherman at Dalton

Sherman began his advance from Chattanooga into Georgia on May 7, 1864. Confederate general Joe Johnston had assumed command of the Army of Tennessee from Braxton Bragg at Dalton, Georgia, a few miles below the Tennessee state line. Johnston, unlike Bragg, was popular with his soldiers.

Although Sherman commanded 100,000 men against Johnston's 62,000, he realized that the Confederate defensive position at Dalton was too strong to attack head on. Sherman was not about to repeat the errors of Ambrose Burnside at Fredericksburg (see Chapter 12) and Joe Hooker at Chancellorsville (see Chapter 14). Instead, he sent a division under James Birdseye McPherson, preceded by a cavalry division under Judson Kilpatrick, to force Johnston to turn his vulnerable flank as Maj. Gen. George Henry Thomas ("The Rock of Chickamauga") proceeded frontally and John M. Schofield menaced the Confederate right.

Except for a protracted skirmish at Rocky Face Ridge (May 5–9), Johnston skillfully maneuvered to avoid major battle. He fell back on Resaca, about 10 miles down the railroad.

Here, once again, Sherman maneuvered to envelop Johnston from the west, and, once again, Johnston wriggled out of a major engagement, although the armies skirmished during May 13–16. Johnston retreated farther south down the railroad, about 25 miles, to Cassville.

Atlanta and vicinity during the Atlanta campaign. The railroad line down which Sherman progressed runs south from Chattanooga to a junction at Dalton, Georgia. All the battle and skirmish sites lie along the rail line. This 1866 map misspells Kennesaw as "Keneshaw" and calls the town of Newnan (at the bottom of the map) "Newman."

(Harper's Pictorial History of the Civil War, *1866)*

Counterattack at Cassville

At Cassville, Johnston decided to concentrate and counterattack Sherman's widely separated corps. He planned to send generals William J. Hardee and Joseph Wheeler against McPherson and Thomas, and John Bell Hood against Schofield. The battle-scarred Hood was a singularly courageous and daring commander, but he was not a sophisticated tactician. Deceived by the positioning of Federal cavalry, he mounted his attack from the wrong direction, creating a delay that fouled the timing of Johnston's intricate plan of coordinated attack. Johnston could do nothing but order a withdrawal to Allatoona Pass, about 12 miles south of Cassville.

Once again, Sherman realized that the Confederates had withdrawn to a point too strong to attack frontally. His army tired from so much fruitless pursuit, he rested his troops for three days, and then undertook a series of maneuvers and skirmishing actions that pushed Johnston to Kennesaw Mountain.

Assault at Kennesaw Mountain

The twin peaks of Big and Little Kennesaw are landmarks just north of Atlanta—uncomfortably *close* landmarks, as far as the citizens of the city were concerned—but in withdrawing to Kennesaw, Johnston had found a very strong position indeed. Using tow ropes, he hauled up his artillery, which thereby commanded the railroad below and much of the level area between Kennesaw and Pine and Lost mountains.

On June 19, Sherman ordered his forces into a position from which he hoped to flank Johnston. Critical to his plan was getting troops south of the Confederate left and in secure possession of the road leading to Marietta. Johnston, however, grasped the situation as well as Sherman did and ordered Hood to defend the road at the farm of the widow of one Valentine Kolb. On June 22, Union forces found themselves checked by Hood at this position.

Then Hood did what he was all too apt to do: He acted rashly and with blind aggression. Instead of holding his strong defensive position, as ordered, he attacked. The result was heavy casualties in a totally unnecessary action. The result, too, was friction within the Confederate as well as Union armies. Johnston reprimanded Hood, who chafed under his commander's apparent reluctance to offer battle as the Yankees drew closer and closer to Atlanta. And Sherman scolded Joseph Hooker, who, he said, had grossly overestimated the enemy at Kolb's Farm, thereby relinquishing the initiative to the rebels.

Sherman was in ill humor. Even as Johnston was being criticized in the Southern press for failing to make a stand and stop Sherman, so the Northern press began printing its doubts about Sherman as a "fighting general." Frustrated and pressured, Sherman decided to risk a frontal assault on Kennesaw Mountain.

Count Off!

Of 16,225 Federals engaged at Kennesaw, 1,999 were killed or wounded, and 52 went missing. Of the 17,333 Confederates engaged, 270 were killed or wounded, and 172 missing.

Words of War _____

Retrograde is military jargon for "backward."

Sites and Sights

Kennesaw Mountain National Battlefield Park, in Kennesaw, Georgia, was the site of Sherman's only serious setback during the Atlanta campaign. Sherman's men never reached their objective, Pigeon Hill, which is now stop #2 on the battlefield tour. The site is beautiful ("too beautiful to be disturbed by the horrors of war," Sherman remarked), with ample hiking opportunities. From I-75 take exit 116, Barrett Parkway, and follow signs to the park. Contact: 1-770-427-4686.

The attack came at 8:00 on the morning of June 27. Miserable weather and tangled underbrush made the uphill attack even more difficult than it would have been under ideal conditions. The attack failed with very heavy losses.

Sherman gained nothing at Kennesaw, but there was no such thing as retreat now. Johnston made yet another *retrograde* (backward) move, to the Chattahoochee River at the outskirts of Atlanta. With each withdrawal, Johnston picked up reinforcements, so he was now stronger than ever. But he had allowed the enemy to approach the threshold of the city.

Hood Succeeds Johnston

What was Joe Johnston about?

He had taken the measure of his man and knew that Sherman was no McClellan or Burnside or Hooker. Johnston knew he could not beat Sherman, but he *could* keep his own army intact and delay the taking of Atlanta long enough to cost Lincoln reelection, thereby bringing in a Democratic administration willing to negotiate a favorable peace.

Under the circumstances, it was a sound strategy. For the only ally the South had now was time. Use up enough of it, and the North might just lose confidence as well as patience.

But the government of Jefferson Davis did not see it this way. It saw only a Yankee army on Atlanta's doorstep. On July 17, 1864, Davis replaced Joseph E. Johnston with John Bell Hood and ordered him to keep Sherman from taking Atlanta.

"War Is Cruelty"

Ringed with earthworks, Atlanta was a formidable objective. Sherman's strategy was not to assault these, but to cut the four rail lines into the city, thereby forcing the Confederates to come out for a fight or to retreat. In executing his plan, however, Sherman had left a gap, between McPherson's Army of the Tennessee and Schofield's Army of the Ohio on the one hand and Thomas's Army of the Cumberland on the other. While Schofield and McPherson approached the city from the east, Thomas was crossing Peachtree Creek, north of the city. It was at this gap that Hood chose to attack, and, on July 20, the savage Battle of Peachtree Creek was fought.

Confederate defensive works outside of Atlanta. Look carefully at the two houses in the middle ground. They have been stripped to their frames for the wood needed to construct obstacles and defenses.

(Library of Congress)

Fortunately for Sherman, Thomas successfully defended against the attack, which might otherwise have destroyed his army before he could join it with the armies of McPherson and Schofield.

Then, on the 22nd, Hood attacked McPherson's Army of the Tennessee, nearly flanking it by swinging around it to the east. This was the beginning of the Battle of Atlanta, and it was one of the hardest fought of the war. McPherson died in the struggle, as his army was attacked simultaneously from the front and the rear, but the Union rallied and, with superior numbers, forced Hood back into his defensive works.

Having succeeded in cutting the rail line north and east, Sherman brought his army down around to the southwest to seize the Macon and Western Railroad. On July 28, Hood emerged again and attacked the Army of the Tennessee, now commanded by O.O. Howard, at Ezra Church, west of the city. In a hard fight, Howard repulsed Hood, inflicting heavy losses.

Sites and Sights

Atlanta's city seal bears the Latin word *resurgens*—rising—above the image of a phoenix emerging from the flames. The modern city bears no trace of the conflict, except for many historical markers placed by the Georgia Historical Commission and the remains of fortifications at Fort Walker in Grant Park. (The park is *not* named for the Union's general-in-chief!) A building in the park houses the largest painting in America, created in 1885–1886 by German artists, an intricately detailed Cyclorama depicting the Battle of Atlanta; a three-dimensional diorama accompanies the painting. A Civil War museum is part of the exhibition, located at 800 Cherokee Avenue, SE, Atlanta, GA 30315; contact: 1-404-624-1071.

Sherman had Atlanta within his grasp. Yet he also knew that, in a sense, he had failed. Johnston's (now Hood's) army was still intact. Worse, if Hood could keep him out of Atlanta sufficiently long, Sherman realized, the Union rear would be vulnerable to Sherman's nemesis, Nathan Bedford Forrest, who, on July 15, had forced Union Maj. Gen. A.J. Smith to withdraw form Tupelo, Mississippi.

Then, on August 25, Sherman summarily halted bombardment of Hood's entrenchments. The next day, most of his army disappeared. Hood rashly concluded that Sherman had retreated. Perhaps it was wishful thinking.

What Sherman *had* done was to swing far to the south, cutting the Macon and Western Railroad, the last rail connection into the city. Forrest, far to the northwest, had indeed performed brilliantly, but, even in defeat, the Union force there kept him occupied, and he was unable to come to Hood's aid. On September 1, Hood realized that Sherman had swung south, and, to avoid being trapped in Atlanta, the Confederate commander evacuated the city. On September 2, the bluecoats marched in.

Sherman was not gentle with those citizens who had chosen to remain in their homes. He ordered the city evacuated of noncombatants, and when Atlanta's mayor and two city councilmen protested the order, Sherman wrote them a letter: "War is cruelty," he wrote. "You might as well appeal against the thunderstorm as against the terrible hardships of war."

Ordered by Sherman to evacuate, these refugees set out from Atlanta.

(National Archives and Records Administration)

Voices

Sherman rejected the plea of Atlanta's mayor and city councilmen to rescind his order of evacuation:

… I assert that our military plans make it necessary for the inhabitants to go away ….

You cannot qualify war in harsher terms than I will. War is cruelty, and you cannot refine it. And those who brought war into our country deserve all the curses and maledictions a people can pour out. I know I had no hand in making this war, and I know I will make more sacrifices today than any of you to secure peace. But you cannot have peace and a division of our country ….

You might as well appeal against the thunderstorm as against the terrible hardships of war. They are inevitable, and the only way the people of Atlanta can hope once more to live in peace and quiet at home is to stop the war ….

… I want peace, and I believe it can only be reached through union and war; and I will ever conduct war purely with a view to perfect an early success. But, my dear sirs, when peace does come, you may call on me for anything. Then will I share with you the last cracker, and watch with you to shield your homes and families against danger from every quarter.

Now you must go, and take with you the old and feeble, feed and nurse them, and build for them in more quiet places proper habitations to shield them against the weather until the mad passions of men cool down and allow the Union and peace once more to settle over your old homes at Atlanta.

Fiery March to the Sea

With the citizens of Atlanta evacuated (only about half actually left), General Sherman set about transforming the Southern city into a Northern fortress. Sherman's victory at Atlanta accomplished three things—only two of which had Sherman and Grant foreseen. The South was deprived of a major rail hub and industrial city, and President Lincoln was assured of reelection. These outcomes had been expected, but now, as a result of the battle, Sherman also found himself unexpectedly rethinking basic strategy. He had concurred with Grant that war would likely continue as long as the South had armies to fight it. Destroy those armies, and the war would end.

Now, however, having taken Atlanta, he saw that the Confederacy was not merely weak. It was hollow. He therefore proposed to Grant a reversal of strategy. Not only would he shift his principal objective away from the destruction of Hood's army, he would effectively *ignore* that army and, instead, advance with 60,000 of his troops southeast to Savannah in a "March to the Sea." This, he proposed to Grant, would accomplish two immediate military objectives: It would cut the Confederacy in two, north and south, just as the victories along the Mississippi River had severed it east from west. It would also allow Sherman to come at Lee's Army of Northern Virginia from the south even as Grant continued to bear down on it from the north—a classic *pincers movement* which would attack the enemy from opposite directions.

Words of War

A **pincers movement** is a strategy of attacking an enemy army from opposite directions, effectively squeezing it between the jaws of a pincers.

But the March to the Sea would accomplish another, even more important, but less immediate, military objective. The Union soldiers would live off the land and would wreck or burn whatever they didn't need to live on, thereby adding to the Confederacy's economic ruin and to its psychological destruction. This would be *total war*. As for the armies of Hood and Forrest, well, they wouldn't be *totally* ignored, but, Sherman pointed out, they could accomplish little, whereas Sherman could demonstrate to the people of the North as well as the South that the Confederate army was powerless to defend the lives, homes, and property of the so-called Confederacy. After some soul-searching, Grant approved Sherman's revised strategy.

Hood's Gamble

Early in October, leaving a corps in Atlanta to hold the city, Sherman pursued Hood, who was trying to disrupt the Federals' greatly extended lines of supply even as Sherman was trying to pin him down for a fight to the finish.

War News

At Allatoona Pass, on October 5, Hood menaced a Federal supply depot commanded by Brig. Gen. John M. Corse. Hood demanded Corse's surrender—"to avoid a needless effusion of blood." The Union brigadier replied that he and his men were ready to shed blood "whenever it is agreeable to you." Sherman, in the meantime, signaled Corse: "Hold the fort." The phrase immediately entered the English language as a common figure of speech and was also the subject and title of a popular ballad of the day. Corse held, and Hood withdrew.

At last, by the middle of November, the armies simply turned away from each other—Sherman to the sea and Hood toward Nashville. Hood's plan now was to work with Nathan Bedford Forrest to overwhelm the 30,000 men under Maj. Gen. George Thomas, who had been sent to clear the Confederates out of Tennessee. This, Hood reasoned, would draw Sherman out of Atlanta to reinforce Thomas. At the very least, it would halt Sherman's raid of the deep South. In the best-case scenario, it might even recover Tennessee for the Confederacy and give Hood a base of operations in Nashville, from which he could launch an invasion of Kentucky and knock at the door of Cincinnati. He might even be able to attack Grant's army from the rear, thereby relieving Lee and Richmond. It was not so much a bold plan as it was a desperate and doomed one.

Who Burned Atlanta?

Anyone who's seen the 1939 movie *Gone with the Wind* (or read the Margaret Mitchell novel on which it is based) knows that Atlanta was put to the torch. The question is, Who did it?

Southerners are quick to answer that the city was burned by order of Sherman, but at least some Northerners will counter that the rebels themselves set the city ablaze.

In fact, both answers are true. After the evacuation of Atlanta, General Hood dispatched men to blow up the Confederate ammunition train to keep it from falling into Union hands. Embers from the blast touched off a large fire in the early morning hours of September 1, 1864. But this was only the first burning of Atlanta. On November 11, Sherman ordered everything of military significance in Atlanta to be destroyed. His men interpreted this liberally and set fire to just about everything that hadn't been destroyed in September. When Sherman marched out of the city on November 16, Atlanta was a smoldering ruin.

Franklin and Nashville

In Nashville, during early November, Maj. Gen. George Thomas strengthened and augmented his forces to some 50,000 men. He was braced for an attack by Hood and Forrest. Hood had been advancing against Union general John M. Schofield, maneuvering him into a vulnerable position at Spring Hill, Tennessee, on November 29 that could have cut off his retreat from Columbia, Tennessee, to Franklin, just south of Nashville. But Hood's plans of envelopment failed in their execution, and Schofield's army continued its withdrawal.

At Franklin, on November 30, a frustrated Hood ordered a frontal assault on Schofield's well-defended position. It was a reckless, futile assault. (Some thought the opiate drugs Hood took to relieve the pain of his wounds befuddled his reasoning.) Of the 18,000 men he fielded in this attack, more than 6,000 were killed or wounded. Schofield continued his withdrawal to Nashville, where he combined with Thomas's force. Hood had fewer men than Thomas to begin with. Now he was outnumbered two to one.

No one could doubt the courage of George Thomas, the "Rock of Chickamauga," but, in contrast to John Bell Hood, Thomas did not confuse rash action with courageous action. He understood that he was in control of the situation around Nashville, and he took his time organizing an attack. When it was delayed by a bad ice storm, however, Grant, back in Virginia, was seized by doubt and became alarmed lest Thomas allow Hood to slip away. Accordingly, he cut an order relieving Major General Thomas of command, but, just before he transmitted the order, during December 15–16, Thomas attacked, decisively defeating Hood. Although brilliant rear-guard action by Forrest prevented the outright destruction of the Army of Tennessee, it was driven from the field, routed, and finished as an effective fighting force.

A Gift for His President

During this period, Sherman marched southeast from Atlanta, toward Savannah, Georgia, cutting a broad, burned swath of destruction and misery as he went. Kilpatrick's cavalry left many barns and homes in ruins, and the notorious army foragers, called *bummers*, were especially ruthless.

Words of War

Bummers were civilian ne'er-do-wells and soldiers who wandered away from their units in search of food and plunder.

On December 22, 1864, Sherman's forces reached the Georgia port city of Savannah. The town surrendered without a fight, and, that evening, the general sent a telegram to Abraham Lincoln: "I beg to present you as a Christmas gift the city of Savannah, with one hundred and fifty heavy guns and plenty of ammunition; also about twenty-five thousand bales of cotton."

Shortly before Sherman's forces left Savannah to invade South Carolina, a fire broke out—apparently set by accident—and spread to a Confederate arsenal. It exploded, touching off a blaze that engulfed much of the city despite the efforts of citizens, freed slaves, and Union troops to put the fires out.

Columbia Burns

Sherman argued that the swath of destruction his troops wrought was a "military necessity," but many subsequent historians have called the March to the Sea nothing less than a campaign of terrorism and have accused Sherman of the equivalent of war crimes. At the very least, some historians argue, Sherman did not—or could not—restrain his troops from gratuitous looting and arson. Other historians claim that the general actively *encouraged* such actions.

If he had promised to "make Georgia howl," Sherman next pledged to "punish South Carolina as she deserves." He said: "The whole army is burning with an insatiable desire to wreck vengeance upon South Carolina. I almost tremble for her fate."

On February 16, 1865, Sherman's army reached the South Carolina capital of Columbia. The mayor surrendered the city on the next day, whereupon fires broke out, razing half the town. Confederate general Wade Hampton, in a letter read before the U.S. Senate in 1866, accused Sherman of burning Columbia "to the ground, deliberately, systematically, and atrociously." Sherman responded that the fires had been started by Confederates in an attempt to destroy valuable cotton bales in order to keep them out of Federal hands.

The Stars and Stripes over Sumter

On February 18, the day after Columbia was occupied, the Confederates abandoned Fort Sumter as Union troops closed on Charleston. This city had stoutly resisted all Union attempts to capture it, but now, with the interior of South Carolina a hollow shell, there was no point in making a stand. Charleston surrendered, and the Stars and Stripes were raised above Fort Sumter for the first time since April 13, 1861. Just now, there was no time for ceremony—Sherman needed to continue his drive northward toward the rear of Robert E. Lee's army—but on April 14, 1865 (a matter of hours before John Wilkes Booth murdered Abraham Lincoln), Maj. Gen. Robert Anderson, who had valiantly, if reluctantly, defended Sumter in the early spring of 1861, returned to raise over the fort the same flag he had taken down four years earlier.

The Least You Need to Know

◆ In the process of taking Atlanta, General Sherman decided to target *civilian* objectives in order to destroy the South's will to fight.

◆ The occupation and destruction of Atlanta and the March to the Sea that followed it were examples of "total war"—war against civilian objectives as well as military ones—which some historians have condemned as terrorism.

◆ Confederate general John Bell Hood sought in vain to draw Sherman away from his massive raid of Georgia and South Carolina by attacking Union forces in Tennessee. But Maj. Gen. George Thomas effectively neutralized Hood's Army of Tennessee at the Battle of Nashville.

Chapter 22

Richmond!

In This Chapter

- ◆ Jubal Early menaces Washington
- ◆ Sheridan wages "total war" in the Shenandoah Valley
- ◆ Confederate terrorism
- ◆ Grant breaks through at Petersburg
- ◆ Davis and his cabinet evacuate Richmond

In terms of military, transportation, and industrial importance, Atlanta was the "second city" of the Confederacy. The primary prize was the capital, Richmond. But while Sherman advanced through Georgia, took Atlanta, invaded South Carolina, and began his roll through North Carolina, Grant's Army of the Potomac was still dug in before Richmond's backdoor, continuing the siege of Petersburg that had begun in June 1864.

While the armies pounded one another from the Petersburg entrenchments, Confederate general Jubal Early dared to menace Washington with his small army of 10,000 to 12,000 infantrymen and 4,000 cavalry troopers. And a far smaller band of Confederates was operating, out of uniform and undercover, to bring the war home to Northern civilians, just as Sherman was bringing it home to their wives, mothers, and children in the South.

Such was the substance of the second-to-last act of the long national tragedy.

Menace in the Shenandoah Valley

Gray-bearded Jubal Early was six feet tall, but he was stooped by arthritis contracted during the Mexican War. Unlike most Southerners, he disavowed all religion, and, unlike many Southerners, he had never favored secession. But his loyalty to the South and the Confederate cause was beyond question, and many thought his skill as a commander was second only to that of Stonewall Jackson and Robert E. Lee, who called him "My Bad Old Man."

Early's Raid

On June 27, 1864, Early set off from Staunton, chief town of the Shenandoah Valley in Virginia, with his army of 14,000 (perhaps as many as 16,000), and invaded Maryland. Not until July 5 did Halleck or Grant take Early's offensive seriously and begin scrambling to reinforce Washington's defenses. On July 9, Early attacked Federal troops under Maj. Gen. Lew Wallace at Monocacy, Maryland, 40 miles northwest of Washington. The Confederates sustained heavy losses, but at the end of the day the Federals were soundly beaten, and Early claimed the only reason he did not pursue them was to avoid burdening his small force with Union POWs. Despite his defeat, Wallace had bought time for the reinforcement of the capital's defenses. In so doing, Grant later said, Wallace accomplished more in defeat than many generals achieve by victory.

Count Off!

Of 6,050 Federal troops engaged at Monocacy, 1,880 were wounded, killed, or missing. Early suffered about 900 casualties, almost all killed or wounded, out of the 14,000 troops he had in action.

After Monocacy, Early menaced Baltimore with a brigade of cavalry as he marched with the main body of his army on Washington. Grant sent men from the Army of the Potomac to defend the capital, which also called on administrative troops and civilians to pitch in. Lincoln asked Grant to consider coming to Washington to direct its defense personally, but the commander persuaded the president that his presence at Petersburg was more important.

On July 11, Early reached the forts defending Washington itself. As the Confederates approached, the War Department cobbled together all available forces, including old soldiers from the Soldiers' Home and disabled veterans from the Invalid Corps. On the verge of ordering a general attack, Early was apparently dismayed by the sudden appearance of the Union's VI Corps, a veteran unit, and withdrew after a brief fight outside the lines of the forts. Early began a general withdrawal during the night of July 12–13, backtracking into the Shenandoah Valley.

War News

On July 11 and 12, President and Mrs. Lincoln, accompanied by political dignitaries, visited Fort Stevens (located in northwest Washington). There was a sharp exchange with rebel sharpshooters, and Lincoln mounted a firing step to peer over the parapet for a view of the action, thereby exposing his head and chest to the enemy fire. A surgeon standing beside Lincoln was wounded, and a young officer shouted to the president, whom he did not recognize: "Get down, you damn fool!"

That officer was Captain Oliver Wendell Holmes, Jr., who would later become the most eloquent and celebrated associate justice ever to sit on the U.S. Supreme Court.

Sheridan the Ruthless

Through the first week of August, Early harried Union units in the Shenandoah until Grant finally dispatched Phil Sheridan with about 48,000 men to defeat Early and to neutralize the Valley, taking the region out of the war once and for all. The Valley was important for two reasons: first, it loomed always as an avenue of invasion, a backdoor to Washington, as well as a means of access to Baltimore and Philadelphia; second, it was incredibly lush and served as the breadbasket of the Confederate armies.

This second fact required Sheridan to wage total war. Grant told him that he wanted the croplands of the Shenandoah devastated so that "a crow flying across the Valley would have to carry its own rations."

Sheridan chased Early up the Shenandoah Valley while burning barns, burning crops, and destroying cattle. In turn, Sheridan's columns were continually harassed by guerrillas, the most famous of which was Col. John Singleton Mosby, the "Gray Ghost of the Confederacy," leading his "Partisan Rangers."

Although Sheridan's forces greatly outnumbered those of Early and guerrilla leaders like Mosby, combat was nevertheless sharp. Sheridan won a major victory at Winchester on September 19 and another at Fisher's Hill on September 22. But Early was far from finished. At dawn on October 19, Early made a surprise attack on the Federal position at Cedar Creek, Virginia, so shocking that troops broke and ran in disordered retreat. Sheridan, who was at Winchester following a visit to

Count Off!

At Cedar Creek, Sheridan lost 5,665 men, killed, wounded, or missing, out of 30,829 engaged, and Early lost 2,910, killed, wounded, or missing, out of 18,410. Early also lost most of his supplies and 43 pieces of artillery.

Washington, galloped to the scene and personally got the troops back into order and into the fight. By 4:00 that afternoon, he staged a furious counterattack, turning a Federal rout into a victory that brought to a successful conclusion Sheridan's Shenandoah Valley campaign.

"Kilcavalry" Raids Richmond

Brig. Gen. Judson Kilpatrick was a twenty-eight-year-old West Pointer with unbounded dreams of glory. Short, slight, sporting ginger-colored mutton-chop whiskers, he wore a rakish hat, a specially tailored cutaway uniform coat, and buff-colored cavalry trousers tucked into high boots. None of this impressed his men, one of whom remarked that it was "hard to look at him without laughing." Worse, Kilpatrick didn't care how many of his troops died in pursuit of his dreams. This earned Kilpatrick the nickname of Kilcavalry. William Tecumseh Sherman simply called him "a hell of a damned fool."

Early in 1864, hearing that the Confederates had left Richmond very thinly defended, Kilpatrick persuaded his superiors to let him stage a lightning cavalry raid against the rebel capital with the purpose of harassing Confederate lines of supply and communication, disrupting government, and liberating the 5,000 Union prisoners languishing in two POW camps, Libby Prison and Belle Isle. When Ulric Dahlgren heard about the raid, he rushed to volunteer as second in command, despite having lost a leg at Gettysburg. At twenty-one, Dahlgren was the youngest colonel in the Union army. He was the son of Rear Admiral John A. Dahlgren, inventor of the famous Dahlgren gun used on most Union warships.

The raiders, 3,585 troopers, set off at 11 P.M. on February 28, 1864. At Spotsylvania, Dahlgren was detached with 500 men to proceed along the James River, upstream from Richmond, while Kilpatrick and the main force approached Richmond directly from the north. As Dahlgren approached from the southwest, Kilpatrick would enter from the north, forcing the defenders to divide their already scant forces.

That was the plan. But Dahlgren never materialized as planned, and Kilpatrick encountered much stiffer resistance than he had anticipated. Just outside of Richmond, Kilpatrick withdrew, stumbling into the 260 survivors of Dahlgren's detachment at a place called Tunstall's Station, near the Pamunkey River. Like Kilpatrick, Dahlgren had encountered heavy resistance and, like Kilpatrick, retreated. Unlike him, however, Dahlgren was killed. Almost half his command were killed or captured.

The Kilpatrick-Dahlgren raid might be remembered as simply a failed military venture were it not for the note Confederates found in Dahlgren's pocket. It was a handwritten speech on Third Division stationery:

You have been selected from brigades and regiments as a picked command to attempt a desperate undertaking ....

We hope to release the prisoners from Belle Island first, and, having seen them fairly started, we will cross the James river into Richmond, destroying the bridges after us, and exhorting the released prisoners to destroy and burn the hateful city, and do not allow the Rebel leader, Davis, and his traitorous crew to escape. ... Jeff Davis and Cabinet [are to be] killed ....

The letter was shown to President Davis, who had it published in the Richmond newspapers as evidence of Northern treachery. The dogs were resorting to assassination!

In response to the newspaper stories and official protests from the Confederacy, Dahlgren's and Kilpatrick's superiors disavowed any knowledge of an assassination plot. Although no Federal conspiracy to assassinate Davis has ever been demonstrated, neither has it been disproved, and the ultimate intention of the Kilpatrick-Dahlgren Raid remains a mystery of the Civil War.

Of Terror and Greek Fire

Northern raiders such as Kilpatrick and Dahlgren were rare. The South made much more extensive use of guerrillas as well as spies and saboteurs.

With the Confederacy crumbling and its depleted army failing, small bands of "irregulars"—spies, infiltrators, raiders, and terrorists—desperately sought to strike a blow against the *people* of the North, just as the *armies* of the North were preying upon Southern civilians.

In the late spring and early summer of 1864, people who lived or fished along the coast of Maine reported seeing "artists" sketching the coastline. These "artists" were, in fact, 50 Confederate topographers making maps of secluded coves and inlets that could harbor two armed steamers, the *Tallahassee* and *Florida*, during a planned terrorist assault along the Northern coast. But word of the operation leaked to the American consul in St. Johns, Quebec, who notified the War Department, which alerted the Home Guard. When the raiders hit the Calais (Maine) National Bank late in July, guardsmen, police, and the Portland marshal were ready for them. The ringleaders were captured, and one of them, Francis Jones, revealed the scope of the entire scheme. Having lost the element of surprise, the seaborne raid of terror fell apart. Jones's revelations led to the arrest of Confederate operatives in Maine, Massachusetts, New York, Pennsylvania, Maryland, Illinois, Missouri, Kentucky, Tennessee, and Ohio.

During this same period, other operatives conspired with Copperhead leader Clement Vallandigham (see Chapter 16) to stage an uprising at the Democratic Convention, set to open in Chicago on August 29, 1864. The principal objective of the operation was Camp Douglas, a prisoner of war facility just outside the city. The plan was to break out the prisoners, arm them, and use them to capture and occupy Chicago. Col. Benjamin Jeffrey Sweet, Eighth Regiment, Veterans' Corps, commandant of Camp Douglas, was sufficiently vigilant to catch word of the scheme and to secure reinforcements to guard the camp and patrol the city. August 29 came and went without incident—although, later, Confederate raiders did manage to torch some federal warehouses in Mattoon, Illinois, and set fire to a number of steamers docked in St. Louis.

The St. Albans Raid

There were other covert Confederate operations in the North during 1864, most of them abortive, many Quixotic. The most successful was the October 19, 1864 raid by about 20 men against three banks in the border town of St. Albans, Vermont. The action, which netted almost $250,000 badly needed by the Confederacy, also resulted in the death of one citizen and the wounding of another. A number of the town's principal buildings were burned to the ground by hurled bottles of an incendiary fluid known as *Greek fire*.

Words of War

Greek fire was a highly flammable fluid consisting of sulfur, charcoal, saltpeter, and possibly quicklime, which burst into flame when suddenly exposed to air. Typically, it was poured into a glass jar, which was then tightly sealed. If suddenly broken, the contents would ignite explosively.

Following the operation, the raiders fled to Canada, which was a headquarters and staging area for Confederate covert operations during the late phases of the war. A posse gave chase, crossed the border, and apprehended eight of the raiders, but had to remand the men to Canadian custody. A team of slick lawyers fought extradition to the United States, and all eight escaped prosecution. Although some nervous New Englanders predicted that St. Albans was merely the overture to a reign of Confederate terror, the northeastern border remained peaceful for the rest of the war.

The Fires of New York

Certainly, there were Confederate agents who *wanted* to do far more than rob banks. The uprising set for August 29 in Chicago had fizzled, but it was now rescheduled for November 8, 1864, election day in the Union, and would target not only Chicago, but

Cincinnati, towns throughout Missouri and Iowa, and, best of all, New York City. Confederate agents called for a program of arson and, in New York, also seizure of the U.S. Sub-Treasury and the liberation of Fort Lafayette, a POW camp. Once again, however, the Chicago operation was aborted as Union counterintelligence rooted out the scheme, and, with the failure of the Chicago uprising, the planned revolts elsewhere likewise came to naught.

But three die-hard agents—Col. Robert Martin and Lt. John W. Headley (both former subordinates of famed raider John Hunt Morgan), plus a shadowy figure known only as Captain Longuemare from Missouri—resolved to act on their own. Their plan was to organize other operatives to check into New York City's 19 most prominent hotels. Each man would go up to his room, set it on fire, and calmly walk out. Longuemare ordered 144 four-ounce bottles of Greek fire from a compliant chemist in Greenwich Village. Headley lugged this heavy and highly combustible load in a carpetbag valise several blocks, boarded a crowded, uptown-bound horsecar, sat behind the conductor, and tucked the valise between his legs. His destination was a Confederate safe house near Central Park (which, in 1864, was still under development).

As the car jostled along the tracks, Headley detected the rotten-egg stench of hydrogen sulfide. He looked down at the valise between his legs, expecting to see a telltale puddle of Greek fire.

But, no.

Then a woman, sniffing, called out: "Something smells dead here! Conductor, something smells dead in that man's valise!"

> ### War News
>
> In addition to the hotels, the arsonists hit the famed Barnum's Museum on lower Broadway, creating a blaze made all the more terrifying by the roar of lions and tigers and the trumpeting of elephants trapped in their cages. The flames drove Barnum's seven-foot-tall giantess into a frenzy, requiring five strong firemen and a physician's sedative to bring her under control.

But nobody did anything. Headley got off the horsecar, walked to the safe house, and distributed the bottles. He and the other agents then left and, beginning about 7:00 in the evening, registered at the hotels. Each signed in, received his key, walked up to his room, and closed the door. Headley later related what he had done at the Astor House: "I hung the bedclothes loosely on the headboard and piled the chairs, drawers of the bureau, and washstand on the bed, then stuffed some newspapers about among the mass and poured a bottle of turpentine over it all." Instead of hurling the bottle of Greek fire against the wall, which would have exploded, attracting immediate attention, he just spilled it on a "pile of rubbish. It blazed up instantly and the whole bed seemed to be in flames before I could get out. I locked the door and … left the key at the office as usual." Walking through the lobby with calm deliberation, he went off to register at the City Hotel, his next target.

After igniting other hotel rooms, Headley strolled along the West Side wharves and hurled Greek fire at a number of vessels tied up there.

For once, a rebel conspiracy seemed to work. Panicked rumors of an invasion buzzed through the streets—and, yet, in an age when frame-built American cities routinely suffered catastrophic fires (the Great Chicago Fire was seven years in the future), no general conflagration developed. Two floors of the Belmont Hotel and the Metropolitan were destroyed, and the St. Nicholas was a complete loss. A dry goods firm was gutted, and a few ships damaged. But that was about all. Perhaps the Greenwich Village chemist had prepared a weak batch of Greek fire, or perhaps the fires in the hotel rooms burned out too quickly because none of the arsonists had thought to open a window to fan the flames; the fires were oxygen starved.

The disappointed conspirators fled back to Canada, and, as the fires died in New York, so, too, the last of the Confederate conspiracies passed into oblivion.

"With Malice Toward None"

No one—not Robert E. Lee, not Joseph E. Johnston, not John Bell Hood, and not a band of determined terrorists—was able to prevent the reelection of Abraham Lincoln, a president committed to fighting the war to total victory. Yet, on Inauguration Day, March 4, 1865, Lincoln made it clear that total victory did not mean wreaking vengeance on the Southland. His brief inaugural address concluded:

> With malice toward none, with charity for all, with firmness in the right as God gives us to see the right, let us strive to finish the work we are in, to bind up the nation's wounds, to care for him who shall have borne the battle and for his widow and his orphan, to do all which may achieve and cherish a just and a lasting peace among ourselves and with all nations.

From the leader of a country on the painful threshold of victory in a war far more costly than either side had ever remotely envisioned, these were remarkable words of justice, compassion, and forgiveness. Eloquent and moving, they must nevertheless have rung hollow in the ears of Southerners whose property was stolen or burned and whose lives were in countless ways shattered.

The war went on.

Breakout from Petersburg

For nine months Petersburg lay under siege. The Army of the Potomac entrenched here numbered about 125,000 men against an Army of Northern Virginia of perhaps half that number. Lee's men were hungrier than ever before (and they had often been hungry before), and their commander knew they were trapped. Jefferson Davis had insisted they stay put. The capital had to be defended at all costs. Now, at last, Lee persuaded the Confederate president that the only chance of averting total defeat and unconditional surrender lay in escape from siege. Lee proposed a breakout from Petersburg and a retreat southeast so that he could unite his forces with the ragged remnants of the Army of Tennessee—since February 22 once again under the command of Joe Johnston—now fighting Sherman in North Carolina.

These Federal soldiers in the Petersburg siege lines await Grant's spring offensive. Union troops here were numerous and well equipped.

(National Archives and Records Administration)

What was the point? Johnston's broken army of 30,000 men was compounded of veteran survivors and homeguardsmen, barely trained, usually overaged, and poorly equipped. Assigned to stop Sherman, Johnston remarked, "I can do no more than annoy him." Lee hoped that, by uniting his forces with Johnston's, they could, together, do far more to Sherman than annoy him. To be sure, Richmond might fall, but it would be perceived as a sacrifice to save the South, the government would therefore remain viable, and the North, having suffered an entirely unexpected reversal, might yet negotiate a favorable peace.

The odds against such an outcome were astronomical, but they *were* odds, and that was more than the Confederacy had with Lee's army starving in the trenches of Petersburg.

Diplomacy and Politics

The Richmond government made two desperate stabs at shortening those odds. Confederate Secretary of State Judah P. Benjamin appealed to France and England for recognition as a sovereign nation on condition that the CSA abolish slavery. It was, of course, too late for such a proposal. Very little of the Confederacy was *left* to recognize. France and England were not interested in Benjamin's proposal. At this remove in time, we cannot know whether the irony of the proposal was apparent to the Richmond government. To avoid surrender, the Confederacy proposed to give up the very institution it had fought to preserve.

In January, Jefferson Davis put out very tentative peace feelers, meeting in Richmond with Francis P. Blair, Sr., father of Lincoln's former postmaster general, Montgomery Blair, and of Francis P. Blair, Jr., one of Sherman's corps commanders. Blair's visit, while approved by Lincoln, was entirely unofficial, but Davis nevertheless seized the opportunity to propose a reunion of the states and then, both bizarrely and irrelevantly, further to propose that the reconstituted nation invade Mexico in order to eject the French-supported regime of Emperor Maximilian.

The latter proposition aside, a semiofficial peace conference was convened on February 3 aboard a Federal steamer in Hampton Roads, Virginia. The Confederacy was represented by its vice president, Alexander Stephens, and two others. The Union delegates were Secretary of State William Seward and President Abraham Lincoln. By definition a high-level conference, it nevertheless came to absolutely nothing.

War News
Many people could not accept that nothing came of the peace conference at Hampton Roads, and a popular myth circulated that Lincoln took a fresh sheet of paper, inscribed the heading "REUNION" at the top, handed it to Stephens, and told him to fill in the rest.
No such thing ever happened.
Lincoln would *accept* no terms and would *offer* only two: The South must lay down its arms and must recognize the absolute authority of the United States government.

"Wake Up. We Are Coming"

At the Petersburg front, Lee assigned Maj. Gen. John Brown Gordon to attack with 12,000 men a hardened Union position called Fort Stedman, a mere 150 yards from the Confederate lines. The idea was to force Grant to contract his lines, thereby creating a breach through which Lee could push a portion of his army and begin the march into North Carolina.

In the wee hours of March 25, the Confederates sent *sappers* with axes to cut down obstructions in front of the fort. An alert Union picket heard the noise and called out, "Who goes there"?

"Never mind, Yank. We are just gathering a little corn," one of the rebels replied.

"All right, Johnny," the Union picket called back. "I'll not shoot at you while you are drawing rations."

At 4:00 A.M., Gordon ordered the quick-thinking soldier to fire a shot to signal the commencement of the assault. When he hesitated, the Confederate general repeated the order. The soldier looked at his general, and then at the Yankee lines.

"Hello, Yank!" he shouted. "Wake up. We are coming."

His conscience thus salved, he fired the shot, and the attack began.

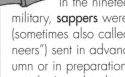

Words of War

In the nineteenth-century military, **sappers** were soldiers (sometimes also called "pioneers") sent in advance of a column or in preparation for an attack. Armed with axes, their mission was to clear debris, undergrowth, and other obstacles to marching or attacking.

Fort Stedman Taken ...

Not only did Fort Stedman quickly fall—with the capture of a thousand Union soldiers and one very surprised Union general—but so did a number of surrounding positions.

Next, Gordon was supposed to capture smaller forts behind Fort Stedman. But two things went wrong. First, Confederate reinforcements were delayed. Second, Gordon was uncertain in which direction to continue his attack—all around him were well-fortified Yankee entrenchments.

... And Lost

Without reinforcements and unable to decide which way to go, Gordon's men were stranded. By 7:30, Union reinforcements poured in, forcing the Confederates back into Fort Stedman. At 8:00, Lee, watching from his lines, ordered a retreat, but by this time the Federals were also raking the Confederate line of retreat with artillery fire. Many rebels surrendered where they stood rather than retreat into certain death. Of 12,000 men engaged, the Confederates lost 4,000 killed, wounded, or captured. And Lee, of course, remained bottled up at Petersburg.

Five Forks

Although the siege at Petersburg had consumed nine months, it was not stalemated. Given the disasters that had befallen Burnside at Fredericksburg, Hooker at Chancellorsville, and Grant himself at Cold Harbor, as well as the lesser reverse Sherman suffered at Kennesaw Mountain, Grant was not about to attempt a frontal assault on the Petersburg lines. Instead, he had been extending his lines westward in order to force Lee to stretch his much thinner lines to the breaking point.

After the exchange at Fort Stedman, it was clear to Grant that Lee's lines had now stretched *beyond* the breaking point. Grant attempted a drive around Lee's right, but was repulsed. Then General Sheridan returned from the Shenandoah Valley with 12,000 cavalry troopers, and, on March 31, headed for Five Forks, a junction not only crucial to the Confederates' contemplated move into North Carolina, but vital to their army's line of supply. Take it, and Lee not only would be cut off from Johnston, but would soon be forced to evacuate Petersburg as well as Richmond.

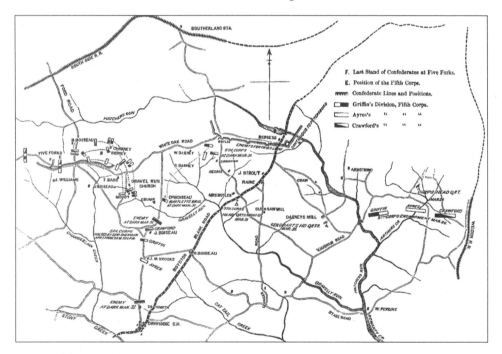

This map of Five Forks shows the South Side Railroad at the upper left. Lee needed this rail line for supply and to get him to Johnston's army in North Carolina.

(Harper's Pictorial History of the Civil War, *1866*)

Lee sent 19,000 (some estimates put this figure at a mere 10,000) men under George Pickett to hold Five Forks, but Sheridan was reinforced by an infantry corps. Outnumbered, Pickett was also outgeneraled. His forces were flanked and routed by Sheridan, some 5,000 men were taken prisoner, and the rest, those not killed or wounded, "skedaddled"—fled.

The disaster at Five Forks has been called "the Waterloo of the Confederacy."

Evacuation

After a nine-month gestation, the birth of victory at Petersburg came suddenly. Grant broke through Lee's lines on April 2 in a quick assault that resulted in the death of Confederate General Ambrose Powell (A.P.) Hill. Lee fell back on Petersburg and evacuated it, retreating west toward Amelia Court House.

At 11:00 on this Sunday morning of April 2, Jefferson Davis was seated in his pew at St. Paul's Church in Richmond. A War Department messenger approached and handed him a telegram from Robert E. Lee. It advised that "all preparation be made for leaving Richmond tonight."

Voices

Edward Pollard, editor of the *Richmond Examiner*, recalled April 2 and 3 in the fallen capital:

> The streets were thronged with fugitives making their way to the railroad depots; pale women and little shoeless children struggled in the crowd; oaths and blasphemous shouts smote the air .... It was proposed to maintain order in the city by two regiments of militia; to destroy every drop of liquor in the warehouses and stores; and to establish a patrol through the night. But the militia ran through the fingers of their officers ..., and in a short while the whole city was plunged into mad confusion and indescribable horrors.

> It was an extraordinary night; disorder, pillage, shouts, mad revelry .... The gutters ran with a liquor freshet [flood], and the fumes filled the air. Some of the straggling soldiers easily managed to get hold of quantities of the liquor.

> Confusion became worse confounded; the sidewalks were encumbered with broken glass; stores were entered at pleasure and stripped from top to bottom; yells of drunken men, shouts of roving pillagers, wild cries of distress filled the air and made night hideous ....

> Morning broke on a scene never to be forgotten .... The smoke and glare of fire mingled with the golden beams of the rising sun .... The fire was reaching to whole blocks of buildings .... Pillagers were busy at their vocation, and in the hot breath of the fire were figures as of demons contending for prey.

Those seated near the Confederate president remarked a "gray pallor" that suddenly crept "over his face" as he read the message. He rose, walked out of church, went to the War Office, then gave orders for evacuation. He and his cabinet would meet that evening and board a train bound for Danville, a Virginia town just north of the North Carolina state line, which would become the new Confederate capital. From the Treasury, Davis ordered that all the Confederacy's ready funds—a mere $528,000 in gold and silver coins and gold and silver ingots—be boxed for shipment to Danville. Davis packed his wife and children off to Charlotte, North Carolina, a location relatively remote from the war.

The Nightmare Gone

The war, which had been measured in agonizing months and years, was now becoming a matter of days. The Confederate government evacuated Richmond on April 2, and Federal troops under Maj. Gen. Godfrey Weitzel were the first to enter the city the next day, trooping into a place that, like so many other Southern cities and towns, was now ablaze. The night before, Confederate authorities blew up the ironclads docked along the James River in order to keep them out of Union hands. The explosions touched off fires in wharfside tobacco warehouses, and those fires spread to large sections of the city before they burned out on the evening of the 3rd.

The ruins of Richmond appear in ghostly silhouette in this period photograph. The fires were touched off when Confederates, evacuating the city, blew up ironclads docked on the James River in order to keep them from being captured.

(National Archives and Records Administration)

On this day, Grant entered Petersburg and was met there by Abraham Lincoln, who strode up to the general, and (as an aide to the general recalled) shook his hand "for some time … pouring out his thanks and congratulations."

Secretary of War Edwin Stanton had sent President Lincoln a telegram advising him to "consider whether you ought to expose the nation to the consequences of any disaster to yourself" in visiting Petersburg. Lincoln replied: "Yours received. Thanks for your caution, but I have already been to Petersburg, stayed with Gen. Grant an hour & a half, and returned here [to Grant's headquarters at City Point]. It is certain now that Richmond is in our hands, and I think I will go there tomorrow. I will take care of myself."

Voices

Lincoln certainly risked assassination when he entered Richmond and walked its streets. A White House guard who accompanied him remembered that "wherever it was possible for a human being to gain a foothold there was some man or woman or boy straining his eyes after the President .... Every window was crowned with heads. Men were hanging from tree-boxes and telegraph poles."

"But," the guard continued, "it was a silent crowd ... thousands of watchers, without a sound either of welcome or hatred."

This was the reaction of the *white* residents of Richmond.

In contrast, black men and women greeted the president effusively: "Bless the Lord, the great Messiah! I knowed him as soon as I seed him. He's been in my heart four long years, and he come at last to free his children from bondage. Glory, hallelujah!"

The man who uttered these words, his hair white with age, then threw himself at Lincoln's feet, as did other now-free slaves, surrounding the president.

"Don't kneel to me," Lincoln gently admonished them. "That is not right. You must kneel to God only, and thank Him for the liberty you will enjoy hereafter."

When he set off for Richmond on the morning of April 4 in David Porter's flagship, Lincoln remarked to the admiral: "Thank God I have lived to see this. It seems to me that I have been dreaming a horrid dream for four years, and now the nightmare is gone."

The Least You Need to Know

- ◆ After Confederate general Jubal Early attacked the outskirts of Washington, General Grant ordered Philip Sheridan to defeat and, in the process, to lay waste to the Shenandoah Valley.

- ◆ Confederate acts of terrorism against the North were conceived on a grand scale, but rarely amounted to much. The most famous raid against the North was the attack on three banks in St. Albans, Vermont, on October 19, 1864.

- The Battle of Five Forks, in which Union commander Philip Sheridan defeated Confederate general George Pickett, has been called the "Waterloo of the Confederacy."

- After Grant's breakthrough at Petersburg, Davis and his government fled Richmond, which instantly fell to the Union. It was the beginning of the war's final act.

- President Lincoln was quick to visit the fallen Confederate capital; his object was to underscore the defeat of the rebel government.

Chapter 23

Appomattox Ending

In This Chapter

- ◆ The pursuit of Lee to Appomattox Court House
- ◆ The decision to surrender
- ◆ Lee surrenders the Army of Northern Virginia
- ◆ The war ends

As the first Union general officer to enter Richmond, Godfrey Weitzel could lay claim to the choicest headquarters, and he did, setting himself up in nothing less than the abandoned Governor's Mansion—for four years the Confederate White House. After walking two miles through the streets of the fallen capital, Abraham Lincoln was tired. Weitzel admitted him into Jefferson Davis's study.

The day before, when Lincoln clasped Grant's hand at Petersburg, the general's aide imagined that "Mr. Lincoln [had never] experienced a happier moment in his life." Today, however, as the president stood in the office of "the enemy," another witness remarked on his "pale and haggard" face, "utterly worn out."

Perhaps it was war weariness or simply the long walk—or something deeper—that prompted Lincoln to slump into Jefferson Davis's chair. He made no speech, no profound pronouncement, just a request: "I wonder if I could get a glass of water?"

During these moments, there was neither rest nor refreshment for Grant, Lee, and their armies. This chapter describes the final pursuit of the Army of Northern Virginia and the last days of the war.

Pursuit

No one knew better than Robert E. Lee that Union victory was now inevitable. If this were a game of chess, Lee, though not checkmated quite yet, would resign—surrender to his opponent. That is what seasoned chess players do when they have run out of options. No reason to play out a foregone conclusion to the bitter end.

But this was no game of chess. At this point, Lee was not motivated by questions of victory or defeat, but by duty. It was, he felt, his duty to continue to fight while he still could to preserve as much of a chance as possible to negotiate surrender terms that were at least something more than abject and unconditional.

Lee took what was left of his army, slightly fewer than 50,000 men, and marched west. To be sure, he was being chased, but he was not so much fleeing as trying to reach Amelia Court House, where he expected to find supplies and gain access to the Danville and Richmond Railroad, which would take his army to that of Johnston. Fighting together, he and Johnston might still prolong the war, giving the Confederacy some basis, some credibility from which to negotiate. By today's standards, we might argue that, by prolonging combat, Lee acted without humanity. By the standards of 1865, however, the loss of honor was perceived as inhumane.

Namozine Church

After Five Forks (see Chapter 22), a brigade of George Armstrong Custer's cavalry pursued a brigade of Confederate cavalry, commanded by Robert E. Lee's nephew Fitzhugh Lee, and fought first at Willicomack Creek, and then at Namozine Church. Here Custer repulsed a desperate Confederate counterpunch. Following this, the Confederates split up, Fitzhugh Lee making for Amelia Court House while his subordinate, William Henry Fitzhugh Lee—called Rooney—headed toward Bevill's Bridge. Rooney was Robert E. Lee's second-eldest son.

War News
George Armstrong Custer was only 23 when he was promoted to brigadier general. Lacking academic skills and self-discipline, he had almost failed to graduate from West Point, but showed such courage on the battlefield—he was especially celebrated for his reckless cavalry charges—that his star rapidly rose. After the war, he earned fame as an Indian fighter in the West commanding the Seventh Cavalry. That fame culminated at the Battle of the Little Big Horn in June 1876. Custer attacked the village of Sitting Bull and Crazy Horse, whose warriors responded by wiping out Custer and more than 200 of his men.

Amelia Springs

By April 5, the bulk of Lee's army was concentrated at Amelia Court House, about 30 miles west of Petersburg. The Confederates were blocked by Sheridan and others from making a break down the Richmond and Danville Railroad. Worse, in the confusion of Richmond's fall, no one had dispatched the promised rations—a fact that hit the half-starved army particularly hard. Sheridan sent a brigade to reconnoiter in the direction of Lee's retreat, and, at Amelia Springs, it attacked a wagon train attached to Lee's army. The Federals took 320 white prisoners and about as many black teamsters, and they set fire to 200 of Lee's wagons, probably destroying all the general's headquarters records in the process.

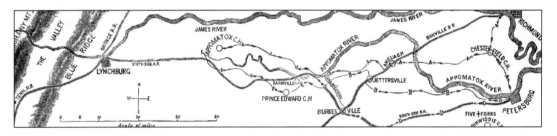

This map shows Lee's route of retreat from Petersburg west to Appomattox Court House. Jetersville (misspelled on this map as Jettersville) is the site of the Amelia Springs battle and is midway between Petersburg and Appomattox Court House (which is also misspelled, as Appomatox).

(Harper's Pictorial History of the Civil War, *1866*)

Sayler's Creek

Having failed to connect with rations and supplies at Amelia Court House and unable to make a rail connection there, Lee turned to the southwest, bound for a place called

Rice Station, where he could get supplies by rail and then push on south to link up with Johnston. Grant, however, ordered attacks, and pursuing Federal forces hit the Confederate wagon train.

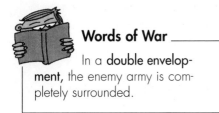

Words of War

In a **double envelopment,** the enemy army is completely surrounded.

At Little Sayler's Creek, Confederate general Richard S. Ewell counterpunched and was able to drive back the Union center, but the arrival of more Federals soon checked this penetration. Then, as Federal strength continued to build, Union forces were able to counterattack and effect a *double envelopment* of Ewell's badly outnumbered command.

Three Confederate commanders—Richard H. Anderson, Bushrod Johnson, and George Pickett—were able to escape, but Ewell remained behind in an effort to lead his troops out of the trap. There was fierce hand-to-hand fighting—certainly not the first in this war, but all the more amazing, given the exhaustion and general emaciation of the Confederate forces.

It was, of course, hopeless. Ewell's men were engulfed, and he was captured, along with five other Confederate commanders, including George Washington Custis Lee, Robert E. Lee's eldest son.

As for Robert E. Lee himself, the commander in chief witnessed the battle—it was a rout—from high ground in the rear. He turned to a subordinate and observed, "General, that half of our army is destroyed."

In truth, Lee had lost a third of his entire forces—which was certainly bad enough.

High Bridge and Farmville

Confederate general John Brown Gordon suffered heavy losses at Sayler's Creek, as did the other rebel commanders; but, unlike them, Gordon successfully rallied his troops and led them farther west to High Bridge, a structure built on 60-foot piers across the Appomattox River at Farmville. There he joined Longstreet in retreating across the bridge, leaving Fitzhugh Lee to fight a rear-guard action.

William "Little Billy" Mahone—commanding a division that was covering Gordon's withdrawal—should have ordered High Bridge put to the torch once all the units had crossed it. But, before the war, Mahone had been a railroad construction engineer and then president of the Southside Railroad, the owner of this particular structure. He did not burn it (skirmishers later tried, without success), and, in consequence, the Federals quickly closed on the rear of Lee's army. Nevertheless, Union forces failed to stop Lee's westward progress here, and the Confederate army even had the opportunity to draw rations at Farmville.

At 10:00 that night, Lee received a message from Ulysses Simpson Grant. It requested the surrender of the Army of Northern Virginia.

Lee said nothing, but passed the note to James Longstreet—his "Old War Horse," who had been the voice of realism when Lee proposed to invade Maryland and, later again, when he resolved to invade Pennsylvania. Now Longstreet read the note, looked at his commander, and said: "Not yet."

Appomattox Station and Appomattox Court House

What drove these battered, hungry men on? The glory of the Noble Southern Cause? The honor of their country? The answer probably lay not in these things, but in the confidence and faith Robert E. Lee continued to inspire.

But what must Lee have been feeling on April 8, when he concentrated the remnant of his ragged, hungry army between Appomattox Station, on the rail line, and Appomattox Court House, a few miles to the northeast? How much farther could he lead these men, who had put their lives in his hands?

General Custer's division moved rapidly against Appomattox Station, drove off two Confederate divisions, and captured their supply train, as well as 30 pieces of artillery. Custer then pressed on toward Appomattox Court House, where he discovered the Confederate defenses just to the southwest of the town. Sheridan, with the main body of troops, caught up with Custer and prepared to launch an attack the next day.

In fact, at 5:00 on the morning of April 9, 1865, it was Lee's generals, John Brown Gordon and Fitzhugh Lee, who attacked first, assaulting hastily constructed Federal breastworks. This proved effective, though the success was short lived. Union cavalry and infantry pressed from the northeast—from Appomattox Court House—and, having gotten across Lee's line of march, also closed in from the southwest, Appomattox Station. At this point, Lee was down to perhaps 30,000 soldiers, of whom only little more than half were still armed.

"I Had Rather Die a Thousand Deaths"

Lee saw that his broken army lay within the jaws of a vise. The army could not go forward. Nor could it retreat. It was time to end it.

"There is nothing left me but to go and see General Grant, and I had rather die a thousand deaths."

But Lee knew that his army had *thirty* thousand deaths yet to die if he did not choose to stop the fighting now.

Like a Wraith of Morning Mist

On April 9, Gen. Joshua Laurence Chamberlain, the former Bowdoin professor of rhetoric who had held Little Round Top and saved the Union army at Gettysburg, was poised for attack with his regiment. He watched the Confederate lines apprehensively, until (as he later wrote) …

> Suddenly rose to sight another form, close in our own front—a soldierly young figure, a Confederate staff officer undoubtedly. Now I see the white flag earnestly borne, and its possible purport sweeps before my inner vision like a wraith of morning mist. He comes steadily on, the mysterious form in gray, my mood so whimsically sensitive that I could even smile at the material of the flag—wondering where in either army was found a towel, and one so white. But it bore a mighty message—that simple emblem of homely service, wafted hitherward above the dark and crimsoned streams that never can wash themselves away.
>
> The messenger draws near, dismounts; with graceful salutation and hardly suppressed emotion delivers his message: "Sir, I am from General Gordon. General Lee desires a cessation of hostilities until he can hear from General Grant as to the proposed surrender."
>
> … "Sir," I answer, "that matter exceeds my authority. I will send to my superior. General Lee is right. He can do no more."

The grim fact is that Lee *could* have done more. A man of lesser moral integrity might have bitterly directed his army to disband, to take to the hills, to fight as partisans and guerrillas, and, in this way, year after year, decade after decade, kill every Yankee they encountered south of the Mason-Dixon Line.

But, instead, Lee directed Col. Charles Marshall "to go forward and find a house where he could meet General Grant." Marshall recalled that the first person he met was a "man named [Wilmer] McLean who used to live on the first battle field of Manassas, at a house about a mile from Manassas Junction. He didn't like the war, and having seen the first battle of Manassas, he thought he would get away where there wouldn't be any more fighting, so he moved to Appomattox Court House."

Marshall asked McLean to show him a house where the generals could meet. McLean took him to a dilapidated shell devoid of furniture. Marshall said it was unsuitable.

"Then [McLean] said, 'Maybe my house will do!'"

*Grant accepted Lee's surren-
der in the McLean house at
Appomattox Court House.
This was McLean's second
house. His first stood on
what became the Bull Run
battlefield—he had moved
to a place he thought would
never see combat.*

(Library of Congress)

In the McLean House

No account of the surrender at Appomattox is clearer, simpler, or more moving than
what Ulysses S. Grant wrote in his *Personal Memoirs*, published in 1885:

> When I had left camp that morning I had not expected so soon the result that
> was then taking place, and consequently was in rough garb. I was without a
> sword, as I usually was when on horseback on the field, and wore a soldier's
> blouse for a coat, with the shoulder straps of my rank to indicate to the army
> who I was. When I went into the house I found General Lee. We greeted each
> other, and after shaking hands took our seats. I had my staff with me, a good
> portion of whom were in the room during the whole of the interview.
>
> What General Lee's feelings were I do not know. As he was a man of much dig-
> nity, with an impassable face, it was impossible to say whether he felt inwardly
> glad that the end had finally come, or felt sad over the result, and was too manly
> to show it. Whatever his feelings, they were entirely concealed from my obser-
> vation; but my own feelings, which had been quite jubilant on the receipt of his
> letter [offering surrender], were sad and depressed. I felt like anything rather
> than rejoicing at the downfall of a foe who had fought so long and valiantly, and
> had suffered so much for a cause, though that cause was, I believe, one of the
> worst for which a people ever fought …

General Lee was dressed in a full uniform which was entirely new, and was wearing a sword of considerable value, very likely the sword which had been presented by the State of Virginia; at all events, it was an entirely different sword from the one that would ordinarily be worn in the field. In my rough traveling suit, the uniform of a private with the straps of a lieutenant-general, I must have contrasted very strangely with a man so handsomely dressed, six feet high and of faultless form ….

We soon fell into a conversation about old army times …. Our conversation grew so pleasant that I almost forgot the object of our meeting. After the conversation had run on in this style for some time, General Lee called my attention to the object of our meeting, and said that he had asked for this interview for the purpose of getting from me the terms I proposed to give his army. I said that I meant merely that his army should lay down their arms, not to take them up again during the continuance of the war unless duly and properly exchanged. He said that he had so understood my letter.

… General Lee [suggested] that the terms I proposed to give his army ought to be written out.

The terms Grant wrote were generous. He would take no prisoners, but simply secure the paroles of officers and men not to take up arms "until properly exchanged"; for although the principal Confederate army had been vanquished, the war was not yet over. Other Confederate troops under other commanders remained in the field. Officers were permitted to retain their sidearms, and officers and men could keep their horses and their personal effects. Everyone would be "allowed to return to their homes, not to be disturbed by United States authority so long as they observe their paroles …"

> **Sites and Sights**
>
> The Appomattox Court House National Historical Park, a 1,325-acre facility centered on the town of Appomattox Court House, includes the fully restored McLean House, furnished as it is supposed to have looked on April 9, 1865, when Lee surrendered the Army of Northern Virginia to Grant. Contact: 1-804-352-8987.

… General Lee, after all was completed and before taking his leave, remarked that his army was in a very bad condition for want of food, and that they were without forage; that his men had been living for some days on parched corn exclusively, and that he would have to ask me for rations and forage. I told him "certainly," and asked for how many men he wanted rations. His answer was "about twenty-five thousand"; and I authorized him to send his own commissary and quartermaster to Appomattox Station, two or three miles away, where he could have, out of the trains we had stopped, all the provisions wanted ….

Voices

On April 10, 1865, Robert E. Lee issued his final order to the Army of Northern Virginia:

> General Order No. 9
> April 10, 1865
>
> After four years of arduous service marked by unsurpassed courage and fortitude, the Army of Northern Virginia has been compelled to yield to overwhelming numbers and resources. I need not tell the brave survivors of so many hard fought battles, who have remained steadfast to the last, that I have consented to this result from no distrust of them; but, feeling that valor and devotion could accomplish nothing that could compensate for the loss that must have attended the continuance of the contest, I have determined to avoid the useless sacrifice of those whose past services have endeared them to their countrymen.
>
> By the terms of the agreement, officers and men can return to their homes and remain there until exchanged. You will take with you the satisfaction that proceeds from the consciousness of duty faithfully performed; and I earnestly pray that a Merciful God will extend to you his blessing and protection.
>
> With an unceasing admiration of your constancy and devotion to your Country, and a grateful remembrance of your kind and generous consideration of myself, I bid you all an affectionate farewell.
>
> (Sgd.)
> R. E. Lee
> Genl.

Coda

Robert E. Lee surrendered an army, not a nation. But the event historian Bruce Catton called the "stillness at Appomattox" did, for all practical purposes, end the Civil War. Except for the desperate, deluded performance of a Southern-sympathizing matinee idol in Washington's Ford's Theatre on the evening of April 14 (see Chapter 24), the rest of the tragedy's last act was an anticlimax.

Montgomery, Alabama, fell to James H. Wilson's Union cavalry on April 12, and Federal troops entered Mobile (long blockaded, but

War News
The tradition of the vanquished commander surrendering his sword is so appealing that rumors soon circulated that Lee surrendered his to Grant and Grant graciously handed it back. In his *Personal Memoirs*, Grant observed that "the much talked of surrendering of Lee's sword and my handing it back, this and much more that has been said about it is the purest romance." It didn't happen.

never captured) the same day. On the 13th, Sherman occupied Raleigh, North Carolina, where, during the 17th and 18th, he sat with Joseph E. Johnston and hammered out a broad armistice that was, in effect, a peace treaty. It traded a blanket amnesty, civil as well as military, for total and absolute military surrender. Unlike Grant, who never asked Lee for his sword, Sherman accepted Johnston's weapon as a symbol of the surrender.

Sherman's veterans pass in grand review down Washington's Pennsylvania Avenue.

(Harper's Pictorial History of the Civil War, *1866)*

Sherman accepted Johnston's surrender at the house of James Bennett in Raleigh, North Carolina.

(Harper's Pictorial History of the Civil War, *1866)*

On April 21, the new president of the United States, Andrew Johnson, and his cabinet rejected and angrily repudiated the Sherman-Johnston document. It was, after all, the generals' province to make war, but the politicians' prerogative to make peace. On the 26th, Johnston accepted a narrower armistice, identical to what Grant had offered Lee, and, also on April 26, the Confederate cabinet held its last meeting, in Charlotte, North Carolina, after which it disbanded or, rather, dissolved. Its members resigned one by one and left to attend to home and family. With the rejection of the Sherman-Johnston armistice, Davis and his ministers were not protected by any amnesty and, in fact, had been branded by President Johnson criminals and fugitives.

Jefferson Davis was captured by Federal troops at dawn on May 10, 1865, near Irwinville, Georgia. He was imprisoned and remained under lock and key for two years. In May 1867, he was released on bail and lived in Canada, awaiting trial for treason. Davis was eager for a trial, which he intended to use as a forum in which to argue that states had a Constitutional right to secede. Perhaps to avoid just such an argument, the government refused to prosecute Davis, and charges were formally dropped on December 25, 1868.

Davis eventually became president of a Memphis-based insurance company; then, in 1877, retired to a small estate near Biloxi, Mississippi, which an admirer provided for him. He died, unrepentant, in 1889.

After the war, in September 1865, Robert E. Lee accepted the presidency of Washington College (today called Washington and Lee College) in Lexington, Virginia. Prematurely aged and plagued by heart disease, he died five years later, on October 12, 1870. His U.S. citizenship was not officially restored until 1975, by act of Congress.

Sites and Sights

The Bennett House, in which General Johnston surrendered to General Sherman, was destroyed by fire in 1921, but was reconstructed in 1958. Although the reconstructed house is furnished with authentic period furnishing, it contains none of the original pieces. Now administered by North Carolina's Division of Historic Sites of the State Department of Archives and History, the house, at 4409 Bennett Memorial Road, Durham, NC 27705, is open to the public free of charge. Contact: 1-919-383-4345

Sites and Sights

Called Beauvoir House, Jefferson Davis's final home is located at 2244 Beach Boulevard, Biloxi, Mississippi 39531, a site that now includes the house, the Jefferson Davis Presidential Library, a Confederate Museum, a historic cemetery, the Tomb of the Unknown Confederate Soldier, and a gift shop. It is open to the public for an admission fee. Contact: 1-228-388-9074 or 1-800-570-3818.

War News

Stand Watie (1806–1871), son of a full-blooded Cherokee father and half-blooded Cherokee mother, was a Confederate brigadier general from Indian Territory—present-day Oklahoma. His unit fought in more battles west of the Mississippi than any other Confederate force, and he was the very last Confederate general officer to surrender, doing so on June 23, 1865, at Doakville, in the Choctaw Nation of the Indian Territory. His Cherokee name, *Degataga,* means "stand firm."

In May, the very last of the fighting ended. Confederate Lt. Gen. Richard Taylor, son of Zachary Taylor, first overall general in the Mexican War and twelfth president of the United States, was in command of the Department of East Louisiana, Mississippi, and Alabama. On May 4, he surrendered to Union general E.R.S. Canby at Citronelle, Alabama.

On May 10, President Andrew Johnson declared that armed resistance was "virtually at an end," but three days later, at Palmito Ranch, near Brownsville, Texas, Confederate troops under Edmund Kirby Smith skirmished with Federals. This small engagement was the last fighting of the war. Ironically, it resulted in the repulse and retreat of the Union troops—a Confederate victory. Kirby Smith surrendered to Canby on May 26.

The Least You Need to Know

♦ After the fall of Petersburg and Richmond, Robert E. Lee hoped to join his forces with those of Joseph E. Johnston in North Carolina in order to prolong the war and give the Confederacy some leverage in peace negotiations.

♦ Lee surrendered the Army of Northern Virginia only when it was trapped and could neither advance nor retreat.

♦ The surrender of the Army of Northern Virginia, the Confederate's principal army, did not officially end the war, but did, in practical terms, end it.

♦ The last fighting unit to surrender was that of Edmund Kirby Smith in Texas, on May 26, 1865, and the last general officer to surrender was the Cherokee Confederate brigadier general Stand Watie, on June 23, 1865.

Part 6

Taps and Reveille

Secure in the knowledge that the Union was saved, but knowing, too, that he now faced the daunting task of "binding the nation's wounds," Abraham Lincoln sought solace in an evening of comedy at Ford's Theatre.

The president's assassination robbed the nation of perhaps the only man capable of guiding it through a process of healing. Lincoln's successor, Andrew Johnson, was beaten into submission by a Congress eager to bring righteous vengeance on the South. The result was a long, bitter period known as Reconstruction, in which the South suffered politically, economically, and emotionally, and in which the newly freed slaves found that their former masters were still powerful and capable of new, even more humiliating, and more terrifying cruelties.

The book concludes with a consideration of the unfinished business of the Civil War, a nation never wholly reunited, and with the role the Civil War continues to play in our collective national memory.

Chapter 24

Malice Toward One

In This Chapter

- ◆ Lincoln is assassinated
- ◆ Andrew Johnson becomes president
- ◆ Johnson battles Congress over Reconstruction
- ◆ Reconstruction legislation and abuses

On April 14, 1865, the day Gen. Robert Anderson ceremonially raised over Fort Sumter the very flag he had taken down four years earlier, President and Mrs. Lincoln invited General Grant and his wife to spend the evening with them in Washington. Mary Todd Lincoln suffered emotionally after the death from an illness of the Lincolns' son Willie in 1862, and was continually assailed by unfair public criticism of her as mistress of the White House. She was jealous of Grant's popularity, which she saw as somehow damaging to her husband. In consequence, Mrs. Lincoln was habitually rude to Julia Grant, and the couple politely declined the invitation to attend, with the Lincolns, a performance of the popular comedy *Our American Cousin* at Ford's Theatre.

Lincoln had much to be happy and grateful for on April 14, but he knew that, at the outset now of his second term, he continued to face the gravest of responsibilities. He had only to look south of the nation's border, to

Central and South America, to see examples of peoples for whom virtually uninterrupted civil war was a way of life, a chronic, bitter guerrilla struggle that never formally began and never formally ended. To ensure that such a bloody twilight would never descend on the reunified United States, Lincoln knew he had to make good on the promises of his Second Inaugural Address: to "bind up the nation's wounds" and to act with "malice toward none and charity for all." Happily, the American people had given him four more years to set this healing work afoot.

An Evening at Ford's Theatre

Those who knew Abraham Lincoln before the war attested to a bright, sly, gentle sense of humor that was, nevertheless, tinged with melancholy. In the depths of the war, that melancholy deepened. He was plagued by nightmares, and, in the Red Room of the Executive Mansion on Tuesday evening, April 11, 1865, he told Mrs. Lincoln, his close friend Ward Hill Lamon, Iowa Senator James Harlan, and a handful of others about a dream he had had.

There was, he said, "a deathlike stillness about me. Then I heard subdued sobs, as if a number of people were weeping. … the mourners were invisible. I went from room to room. No living person was in sight …. It was light in all the rooms; every object was familiar to me, but where were all the people who were grieving as if their hearts would break?"

The dreaming Lincoln, determined to find the source of the weeping, looked in each room until he entered the East Room.

"Before me was a catafalque, on which rested a corpse in funeral vestments. Around it were stationed soldiers who were acting as guards: and there was a throng of people, some gazing mournfully upon the corpse, whose face was covered, others weeping pitifully.

"'Who is dead in the White House?' I demanded of one of the soldiers.

"'The President,' was his answer. 'He was killed by an assassin.'"

Matinee Idol

John Wilkes Booth was born in 1838 near Bel Air, Maryland, the ninth of ten children of the celebrated American actor Junius Brutus Booth. Young Booth debuted to little acclaim in Baltimore in 1856, then played minor roles in Philadelphia through 1859, until he joined a Shakespearean company in Richmond. This was his breakthrough. Southern audiences loved him, and Southern belles in particular loved his energetic performance and dark good looks.

John Wilkes Booth, photographed when he was a successful actor in Richmond.

(National Archives and Records Administration)

Southerners appreciated, too, Booth's outspoken advocacy of the Confederate cause (he had served as a volunteer in the Richmond militia that hanged John Brown in 1859) and his equally outspoken hatred of Abraham Lincoln.

Late in 1864, he resolved to transform his words into deed and gathered about him a small group of conspirators. They were miscellaneous misfits, really, although one, John Surratt, was a courier who regularly worked for the Confederate "secret service." They met in the Washington boarding house of Surratt's mother, Mary, where Booth laid out a bold plan to kidnap Lincoln and hold him hostage. The ransom price? Liberation of all Confederate prisoners of war.

Like so many other undercover Confederate plots, the plan came to nothing. But Booth hatched a second scheme, this time to abduct the president at Ford's Theatre on January 18, 1865. He would station Surratt at the master gas valve beneath the stage of Ford's. At a signal, Surratt would turn the valve, plunging the gas-lit theater into darkness. Booth, his gun to Lincoln's head, would gag and bind the president, tie a rope to him, and lower him from his box onto the stage. Booth would climb down the same rope, bundle Lincoln into a waiting wagon, then spirit him off to Richmond via Maryland.

But Lincoln didn't attend the theater that evening, and the disappointed conspirators dispersed.

Still Waters Run Deep

The next month, a new conspirator joined Booth's band, which now included the courier Surratt, Michael O'Laughlin and Sam Arnold (boyhood friends of Booth), George A. Atzerodt (a Maryland carriage maker), and David Herold (a drugstore clerk, aged 23, but who seemed almost childlike in his insatiable desire to please). The newcomer was a powerfully built former Confederate soldier who called himself Lewis Paine, but whose real name was Louis Thornton Powell. By the middle of the next month, Booth had a new plot for them all.

President and Mrs. Lincoln were scheduled to attend a matinee performance of *Still Waters Run Deep* to be given at Campbell Hospital, just north of the city. John Surratt called at the tavern in Surrattsville that his father had once owned and that his widowed mother subsequently leased to a dipsomaniac innkeeper named John M. Lloyd. Against Lloyd's wishes, Surratt secreted in the tavern two army carbines, some rope, and a monkey wrench. The plan was to waylay the president's carriage as it passed out of the city, kidnap Lincoln, and ransom him for the Confederate POWs.

Booth, Surratt, Paine, Atzerodt, Arnold, and O'Laughlin waited in ambush. When the carriage approached, Booth and Surratt rode out to overtake it. But when they peered inside, it was clear that the president was not a passenger. Once again, the conspirators went home disappointed.

Booth was in a black mood. He had been supporting his band and was now running out of money. All about him, the people of Washington were celebrating the fall of Richmond and then, even worse, the surrender of Lee. The curtain was ringing down on the great drama of the Civil War, and John Wilkes Booth had yet to play a part.

But what part was there left to play? Kidnapping Lincoln was to have forced the release of Confederate prisoners. The war was about to end, there was no more army, and the prisoners would go home. What could John Wilkes Booth do to Abraham Lincoln now?

He could kill him.

Besides, it was easier to kill a man than to kidnap one.

Sites and Sights

Located at 511 and 516 Tenth Street, NW, Washington, D.C., Ford's Theatre National Historic Site encompasses both the theater and the Petersen House across the street, where Lincoln was taken after he was shot. Ford's Theatre is a working playhouse and is closed to tours during rehearsals and performances. Otherwise, the theater and Petersen House are open for touring from 9:00 to 5:00 every day but Christmas. Contact: 1-202-426-6924.

"Sic Semper Tyrannis!"

During the two or three days before Good Friday, April 14, John Wilkes Booth was mostly drunk. Of his original band, only Paine, Herold, and Atzerodt were left. Booth assigned Atzerodt to kill Vice President Andrew Johnson. Paine and Herold would murder Secretary of State William H. Seward—an easy mark, since the old man was convalescing from serious injuries sustained in a carriage accident. Booth would shoot the president.

Things went wrong from the beginning. Atzerodt backed out and never tried to kill Johnson. As to Paine, while Herold waited outside holding his horse, he entered Seward's house bearing a package of "medicine." Seward's son Frederick told Paine that his father was sleeping and could not take medicine at this time. When Paine insisted, Seward ordered him to leave, whereupon Paine pulled a pistol, placed it to young Seward's head, and pulled the trigger.

Click. A misfire.

Paine turned the gun in his hand and repeatedly brought the butt down on Frederick Seward's head, cracking his skull. He then withdrew a large knife from the package and entered the secretary's darkened bedroom, where he found Seward's young daughter, Fanny, and a male military nurse, George T. Robinson. Seeing the knife, Robinson leaped to his feet and rushed Paine—described as a giant of a man—who slashed him across the forehead and knocked him to the floor before striking Fanny Seward and knocking her unconscious.

Paine threw himself on Seward's bed, stabbing the old man again and again—tearing a gaping hole in his cheek—until Seward rolled off and under the bed. At this moment, Robinson revived sufficiently to attack Paine, who then stabbed Robinson. Into the room burst another of Seward's sons, Maj. Augustus Seward, awakened by the commotion. Paine slashed his forehead and hand, then bounded out of the room and down the stairs—in time to encounter a State Department messenger, who he also slashed before running out the front door screaming, "I am mad! I am mad!"

Incredibly, all of those Paine assaulted recovered, and, in 1867, as secretary of state in the cabinet of Andrew Johnson, Seward would go on to negotiate the controversial purchase of Alaska from the czar of Russia.

> ### War News
>
> Washington policeman John F. Parker was supposed to be on post outside the door leading to the hall that opened on the presidential box. He was absent when Booth entered. He later explained that the play bored him, and he had gone next door to the saloon to get a drink. Parker was neither prosecuted for dereliction of duty, nor even dismissed from the police force.

As for Booth, he calmly entered the president's box at Ford's Theatre at about 10:00 P.M. The lock on the door of the box had been broken a few days earlier, but nobody bothered to report it, let alone fix it. Nor had Booth, a familiar face at Ford's, met with any challenge from the men who should have been guarding the president.

Booth entered the box, quietly leveled his *derringer* between Lincoln's left ear and spine, and squeezed the trigger.

Few among the 1,675 members of the audience heard the report of the diminutive weapon. Even Mrs. Lincoln, seated next to her husband, and Maj. Henry Rathbone, seated in the presidential box with his fiancée, Clara Harris, were not much startled by the dull pop. Booth knew the script of *Our American Cousin* well, and he had timed his shot to coincide with the play's biggest laugh—just after actor Harry Hawk, playing Mr. Trenchard, drawls, "Wal, I guess I know enough to turn you inside out, you sockdologizing old mantrap."

After tangling with Rathbone, whom he stabbed in the arm, Booth leaped down from the box to the stage, catching his right spur in the Treasury Regiment flag that festooned the box. His left leg took the full impact of his fall, and the bone snapped just above the instep. Turning to the audience, Booth shouted "Sic semper tyrannis!"—*Thus ever to tyrants*, the state motto of Virginia. The actor-assassin limped into the wings, fell, recovered, and lurched offstage. Stunned by the spectacle, no one gave chase.

Death Watch

A 23-year-old surgeon, Dr. Charles Augustus Leale, was in the theater and came to Lincoln's aid. He was quickly joined by another physician, Dr. Charles Sabin Taft, and the two attempted to revive the president. At length, Leale, in tears, said to Taft: "I can't save him. His wound is mortal. It is impossible for him to recover."

Lincoln was borne out of the theater and across the street to a house owned by a German tailor named William Petersen. At over six-foot-four, Lincoln was too tall for the bed on which he was placed, so the doctors positioned him diagonally across it.

April 15, 1865, 7:22 A.M.

Among those who watched the president's life ebb during the night of the 14th and the early morning of the 15th was Secretary of War Edwin Stanton. At 7:22 A.M., the doctors pronounced Lincoln dead, and Stanton raised his hand with great solemnity, put his hat on his head, then, majestically, removed it. Turning to Lincoln's clergy-man, he said, "Doctor, lead us in prayer." After this, as the officials present began to file out, Stanton went about the room, darkening the windows.

"Now he belongs to the ages," said the secretary of war.

"Useless, Useless"

For 11 days, John Wilkes Booth eluded the army of troopers, policemen, and detec-tives sent in pursuit of him. At last, after midnight, on April 26, a detachment of Federal cavalry ran him to ground at a tobacco farm near Port Royal, Virginia. Booth and Herold were in a tobacco barn. Herold surrendered, but Booth resolved to shoot it out, whereupon the troopers set fire to the structure.

They all saw the assassin's silhouette against the flames, a man leaning on a crutch and carrying a carbine. With his revolver, Sgt. Boston Corbett fired a shot that passed through the actor's neck.

Booth was dragged out of the blazing barn and was set down on the porch of the Garrett house. The bullet having severed his spinal cord, the actor was paralyzed.

"I thought I did for the best," he managed to gasp out.

He asked that someone lift his lifeless hands so that he might look at them. This was done. He gazed at his hands.

"Useless, useless."

These were Booth's last words, uttered at sunup on the day Gen. Kirby Smith surrendered to Gen. E.R.S. Canby, the last day of the Civil War.

> **War News**
>
> For years, rumors persisted that the man shot and killed was not Booth, and that Booth got away. These tales have never been entirely put to rest, but accept-able evidence has yet to surface in support of them. The man slain—presumably Booth—is buried in Green Mount Cemetery in Baltimore. His grave is un-marked.

Accomplices All

With the exception of John Surratt, all of Booth's co-conspirators were rounded up. Paine, Herold, Atzerodt, and Mary Surratt (John's mother and the owner of the boarding house in which the conspirators met) were all sentenced to hang and were executed together on July 7, 1865. Mary Surratt had the dubious distinction of being the first woman ever executed by hanging in the United States.

Michael O'Laughlin and Sam Arnold were sentenced to life imprisonment, as was Samuel Mudd, a Maryland physician who had patched up Booth's broken leg when the actor stopped by his Charles County farmhouse in the wee hours of the morning after the assassination. (Mudd was pardoned by Andrew Johnson in 1868 after he saved many lives during a prison epidemic. Arnold was paroled the following year. O'Laughlin died in prison.) Edward Spangler, a Ford's Theatre carpenter convicted on dubious evidence of having assisted Booth, was sentenced to six years.

After the assassination, John Surratt fled to Canada, thence to England, and then to Italy, where he joined the Papal Zouaves, Swiss mercenary troops who guarded the Pope. A fellow Zouave turned him in, and he was arrested on November 8, 1866, but escaped and fled to Egypt. He was apprehended there and was returned to the United States on June 10, 1867. Put on trial, he was acquitted of complicity in the assassination.

The fate of Maj. Henry Rathbone, who was unable to stop Booth, was more cruel. He married Clara Harris, with whom he had sat in the presidential box, but in 1894 he murdered her because, he said, he was jealous of her love for their children. Confined to an asylum for the criminally insane, he died in 1911. His last words were: "The man with the knife! I can't stop him! I can't stop him!"

Those found guilty of conspiracy in the assassination of Abraham Lincoln were executed on July 7, 1865. Among them was Mary Surratt, mother of Booth associate John Surratt and owner of the Washington boarding house in which the conspirators met. She was the first woman hanged in the United States.

(National Archives and Records Administration)

Odor of Conspiracy

Beginning on November 22, 1963, the day John Fitzgerald Kennedy was assassinated in Dallas, an industry developed, dedicated to proving that the president had been a victim of this or that conspiracy, as shadowy as it was massive. A similar conspiracy industry had grown up after the Lincoln assassination, and although most historians simply dismiss the various conspiracy theories, a few attempt seriously to investigate them.

As with the JFK conspiracy theories, the most persistent Lincoln conspiracy theory climbs to the highest levels of government.

"Lieutenant, We Have Got a Sure Thing"

On the day Lincoln died, the day after that night at Ford's Theatre, Secretary of War Edwin M. Stanton sent a message to Lafayette C. Baker, colonel of the 1st District of Columbia Cavalry and chief of a 30-man force Baker himself decided to call the National Detective Police. "Come here immediately and see if you can find the murderer of the President," the note said.

Nine days passed before Baker deployed a band of 25 men into the field. By that time, a dragnet of some 1,400 soldiers and police investigators had been combing Maryland and Virginia without finding Booth.

"You are going after Booth," Baker told his cousin Luther, a junior officer in the Union army. "Lieutenant, we have got a sure thing."

And then Baker told the young man precisely where to find the assassin, holed up in the tobacco shed of the Garrett family farm near Port Royal, Virginia.

That Scoundrel Baker

How did Baker, out of so many searching for John Wilkes Booth, know where to find him?

Some believe he had access to good intelligence. Others think he was just plain lucky. And still others have concluded that Baker was, in truth, a key figure in an assassination conspiracy involving Edwin M. Stanton, Vice President Andrew Johnson, and others. Why did Baker know where to find Booth? Because, they claim, Baker had hired him.

Certainly, Baker had an unsavory enough reputation. Born in Stafford, New York, in 1826, he wandered, as an adult, through New York, Philadelphia, and, finally, California, where, during the Gold Rush, he was rumored to have been a claim jumper. However, he also organized an effective vigilante force for lawless San Francisco, and he became acquainted with influential politicians. Through a political connection, he obtained an audience with the Union army's general-in-chief, Winfield Scott, during the early days of the war and volunteered as a spy. He functioned in this capacity briefly before he was more or less officially authorized to set up the "secret service" bureau he himself christened the National Detective Police. For the rest of the war, Baker engaged in counterespionage, operating so high-handedly that Lucius E. Chittenden, Register of the Treasury, claimed that he "became a law unto himself. He instituted a veritable Reign of Terror. ... He did not require the formality of a written charge; it was quite sufficient for any person to suggest to Baker that a citizen might be doing something that was against the law. He was immediately arrested, hand-cuffed, and brought to Baker's office [where] he was subjected to a browbeating examination. ... Men were kept in his rooms for weeks, without warrant, affidavit, or other semblance of authority."

He was despised by practically everyone of any consequence during the war, and, after it, he went to work as Stanton's spy on President Andrew Johnson, gathering evidence to help impeach Johnson.

The Very Highest Levels

In 1961, Ray A. Neff, a professional chemist and amateur Civil War buff, published an extraordinary discovery in the popular historical journal *Civil War Times*. Perusing an 1864 bound volume of *Colburn's United Service Magazine*, a British military journal he had purchased for fifty cents in a secondhand bookstore in Philadelphia, Neff discovered two handwritten elementary cipher messages. He decoded them, and what they said was astonishing enough. Then this chemist examined the rest of the volume for more messages, but found only some brownish spots. These he examined under ultraviolet light. One of the spots now glowed purple, and Neff applied a solution of tannic acid to it. The faded signature "L. C. Baker" emerged, revealing the owner of the volume.

The messages detailed a conspiracy to assassinate Lincoln that involved Stanton, Andrew Johnson, and (Baker wrote) "at least eleven members of Congress, ... no less than twelve Army officers, three Naval officers and at least 24 civilians, of which one was a governor of a loyal state. ... There were probably more that I know nothing of."

Those who relish conspiracy theories point to the "Neff cipher" as the smoking gun, the most damning evidence of a Radical Republican plot to eliminate Abraham Lincoln, the man who had pledged to reconcile charitably with the South. A few historians suggest that Neff fabricated the evidence of the conspiracy, but most (among the few who address the matter at all) accept the Neff material; however, they believe that the cipher was Baker's scheme for discrediting both Stanton and Johnson, whom he hated.

Reconstruction Without Lincoln

Perhaps the Baker claims will never be definitively proved or disproved; what does seem certain to many historians is that John Wilkes Booth had killed quite probably the only man capable of beginning to heal the nation. At the time, Northerners felt the tragedy of loss keenly and personally, but, in the end, it would be the South that would suffer most as a result of the president's assassination.

The New President: A Tailor by Trade

Although Abraham Lincoln had been willing to fight the war without compromise and to absolute victory, he was a moderate in comparison with the radical faction of his Republican party. The Radical Republicans wanted the South punished and those who led the rebellion arrested and tried for treason. Lincoln favored amnesty and, in general, an effort to heal.

In choosing a running mate for Lincoln in 1864, the Republicans had purposely avoided pairing him with a Radical Republican. They did not want to scare off moderate voters. In a gesture of national unity and healing, a *Democrat* was chosen as the vice presidential candidate. It seemed safe enough—truly a *gesture* only—for vice presidents, in the 1860s as now, had little power or influence, and while some presidents had died in office, Lincoln, at 55, was relatively young. Before 1865, presidential assassination was almost unknown in the United States—although in 1835 a man did fire twice at Andrew Jackson at point-blank range; the improperly loaded pistols failed to discharge.

War News

In the early 1960s, a physician published a paper in which he diagnosed Abraham Lincoln as a victim of Marfan's syndrome, a disorder of the connective tissue. The diagnosis was based largely on Lincoln's appearance: tall, thin, loose-jointed, arms and legs unusually and disproportionately long, big hands, big feet, long and slender fingers. The diagnosis has been subject to debate, but if Lincoln did suffer from this syndrome, it is likely that he would have succumbed to heart disease (a weakened aorta, liable to bursting, or a failed mitral valve) and might not have lived out his second term, even if he had escaped assassination.

Born in North Carolina in 1808, Johnson spent his youth in Tennessee. Lacking formal education, he was a tailor by vocation and a politician by avocation, becoming mayor of his town before he was 21, a state legislator for eight years (1835–1843), a Congressman for 10 (1843–1853), then governor of Tennessee 1853–1857). He was elected to the U.S. Senate in 1856 and cleaved to the conventional Democratic Party line until 1860, when he came out against Southern secession. When Tennessee seceded in June 1861, Johnson was the only Southern senator who remained in the Senate and refused to join the Confederacy. In acknowledgment of his loyalty to the Union, Lincoln appointed Johnson military governor of federally occupied Tennessee in May 1862.

Andrew Johnson, 17th president of the United States, battled Congress, impotently and bitterly, over Reconstruction policy.

(Harper's Pictorial History of the Civil War, *1866)*

"I'm Ready"

Thrust so unexpectedly into office, Johnson was determined to carry out what he saw as Lincoln's mild program of reconciliation—no more and no less. As the war wound down, Lincoln drew up plans to create loyal governments in the Southern states quickly. Even before Lincoln's murder, new governments had been set up in Louisiana, Tennessee, and Arkansas, and Johnson was eager to see this work proceed.

But Johnson was no Lincoln. Whereas the martyred president radiated an endearingly homespun wisdom and soft-spoken intelligence, Johnson was loud, boorish, abrasive, sour, and ineloquent. If Lincoln was a man difficult not to like, Johnson invited contempt. Although there is some evidence that Johnson briefly visited the bedside of the mortally wounded Lincoln, he slept through most of the night of April 14–15, and, only after Lincoln actually died did anyone think of swearing him in. Senator Solomon Foot of Vermont escorted Salmon P. Chase, now (thanks to Lincoln) chief justice of the Supreme Court, to Johnson's residence.

Foot pounded on Johnson's bedroom door. At length, Johnson opened it, hair matted, eyes heavy with sleep, feet bare, and breath redolent of whiskey. Chase said, "The president has been assassinated. He died this morning, and I have come to administer the oath of office to you."

Johnson rose from the chair into which he had slumped, raised his right hand, and in a voice thick with sleep and booze, announced: "I'm ready."

Wade-Davis Plan

Congress had refused to recognize the new governments set up for Louisiana, Tennessee, and Arkansas, and, instead passed the Wade-Davis Bill, sponsored by Radical Republican senators Benjamin F. Wade and Henry W. Davis, which provided for the appointment of provisional military governors in the seceded states. Only after a majority of a state's white citizens swore allegiance to the Union could a constitutional convention be called. Each state constitution would be required to abolish slavery, repudiate secession, and bar all former Confederate officials from holding office or even voting. Moreover, to qualify for the vote, each and every citizen would be required to swear an oath that he had never voluntarily given aid to the Confederacy; this, of course, would exclude former Confederate soldiers and, in truth, anyone who had actively supported the government of Jefferson Davis.

President Lincoln exercised a *pocket veto* of the bill, and, after he assumed office, President Johnson modified the Wade-Davis plan by issuing an outright amnesty to anyone who took an oath to be loyal to the Union *from now on*; moreover, the creation of state governments would not be made contingent on a majority's taking these oaths. Johnson did require that states ratify the new Thirteenth Amendment, which abolished slavery, and further required states to forbid slavery in their own constitutions, repudiate debts incurred during the rebellion (so that the federal government would not be responsible for them), and explicitly declare secession null and void. By the end of 1865, all the former Confederate states had complied, except Texas, which at last fell into line the following year.

Words of War

If a bill is presented for presidential signature within 10 days of congressional adjournment, the president may indirectly veto it by holding it, unsigned, until after Congress adjourns. This is a **pocket veto.**

Congress Acts

Abraham Lincoln would have faced a difficult struggle in opposing Wade-Davis. For Johnson, the battle soon became hopeless. Congress not only feared and resented restoring power to the very individuals who had brought about the rebellion, it was loath to allow the Democratic Party to revive. There was also great outrage over the way in which the former Confederate states, while ostensibly freeing the slaves, kept them in subservience, effectively denying them the vote and other rights.

Freedmen's Bureau and Civil Rights

In 1866, Congress passed the Freedmen's Bureau Act and the Civil Rights Act. The *Freedmen's Bureau* was designed to assist blacks in their transition from slave life to freedom, and the Civil Rights Act defined African Americans as citizens of the United States, declaring specifically that states could not restrict their rights to testify in court or to own property. President Johnson vetoed both measures, but Congress easily overrode the vetoes.

Fourteenth Amendment

When Congress overrode the presidential veto on April 9, 1866, it effectively seized control of *Reconstruction* from the executive branch. All hope for compromise and moderation evaporated as the Radical Republicans self-righteously seized the helm.

Words of War

The **Freedmen's Bureau** was the popular name for the United States Bureau of Refugees, Freedmen, and Abandoned Lands, which was established by Congress to provide practical aid to newly freed African Americans in their transition from slavery to freedom. **Reconstruction** is the general term for the transition of the former Confederate states from Federal control to restoration of statehood. The period of Reconstruction spanned 1865 to 1877.

To be sure, much of Reconstruction was motivated by the noblest of purposes: to ensure that slavery would never again become an issue in American society and government (hence the Thirteenth Amendment), and to aid blacks in the formidable transition from slavery to freedom (with the Freedmen's Bureau and the Civil Rights Act).

Another act of Reconstruction, the Fourteenth Amendment, explicitly defined citizenship to extend to everyone "born or naturalized in the United States," forbade states from enacting laws "which shall abridge the privileges or immunities of citizens of the United States," and guaranteed the voting rights of all citizens. Section 2 of the amendment stipulated that if any state prohibited any part of the adult male population from voting, that state's representation in Congress would be proportionately decreased.

Yet like Reconstruction itself, the Fourteenth Amendment was a mixture of noble purpose and naked vengeance. Section 3 of the amendment barred former Confederates from holding federal—*or state*—offices unless individually pardoned by a two-thirds vote of Congress, and Section 4 repudiated debts incurred by the former Confederate government and also repudiated compensation for "the loss or emancipation of any slave." By law, slaves *had* been property, and now (as many in the South saw it), with neither compensation nor due process of law, this property had been seized.

Military Government

The Fourteenth Amendment brought about a new rebellion—of sorts. The only former Confederate state to ratify the amendment was Tennessee; the others refused. Congress responded with a harsh series of Reconstruction Acts. The first, passed on March 2, 1867, put all of the South, save Tennessee, under military government, with a major general serving as chief executive of each state. The only escape from under military rule was to draft and ratify a state constitution providing for enfranchisement of African Americans and disenfranchisement of ex-Confederates; moreover, Congress would withhold approval of a state's constitution pending that state's ratification of the Fourteenth Amendment.

A second Reconstruction Act authorized the military government of each state to use soldiers and officers to aid in the registration of voters and to supervise the election of delegates to the state constitutional conventions. Even after constitutions were duly drafted, a majority of white Southerners decided to defeat them simply by registering to vote but refraining from voting. Congress then enacted legislation changing the requirement for ratification of the constitutions from a majority of *registered* voters to a majority of those who cast ballots.

In June 1868, Arkansas was readmitted to the Union, and its military government stepped down. In July 1870, Georgia became the last state to be readmitted. But the feelings of bitterness, the acts of injustice, and the attitudes of inequality could not be erased by a handful votes and few strokes of the pen.

The Least You Need to Know

- John Wilkes Booth assassinated Abraham Lincoln to avenge the South; in truth, the murder of Lincoln deprived the South of a chief executive who would have treated the region with constructive compassion and healing forgiveness.

- Andrew Johnson tried to carry out what he saw as Lincoln's program of Reconstruction, but he was repeatedly blocked by an uncompromising Congress.

- Reconstruction was motivated in Congress by mixed objectives: on the one hand were such noble purposes as achieving full citizenship rights and equality for the freed slaves, and on the other hand was the desire simply to destroy the Democratic Party by keeping Southern Democrats out of office.

- In the end, the Reconstruction program Congress forced upon the South was, for the most part, vengeful, punitive, and humiliating.

Chapter 25

War Without End

In This Chapter

- ◆ Impeachment and acquittal of Andrew Johnson
- ◆ The effects of Reconstruction on the South
- ◆ The Ku Klux Klan is born
- ◆ The struggle for civil rights
- ◆ Continued fascination with the Civil War

It is difficult to study the Reconstruction period without sadness. Thousands had sacrificed lives, health, and property to achieve a victory that won—what? The slaves were freed, but they were hardly treated as equal citizens of the United States. The white people of the South were impoverished, punished, and humiliated. Harsh Reconstruction laws intended to "put them in their place" created a climate of sectional division and resentment that endured well into the twentieth century and, to some extent, lingers today. Worse, Reconstruction cast Southern blacks into the unwilling role of scapegoat, the minority against which the white majority vented a rage and intolerance born of powerlessness, frustration, and loss.

The long aftermath of the Civil War left a bad enough legacy—but that could have been worse. Much as the American War of Independence is almost unique as a truly successful revolution, one that actually succeeded in achieving liberty, so the Civil War proved highly exceptional. For few civil wars end. The formal battles might cease, but one faction or another typically continues to resist, waging chronic and debilitating guerrilla warfare.

It is true that Reconstruction brought much misery, that for the latter nineteenth century (and much of the twentieth) the South existed in the political and economic shadow of the North, and that African Americans endured greater economic, social, legal, physical, and emotional hardships in the South than they did in the North. Yet, despite its difficult aftermath, the Civil War, as a *war*, did end.

It has had continued resonance, however, in American life and politics, and, as the next chapter shows, in the collective American memory as well.

Words of War

Separation of powers is the Constitutional division of U.S. federal authority and responsibility among the three branches of government: executive (presidential), legislative (congressional), and judicial (the federal courts).

Words of War

The **Tenure of Office Act** (March 2, 1867) barred the president from dismissing, without consent of the Senate, any civil officer who had been appointed with Senate approval. When President Andrew Johnson dismissed Secretary of War Edwin Stanton, Congress impeached him on charges of violation of the act. The act was repealed in part in 1869 and entirely in 1887. In 1926, the U.S. Supreme Court declared it to have been unconstitutional.

Articles of Impeachment

The Civil War might have ended, but the war between Andrew Johnson and the U.S. Congress was just getting started. As the war between North and South had challenged ideas basic to the *union* of the United States, so the conflict between the president and the legislators threatened the concept of *separation of powers* central to American government. Congress sought to assume executive (presidential) powers, even as the president sought to thwart Congress by purposely interfering with the execution of the Reconstruction laws it had passed.

On March 2, 1867, over President Johnson's veto, Congress passed the Tenure of Office Act, which barred the president from dismissing, without senatorial approval, any civil office holder who had been appointed with senatorial consent. The act was part of the general effort of Congress to usurp as many executive prerogatives as possible, but, more specifically, it was aimed at preventing Johnson from removing Secretary of War Edwin Stanton, who was strongly allied to the cause of the Radical Republicans. When a defiant Johnson dismissed Stanton in 1868 despite the law, the House of Representatives voted to *impeach* the president.

Under our Constitution, only the House of Representatives may bring impeachment charges against the president, who is then tried before the Senate. The charges against Johnson were weak and transparently motivated by partisan purposes. The Tenure of Office Act was a dubious law, and Johnson had defied it, in large part, to bring it to a Constitutional challenge before the Supreme Court. That is the arena in which the next stage of the debate should have been held. Instead, there was a trial in the Senate spanning March through May 1868. The key votes, on May 16 and 26, 1868, fell one short of the two thirds required for conviction. Seven Republicans, men of conscience, voted with Johnson's Democratic supporters.

Words of War

Impeachment is often misunderstood to mean *removal* from office. In fact, to *impeach* is merely to *charge* a public official with misconduct in office before a legally constituted tribunal. President Johnson, like Bill Clinton 131 years later, was *impeached*, but, like Clinton, was acquitted of wrongdoing and was not removed from office.

Reconstruction—or Deconstruction

Johnson's acquittal was a triumph for the system of checks and balances, but the gulf between him and Congress was so deep that he was effectively neutralized as a political leader. With Johnson still in office, but essentially powerless, the Radical Republican Congress tore into the South more aggressively than ever, using Federal troops to enforce a Reconstruction program that was both genuinely reform-minded and frankly punitive.

Political Agenda

Although it is true that, in the course of Reconstruction, a series of laws were passed to achieve equal rights for African American citizens, to establish state-supported free public schools, to provide more equitable conditions for labor, and to apportion taxes more equitably, the frenzy of radical Reconstruction also levied many heavy taxes and led to widespread local corruption. In a punitive spirit, those who administered Reconstruction thrust illiterate former slaves into high-level positions in state and local government, for which they were entirely unprepared. The result was more chaos, corruption, and self-righteous bitterness.

The political agenda of Reconstruction was hardly subtle. It was to take vengeance on the former Confederacy while simultaneously destroying the Democratic Party.

Carpetbaggers

Into the Southland poured a horde of Northern politicians and unscrupulous financial adventurers eager to exploit the newly enfranchised freedmen in order to either obtain political office or make a quick buck. They were called *carpetbaggers*—unwelcome visitors who brought with them nothing other than what they could carry in a "carpetbag" satchel. And they did not leave without taking away far more than they had brought.

Words of War

Carpetbaggers were Northerners who descended on the South after the war, usually to exploit the freedmen in order to control local governments and profit from corruption. Unwelcome visitors, they brought with them only what they could carry in their "carpetbag" satchels. **Scalawags** were white Southerners who aided and abetted the carpetbaggers.

Scalawags

As much as Southerners despised the carpetbaggers, the Northern interlopers and opportunists, they hated even more those fellow Southerners who sold themselves out to the carpetbaggers, cooperating with them in their schemes. Scalawags, they were called, and they were regarded as traitors to the region and to the memory of the great war just ended.

Forrest and the KKK

The South felt besieged—economically and, what was worse, culturally. Northerners were telling Southern people how to live their lives, and the Yankees delighted in putting former slaves in positions of power and authority, as if to make the humiliation of the South complete.

A grassroots resistance movement grew up in response to the abuses of Reconstruction, and Nathan Bedford Forrest, late of the Confederate army, was one of its prime movers. In 1866, in Pulaski, Tennessee, a band of Confederate veterans formed a social club. Like many self-respecting fraternities, it looked to classical Greece for its name, transforming the Greek word for circle, *kyklos*, into *Ku Klux*, and adding, for good measure, the alliterative *Klan* to the end of it.

Within a remarkably short time, the Ku Klux Klan (together with a similar organization, the Knights of the White Camelia—this is how the "knights" spelled the name of the flower—formed in Louisiana in 1867) became the principal vehicle for covert resistance to Radical Reconstruction. In the summer of 1867, the Klan met in Nashville, where it was styled as the "Invisible Empire of the South." Its first leader, or "Grand Wizard," was Forrest, under whom the Klan became a kind of shadow government, a combination vigilante force (for violent lawlessness was rampant in the postwar South) and terrorist army.

The objects of KKK terrorism were the newly freed, newly enfranchised Southern blacks. At first, terror was achieved primarily by means of the robes, sheets, and other secret society mumbo jumbo—all intended to play on the superstitions of uneducated blacks while also providing a disguise against detection by Federal troops and other officials. Soon, the psychological terror turned physical; Klansmen engaged in "night rides," whipping, beating, even murdering freedmen and any whites who supported them.

Ratification of the Fifteenth Amendment, which explicitly prohibited states from denying the vote to persons on the basis of "race, color, or previous condition of servitude," came in March 1870 and served, in some parts of the South, to increase the influence and power of the KKK. Largely because of the Klan, white rule was restored in North Carolina, Tennessee, and Georgia. However, by 1869, Forrest was convinced that KKK violence had gotten out of hand, and he disbanded the organization. In defiance of this order, local branches ("klaverns") continued to flourish, prompting Congress to pass the Force Act in 1870 and the Ku Klux Act in 1871, which authorized the president to suspend the writ of habeas corpus, suppress disturbances by force, and impose other penalties on terrorist organizations.

The Elevation of "His Fraudulency"

Andrew Johnson's term ended in 1869, and Ulysses S. Grant, elected the year before, assumed office. The corruption that had taken root in the South bloomed fiercely nationwide in the Grant administration. Although the former Union general-in-chief was personally honorable, he was inattentive to the fraud, chicanery, and outright larceny that flourished during his two terms in office—some of the most spectacular revolving around the financing and construction of the great Central Pacific-Union Pacific transcontinental railroad.

War News

A new Ku Klux Klan reappeared in the twentieth century, organized in 1915 by Col. William J. Simmons. Although blacks were still a prime target of the Klan, so were "Bolsheviks," immigrants, Catholics, Jews, and organized labor. By the 1920s, the Klan boasted over four million members. Klan membership declined during the Depression, and the KKK even officially disbanded in 1944. It was revived in the South during the early 1960s as the civil rights movement developed. The KKK was involved in numerous bombings, whippings, and shootings in Southern states. Today, the Klan is relatively small and fragmented, occasionally associated with other right-wing extremist and neo-Nazi groups.

This illustration, a romantic glorification of the Ku Klux Klan, is from Thomas Dixon, Jr.'s 1905 racist novel The Clansman, *the book on which D.W. Griffith based his epic Civil War film,* The Birth of a Nation *(1915).*

(Author's collection)

As Grant paid little heed to the lawlessness of his political subordinates and associates, so was he lax in exercising the authority Congress had provided for dealing with the KKK. Although he did send Federal troops into the areas of most intense Klan activity, suspended *habeas corpus* in nine South Carolina counties, and arrested many Southerners, local Klan activity remained widespread and, during the 1870s, achieved most of what the "Invisible Empire" had set out to do: It terrorized blacks into submission. This accomplished, the KKK disappeared during the 1880s.

Words of War

Redeemers were Southern political activists who promoted passage of **Jim Crow laws,** state and local ordinances that enforced racial segregation and other forms of discrimination aimed at subjugating African Americans. They were named after a racially demeaning song and dance familiar from blackface minstrel shows.

Indeed, during the 1870s, the white supremacy movement was becoming open and public in the South. There was little need for robes and hoods. So-called *redeemers*—open political activists—managed to enact state laws that institutionalized the social, legal, and economic subjugation of blacks. Such legislation came to be called *Jim Crow* laws, taking their name from a racially demeaning song and dance performed in the blackface minstrel shows popular in the North as well as the South.

By 1876, the political clout of the redeemers reached the national level. In that year, Democrat Samuel J. Tilden captured the vote of the *solid South* and outpolled

Republican presidential candidate Rutherford B. Hayes by 250,000 votes. But the Republicans used Reconstruction laws to reverse the electoral tally in three Southern states, on the grounds that blacks had been intimidated to keep them from voting, and thereby challenged the outcome of the election.

The election was thrown into the House of Representatives, which failed to resolve it as Inauguration Day, March 4, loomed. There was talk of authorizing the current secretary of state to serve as interim chief executive, and many in the South were actually talking about secession and were already setting up rival governments.

Just two days before the inauguration deadline, Congress authorized a bipartisan Electoral Commission while legislators negotiated a behind-the-scenes deal to decide the issue. Republican politicians struck a deal with Southern Democrats: admit Hayes into office, and no Republican administration would ever again disturb the Southern world of segregation and Jim Crow.

The deal was made, Reconstruction came to an abrupt end, and even Hayes's friends and supporters took to calling the new president, with cruel humor, "Your Fraudulency."

Words of War

The **Solid South** referred to the unified Democratic voting bloc that dominated the Southern states from the 1870s through the late 1960s, making the South virtually a region of one-party politics.

Separate and Unequal

The election of 1876 made it apparent that Radical Reconstruction had backfired. The price of Hayes's presidency was three quarters of a century of legally sanctioned and institutionalized racism and racial segregation in the South, bolstered by custom and enforced by intimidation and terror.

The Cotton States

After the destruction of war, the economy of the South recovered very, very slowly. Crop-lands were torn up or burned, livestock destroyed, miles of railroad twisted into pretzel-like *Sherman neckties*, and untold billions in slave "property" investments wiped out.

Most of the South reverted to an economy based on its traditional staple crops: tobacco,

Words of War

Sherman's troops destroyed hundreds of miles of Southern railroad by ripping up rails, heating them over open fires, and twisting them into pretzel-like shapes that made them impossible to repair. Such a piece of ruined rail was called a **Sherman necktie.**

rice, and, above all, cotton. For labor, the region replaced slavery with *sharecropping*, in which relatively few landowners parceled out their property to black as well as poor white tenant farmers. The South settled into a strictly enforced policy of racial segregation, supported by a one-party (Democratic) political system, dominated by locally and regionally powerful political bosses. Blacks, no longer slaves, were now a kind of permanent underclass, the American equivalent of a feudal peasantry.

The South's new feudalism was a heavy drag on its economic recovery, and, not surprisingly, it was among the regions hit hardest by the Great Depression of the 1930s, which essentially bankrupted the cotton economy.

Lynch Law

President Franklin D. Roosevelt's Depression-era economic-recovery programs brought some relief and recovery to the South, but failure to diversify economically and, even more important, failure to reform socially kept many of its citizens in poverty. Because of its institutionalized bigotry, the South was shunned by the North, and many Americans felt that the United States was really two nations almost as separate as the Union and the Confederacy had been.

Under a barrage of criticism, Southerners frequently pointed to the hypocrisy of the North, in whose cities African Americans were segregated and discriminated against not by law, but by custom and common consent. This was true. But the South *was* nevertheless quite different. There, racial inequality was a matter of *law*, and when state-constituted law proved insufficient to enforce bigotry and subjugation, some Southerners turned to *lynch law* (the work of vigilantes who summarily abducted and executed those they considered wrongdoers).

If discriminatory Jim Crow laws were the everyday means of enforcing the social status quo in the South, lynching was the ultimate weapon of terrorism. Blacks who spoke out against local whites or against discrimination and injustice or who attempted to organize others for social change were often marked for death by the KKK and other white mobs. Between 1882 (the first year for which we have reliable figures) and 1968 (when lynchings became rare), 4,743 persons were murdered by lynching, of whom 3,446 were African Americans. And these figures represent only *recorded* lynchings; certainly, many more must have occurred.

Count Off!

The numbers of blacks and whites who were lynched during 1882–1968 are represented here:

State	Blacks	Whites
Mississippi	539	42
Georgia	492	39
Texas	352	141
Louisiana	335	56
Alabama	299	48

The great African American jazz singer Billie Holiday (1915–1959) sang about lynching in a haunting song called "Strange Fruit," which evoked images of black men dangling from tree-tied nooses in the South. Well into the twentieth century, the Civil War had ended, but racially motivated killing had not.

From the Back of the Bus

The manufacturing and agricultural demands of World War II brought a measure of prosperity to the South as it did to the rest of the nation. The war also brought the beginnings of social change. Although World War II–era armed forces were racially segregated, blacks and whites did serve and work together, and—in many cases for the first time—white and black Southerners got to know one another more or less as equals. After the war, on July 26, 1948, President Harry S Truman signed Executive Order 9981, which mandated "equality of treatment and opportunity" in the armed forces regardless of race. The integration of the armed forces was a modest degree of social change that gradually spread to civilian society.

On May 17, 1954, the U.S. Supreme Court ruled in the case of *Brown v. The Board of Education of Topeka* that public-school segregation was unconstitutional. The following year, in Montgomery, Alabama, an African American seamstress named Rosa Parks

(1913–) boarded a city bus, and, in defiance of city ordinance, refused to yield her seat to a white passenger. Her arrest triggered a black boycott of Montgomery city buses, which in turn focused national attention on civil rights in the South.

After Rosa Parks's ride and arrest, Martin Luther King, Jr., and others shaped an intensive civil rights movement that dominated the late 1950s and early 1960s and that helped to bring down many racial barriers in the South. In 1959, President Dwight D. Eisenhower federalized the National Guard to enforce integration in the schools of Little Rock, Arkansas, and, in 1964, a new, sweeping Civil Rights Act was passed, followed by the Voting Rights Act in 1965.

Change, of course, was resisted, and often violently. But change came, and it is no coincidence that, with social change, the economic position of the entire South, white and black, greatly improved. By the 1970s, many American industries and people eagerly flocked to an area no longer called the Cotton Belt, but, more invitingly now, the Sun Belt.

No one who drives through America's cities, North or South, can deny that the United States is still a divided nation. Segregation along racial, ethnic, and economic lines, though no longer sanctioned by law, is still very real. Yet real progress has also been made, and perhaps the most real progress has come in attitude. Social inequality and injustice might persist, but few people, North or South, openly defend such conditions. Most of us think that they're wrong and want to see them changed.

The Least You Need to Know

♦ The impeachment of Andrew Johnson threatened the principles of American government almost as profoundly as secession did.

♦ The Radical Republican program of Reconstruction brought some benefits to Southern blacks, but, ultimately, created a climate of corruption and bitterness that doomed the majority of Southern African Americans to decades of inequality, injustice, and even terror.

♦ The South's recovery from the devastation of war was retarded by its persecution of African Americans.

♦ The civil rights movement that began in the 1950s, bitterly resisted in the South, ultimately helped to return much of the region to prosperity.

Chapter 26

Memory

In This Chapter

- ◆ Civil War legacy
- ◆ Historical approaches
- ◆ Civil War genealogy, reenactments, and other passions
- ◆ The war in popular literature and film

"We are not enemies, but friends. We must not be enemies." The words near the end of Abraham Lincoln's *First Inaugural Address* echo with a heartbreaking poignancy. For, of course, war did come, and it came with a violence and bitterness far greater than anyone—save, perhaps, William Tecumseh Sherman—ever imagined possible.

And yet the rest of the close of the inaugural address proved, in the long run, prophetic: "Though passion may have strained it must not break our bonds of affection. The mystic chords of memory, stretching from every battlefield and patriot grave to every living heart and hearthstone all over this broad land, will yet swell the chorus of the Union, when again touched, as surely they will be, by the better angels of our nature." In the preceding chapter, we saw the destructive legacy of the war, first in a corrupt program of Reconstruction and then in a long regime of racial oppression. But the bloody and bitter conflict also created a far more positive legacy. Not only did it forge the ultimate unity of the United States as one nation, indivisible, it has also figured as a subject of continual fascination to millions of Americans. No other war—although World War II comes closest—draws so much active popular inquiry and interest. From no other historical era do the "mystic chords of memory" sound more clearly, more hauntingly, more arrestingly.

From Killing Fields to Subdivisions

If we still taste something of the bitterness that once tore a nation in two, the physical scars of the old wounds have long since healed. Many major battlefields have become national parks, and Manassas, for example, site of the first and second battles of Bull Run, is now a pleasant Washington suburb, whereas the area of Atlanta that saw the most intense combat of the Atlanta campaign, the vicinity of Peachtree Creek, is now an elegant urban neighborhood called Peachtree Battle. Other hallowed grounds have been lost to suburban sprawl, inspiring a preservation movement.

Yet no matter how the landscape might change, the Civil War is unlikely ever to fade from our collective memory. Since 1865, more than 65,000 books have been published on the subject. To this add numerous movies, television shows, and, nowadays, more than a dozen popular interactive Civil War battle and strategy computer games. Thousands of enthusiasts regularly meet at "Civil War Roundtables" to discuss arcane aspects of the conflict, and an estimated 45,000 more periodically don impeccable reproduction period uniforms and tote reproduction period weapons into reenactments of key Civil War engagements. Americans, it seems, never tire of reading, talking, thinking about, and even reliving the Civil War.

Birth of a Nation and *Gone with the Wind*

Generations of dry-as-dust school texts have done nothing to kill our national fascination with the Civil War, which has been stoked by many other more vivid renditions of the war and its aftermath.

The film that marked the transition from the infancy of motion pictures to its early maturity as a vivid storytelling art form, *The Birth of a Nation*, debuted on February 8, 1915 in Los Angeles. The work of D.W. Griffith, son of a former Confederate colonel, it tells the epic story of two families during the Civil War and Reconstruction. Controversial (and even censored in some areas because of its sympathetic portrayal of the Ku Klux Klan), the film cost $110,000 to produce—a staggering budget in 1915—but brought untold millions in profits. Film historians believe it still holds the record as the most profitable film of all time.

Confederate Civil War reenactors at the 1997 Civil War Encampment, Atlanta History Center: One Johnny Reb prepares lunch (left), while another explains the intricacies of his musket to visitors.

(Author's collection)

There is no need to guess about the financial success of the most famous of all Civil War movies. *Gone with the Wind*, based on Atlanta author Margaret Mitchell's best-selling novel, used three directors, 15 screenwriters, and extravagantly re-created the burning of Atlanta, but returned $24 million in revenues during its first release in a day when most tickets were under a dollar each. Some 25 million people saw the movie. It has been rereleased several times since 1939, always to great profit.

> ### War News
>
> President Woodrow Wilson, who saw *The Birth of a Nation* at a private White House screening, remarked that it was "like writing history with lightning. And my only regret is that it is all terribly true."

Defending the Flag

At times, the Civil War resurfaces as a subject of more than mere fascination. In 1962, the all-white South Carolina state legislature voted to fly the Confederate battle flag from the top of the statehouse. Over the years, other Southern states removed similar flags from their statehouses, but South Carolina held on and held out. Partisans of the flag argued that it honored the valor of the veterans of the Civil War and was, therefore, a treasured emblem of South Carolina heritage. Others, including many African Americans, saw the battle flag as an inflammatory emblem of slavery, and the National Association for the Advancement of Colored People (NAACP) organized a national economic boycott against South Carolina's $14 billion-a-year tourism industry. Between 1999 and 2000, more than 100 conventions and business organizations joined the boycott. Finally, on April 12, 2000, the South Carolina state senate voted, 36 to 7, to remove the flag and to substitute a "more traditional version" of the battle flag (square, not rectangular) to be flown in front of the Capitol, next to a monument honoring fallen Confederate soldiers. The House passed the bill on May 18, 66 to 43, and on July 1, the flag was removed from the South Carolina statehouse.

Georgia experienced similar controversy with its state flag. In 1956, Georgia House floor leader Denmark Groover sponsored legislation to add the Southern Cross— the battle flag emblem—to the state flag. In later years, Groover freely admitted that he and many other Georgia legislators had been frank segregationists who added the Confederate symbol to the flag in defiant protest against federal legislation and orders flowing chiefly from the historic 1954 Supreme Court decision in *Brown* v. *The Board of Education of Topeka, Kansas*, ordering the racial integration of public schools and opening the door to general desegregation. On January 30, 2001, the Georgia state legislature adopted a new flag, prominently featuring the state seal and running small images of "Georgia's historical flags," including the 1956 design, below it.

> **War News**
>
> In 2001, 45 years after he sponsored the Southern Cross flag, Groover, long retired, voiced his approval of the removal of the symbol. He called it divisive.

As of early 2003, Mississippi was the only Southern state whose flag prominently retains the Southern Cross; in a referendum on April 17, 2001, Mississippians overwhelmingly voted to retain the flag, which had been adopted in 1894. But the controversy in Georgia had not died. Many attributed the defeat of Democratic governor Roy Barnes in his 2002 reelection bid to his support of the new flag. His opponent, Sonny Perdue—who became the state's first Republican governor since the end of Reconstruction—had run on a pledge to conduct a popular referendum on the flag.

The Historians

Although many Civil War books are fiction and others are memoirs by politicians and generals, most are the work of historians. The most distinguished popular general works on the war are those by Bruce Catton (*Mr. Lincoln's Army, Glory Road,*

A Stillness at Appomattox, *The Coming Fury*, *Terrible Swift Sword*, and *Never Call Retreat*) and Shelby Foote (*The Civil War: A Narrative*, published in three volumes). Catton's *A Stillness at Appomattox* was awarded both a Pulitzer Prize and a National Book Award, and Foote's trilogy was the basis of a detailed and moving film documentary series by Ken Burns, which first aired on public television in 1990 and brought the Civil War home to yet another generation.

War News

The great American humorist Mark Twain owned a controlling interest in a publishing company and solicited from Ulysses Simpson Grant a book of memoirs. Bankrupt, in political disrepute, and dying of throat cancer, Grant accepted the offer and began writing in the summer of 1884. He finished proofreading galleys on July 14, 1885, then died on the 23rd. *Personal Memoirs of U.S. Grant* is the greatest firsthand account of the Civil War and, as Twain himself opined, "the best of any general's [memoirs] since Caesar." A literary masterpiece, the book was also a financial triumph, netting Grant's widow more than a half-million dollars in royalties.

The Presence of the Past

Most historians say that we're fascinated by the Civil War because, even more than the American Revolution, it shaped our nation and national character. That is certainly a good reason to be interested in the war. Of course, the war also presents a gripping, exciting, moving, tragic, epic story, displaying, all at once, the meanness, brutality, compassion, and greatness of which human beings are capable. It is also, as this chapter and the previous one suggest, an unfinished story. The divisions and injustices that spawned the war have yet to be eradicated, and debate concerning virtually every aspect of the war continues to be lively.

War News

You'll find recommendations for historical reading in Appendix E, "A Civil War Library," at the back of this book.

Civil War Archaeology

Many of us think archaeology is something that is done only in places like Egypt and is concerned with the ancient past. In fact, archaeologists work wherever they believe the physical evidence of the past may be found—and that is just about everywhere. The process of fighting the Civil War produced untold quantities of debris, the physical evidence of historical events.

Among the many archaeological projects devoted to Civil War study was the work of the Southeast Archaeological Center of the National Park Service at the site of Georgia's notorious Andersonville POW camp during 1987–1990. The work enabled a fuller understanding of the construction of the camp and its buildings, which contributed to more accurate reconstruction and interpretation of the site. Artifacts recovered ranged from buttons, buckles, and tools to animal bones, which revealed much about what prisoners and slaves (who worked as laborers in the camp) ate. Archaeologists were also able to determine the exact location of the infamous "Dead Line"—prisoners attempting to cross this barrier were shot without warning—and they uncovered an escape tunnel.

A number of battlefields, ranging from major sites such as Gettysburg to more minor ones, such as Monroe's Cross in Hoke County, North Carolina (scene of one of the war's few all-cavalry clashes), have been investigated archaeologically in an effort to augment, with physical evidence, eyewitness accounts of battles and accounts gathered from official records.

The Enthusiasts

In contrast to many other specialized fields, Civil War study is not the exclusive province of historians and archaeologists. A lot of ordinary people, without advanced training but with plenty of passion and curiosity, take an extraordinary interest in the war.

Do-It-Yourself Scholarship: The Sources

In addition to the many thousands of books devoted to the Civil War, anyone interested in learning more can find a great many scholarly resources readily available—no special credentials required.

Those interested in a particular battle or other event should begin by finding out if the battlefield or other site can be visited. Many of the important sites have been, in varying degrees, preserved and interpreted, and they usually welcome visitors.

The Library of Congress, in Washington, D.C. (www.loc.gov), maintains an unparalleled collection of Civil War research materials, including documents, images, maps, and sheet music. Also based in the nation's capital are the National Archives and Records Administration (www.nara.gov), which holds detailed records relating to the war and the soldiers and sailors who fought it, both Union and Confederate.

Important sources of records, artifacts, and other materials are located in various states. Some of the most important include the following:

- Alderman Memorial Library at the University of Virginia, Charlottesville (www. lib.virginia.edu)

- Atlanta History Center, in Atlanta, Georgia (www.athist.org)

- Bowling Green State University Center for Archival Collections, Bowling Green, Ohio (www.bgsu.edu/colleges/library/cac/cac.html)

- Center for American History, at the University of Texas, Austin (www.cah. utexas.edu)

- Charleston Museum, Charleston, South Carolina (www.charlestonmuseum.com)

- Chicago Historical Society (www.chicagohs.org)

- Civil War Center at Louisiana State University, Baton Rouge (www.cwc.lsu. edu/cwc)

- Civil War Library and Museum, Philadelphia (www.netreach.net/~cwlm)

- Colonel Eli Lilly Civil War Museum, Indianapolis, Indiana (www.state.in. us/iwm/civilwar)

- Confederate Museum (Memorial Hall), in New Orleans (www. confederatemuseum.com)

- Filson Club Historical Society, in Louisville, Kentucky (www.filsonhistorical.org)

- Maine State Archives, in Augusta (www.state.me.us/sos/arc/archives/military/ civilwar/civilwar.htm)

- Mariner's Museum, Newport News, Virginia (www.mariner.org)

- Museum of the Confederacy, Richmond, Virginia (www.moc.org)

- National Civil War Museum, Harrisburg, Pennsylvania (www. nationalcivilwarmuseum.org)

- National Museum of Civil War Medicine, in Frederick, Maryland (www. civilwarmed.org)

- New York Public Library, New York City (www.nypl.org)

- U.S. Army Military History Institute, at the Army War College, Carlisle, Pennsylvania (carlisle-www.army.mil/usamhi)

- Virginia Historical Society, Richmond (www.vahistory.org)

- VMI Archives at the Virginia Military Institute, Lexington (www.vmi. edu/~archtml)

◆ West Point Museum at the United States Military Academy, West Point, New York (www.usma.edu/Museum)

◆ William L. Clements Library at the University of Michigan, Ann Arbor (www.clements.umich.edu)

◆ Wilson Library at the University of North Carolina, Chapel Hill (www.lib.unc.edu/wilson)

A Confederate (or Yankee) in the Attic

Perhaps you have a connection with the Civil War that goes well beyond intellectual interest and imaginative affinity. If you know or believe that you are a relative of someone who fought in the Civil War, you can investigate—or discover—your ancestor or ancestors through genealogical research.

A good way to begin is to consult "A Brief Introduction to Genealogy and the American Civil War," a website at www.illinoiscivilwar.org/cwgeneal.html, and Bertram H. Groene's helpful book, *Tracing Your Civil War Ancestor* (Winston-Salem, N.C.: John F. Blair, 1987).

Those Civil War descendants who are interested in meeting with others might want to contact and perhaps join an organization of descendants. The largest of these are the following:

◆ Dames of the Loyal Legion of the United States (http://suvcw.org/millus/dollus/home.htm)

◆ Daughters of Union Veterans of the Civil War 1861–1865 (www.duvcw.org)

◆ Military Order of the Loyal Legion of the United States (suvcw.org/mollus)

◆ Military Order of the Stars and Bars (scv.org/mosb)

◆ Sons and Daughters of United States Colored Troops (members.aol.com/sdusct)

◆ Sons of Confederate Veterans (scv.org/scvinfo.htm)

◆ Sons of Union Veterans of the Civil War (suvcw.org)

◆ United Daughters of the Confederacy (www.hqudc.org)

Reenactors and Reenactments

"Learn by doing" is a time-honored maxim among educators, and some 45,000 enthusiasts have taken this to heart to enhance their knowledge and understanding of the Civil War. These individuals participate in various reenactment projects, ranging from Civil War blacksmithing, Civil War cooking, Civil War sewing, to Civil War "encampments" (living-history recreations of life in soldiers' camps), to full-scale, historically faithful reenactments of battles.

For those committed to reenactments in a big way, a considerable investment of time, energy, and money is required. Reproduction uniforms, weapons, and accouterments can be quite costly.

War News

You don't have to be a reenactor to get together with others interested in the Civil War. Since 1940, when a group began to assemble regularly at Chicago's Abraham Lincoln Book Shop to discuss the Civil War, "Civil War Round Tables" have been popular vehicles for sharing information and interpretations and for organizing various activities, such as battlefield tours and scholarly lectures. As of 2003, there were about 400 Civil War Round Tables ongoing nationwide (and in some foreign countries as well). Most of these groups are affiliated with Civil War Round Table Associates, a national organization that can be contacted at CWRTA; P.O. Box 7388; Little Rock, Arkansas 72217.

Perhaps the best way to find out more about—or get started in—Civil War reenactments is by consulting the "Civil War Reenactment Organizations and Related Links" page of the website maintained by the Sons of Union Veterans of the Civil War: suvcw.org/reenact.htm. Also check out the following websites:

- Civil War Reenactors (www.cwreenactors.com)
- Civil War Shows (www.civilwarshows.com)
- Living the Memory (www.cw-reenactors.com)

Yesterday Everyday

As the Civil War remains a fertile field for historians and archaeologists, as well as those with strong political convictions (as the ongoing Confederate state flag controversies attest) and passionate enthusiasts of all kinds, so it has served and continues to serve as a source of material for modern historical fiction and film.

Civil War Lit

Some key non-fiction books on the Civil War will be found in Appendix E, but the war also gave rise to a large number of novels. *Uncle Tom's Cabin* (1852) was discussed in Chapter 3, and many other novels came out during and shortly after the war. While most of these are of interest mainly to literary historians, there are exceptions of enduring general appeal. John W. De Forest's *Miss Ravenel's Conversion* (1867), a story of a New Orleans physician who moves to Boston because he abhors slavery, is fascinating literature with some thrilling battle scenes. Ambrose Bierce's wry, bitter, and extraordinary short stories collected in his *Tales of Soldiers and Civilians* (1891) are not to be missed. Most important of all nineteenth-century Civil War novels is *The Red Badge of Courage*, published in 1895 by Stephen Crane. This literary classic presents a soldier's-eye view of battle so stunningly real that many assumed its author was a veteran. Crane, however, was born in 1871.

More recent "must-read" Civil War fiction includes the following:

- *Andersonville* (1955) by MacKinlay Kantor, a novel of life and death in the notorious POW camp

- *Cold Mountain* (1997) by Charles Frazier, about the struggle of a wounded soldier to return home

- *Gods and Generals* (1996), by Jeff Shaara, the "prequel" to the great novel of Gettysburg

- *The Killer Angels* (1974), by Shaara's father, Michael

- *Gone with the Wind* (1936), by Margaret Mitchell, the most famous of all Civil War novels and not to be missed if all you know is the 1939 film

- *Jubilee* (1966), by Margaret Walker, the story of a slave family during the war period

- *The Oldest Living Confederate Widow Tells All* (1989), by Allan Gurganus, a yarn spun by a 100-year-old woman

- *The Unvanquished* (1938), by William Faulkner, a tale of Mississippians who refuse to surrender after the fall of the Confederacy

Hollywood Battlefield

The Civil War and the years on either side of it were the subject of what most film historians regard as the greatest movie of the silent era, D.W. Griffith's *Birth of a*

Nation (1915), discussed earlier in this chapter. Another Civil War classic of film's silent era is, unlikely enough, a classic comedy: Buster Keaton's *The General* (1927), based on the exploits of Union raiders who stole a Confederate locomotive.

Sites and Sights

In April 1862, 22 Union raiders, including leader James J. Andrews, a civilian, hijacked *The General*, a locomotive owned by the Western and Atlantic Railroad, in an effort to disrupt Confederate supply lines. This precipitated the "Great Locomotive Chase" on April 12, which began a spree of sabotage against Confederate railroad track and bridges. *The General* and other artifacts can be seen at the Southern Museum of Civil War and Locomotive History in Kennesaw, Georgia. Contact the Kennesaw Civil War Museum, 2829 Cherokee St., Kennesaw, GA 30144; 1-770-975-0877.

Other notable Civil War movies include the following:

◆ *Friendly Persuasion* (1956), adopted from the novel by Jessamyn West, the story of a Quaker family struggling to remain at peace while the nation is at war

◆ *Gettysburg* (1993), a meticulous, if sometimes overly literal, adaptation of Michael Shaara's novel, *The Killer Angels*

◆ *Glory* (1989), the inspiring story of 54th Massachusetts, the war's most famous African American regiment

◆ *Gods and Generals* (2003), the film version of Jeff Shaara's "prequel" to his father's *The Killer Angels*.

◆ *Gone with the Wind* (1939), which, long as it is, omits a good deal of Margaret Mitchell's famed novel, but is a must-see nevertheless

◆ *The Red Badge of Courage* (1951), an extraordinary, starkly straightforward adaptation of Stephen Crane's classic novel

One Nation, Indivisible

For us, today, the Civil War is an opportunity to learn more about who we are as a nation. That statement, although true, is also, like most abstract statements, rather flat and dull. For it is not "history" that study of the Civil War teaches, but the real *meaning* behind that history. The war was an event enacted by men and women with whom we cannot help but feel a profound kinship and sympathy.

The people who passed through the crucible of the Civil War were not, for the most part, professional soldiers, and they were certainly not hirelings of a warlike state. America, North and South, has never been a military or militaristic society.

The people of the Civil War were doctors, lawyers, clerks, brokers, farmers, brothers, sisters, fathers, mothers, sons, daughters, husbands, wives, lovers. They were people like us, and their lives were like the lives most of us live. Only theirs were fiercely moved by patriotic passions, pierced by bugle calls, shattered by bullets, torn by the cries of the wounded, and, perhaps, buried in the silence of the slain. But for the accident of time, we could have been them and they us.

The Least You Need to Know

- No event or period in American history commands more and more enduring modern interest than the Civil War.

- The war is the focus of historical and archaeological specialists, as well as legions of amateur enthusiasts, including reenactors, nonprofessional scholars, and amateur genealogists.

- The Civil War remains a fertile source of popular culture, including many novels and movies.

- The Civil War continues to fascinate us because we identify strongly with its issues and its people.

Words of War

abolitionists   Those who advocated abolishing slavery altogether. To many Northerners, the label was a badge of honor; to most Southerners, it was a mark of scorn.

agent provocateur   An undercover enemy operative who works to provoke some destructive action.

Anaconda   The nickname of the Union's naval blockade of the South.

battalion   An operational unit composed of two or more companies or (in the case of an artillery battalion) batteries. In the Civil War, two or more battalions were organized into regiments. (Battalions were not used as operational units in infantry regiments.) *See also* battery, company, and regiment.

battery   In a Civil War artillery regiment, the operational unit comprising four to six cannon, equivalent to a company in an infantry or cavalry regiment. *See also* company.

beat to quarters   To order a ship's crew to prepare for battle and assume their battle stations. In the eighteenth and nineteenth centuries, the signal was a continuous drum roll—hence the expression to *beat* to quarters.

Billy Yank   What Union soldiers sometimes were called and called themselves. Civil War equivalent of World War II's "G.I. Joe" as a name for the common soldier. *See also* Johnny Reb.

bivouac   A temporary encampment.

blockade runner A vessel—or its captain—specializing in evasion of the Union naval blockade of the South. The ships were generally small, sleek cargo vessels built for speed, with a sufficiently shallow draft to negotiate the treacherous waters along Southern coastlines without running aground.

border ruffians Proslavery Missourians who periodically raided eastern Kansas, intimidating and sometimes murdering antislavery settlers. For the border ruffians, the slavery issue was often little more than an excuse for robbery.

border states Slave states that did not secede. They included Delaware, Maryland, Kentucky, and Missouri. The counties forming present-day West Virginia declared themselves loyal to the Union and seceded from the rest of Virginia when that state left the Union. On June 20, 1863, West Virginia was admitted to the Union as a new slave state; it is usually counted among the border states.

breastworks Temporary, improvised defensive barriers, made of earth, stone, wood— whatever materials are available—usually affording protection that is breast high.

brevet A promotion for conspicuous bravery or meritorious service. The promotion usually comes without an increase in pay and is often of an honorary (and temporary) nature.

brigade In the Civil War, an operational unit consisting of two or more regiments. Union brigades averaged 2,000 men, whereas Confederate brigades averaged 1,850. Two or more brigades were organized into a division. *See also* battalion, battery, company, and division.

bummers Renegade soldier foragers, and sometimes civilians, attached to General Sherman's columns during the March to the Sea, partaking in the looting and destruction visited by the Union army.

bushwhacker The generic term for pro-Confederate guerrillas active in the Kansas-Missouri border region.

canister shot (or **canister**) A type of artillery shell designed to explode upon firing, spraying out the lead or iron shot that was packed within the canister. It was a cruelly effective antipersonnel weapon, generally used at close range.

carpetbaggers Northerners who descended on the South after the war, usually to exploit the freedmen in order to control local governments and profit from corruption. Unwelcome visitors, they brought with them only what they could carry in their "carpetbag" satchels. *See also* scalawags.

commerce raider A private, civilian vessel authorized by the Confederate government to intercept U.S. merchant ships and seize their cargo. Commerce raiding was, in effect, government-sanctioned piracy.

commissary   In the military jargon of the period, the store from which rations were drawn, as well as the officer in charge of provisions.

company   The basic operational unit in the Civil War–era army. In the Union army, it consisted of 30 to 60 officers and men, including one captain, one first lieutenant, one second lieutenant, one first sergeant, four sergeants, eight corporals, two musicians, and one wagoner; the remaining personnel were privates. Confederate practice sometimes varied from this. *See also* battalion, battery, and regiment.

Copperhead   The disparaging term applied to Peace Democrats. It evoked the image of a venomous snake in the grass and might also have been derived from party badges worn by Peace Democrats, which were fashioned from copper coins. *See also* Peace Democrat.

corps   In the Civil War, an operational unit consisting of two or more divisions and commanded by a major general. *See also* division.

cotton gin   A device, invented by Eli Whitney (1765–1825) in 1793, for separating the seeds from cotton fiber so that the fiber could be woven into cloth. "Gin," short for *engine*, was what people of the eighteenth century called any labor-saving mechanical device.

counterreconnaissance   An effort to foil the attempt of the enemy to carry out his reconnaissance mission. Like reconnaissance, counterreconnaissance was typically assigned to the cavalry. *See also* reconnaissance.

cracker barrels   Crates or barrels used to store crackers or hardtack—and often used as impromptu camp furniture.

crackers   Hardtack biscuits made with flour and water. Soldiers called these basic ration items "teeth dullers." Crackers were stored in crates or barrels—in either case called cracker barrels.

defeat in detail   The time-honored strategy of attacking the spread-out elements of an enemy force one by one, before they have time to concentrate into a single, more powerful unit.

derringer   A pocket-sized handgun with a short barrel and large bore. It is named for gunsmith Henry Deringer (whose name is spelled with one *r*).

division   In the Civil War, an operational unit consisting of two or more brigades and manned, on average, by 6,200 officers and men, in the Union army, and 8,700 in the Confederate army. Two or more divisions made up an army corps. *See also* battalion, battery, brigade, and company.

double envelopment   A tactic in which the enemy army is completely surrounded.

earthworks   Entrenchments and/or mounded earth parapets used as defensive positions.

emancipate   To free from bondage or involuntary servitude.

embargo   A government-imposed ban on the exportation or importation of certain goods or on trade with certain other countries.

endemic disease   A disease chronically characteristic of a certain place or population. *See also* epidemic disease.

epidemic disease   An acute, severe, and widespread outbreak of a disease among a certain population. *See also* endemic disease.

fatigue duty   Military jargon for manual labor.

Federal army   The most commonly used term, on both sides, for the Union army.

fire-eater   A Southerner who enthusiastically and unconditionally advocated secession.

flag officer   During the Civil War, a naval rank intermediate between captain and rear admiral. (Today, a flag officer in the U.S. Navy or Coast Guard is a generic term for anyone holding a rank above captain, such as a rear admiral, vice admiral, or admiral.)

flank   As a noun, the right or left elements of a body of troops; as a verb, to attack from a vulnerable side, usually a lightly defended side.

foreign secretary   The British government equivalent of the secretary of state in the government of the United States.

Freedmen's Bureau   The popular name for the United States Bureau of Refugees, Freedmen, and Abandoned Lands, which was established by Congress to provide practical aid to newly freed African Americans in their transition from slavery to freedom.

frigate   In the middle nineteenth century, any high-speed, medium-sized warship.

gentlemen's agreement   As used in diplomacy, an understanding between two nations, usually drawn up in the form of a diplomatic letter rather than a fully binding treaty.

grape or **grapeshot**   A type of ammunition, usually used on warships, consisting of a cluster of small iron balls used as a cannon charge. Like canister ammunition, grapeshot was intended to spray out and kill personnel.

graving dock   A dry dock where major work is done on ships.

Greek fire   A highly flammable fluid that bursts into flame when suddenly exposed to air. Typically, it was poured into a glass jar, which was then tightly sealed. If suddenly broken, the contents ignited explosively.

gunboat   In the Civil War era, a squat, shallow-draft vessel, often clad in iron plates to deflect cannonballs, and designed mainly for use on rivers as a floating artillery platform.

high ground   Any elevated ground, such as a hill, on which troops can be placed so as to command clear fields of vision and fire over the ground below. Occupying the high ground almost always confers a tactical advantage.

impeachment   Often misunderstood to mean *removal* from office, to *impeach* is merely to *charge* a public official with misconduct in office before a legally constituted tribunal. President Johnson, like President Bill Clinton 130 years later, was *impeached*, but was acquitted of wrongdoing and was not removed from office.

indentured servitude   A colonial-era form of voluntary servitude, in which a person bound himself to work for another for a fixed period (usually seven years) in return for passage to the New World.

independent command   The label applied to the highest military ranks, in which commanders must determine overall strategy as well as specific tactics. *See also* subordinate command.

Jayhawkers   Self-appointed abolitionist guerrillas active in the Kansas-Missouri border region. The most aggressive of them were called "Red Legs," after the red leggings they wore as their only uniform.

Jim Crow laws   Named after a racially demeaning song and dance from blackface minstrel shows, *Jim Crow laws* were state and local ordinances that enforced racial segregation and other forms of discrimination aimed at subjugating African Americans.

Johnny Reb   What Confederate soldiers sometimes were called and called themselves. Civil War equivalent of World War II's "G.I. Joe" as a name for the common soldier. *See also* Billy Yank.

line officers   Military field commanders who execute the orders of the overall commander in charge.

Louisiana Purchase   In 1803, the United States acquired from France territory extending from the Mississippi River to the Rocky Mountains between the Gulf of Mexico and the Canadian border for the bargain price of $15 million.

minister   In the eighteenth and nineteenth centuries, U.S. ambassadors were generally called *ministers*.

monitor   Borrowed from the name of the first Union steel-hulled warship, the term was applied generically to all steel-built or ironclad vessels with gun turrets, especially those designed for coastal bombardment.

mortar   A short, thick-walled artillery piece designed to lob a heavy projectile in a steep, high trajectory; it was most often used against high-walled forts.

National army   A contemporary synonym for the Union army.

nullification   The principle that a state may nullify and refuse to obey or enforce any federal law it considers unconstitutional. The concept rested on the related principle of states' rights.

parole   From the French word for *word* or *promise*, it meant, during the Civil War, the act of releasing a POW to his own lines on condition that he give his word of honor not to fight until he was officially exchanged for a prisoner held by the enemy.

Peace Democrat   Any Northerner who advocated a negotiated settlement of the war, with concessions to the South. *See also* Copperhead.

peculiar institution   The euphemism Southerners (and some others) adopted when referring to slavery.

picket   During the Civil War, a synonym for a guard or sentry.

picket line   The outer perimeter, usually around a camp, which was patrolled by sentries ("pickets").

pincers movement   A tactic of attacking an enemy army from opposite directions, effectively squeezing it between the jaws of a pincers.

plug uglies   Pro-Confederate thugs who attacked Union troops when they marched through Baltimore to Washington at the beginning of the war. Some authorities trace the name to the days when private fire-fighting companies actually competed to put out fires; plug uglies were toughs dispatched to guard city fire plugs to prevent rival fire companies from using them. They not only rioted in Baltimore, but also wreaked havoc throughout Maryland.

pocket veto   When a bill is presented for presidential signature within 10 days of congressional adjournment, the president may indirectly veto it by holding it, unsigned, until after Congress adjourns; this is a *pocket veto*.

political generals   Inexperienced commanders taken from civilian life and given high military rank as a reward for political services.

pontoon bridge   A transportable temporary bridge resting on floating pontoons or pontoon boats rather than permanent piers or pilings.

popular sovereignty   The doctrine and policy introduced in the Compromise of 1850 that provided for the people of a territory to vote on whether the territory would apply for admission to the Union as a free state or a slave state. The federal government would be bound by the people's decision.

privateer   A privately owned armed vessel commissioned by a warring state to attack enemy vessels of commerce. The word can also be applied to the captain of the privateer vessel. Captains and crews were generally not paid by the government, but were entitled to claim captured ships as prizes for their own profit.

prize   In naval jargon, a captured vessel and any and all cargo it carries.

protective tariff   A tax imposed on imported goods with the purpose of discouraging importation and, therefore, promoting the manufacture and sale of domestic goods.

provost marshal   Effectively, the chief of the military police, whose job is to maintain both security and order.

Pyrrhic victory   Victory at a self-defeating cost. The word derives from Pyrrhus (319–272 B.C.E.), king of Epirus, who defeated a Roman army at the Battle of Heraclea (280 B.C.E.), but lost so many men in the triumph that he remarked, "One more such victory and I shall be lost."

Quaker gun   A log positioned and painted to look like a cannon barrel. The Confederates used Quaker guns to deceive Union commanders into inflating estimates of their strength.

quartermaster   The officer in charge of procurement and supply for army units.

Radical Republicans   Northerners who advocated continuation of the war to absolute, total victory, and who further proposed severe punishment for the South following its defeat.

ram   A vessel built with a specially reinforced prow (or "beak") expressly for the purpose of deliberate collision with other ships. A ram sinks enemy vessels by punching through the enemy's hull at or below the water line.

rebels, rebel army   Terms often used by Union forces and the Union government to refer to the Confederates and Confederate army.

reconnaissance   An exploration to ascertain military information. During the Civil War, typically the mission of cavalry.

Reconstruction   The general term for the transition of the former Confederate states from federal control to restoration of statehood. The period of Reconstruction spanned 1865 to 1877.

redeemers   Late nineteenth-century Southern political activists who promoted passage of "Jim Crow laws" aimed at curtailing the civil rights of African Americans.

regiment   In the Civil War, infantry regiments were units consisting of ten companies, and cavalry (as well as heavy artillery regiments retrained as infantry) had 12 companies. Two or more regiments were organized into a brigade. See also battalion, battery, brigade, and company.

retreat   The orderly withdrawal of troops from battle. *See also* rout.

retrograde   Military jargon for movement backward.

rifle pit   The Civil War equivalent of World War II's foxhole; a hastily dug emplacement that afforded riflemen a degree of protection.

rout   Withdrawal in panic and disorder, typically accompanied by a high rate of casualties. *See also* retreat.

rump   In political terms, a legislature having only a fraction of its original membership; it has no legal authority, but acts as if it did.

salient   Any strong or strongly fortified position or concentration of troops projecting from the main line.

sambo   One of the many offensive and demeaning names whites applied to African Americans during the nineteenth century. Some linguists have suggested that the term might be derived from the Fulani (Senegalese) word for uncle.

sappers   In eighteenth- and nineteenth-century armies, soldiers sent in advance of a column or in preparation for an attack. Armed with axes, the sappers' mission was to clear debris, undergrowth, obstructions, and other obstacles to marching or attacking. Also called *pioneers*.

scalawags   White Southerners who aided and abetted carpetbaggers. *See also* carpetbaggers.

schooner   A fore-and-aft-rigged sailing vessel.

scow   A large flat-bottomed boat with square ends fore and aft, used for transporting freight.

screw sloop   A small armed vessel powered by a steam-driven propeller ("screw").

secede   To withdraw from membership in an organization, association, alliance, or, in the case of what became the eleven Confederate states, from the union that was the United States.

separation of powers   The Constitutional division of U.S. federal authority and responsibility among the three branches of government: executive (presidential), legislative (congressional), and judicial (the federal courts).

servile insurrection   A period synonym for slave rebellion.

sharecropping   The practice of tenant farming, in which the tenant gives to the landlord a share of the crops he raises in lieu of cash rent.

Sherman necktie   General Sherman's troops destroyed hundreds of miles of Southern railroad by ripping up rails, heating them over open fires, and twisting them into pretzel-like shapes that made them impossible to repair. Such a piece of ruined rail was called a *Sherman necktie*.

shoddy   Today an adjective meaning cheap, poorly made, and generally faulty, the word is derived from a Civil War–era noun meaning a kind of cloth made from scraps of material felted together—compounded and glued—rather than woven and, therefore, subject to disintegration. Uniforms made of shoddy were sometimes sold to the federal government by corrupt contractors.

skedaddle   The word soldiers used to describe the act of fleeing under fire.

soldier's battle   A battle in which the outcome is determined more by the action of the enlisted soldiers and the junior officers than by the leadership of principal commanders.

Solid South   The unified Democratic voting bloc that dominated the Southern states from the 1870s through the late 1960s, making the South virtually a region of one-party politics.

staff officers   Assistants to a commander in performing planning and administrative functions. Staff officers are often responsible for ensuring that the commander's decisions are correctly implemented by the line officers.

states' rights   The doctrine that the individual states command all powers and authority not *explicitly* assigned to the federal government by the Constitution. It was the basis of nullification.

straggler   Slang for a soldier who lags behind or wanders away from his unit. Unlike deserters, stragglers usually caught up with their unit.

subordinate command   The label applied to command positions responsible for executing the orders and achieving the objectives issued by those in independent command positions.

Tenure of Office Act   Enacted on March 2, 1867, the law barred the president from dismissing, without consent of the Senate, any civil officer who had been appointed with Senate approval. When President Andrew Johnson dismissed Secretary of War Edwin Stanton, Congress impeached him on charges of violation of the act. The act was repealed in part in 1869 and entirely in 1887. In 1926, the U.S. Supreme Court declared it to have been unconstitutional.

Three-Fifths Compromise   Article I, Section 2.3 of the U.S. Constitution stipulated that slaves (although that word is not used) may be counted as three-fifths of a person for purposes of levying taxes and apportioning representation in Congress. This provision was a compromise made by the framers of the Constitution between Northern interests (which did not want slaves counted at all) and Southern interests (which wanted slaves counted as persons).

torpedo   At the time of the Civil War, a *torpedo* was not a waterborne projectile, but a stationary mine, often no more elaborate than a beer barrel made watertight and tightly packed with explosive black powder. The torpedo would explode when struck by a vessel.

total war   Combat waged against civilian as well as military targets with the object not only of destroying the enemy's capacity to fight, but also his will to fight.

Underground Railroad   A secret network that helped fugitive slaves escape from the South to the free states of the North and, sometimes, into Canada.

works   Fortifications. *See also* breastworks and earthworks.

Who Was Who in the Civil War

This is a highly selective alphabetical list of personalities who played key roles in the Civil War.

For military figures, entries include the subject's affiliation (**CSA**, Confederate States Army; **CSN**, Confederate States Navy; **USA**, U.S. Army; **USN**, U.S. Navy) and the highest rank the subject attained by the end of the war. If the subject held command of a major military unit, the unit is listed followed by the nature of the command (in parentheses, sometimes with time served) and the major engagement(s) in which the subject fought. For example,

> **Bragg, Braxton (1817–76), General CSA**   Army of Mississippi (corps commander): Shiloh; Army of Mississippi (commander): Perryville; Army of Tennessee (commander): Murfreesboro, Chickamauga, Chattanooga; adviser to Jefferson Davis, February 1864–January 1865

This means that Bragg was a general in the Confederate States Army, a corps commander in the Army of Mississippi at the battle of Shiloh, commander of that army at Perryville; then commander of the Army of Tennessee at Murfreesburo, Chickamauga, and Chattanooga; after this, he was an adviser to Davis.

If the subject held no overall command of a major unit, but participated in a major battle, only the battle is noted. For example, George A. Custer first distinguished himself at the First Battle of Bull Run, but did not hold any overall command in that engagement.

Finally, early in the war, commanders were not always assigned to specific military units; thus, for example, you will note that the entry for P.G.T. Beauregard begins "Received surrender of Fort Sumter; had field command at First Bull Run"; only after this was he assigned command of the Army of Mississippi.

Adams, Charles Francis (1807–86) U.S. minister (ambassador) to Great Britain (1861–68).

Anderson, Robert (1805–71), Maj. Gen. USA Surrendered Fort Sumter.

Baker, Lafayette C. (1826–68) Union spy and spymaster; instrumental in capture of John Wilkes Booth; implicated self in a conspiracy to assassinate Lincoln (a hoax?).

Banks, Nathaniel P. (1816–94), Maj. Gen. USA Massachusetts governor 1858–61; Army of the Potomac (corps commander): Shenandoah Valley, 1862; Army of Virginia (corps commander): Cedar Mountain; Department of the Gulf (commander): Port Hudson, Red River Campaign.

Barton, Clara (1821–1912) "Angel of the Battlefield"; solicited and distributed medical supplies for the wounded; founder and first president of the American Red Cross, 1881.

Beauregard, P.G.T. (1818–93), General CSA Received surrender of Fort Sumter; had field command at First Bull Run; Army of Mississippi (commander): Shiloh; Departments of South Carolina, Georgia, and Florida (commander), August 1862–April 1864; Departments of North Carolina and Southern Virginia (commander, April 1864–March 1865): Petersburg, Carolinas.

Benjamin, Judah P. (1811–84) Confederate secretary of war, September 1861–February 1862; secretary of state, March 1862–April 1865.

Booth, John Wilkes (1838–65) Assassin of Lincoln, April 14, 1865.

Bragg, Braxton (1817–76), General CSA Army of Mississippi (corps commander): Shiloh; Army of Mississippi (commander): Perryville; Army of Tennessee (commander): Murfreesboro, Chickamauga, Chattanooga; adviser to Jefferson Davis, February 1864–January 1865.

Breckinridge, John C. (1821–75), Maj. Gen. CSA U.S. vice president, 1857–61; Army of Mississippi (corps commander): Shiloh; Army of Tennessee (division commander): Murfreesboro, Chickamauga; Army of Tennessee (corps commander):

Chattanooga; Army of Northern Virginia (division commander): Cold Harbor; Confederate secretary of war, February 1864–April 1865.

Buchanan, Franklin (1800–74), Admiral CSN   First superintendent of U.S. Naval Academy (Annapolis), 1845–47; became a Confederate and commanded ironclads USS *Merrimac* at Hampton Roads, March 8, 1862, and USS *Tennessee* at Mobile Bay, August 5, 1864.

Buchanan, James (1791–1868)   Fifteenth U.S. President, 1857–61; blamed for doing nothing to prevent the Civil War.

Buckner, Simon Bolivar (1823–1914), Lt. Gen. CSA   Surrendered Fort Donelson; Army of Mississippi (division commander): Perryville; Army of Tennessee (corps commander): Chickamauga.

Buell, Don Carlos (1818–98), Maj. Gen. USA   Department of the Ohio (commander, November 1861–March 1862); Army of the Ohio (commander): Shiloh, Perryville; relieved of command, October 1862; resigned, June 1864.

Buford, John (1826–63), Maj. Gen. USA   Army of Virginia (cavalry brigade commander): Second Bull Run; Army of the Potomac (chief of cavalry): Antietam, Fredericksburg; Army of the Potomac (cavalry division commander): Gettysburg.

Burnside, Ambrose E. (1824–81), Maj. Gen. USA   Brigade commander: First Bull Run; Roanoke Island; Army of the Potomac (corps commander): Antietam; Army of the Potomac (commander): Fredericksburg; Army of the Ohio (commander): Knoxville; Army of the Potomac (corps commander): the Wilderness, Spotsylvania, Cold Harbor, Petersburg; relieved of command, August 1864.

Butler, Benjamin F. (1818–93), Maj. Gen. USA   Occupation of Baltimore; occupation of New Orleans ("Beast" Butler); Army of the James (commander): Bermuda Hundred, Fort Fisher; relieved, January 1865.

Cameron, Simon (1799–1889)   Corrupt U.S. secretary of war, March 1861–January 1862; minister to Russia, 1862.

Canby, Edward R.S. (1817–73), Maj. Gen. USA   Military Division of West Mississippi commander: capture of Mobile; received surrender of the last Confederate armies.

Chase, Salmon P. (1808–73)   Ohio governor, 1855–59; U.S. secretary of the treasury, March 1861–June 1864; chief justice of the United States, 1864–73.

Crittenden, George B. (1812–80), Maj. Gen. CSA   Son of John J. Crittenden; defeated at Mill Springs; resigned, October 1862.

Crittenden, John J. (1787–1863) U.S. senator from Kentucky, 1854–61; proposed Crittenden Compromise to avert war, December 1860; U.S. congressman, 1861–63; his Crittenden Resolution declared the preservation of the Union as the sole war aim, July 25, 1861; father of a Confederate and a Union general.

Crittenden, Thomas L. (1819–93), Maj. Gen. USA Son of John J. Crittenden; Army of the Ohio (division commander): Shiloh; Army of the Cumberland (left wing commander): Murfreesboro; Army of the Cumberland (corps commander): Chickamauga; resigned, December 1864.

Custer, George A. (1839–76), Maj. Gen. USA First Bull Run; Army of the Potomac (cavalry brigade commander): Peninsula to Petersburg; Army of the Shenandoah (cavalry division commander): Shenandoah Valley; Appomattox; slain at Little Big Horn River, Montana, 1876.

Dahlgren, John A. (1809–70), Rear Adm. USN Inventor of Dahlgren naval gun; South Atlantic Blockading Squadron commander, July 1863–July 1865.

Davis, Jefferson (1808–89) U.S. senator (Miss.), 1847–51 and 1857–61; U.S. Secretary of War, 1853–57; Confederate president.

Du Pont, Samuel F. (1803–65), Rear Adm. USN Port Royal; directed attacks on Charleston, April–July 1863; relieved, July 1863.

Early, Jubal A. (1816–94), Lt. Gen. CSA Brigade commander: First Bull Run; Army of Northern Virginia (brigade commander): Peninsula, Second Bull Run; Army of Northern Virginia (division commander): Antietam, Fredericksburg, Chancellorsville, Gettysburg, the Wilderness, Spotsylvania; Army of Northern Virginia (corps commander): Cold Harbor, Shenandoah Valley.

Ericsson, John (1803–89) Designer and builder of the Union ironclad USS *Monitor*.

Ewell, Richard S. (1817–72), Lt. Gen. CSA Army of Northern Virginia (division commander): Shenandoah Valley, Peninsula, Second Bull Run; Army of Northern Virginia (corps commander): Gettysburg, the Wilderness, Spotsylvania, Richmond defenses; captured at Sayler's Creek, April 6, 1865.

Farragut, David G. (1801–70), Vice Adm. USN West Gulf Blockading Squadron (commander): capture of New Orleans, bombardment of Vicksburg, Port Hudson, Mobile Bay.

Foote, Andrew (1806–63), Rear Adm. USN Upper Mississippi River fleet (commander), August 1861–May 1862; capture of Fort Henry, Fort Donelson, Island No. 10.

Frémont, John C. (1813–90), Maj. Gen. USA Western Department (commander, July–November 1861); relieved, November 1861; Mountain Department (commander, March–June 1862): Shenandoah Valley (1862); relieved, June 1862; Republican nominee for president, May 31, 1864; withdrew, September 22, 1864.

Gibbon, John (1827–96), Maj. Gen. USA Army of Virginia (brigade commander): Second Bull Run; Army of the Potomac (brigade commander): Antietam; Army of the Potomac (division commander): Fredericksburg; Army of the Potomac (corps commander): Gettysburg; Army of the Potomac (division commander): the Wilderness, Spotsylvania, Petersburg, Cold Harbor; Army of the James (corps commander): Appomattox.

Gordon, John B. (1832–1904), Maj. Gen. CSA Army of Northern Virginia: Peninsula, Antietam; Army of Northern Virginia (brigade commander): Chancellorsville, Gettysburg, the Wilderness, Spotsylvania; Army of Northern Virginia (division commander): Shenandoah Valley, 1864; Army of Northern Virginia (corps commander): Petersburg, Appomattox.

Grant, Ulysses S. (1822–85), Lt. Gen. USA Commander: Belmont, Fort Henry, and Fort Donelson; Army of the Tennessee (commander): Shiloh, Vicksburg; Military Division of the Mississippi (commander): Chattanooga; general-in-chief of Union armies, March 12, 1864; directed campaigns of Army of the Potomac, 1864–65; received Lee's surrender at Appomattox, April 9, 1865.

Greeley, Horace (1811–72) Abolitionist editor of the New York *Tribune*, 1841–72; condemned Lincoln's lukewarm abolition policies in "The Prayer of Twenty Million" editorial, August 20, 1862.

Halleck, Henry Wager ("Old Brains") **(1815–72), Maj. Gen. USA** Department of the Missouri (commander, November 1861–March 1862); Department of the Mississippi (commander, March–July 1862); general-in-chief of Union armies, July 1862–March 1864; chief of staff, March 1864–April 1865.

Hamlin, Hannibal (1809–91) U.S. vice president during Lincoln's first term, 1861–65.

Hancock, Winfield Scott (1824–86), Maj. Gen. USA Army of the Potomac (brigade commander): Peninsula; Army of the Potomac (division commander): Antietam, Fredericksburg, Chancellorsville; Army of the Potomac (corps commander): Gettysburg, the Wilderness, Spotsylvania, Cold Harbor, Petersburg.

Hardee, William J. (1815–73), Lt. Gen. CSA Army of Mississippi (corps commander): Shiloh; (left wing commander): Perryville; Army of Tennessee (corps commander): Murfreesboro, Chattanooga, Atlanta, Carolinas; Department of South Carolina, Georgia, and Florida (commander, September 1864–April 1865).

Heth, Henry (1825–99), Maj. Gen. CSA Army of Mississippi (division commander): Perryville; Army of Northern Virginia (division commander): Chancellorsville, Gettysburg, the Wilderness, Spotsylvania, Petersburg, Appomattox.

Hill, Ambrose Powell (1825–65), Lt. Gen. CSA Army of Northern Virginia (division commander): Peninsula, First and Second Bull Run, Antietam, Fredericksburg, Chancellorsville; Army of Northern Virginia (corps commander): Gettysburg, the Wilderness, Cold Harbor, Petersburg; killed at Petersburg, April 2, 1865.

Hill, Daniel Harvey (1821–89), Lt. Gen. CSA Big Bethel; Army of Northern Virginia (division commander): Peninsula, Antietam; Army of Tennessee (corps commander): Chickamauga; relieved Oct. 1863; Army of Tennessee (division commander): Carolinas.

Hood, John Bell (1831–79), General CSA Army of Northern Virginia (brigade commander): Peninsula; Army of Northern Virginia (division commander): Second Bull Run, Antietam, Fredericksburg, Gettysburg; Longstreet's corps (commander): Chickamauga; Army of Tennessee (corps commander): Atlanta; Army of Tennessee (commander): Atlanta, Franklin and Nashville; voluntarily relieved, January 1865.

Hooker, Joseph (1814–79), Maj. Gen. USA Army of the Potomac (division commander): Peninsula, Second Bull Run; Army of the Potomac (corps commander): Antietam; Army of the Potomac (Center Grand Division commander): Fredericksburg; Army of the Potomac (commander): Chancellorsville; Army of the Cumberland (corps commander): Chattanooga, Atlanta; voluntarily relieved, July 1864.

Howard, Oliver O. (1830–1909), Maj. Gen. USA Brigade commander: First Bull Run; Army of the Potomac (brigade commander): Peninsula; Army of the Potomac (division commander): Antietam, Fredericksburg; Army of the Potomac (corps commander): Chancellorsville, Gettysburg; Army of the Cumberland (corps commander): Chattanooga, Atlanta; Army of the Tennessee (commander): Atlanta, March to the Sea, Carolinas.

Jackson, Thomas J. "Stonewall" (1824–63), Lt. Gen. CSA Brigade commander: First Bull Run; commander: Shenandoah Valley (1862); Army of Northern Virginia (division commander): Peninsula; Army of Northern Virginia (left wing commander): Second Bull Run; Army of Northern Virginia, "Jackson's Command": Antietam; Army of Northern Virginia (corps commander): Fredericksburg, Chancellorsville; victim of friendly fire at Chancellorsville, May 2, 1863; died, May 10, 1863.

Johnson, Andrew (1808–75) Governor of Tennessee, 1853–57; U.S. senator, 1857–62; member, Joint Committee on the Conduct of the War; military governor of Tennessee, 1862–65; U.S. vice president, November 8, 1864; succeeded to the presidency, April 15, 1865.

Johnston, Albert Sidney (1803–62), General CSA   Western Department (commander, September 1861–April 1862); Army of Mississippi (commander): Shiloh; killed at Shiloh, April 6, 1862.

Johnston, Joseph E. (1807–91), General CSA   Commander: First Bull Run, Fair Oaks; Division of the West (commander, November 1862–December 1863); Army of Tennessee (commander, December 1863–July 1864): Atlanta; Army of Tennessee (commander, February–April 1865): Carolinas.

Lee, Fitzhugh (1835–1905), Maj. Gen. CSA   Army of Northern Virginia (cavalry commander): Peninsula; Army of Northern Virginia (cavalry brigade commander): Antietam, Chancellorsville, Gettysburg; Army of Northern Virginia (cavalry division commander): Spotsylvania, Shenandoah Valley (1864); Army of Northern Virginia (cavalry corps commander): Appomattox.

Lee, Robert E. (1807–70), General CSA   Commander of Virginia troops, April–November 1861; Department of South Carolina, Georgia, and Florida (commander, November 1861–March 1862); adviser to Jefferson Davis, March–June 1862; Army of Northern Virginia (commander, June 1, 1862–April 9, 1865): Peninsula to Appomattox; named Confederate general-in-chief, February 6, 1865; surrendered to Grant, April 9, 1865.

Lincoln, Abraham (1809–65)   Sixteenth president of the United States, 1861–65; assassinated April 14, 1865.

Longstreet, James (1821–1904), Lt. Gen. CSA   Brigade commander: First Bull Run; Army of Northern Virginia (division commander): Peninsula; Army of Northern Virginia (right wing commander): Second Bull Run; Army of Northern Virginia, "Longstreet's Command": Antietam; Army of Northern Virginia (corps commander): Fredericksburg, Gettysburg; Army of Tennessee (left wing commander): Chickamauga; Confederate commander: Knoxville; Army of Northern Virginia (corps commander): the Wilderness, Petersburg, Appomattox.

Lyon, Nathaniel (1818–61), Brig. Gen. USA   Department of the West (commander, May–July 1861); killed at Wilson's Creek, August 10, 1861.

McClellan, George B. (1826–85), Maj. Gen. USA   Department of the Ohio (commander, May–July 1861): Philippi, Rich Mountain; District of the Potomac (commander, July–August 1861); Army of the Potomac (commander, August 1861–November 1862): Peninsula, Antietam; Union army general-in-chief, November 1861–July 1862; relieved, November 1862; Democratic candidate for president, 1864.

McDowell, Irvin (1818–85), Maj. Gen. USA   Army of the Potomac (division and corps commander): First Bull Run; October 1861–April 1862; Army of the

Rappahannock (commander, April–June 1862); Army of Virginia (corps commander): Second Bull Run; relieved, September 1862.

McPherson, James B. (1828–64), Maj. Gen. USA   Chief engineer: Fort Henry and Fort Donelson, Shiloh; Army of the Tennessee (brigade commander): Iuka; Army of the Tennessee (division commander, October 1862–January 1863); Army of the Tennessee (corps commander): Vicksburg; Army of the Tennessee (commander): Atlanta; killed at Atlanta (Battle of Peachtree Creek), July 22, 1864.

Magruder, John B. (1810–71), Maj. Gen. CSA   Commander: Big Bethel; Army of Northern Virginia, "Magruder's Command": Peninsula; district commander, Texas and Arkansas, October 1862–May 1865.

Mallory, Stephen R. (1813–73)   Confederate secretary of the Navy, 1861–65.

Mason, James M. (1798–1871)   Confederate commissioner to Great Britain, August 1861; captured in *Trent* Affair, November 8, 1861.

Meade, George Gordon (1815–72), Maj. Gen. USA   Army of the Potomac (brigade commander): Peninsula, Second Bull Run; Army of the Potomac (division commander): Antietam, Fredericksburg; Army of the Potomac (corps commander): Chancellorsville; Army of the Potomac (commander, June 1863–April 1865): Gettysburg to Appomattox.

Morgan, John Hunt (1825–64), Brig. Gen. CSA   Shiloh; led Kentucky raids, July, October, December 1862; led Ohio Raid, July 1863; captured and escaped (July 26–November 26, 1863; killed at Greeneville, Tenn., September 4, 1864.

Mosby, John S. (1833–1916), Col. CSA   First Bull Run; Shenandoah (1862); commander of Partisan Rangers, January 1863–April 1865; "Gray Ghost" of the Confederacy.

Ord, Edward O.C. (1818–83), Maj. Gen. USA   Commanded Washington defenses, October 1861–March 1862; Army of the Tennessee (division and district commander, June–Oct. 1862); Army of the Tennessee (corps commander): Vicksburg; Department of the Gulf (corps commander, September 1863–February 1864); Army of the James (corps commander): Petersburg; Army of the James (commander): Appomattox.

Paine, Lewis (1845–65)   Booth co-conspirator; attempted assassination of Secretary of State Seward, April 14, 1865; hanged, July 7, 1865.

Pickett, George E. (1825–75), Maj. Gen. CSA   Army of Northern Virginia (brigade commander): Peninsula; Army of Northern Virginia (division commander):

Fredericksburg, Gettysburg; Department of Virginia and North Carolina (commander, September 1863–May 1864): Drewry's Bluff; Army of Northern Virginia (division commander): Cold Harbor, Petersburg, Appomattox.

Pinkerton, Allan (1819–84)   Union detective/spy/counterespionage agent; Army of the Potomac (chief detective, August 1861–November 1862).

Pleasonton, Alfred (1824–97), Maj. Gen. USA   Peninsula; Army of the Potomac (cavalry division commander): Antietam, Fredericksburg, Chancellorsville; Army of the Potomac (cavalry corps commander): Gettysburg.

Polk, Leonidas (1806–64), Lt. Gen. CSA   Western Department (commander, July–September 1861): Belmont; Army of Mississippi (corps commander): Shiloh; Army of Mississippi (commander): Perryville; Army of Tennessee (corps commander): Murfreesboro; Army of Tennessee (right wing commander): Chickamauga; Army of Tennessee (corps commander): Atlanta; killed at Pine Mountain, Ga., June 14, 1864.

Pope, John (1822–92), Maj. Gen. USA   Army of the Mississippi (commander, February–June 1862): New Madrid, Island No. 10; Army of Virginia (commander): Second Bull Run; Department of the Northwest (commander, September–November 1862 and February 1863–February 1865).

Porter, David Dixon (1813–91), Rear Adm. USN   Capture of New Orleans; Mississippi Squadron (commander, October 1862–July 1863): Fort Hindman, Vicksburg; Lower Mississippi River fleet (commander, August 1863–October 1864): Red River; North Atlantic Blockading Squadron (commander, October 1864–April 1865): Fort Fisher.

Porter, Fitz-John (1822–1901), Maj. Gen. USA   Army of the Potomac (division commander): Yorktown siege; Army of the Potomac (corps commander): Peninsula, Second Bull Run, Antietam; relieved, November 1862; removed, January 1863, for conduct at Second Bull Run; exonerated, May 1882.

Price, Sterling (1809–67), Maj. Gen. CSA   Missouri State Guard (commander): Wilson's Creek, Lexington, Pea Ridge; Army of the West (commander): Iuka; Army of West Tennessee (corps commander): Corinth; led Price's Missouri Raid.

Quantrill, William C. (1837–65), Col. CSA   Wilson's Creek; led guerrilla raids: Independence, Mo., Lawrence, Kan., and Baxter Springs, Kan.; killed in Kentucky, May 10, 1865.

Reynolds, John F. (1820–63), Maj. Gen. USA   Army of the Potomac (brigade commander): Peninsula; Army of the Potomac (division commander): Second Bull Run; Army of the Potomac (corps commander): Fredericksburg, Chancellorsville, Gettysburg; killed at Gettysburg, July 1, 1863.

Rosecrans, William S. (1819–98), Maj. Gen. USA   Rich Mountain; Army of Occupation and Department of West Virginia, July 1861–March 1862; Army of the Mississippi (commander): Iuka, Corinth; Army of the Cumberland (commander): Murfreesboro, Chickamauga; relieved October 1863.

Ruffin, Edmund (1794–1865)   Rabid Virginia secessionist; credited with firing first shot at Fort Sumter; committed suicide, June 18, 1865.

Schofield, John McA. (1831–1906), Maj. Gen. USA   Wilson's Creek; Missouri district and department commander, November 1861–January 1864; Army of the Ohio (commander): Atlanta, Franklin and Nashville, Carolinas.

Schurz, Carl (1829–1906), Brig. Gen. USA   U.S. minister to Spain, 1861–62; Army of Virginia (division commander): Second Bull Run; Army of the Potomac (division commander): Chancellorsville; Army of the Cumberland (division commander): Chattanooga; voluntarily relieved, 1864.

Scott, Winfield (1786–1866), Lt. Gen. USA   General-in-chief, USA, 1841–61; crafted Anaconda Plan; retired, 1861.

Seddon, James A. (1815–80)   Confederate secretary of war, November 1862–February 1865.

Semmes, Raphael (1809–77), Rear Adm. CSN   Commander of Confederate commerce raiders *Sumter,* June 1861–January 1862, and *Alabama,* August 1862–June 1864; lost naval battle with *Kearsarge* off French coast, June 19, 1864; returned to Confederacy to assume command of James River squadron until April 1865.

Seward, William H. (1801–72)   U.S. secretary of state, 1861–69; wounded in assassination attempt, April 14, 1865.

Sheridan, Philip H. (1831–88), Maj. Gen. USA   Army of the Ohio (division commander): Perryville; Army of the Cumberland (division commander): Murfreesboro, Chickamauga, Chattanooga; Army of the Potomac (cavalry corps commander): the Wilderness, Spotsylvania, Richmond Raid, Cold Harbor, Appomattox; Army of the Shenandoah (commander, August 1864–March 1865).

Sherman, William Tecumseh (1820–91), Maj. Gen. USA   Brigade commander: First Bull Run; Department of the Cumberland (commander, October–November 1861); Army of the Tennessee (division commander): Shiloh; Army of the Tennessee (corps commander): Chickasaw Bluffs, Fort Hindman, Vicksburg; Army of the Tennessee (commander, October 1863–March 1864): Chattanooga, Meridian; Military Division of the Mississippi (commander, March 1864–April 1865): Atlanta, March to the Sea, Carolinas.

Sickles, Daniel E. (1825–1914), Maj. Gen. USA   Army of the Potomac (brigade commander): Peninsula; Army of the Potomac (division commander): Fredericksburg; Army of the Potomac (corps commander): Chancellorsville, Gettysburg.

Sigel, Franz (1824–1902), Maj. Gen. USA   Organizer of German-American troops and war support; Wilson's Creek; division commander: Pea Ridge; Army of Virginia (corps commander): Second Bull Run; Army of the Potomac (corps commander, September 1862–February 1863); Department of West Virginia (commander, March–May 1864): New Market; relieved, July 1864.

Slidell, John (1793–1871)   Confederate commissioner to France, August 1861; captured in *Trent* affair, November 8, 1861.

Smith, Edmund Kirby (1824–93), General CSA   Brigade commander: First Bull Run; Department of East Tennessee (commander): invasion of Kentucky; Trans-Mississippi Department (commander, March 1863–May 1865): Red River; commander of last Confederate operational unit to surrender, May 26, 1865.

Stanton, Edwin McMasters (1814–69)   U.S. attorney general, December 1860–March 1861; U.S. secretary of war, January 1862–May 1868.

Stephens, Alexander H. (1812–83)   Confederate vice president.

Stevens, Thaddeus (1792–1868)   U.S. congressman from Pennsylvania and leader of the Radical Republicans.

Stoneman, George (1822–94), Maj. Gen. USA   Army of the Potomac (cavalry division commander): Peninsula; Army of the Potomac (corps commander): Fredericksburg; Army of the Potomac (cavalry corps commander): Chancellorsville; Cavalry Bureau chief, July 1863–January 1864; Army of the Ohio (cavalry division commander): Atlanta; captured near Macon, Ga., July 30 1864, and exchanged; Department of the Ohio (commander, November 1864–January 1865); District of East Tennessee (commander, March–April 1865).

Stuart, J.E.B. (1833–64), Maj. Gen. CSA   First Bull Run; Army of Northern Virginia (cavalry commander): Peninsula, first ride around McClellan, Second Bull Run, Antietam, second ride around McClellan, Fredericksburg, Chancellorsville; temporary command of Jackson's corps: Brandy Station, Gettysburg Raid, the Wilderness, Spotsylvania; mortally wounded at Yellow Tavern, May 11, 1864; died May 12, 1864.

Sumner, Charles (1811–74)   U.S. senator from Massachusetts, 1851–74; leading abolitionist and Radical Republican; caned in Senate by Rep. Preston S. Brooks of South Carolina, 1856.

Sumner, Edwin V. (1797–1863), Maj. Gen. USA   Army of the Potomac (corps commander): Peninsula, Antietam; Army of the Potomac (Right Grand Division commander): Fredericksburg; voluntarily relieved, January 1863.

Thomas, George H. (1816–70), Maj. Gen. USA   Army of the Ohio (division commander): Mill Springs; Army of the Ohio (second in command): Perryville; Army of the Cumberland (commander of the center): Murfreesboro; Army of the Cumberland (corps commander): Chickamauga ("Rock of Chickamauga"); Army of the Cumberland (commander): Chattanooga, Atlanta, Franklin and Nashville.

Toombs, Robert (1810–85), Brig. Gen. CSA   Confederate secretary of state, March–July 1861; Army of Northern Virginia (brigade commander): Peninsula, Second Bull Run, Antietam; resigned March 1863.

Vallandigham, Clement L. (1820–71)   U.S. congressman from Ohio, 1858–63; leader of Copperhead Democrats; banished to the South, May 1863; ran in absentia for Ohio governorship, October 1863; defeated, returned to the North to write peace platform at Democratic convention, August 1864.

Van Dorn, Earl (1820–63), Maj. Gen. CSA   Army of the West (commander): Pea Ridge; Army of West Tennessee (commander): Corinth, Holly Springs; murdered by a civilian, May 8, 1863.

Wallace, Lew (1827–1905), Maj. Gen. USA   Division commander: Fort Donelson; Army of the Tennessee (division commander): Shiloh; Monocacy; served on court-martial of Lincoln's assassins and was president of court-martial that convicted Andersonville Commandant Henry Wirz.

Welles, Gideon (1802–78)   U.S. secretary of the navy, March 1861–March 1869.

Wheeler, Joseph (1836–1906), Lt. Gen. CSA   Shiloh; Army of Mississippi (cavalry brigade commander): Perryville; Army of Tennessee (cavalry brigade commander): Murfreesboro; Army of Tennessee (cavalry corps commander): Chickamauga, Knoxville, Atlanta, March to the Sea, Carolinas.

Wilkes, Charles (1798–1877), Commodore USN   Captain of USS *San Jacinto* who removed Confederate commissioners James M. Mason and John Slidell from British vessel *Trent*, November 8, 1861.

Wirz, Henry (1822–65), Maj. CSA   Andersonville Prison commandant, January 1864–April 1865; convicted of responsibility for inhuman prison conditions and executed, November 10, 1865—the only person executed after the war for actions during the war.

Major Civil War Sites and Sights

This is a highly selective alphabetical list of key Civil War attractions, sites, and sights.

Abraham Lincoln Birthplace
2995 Lincoln Farm Road
Hodgenville, KY 42748
1-502-358-3137

Andersonville National Historic Site
GA 49, 10 miles northeast of Americus, Georgia
1-912-924-0343
The notorious Confederate POW camp.

Andrew Johnson National Historic Site
Depot and College Streets
Greenville, Tennessee
1-615-638-3551

Antietam National Battlefield and National Cemetery
On MD 65 and MD 34, immediately to the north and northeast of
Sharpsburg
1-301-432-5124
Site of the battle that preceded the Emancipation Proclamation and was
the bloodiest single day of the war.

Appomattox Court House National Historical Park
(includes McLean House)
Appomattox Court House, Virginia
1-804-352-8987
Site of Lee's surrender.

Arlington House, the Robert E. Lee Memorial
George Washington Memorial Parkway
Arlington, VA
1-703-235-1530
The most important house associated with Lee; Arlington National Cemetery was
established on grounds formerly belonging to the house.

Atlanta Campaign
Atlanta Cyclorama
800 Cherokee Avenue, SE, Atlanta, GA 30315
404-624-1071
A giant panoramic painting (with 3-D elements) commemorating the Battle of Atlanta.

Boston African American National Historic Site
A collection of historic sites along the Black Heritage Trail relating to the abolition
movement and the organization of the 54th Massachusetts Regiment; consult
www.nps.gov/boaf for complete information.

Bull Run Battles
Manassas National Battlefield Park
VA 234 off I-66
1-703-361-1334
Two Union defeats, the first one the first major battle of the war, about 25 miles south-
west of Washington, D.C.

Chancellorsville Battlefield Unit
Fredericksburg and Spotsylvania County Battlefields Memorial National Military Park
Visitor Center, Chancellorsville Battlefield Unit, north of VA 3 on Bullock Road
Site of "Lee's masterpiece," Hooker's catastrophic defeat, and the mortal wounding of
Stonewall Jackson.

Chickamauga and Chattanooga
Chickamauga and Chattanooga National Military Park
P.O. Box 2128
Fort Ogelthorpe, GA 30742
1-706-866-9241
A fight in the lowlands and a "Battle above the Clouds."

Clara Barton National Historic Site
5801 Oxford Road
Glen Echo, MD 20812
1-301-492-6245
Home of the founder of the American Red Cross.

Ford's Theatre and the Petersen House
Ford's Theatre National Historic Site 511 and 516 Tenth Street NW
Washington, D.C. 20004
1-202-426-6924
Site of Lincoln's assassination.

Fort Donelson National Battlefield
P.O. Box 434
Dover, TN 37058
1-615-232-5348
Scene of Grant's first victories.

Fort Sumter
Charleston Harbor
Park Superintendent, Drawer R
Sullivan's Island, SC 29482
Ferry service: Fort Sumter Tours, Inc., 1-803-722-1691
Where the war began.

Frederick Douglass National Historic Site
1411 W. Street SE
Washington, D.C. 20020
1-202-426-5961
Home of the great black abolitionist.

Fredericksburg
Fredericksburg and Spotsylvania County Battlefields Memorial National Military Park
Burnside suffered a disastrous defeat here.
For comprehensive information on Fredericksburg, Spotsylvania, and Wilderness campaign attractions in the area, contact:
Spotsylvania Visitors' Center
4707 Southpoint Parkway
Fredericksburg, VA 22407
1-703-891-TOUR/1-800-654-4118

Gettysburg National Military Park
Visitors' Center
97 Taneytown Road
Gettysburg, PA 17325
1-717-334-1124
The largest battle ever fought in the Western hemisphere, and the turning point of the war.

Grant's Tomb (General Grant National Memorial)
Riverside Drive at 123rd Street
New York City
The final resting place of Grant and his wife, Julia.

Harpers Ferry National Historical Park
P.O. Box 65
Harpers Ferry, WV 25425
1-304-535-6298
Scene of John Brown's 1859 raid.

Kennesaw Mountain National Battlefield Park
Kennesaw, Georgia
From I-75 take exit 116, Barrett Parkway, and follow signs to the park
1-770-427-4686
Prelude to the Battle of Atlanta.

Monocacy National Battlefield
4801 Urbana Pike
Frederick, MD 21704-7307
1-301-662-3515
Jubal Early's victory here (July 9, 1864) brought his raiders to the doorstep of Washington, D.C.

Pea Ridge National Military Park
P.O. Box 700
Pea Ridge, AR 72751-0700
1-479-451-8122
Site of the battle that saved Missouri for the Union.

Petersburg National Battlefield
Petersburg Visitor Center
15 West Bank Street
Stony Creek, VA 23882
1-804-246-2226
Site of 10 months of trench warfare—Grant's long siege prior to the fall of Richmond.

Richmond National Battlefield Park
Metro Richmond Visitors' Center
550 East Marshall Street
Richmond, VA 23219
1-804-782-2777
The battle for the rebel capital.

Shiloh National Military Park
22 miles northeast of Corinth, MS, on TN 22
1-901-689-5275
Grant's near catastrophe.

Spotsylvania
Fredericksburg and Spotsylvania County Battlefields Memorial National Military Park
Spotsylvania Visitors' Center
4707 Southpoint Parkway
Fredericksburg, VA 22407
1-703-891-TOUR/1-800-654-4118
One battle in the long campaign in which Grant earned the nickname "The Butcher."

Ulysses S. Grant National Historic Site
7400 Grant Road
St. Louis, MO 63123
1-314-842-3298
The home of Ulysses and Julia Dent Grant, the site commemorates the life and career of the Union general and 18th president of the United States.

USS *Merrimac*
Artifacts relating to the USS *Merrimac* (CSS *Virginia*) are housed in
The Portsmouth Naval Shipyard Museum
2 High Street
Portsmouth, VA 23704
1-804-393-8591
and
The Hampton Roads Naval Museum
333 Waterside Drive
Norfolk, VA 23510
1-804-444-8971)

USS *Monitor*
USS *Monitor* artifacts are exhibited at
The Mariners' Museum
100 Museum Drive
Newport News, VA 23606
1-804-595-0368
Relics of the war's great ironclads.

Vicksburg National Military Park
Vicksburg, Mississippi
1-601-636-0583
Grant's successful siege was the key to Union victory in the West.

The Wilderness
Fredericksburg and Spotsylvania County Battlefields Memorial National Military Park
Spotsylvania Visitors' Center
4707 Southpoint Parkway
Fredericksburg, VA 22407
1-703-891-TOUR/1-800-654-4118
Another bloody step toward Richmond.

Appendix D

Civil War Weapons

The following are the most commonly used weapons in the Civil War. The list is by no means exhaustive. Those with a specialized interest in Civil War weapons should consult James B. Whisker, *U.S. and Confederate Arms and Armories During the American Civil War* (Lewiston, N.Y.: Edwin Mellen Press, 2002).

Long Arms: Rifle-Muskets, Rifles, and Muskets

U.S. Rifle-Musket, Model 1861 ("1861 Springfield"). .58 cal., muzzle-loader. The most numerous Union army weapon: 265,129 manufactured at the Springfield Arsenal, and 643,439 manufactured by private contractors.

U.S. Rifle-Musket, Models 1863 and 1864. .58 cal., muzzle-loader. 255,040 delivered to the Union army.

Muskets, Patterns 1839 and 1842. British-made .753 cal. Muzzle-loading smoothbore weapons. Unknown quantities imported by the Confederacy.

Fayetteville Rifle. .58 cal. muzzle-loader. About 20,000 were manufactured by Fayetteville, North Carolina, Armory and Arsenal for the Confederacy.

Richmond Rifle-Musket ("C.S. Richmond"). .58 cal. muzzle-loader. About 42,000 were manufactured by Richmond Armory and Arsenal for the Confederacy.

Tyler, Texas, Enfield Rifle. .577 cal. muzzle-loader. Unknown quantities manufactured for the Confederacy.

Austrian Rifle. .54 cal. muzzle-loader. Unknown quantities manufactured for the Confederacy by the armory at Tyler, Texas, after an Austrian design.

Cook Infantry Rifle. .577 cal. muzzle-loader. At least 20,000 manufactured for the Confederacy.

In addition to these weapons, the Confederacy imported many long arms from a variety of European manufacturers.

Long Arms: Carbines and Musketoons

At four or five feet long, rifles and muskets were impractical for cavalry troops, who used instead short-barrel carbines and musketoons. The best for mounted troops were breech loaders.

U.S. Cavalry Rifled Carbine, model 1855. .54 cal. muzzle-loader.

Burnside Carbine, models 1-5, 1861–1864. .54 cal. breech-loader, designed by Gen. Ambrose Burnside; 55,000 of models 4 and 5 were acquired for the Union army.

Gallager Carbine, Model 1860. .50 cal. breech-loader; 17,782 purchased for the Union.

Maynard "Second Model" Sharps Carbine, Models 1852, 1859, and 1863. .52 cal. breech-loader. The most popular carbine of the war, 80,000 were purchased for Union forces.

Smith Carbine. .50 cal. breech-loader invented by a Northern dentist and purchased in a quantity of some 30,000 for Union forces.

Richmond Carbine. .577 cal. muzzle-loader. More than 2,500 were manufactured by the Richmond Armory and Arsenal for the Confederacy.

Confederate (Richmond) Sharps Carbine. .52 cal. breech-loader. About 3,000 of these copies of the Union's Sharps carbine were made by the S.C. Robinson firm in Richmond.

Revolvers

Colt Army Revolver, Model 1860 ("New Model Army"). .44 cal., six shots. More than 100,000 were purchased for Union forces.

Remington "New Model" Army Revolver (1863). .44 cal., six shots. 125,314 purchased for Union use.

Rigdon, Ansley & Co. Revolver. .36 cal., six shots. A Confederate copy of the Colt Navy Revolver.

Griswold & Gunnison Revolver. .36 cal., six shots. Another Confederate copy of the Colt Navy Revolver.

Spiller & Burr Revolver. .36 cal., six shots. Only 1,400 of the contracted 15,000 were delivered to the Confederacy.

Both the Union and the Confederacy also imported quantities of revolvers from foreign manufacturers.

Artillery: Field Weapons

Field artillery, also called light artillery, consisted of readily movable weapons and included, most commonly, the following:

The "Napoleon." This "Twelve-Pounder Field Gun, Model 1857" was the workhorse of the Union army. The Tredegar Iron Works, in Richmond, made copies for the Confederacy. Cast from brass, the smoothbore weapon fired a 12-pound, 4.2-inch projectile. About 1,000 were manufactured for the Union and a little more than half that number for the Confederacy.

The Parrott Gun. Designed by Robert P. Parrott, this cast-iron rifled gun was reinforced with wrought-iron bands. It was made in a 10-pounder and 20-pounder version. The rifling enabled greater accuracy, and the reinforcements permitted the use of larger charges without danger of the weapon exploding. The latter benefit, unfortunately, was unreliable, as a significant number of these weapons did burst, often with catastrophic results. The Parrott Gun was a Union weapon.

The Ordnance Rifle. A wrought-iron weapon, the Ordnance Rifle, patented by John Griffen in 1855, was similar to the Parrott Gun (although its range was somewhat shorter) but far more reliable—it didn't burst—and was highly prized by Union artillerists.

The Confederacy relied primarily on Napoleons and obsolete brass howitzers (small, highly mobile, short-barrel cannon). In addition, both the Union and the Confederacy imported some artillery, especially the Whitworth Gun, imported from the British firm of Sir Joseph Whitworth. These were 6-pounder and 12-pounder rifled cannon with a unique hexagonal (rather than round) bore. Whitworth Guns fired long projectiles called bolts and could achieve excellent range with great accuracy.

Heavy Artillery

Heavy artillery included large cannons, used in forts and seacoast defense, and mortars and other siege weapons.

The major fortress or seacoast weapon was the Columbiad, which had a bottle shape designed to keep the weapon from bursting. The Union used three principal models: The Model 1844 (8-inch and 10-inch, with a range of 1,800 yards), the Model 1858 (8-inch and 10-inch, with similar range), and the Model 1861 Rodman (8-inch, 10-inch, and 15-inch, with a maximum range of 4,680 yards.

The Confederacy copied the Rodman in its 8-inch and 10-inch versions. Confederate forces also used 32-pounder and 42-pounder heavy seacoast guns, smoothbore weapons that had a range of more than a mile.

Parrot Guns were also adopted for heavy artillery use and could fire 10-inch projectiles weighing up to 300 pounds to about 8,000 yards. Unfortunately, these weapons were unreliable and often burst.

Mortars were extremely short-barreled weapons with wide bores and very thick barrels. They fired very heavy projectiles at very high trajectories and were used for seacoast defense as well as siege work. The Union's model 1861 had a 13-inch bore and fired 200-pound projectiles more than two miles. Very heavy[md]it weighed 17,000 pounds—it could be transported by rail and fired from a specially reinforced flatcar. The most famous Model 1861 mortar was the "Dictator," used by the First Connecticut Heavy Artillery at the siege of Petersburg.

Mortars fired explosive shells, not mere cannonballs. Some of these projectiles were designed to detonate on impact. Others were fused and designed to detonate in midair, broadcasting shrapnel over a wide area.

The Confederacy had few mortars.

Naval Artillery

The most important innovation in naval artillery was the Dahlgren Gun, designed by Rear Adm. John A. Dahlgren of the U.S. Navy in 1855. The bottle-shaped weapon, usually manufactured in 9- and 11-inch versions (though 15- and 20-inch models were also produced), was the principal ship-mounted gun in the Union navy.

A Civil War Library

Since 1865, more than 65,000 books have been devoted to the Civil War. The following is intended to whet—not to satisfy—the historical appetite of anyone who wants to read beyond *The Complete Idiot's Guide to the Civil War, Second Edition.* Only nonfiction books are listed here; for some recommendations on Civil War fiction, see "Civil War Lit" in Chapter 26, "Memory."

Axelrod, Alan. *The War Between the Spies: A History of Espionage During the American Civil War.* New York: Atlantic Monthly Press, 1992.

Billings, John D. *Hard Tack and Coffee: The Unwritten Story of Army Life.* 1887; reprinted, Lincoln: University of Nebraska Press/Bison Books, 1993.

Boatner, Mark Mayo, III. *The Civil War Dictionary*, rev. ed. New York: David McKay, 1959.

Boritt, Gabor S. *Lincoln's Generals.* New York: Oxford University Press, 1994.

Boritt, Gabor S., ed. *Why the Confederacy Lost.* New York: Oxford University Press, 1992.

Catton, Bruce. *The Coming Fury.* Garden City, N.Y., 1961.

—*Glory Road*. Garden City, N.Y.: Doubleday, 1952; reprinted, New York: Anchor Books, 1990.

—*Mr. Lincoln's Army*. Garden City, N.Y.: Doubleday, 1951; reprinted, New York: Anchor Books, 1990.

—*Never Call Retreat*. Garden City, N.Y.: Doubleday, 1965.

—*A Stillness at Appomattox*. Garden City, N.Y.: Doubleday, 1953; reprinted, New York: Anchor Books, 1990.

—*Terrible Swift Sword*. Garden City, N.Y.: Doubleday, 1963.

—*This Hallowed Ground*. Garden City, N.Y.: Doubleday, 1955.

Cornish, Dudley Taylor. *The Sable Arm: Black Troops in the Union Army, 1861–1865*. Lawrence: University of Kansas Press, 1987.

Current, Richard N., Paul D. Escott, Lawrence N. Powell, James I. Robertson, Jr., and Emory M. Thomas, eds. *Encyclopedia of the Confederacy*. New York: Simon and Schuster, 1993.

Davis, Burke. *Sherman's March*. New York: Random House, 1980.

Davis, William C. *The Commanders of the Civil War*. New York: Salamander Books, 1990.

Davis, William C., ed. *The Image of War, 1861–1865*. New York: Doubleday, 1981–1984.

—*Jefferson Davis: The Man and His Hour*. New York: HarperCollins, 1991.

Denney, Robert F. *The Civil War Years: A Day-by-Day Chronicle of the Life of a Nation*. New York: Sterling, 1992.

Donald, David Herbert. *Lincoln*. New York: Simon & Schuster, 1995.

Douglass, Frederick. *Narrative of the Life of Frederick Douglass: An American Slave*. 1845; reprinted New York: Signet Books, 1968.

Duncan, Russell, ed. *Blue-Eyed Child of Fortune: The Civil War Letters of Colonel Robert Gould Shaw*. Athens: University of Georgia Press, 1992.

Dupuy, R. Ernest, and Trevor N. Dupuy. *The Compact History of the Civil War*. New York: Warner Books, 1993.

Dyer, Frederick H. *A Compendium of the War of the Rebellion: From Official Records of the Union and Confederate Armies, Reports of the Adjutant Generals of the Several States, the Army Registers, and Other Reliable Documents and Sources.* 1911; reprint ed., New York: T. Yoseloff, 1959.

Eicher, David J. *The Civil War in Books*. Champaign-Urbana: University of Illinois Press, 1997.

Fehrenbacher, Don E., ed. *Lincoln: Speeches and Writings, 1859–1865*. New York: Library of America, 1989.

Foote, Shelby. *The Civil War: A Narrative, Vol. 1, Fort Sumter to Perryville*. New York: Random House, 1958. *Vol. 2, Fredericksburg to Meridian*. New York: Random House, 1963. *Vol. 3, Red River to Appomattox*. New York: Random House, 1974. All reprinted, New York: Vintage, 1986.

Freeman, Douglas Southall. *Lee*. New York: Scribner's, 1934.

Furgurson, Ernest B. *Chancellorsville 1863: The Souls of the Brave*. New York: Knopf, 1992.

Gragg, Rod. *The Illustrated Confederate Reader*. New York: Harper & Row, 1989; reprinted, New York: Harper Perennial, 1991.

Harwell, Richard B. *The Confederate Reader: How the South Saw the War*. New York: Longmans, Green & Co., 1957; reprinted, New York: Dover, 1989.

Hedrick, Joan D. *Harriet Beecher Stowe: A Life*. New York: Oxford University Press, 1994.

Heidler, David S., and Jeane T. Heidler, eds. *Encyclopedia of the American Civil War: A Political, Social, and Military History*. Santa Barbara, Calif.: ABC-CLIO, 2000.

Hennessy, John J. *Return to Bull Run: The Campaign and Battle of Second Manassas*. New York: Simon & Schuster, 1993.

Hurst, Jack. *Nathan Bedford Forrest: A Biography*. New York: Knopf, 1993.

Long, E.B., and Barbara Long. *The Civil War Day by Day*. New York: Doubleday, 1971.

Marszalek, John F. *Sherman: A Soldier's Passion for Order*. New York: Free Press, 1993.

McFeely, William S. *Grant: A Biography*. New York: Norton, 1981.

McPherson, James M. *Abraham Lincoln and the Second American Revolution*. New York: Oxford University Press, 1990.

—*Battle Cry of Freedom*. New York: Oxford University Press, 1988.

McPherson, James M., ed. *The Atlas of the Civil War*. New York: Macmillan, 1994.

Morris, Roy, Jr. *Sheridan: The Life and Wars of General Philip Sheridan*. New York: Crown, 1992.

Nevins, Allan. *Ordeal of the Union*. New York: Scribner's, 1947–1971.

Nolan, Alan T. *Lee Considered: General Robert F. Lee and Civil War History*. Chapel Hill: University of North Carolina Press, 1991.

Oates, Stephen B. *A Woman of Valor: Clara Barton and the Civil War*. New York: Free Press, 1994.

Phillips, Charles, and Alan Axelrod. *My Brother's Face: Portraits of the Civil War*. San Francisco: Chronicle Books, 1992.

Robertson, James I., Jr. *Soldiers Blue and Gray*. Columbia: University of South Carolina Press, 1988.

—*Stonewall Jackson: The Man, the Soldier, the Legend*. New York: Macmillan General Reference, 1997.

Sears, Stephen W. *George B. McClellan: The Young Napoleon*. New York: Ticknor & Fields, 1988.

—*Landscape Turned Red: The Battle of Antietam*. New York: Ticknor & Fields, 1982.

—*Campaign*. New York: Ticknor & Fields, 1992.

Sifakis, Stewart. *Who Was Who in the Civil War*. New York: Facts On File, 1988.

Thomas, Emory M. *Bold Dragoon: The Life of J.E.B. Stuart*. New York: Random House, 1986.

—*Robert E. Lee: A Biography*. New York: Norton, 1995.

Thomas, William G., and Alice E. Carter. *The Civil War on the Web: A Guide to the Very Best*. Wilmington, Del.: SR Books, 2001.

United States War Department. *The War of the Rebellion: A Compilation of the Official Records of the Union and Confederate Armies*. Washington, D.C.: Government Printing Office, 1880–1901. Also available on CD-ROM from The Guild Press of Indiana, Inc.; 10665 Andrade Drive, Zionsville, IN 46077.

Wagner, Margaret, Gary W. Gallagher, and Paul Finkelman. *The Library of Congress Civil War Desk Reference*. New York: Simon and Schuster, 2002.

Ward, Geoffrey C., with Ric Burns and Ken Burns. *The Civil War*. New York: Knopf, 1990.

Warren, Robert Penn. *John Brown: The Making of a Martyr*. Payson & Clarke, 1929; reprinted, Nashville: J. F. Sanders, 1993.

Watkins, Sam R. *"Co. Aytch": A Side Show of the Big Show*. New York: Macmillan, 1962.

Wertz, Jay, and Edwin C. Bearss. *Smithsonian's Great Battles and Battlefields of the Civil War*. New York: Morrow, 1997.

Wheeler, Richard. *Voices of the Civil War*. New York: Crowell, 1976; reprinted, New York: Meridian, 1990.

Wiley, Bell Irvin. *The Life of Billy Yank: The Common Soldier of the Union*. 1953; reprinted, Baton Rouge: Louisiana State University Press, 1978.

—*The Life of Johnny Reb: The Common Soldier of the Confederacy*. 1943; reprinted, Baton Rouge: Louisiana State University Press, 1978.

Williams, T. Harry. *Lincoln and His Generals*. New York: Knopf, 1952.

Wills, Garry. *Lincoln at Gettysburg: The Words That Remade America*. New York: Simon & Schuster, 1992.

Woodward, C. Vann, ed. *Mary Chesnut's Civil War*. New Haven: Yale University Press, 1981.

Woodworth, Steven E., ed. *The American Civil War: A Handbook of Literature and Research*. Westport, Conn.: Greenwood Press, 1995.

Index

Numbers